AGENTS OF CHAOS

ALSO BY SEAN HOWE

Marvel Comics: The Untold Story

AGENTS of CHAOS

THOMAS KING FORÇADE, HIGH TIMES, AND THE PARANOID END OF THE 1970S

SEAN HOWE

hachette
BOOKS

NEW YORK

Hachette Books
Hachette Book Group
1290 Avenue of the Americas
New York, NY 10104
HachetteBooks.com
Twitter.com/HachetteBooks
Instagram.com/HachetteBooks

First Edition: August 2023

Published by Hachette Books, an imprint of Hachette Book Group, Inc. The Hachette Books name and logo are trademarks of the Hachette Book Group.

The Hachette Speakers Bureau provides a wide range of authors for speaking events. To find out more, visit hachettespeakersbureau.com or email HachetteSpeakers@hbgusa.com.

Books by Hachette Books may be purchased in bulk for business, educational, or promotional use. For information, please contact your local bookseller or email the Hachette Book Group Special Markets Department at Special.Markets@hbgusa.com.

The publisher is not responsible for websites (or their content) that are not owned by the publisher.

Print book interior design by Jeff Williams

Library of Congress Cataloging-in-Publication Data

Name: Howe, Sean, author.
Title: Agents of chaos: Thomas King Forçade, High Times, and the paranoid end of the
    1970s / Sean Howe.
Description: New York: Hachette Books, 2023. | Includes bibliographical references and index.
Identifiers: LCCN 2023010876 | ISBN 9780306923913 (hardcover) |
    ISBN 9780306923920 (trade paperback) | ISBN 9780306923937 (ebook)
Subjects: LCSH: Forçade, Thomas King. | Underground Press Syndicate. | High Times. |
    Journalists—United States—Biography. | Marijuana—Social aspects—United States. |
    Marijuana—Law and legislation—United States. | Drug legalization—United States.
Classification: LCC PN4874.F5185 H69 2023 | DDC 070.92
    [B]—dc23/eng/20230414
LC record available at https://lccn.loc.gov/2023010876

ISBNs: 978-0-306-92391-3 (hardcover), 978-0-306-92393-7 (ebook)

Printed in the United States of America

LSC-C

Printing 1, 2023

CONTENTS

FLOWERING,
1969–1972

CHAPTER 1

AT THE END OF FEBRUARY 1969, THE MARIJUANA LEGALIZATION GROUP LEMAR held a three-day "New World Drug Symposium" on the State University of Buffalo campus.

The group had formed five years earlier, after a goateed-and-leather-jacketed twenty-seven-year-old auto mechanic named Lowell Eggemeier strolled into a San Francisco police station, lit a joint, and exhaled at a detective. "I am starting a campaign to legalize marijuana smoking," Eggemeier declared. "I wish to be arrested."

His attorney quickly announced the foundation of LEMAR, for "Legalize Marijuana," and picket-sign protests in the city followed—first gathering ten and then a couple hundred activists. Within six months, another LEMAR chapter had formed in New York City with the involvement of such luminaries as the poet Allen Ginsberg; a LEMAR-affiliated mimeograph, the *Marijuana Newsletter*, began publication soon afterward. Ginsberg zeroed in on the ways in which smoking the forbidden plant, cultivated for its medicinal and psychoactive properties for thousands of years in Africa and Asia but outlawed in twentieth-century America, might lead to revolution: "When the citizens of this country see that such an old-time, taken-for-granted, flag-waving, reactionary truism of police, press, and law as the 'reefer menace' is in fact a creepy hoax, a scarecrow, what will they begin to think of the whole of taken-for-granted public REALITY? What of other issues filled with the same threatening hysteria? The specter of Communism? Respect for the police and courts? Respect for the Treasury Department? If marijuana is a hoax, what is Money? What is the War in Vietnam? What are the Mass Media?" By 1967, there were LEMAR chapters in Buffalo, Detroit, Los Angeles, and Toronto; during that year of so many Be-Ins and Love-Ins, a number of "smoke-ins" occurred, with pounds of marijuana chopped up and rolled into hundreds of joints and distributed.

Those events had, unsurprisingly, attracted police attention, and early publicity guaranteed that the 1969 Buffalo gathering would too. "Let's go and get high and listen to some music, and FUCK!" raved the underground newspaper *Ann Arbor Sun* a month in advance.

On the symposium's first day, agents of the US Postal Service, FBI, Customs, and Bureau of Narcotics and Dangerous Drugs all descended on a university classroom to arrest a student suspected of smuggling hashish.

This made Michael Aldrich, the local LEMAR organizer, nervous. Along with the distinguished MDs and PhDs invited to attend the seminar were several high-profile icons of the counterculture, many of whom had tangled with the law: LSD evangelist Timothy Leary was already appealing a thirty-year jail sentence and a $30,000 fine for possession and transportation of marijuana. Abbie Hoffman and Jerry Rubin of the Youth International Party (YIP) had been called before the House Committee on Un-American Activities. The MC5, the weekend's musical entertainment, had recently performed a concert that was surreptitiously filmed by the FBI; their manager, John Sinclair, was awaiting sentencing on charges of assaulting a police officer at one of their shows. Nearly fifty members—five busloads—of the Hog Farm, a commune-turned-hippie-caravan, had been recently detained in a Pennsylvania narcotics raid. Allen Ginsberg had a criminal record in multiple countries. Even the eminent literary critic Leslie Fiedler, a professor at Buffalo and faculty advisor to the local LEMAR chapter, had been arrested on drug charges—along with his wife, son, and daughter-in-law—when police raided his wiretapped home.

So Aldrich, not taking any chances, kept his guests holed up and away from public view. "If you try to see any of these people in their rooms," he told a local reporter, "I'll take your press pass away."

"We were all put up in these dormitories, they were like Holiday Inn rooms," recalled Ken Kelley, a militant activist who'd traveled to Buffalo with the MC5. "And all the sudden this guy in a hat comes in, makes a point of taking off his coat, taking out a pistol, and putting it on the bed.

"Everybody fucking freaks out, and he announces, 'I'm Tom Forcade, the head of the Underground Press Syndicate.'

"Everybody goes, *Uh oh! A-gent!*"

Three months later, and two thousand miles to the southwest, the *Arizona Republic* informed its readers that revolution was afoot in Phoenix.

"Although local evidence to the fact is scarce, the fourth largest underground publication in the country is edited right here in Phoenix," wrote columnist Paul Schatt. "*Orpheus Magazine*, the digest of the undergrounds, is produced here or on the road in a 1946 Chevrolet school bus that has been converted into an office on wheels."

A mysterious group, Schatt reported, was behind not just *Orpheus* but also the entire Underground Press Syndicate, "the international association of all underground papers," which included the *Los Angeles Free Times*, *Chicago Seed*, *East Village Other*, and *Berkeley Barb*. An anonymous source at *Orpheus* told Schatt that the group—at the behest of its leader, one Tom K. Forcade—had purposely kept its local circulation to a minimum even as it sold heavily in other parts of the country and overseas.

"We, however, think this is a mistake," the source told Schatt, "and detrimental both to the staff and to Phoenix, for us to have to operate quasi-secretly and for Phoenix not to accept that an operation of this scope is taking place in Phoenix. We are nonviolent, don't bother anyone, and feel that Phoenix should know the good we're doing—or bad, if they feel that way."

In truth, it was highly unlikely that the underground press would receive a warm reception in conservative Arizona. "You shouldn't talk so freely about sexuality," an *Arizona Republic* reporter had recently sneered to a visiting Allen Ginsberg; when Ginsberg responded with a curse, the newsman punched the poet in the mouth. The week that the *Republic*'s column on *Orpheus* ran, one of the shops that sold the magazine was evicted. "You are dirty people," the owners of the Hip Pocket Emporium were told, "and your clientele are an undesirable element."

The *Orpheus* manifesto from which Schatt quoted indicated that the group was already braced for any hostilities that might arise:

> *Orpheus* herewith announces its intention of moving its offices to a free zone, located on a delta of the Colorado River. Since the status of these deltas is ambiguous, we will declare it a free liberated zone, and inhabitants will not be obliged to follow any of the irrational laws now in force in the unliberated zone.

Schatt closed his column with a promise that the *Republic* would "report from time to time on the progress made in establishing this beachhead." Within days, the paper made good on that promise and sent a journalist to visit *Orpheus* headquarters: a rundown, single-story, twelve-room house on the west side of downtown Phoenix, in the shadow of the State Capitol Building.

A hippie greeted the reporter at the front steps, quickly barred shut the heavy door behind them, and ushered him into the living room to meet the mysterious Tom Forcade, who pronounced his name like "façade."*

The diminutive Forcade was sitting in the corner, wearing a black suit, moccasins, and a wide-brim brown hat with bunting that appeared to be fashioned from an American flag. When the hat tilted up, his piercing blue eyes were revealed. "Did you notice the charred marks on the house when you came in?" he asked, sipping milk from a carton. "Two weeks ago, someone threw a bomb on the porch. We found another bomb that didn't go off."

The reporter noted that Forcade was himself clean-shaven, with short hair. "Occasionally," Forcade explained, "I have to go out when they want someone to play straight." But he declined to answer other questions about himself, and spoke slowly, as if searching for exaction with every word.

"We don't break any laws or confront the establishment," he insisted, and explained that the Underground Press Syndicate was simply a kind of Associated Press for a movement with "its own music, art, theater, vocabulary, fads, religions, entrepreneurs and, of course, its own politics and mass media."

And yet, Forcade said, they were faced with constant hostilities. "We have a hard time staying alive, and have to fight back the people who have a negative attitude against us." Other underground newspaper offices, he said, had been "ripped up with axes" or otherwise sabotaged. "Usually, it's the action of some yo-yo politician out to make a name for himself. But no underground paper which has been suppressed has lost when its case has been taken to a higher court."

Forcade gave the reporter a tour of the house, showing off a darkroom, an offset printing press, and the largest underground-newspaper

---

* Thomas King Forcade sometimes spelled his last name "Forçade." The cedilla appears in this book's title to signal his preferred pronunciation and intentional echo of "façade," but the name is rendered throughout the text as "Forcade," as it usually was during his lifetime.

library in the world. Stacks of papers filled shelves and spilled onto the floor. "Although newspaper offices are destroyed," Forcade said, "they know at least one copy of their paper will exist." He pointed out the old school bus that had been mentioned in Paul Schatt's column, the one that served as an "office on wheels." Sometimes they loaded the printing press onto the bus, Forcade said, when they deemed it necessary to "go to centers of awareness and have contact with people with their advanced minds and followers."

At the end of the visit, he walked the reporter to the door. "Today you can't be concerned with what is constitutional but what is right," Forcade mused. "If all the laws in the United States were strictly enforced everyone would be in jail."

HOUSE NEAR STATE CAPITOL LINKS UNDERGROUND PRESS ran the headline in the *Republic*; the story noted that Forcade had refused to be photographed (instead there appeared a picture of Benny Alvarez, a longhaired Chicano youth who volunteered for *Orpheus*, operating the magazine's printing press).

If that didn't sow suspicion in the minds of the Phoenix readership, surely the story that shared the page—ALARMED EXPERT RANKS PHOENIX AMONG WIDEST OPEN DRUG TOWNS—would drive home the idea that the city was under threat. That article quoted a local psychologist warning that proximity to the Mexican border and a lack of public funding for narcotics control put Phoenicians at risk. The local marijuana, he contended, was in fact hashish, which caused such powerful hallucinations and disturbances that users turned to morphine or barbiturates to calm down. Worse, he said, much of the LSD was cut with amphetamines, strychnine, and mescaline. And the valley was flooding with heroin.

In Phoenix, where narcotics arrests had risen by 500 percent in two years, the drug scare had flared into hysteria, and authorities linked the threat to political insurgencies. Charles Tignor, the director of Arizona's State Narcotics Enforcement Division, told a Rotary Club luncheon crowd that campus unrest and hallucinogens were two prongs of a Communist strategy to "morally corrupt the youth of this country," and he traced the problem back to 1965, "when the New Left became active on campuses" and pro-LSD "propaganda" bombarded the youth.

"It's hard to believe that this could happen in our community and in all other communities across the nation by accident," the assistant police chief of Phoenix told one PTA meeting. Surely the rise of drug use was the result of "small groups working to destroy our way of life without offering anything better to replace it. They are small groups, but they are influencing very large numbers of young people. I have to wonder, is this accidental?"

On June 17, a few weeks after the *Arizona Republic* profile of *Orpheus* was published, the Special Investigations unit of the Phoenix police paid its own visit to the house on the west side of the city. They removed seven tablets of LSD from the refrigerator and arrested an *Orpheus* volunteer who lived in a trailer parked in the backyard. They also put out a warrant for Forcade, who wasn't there.

According to Forcade's account, when he returned to the house it was so utterly destroyed that he suspected a prankster had let loose wild javelinas. Boxes and drawers had been dumped on the floor; water was poured over files. Every piece of furniture was overturned, the stereo was destroyed, and the mail was ripped open. Worst of all was the damage to the UPS library, the largest collection of underground periodicals in the world.

"The only LSD in our office was the LSD the police put there," Forcade responded, after turning himself in to police. "It would have been much more imaginative and equally realistic to charge that the entire building was constructed of marijuana bricks and then haul it away with house-moving equipment, as evidence."

Forcade asserted that the police had found it necessary to create an excuse to destroy the UPS office because they would never actually catch him breaking the law. "I don't smoke, drink, or use medication or drugs of any kind, legal or illegal," he claimed. "I learned that out of the Bible."

The raid, he said, was a political attempt to silence a free press, and the area newspapers, which had not asked UPS for its side of the story, were complicit.

"The local media continually rant on law and order and upholding the Constitution. Talk is cheap."

Perhaps looking to establish his credibility as a man of God, Forcade submitted an article about the dangers of drugs to a small local newspaper called the *North Mountain News* and signed it "The Reverend Thomas King Forcade." But it was largely plagiarized from an article that had been written by the army and circulated on various military bases. In an editorial, the publisher of the *North Mountain News* vouched for him as well, noting that Forcade "has a bachelor's degree from Brigham Young University and at 23 is undoubtedly one of the most talented advertising men and publishers in the United States. He has worked for the past two years under the handicap of having his phone tapped, his mail opened, and his business establishment raided by narcotics agents. [Forcade] is a Mormon and neither drinks, smokes, nor uses narcotics. If there really was LSD found in his establishment, it was put there without his knowledge—or, very simply, he is being framed."

Some of this was true.

The Underground Press Syndicate was founded in 1966, a consortium of the largest and most influential independent newspapers—the *Los Angeles Free Press*, the *East Village Other* in New York City, the *Berkeley Barb*, the *Paper* in East Lansing, and the *Fifth Estate* in Detroit—that had sprung up in just a couple of years alongside the rise of New Left politics, anti-war sentiment, and the burgeoning psychedelic counterculture. Part of the goal of the UPS was simply for appearances' sake: to present a united front of freaks, and stave off feelings of alienation throughout the sprawling underground community. But it was also practical: a way for budget-crunched papers to freely share editorial content with one another, and to set up national advertising deals.

In August 1967, Forcade, a twenty-one-year-old Arizona resident with a degree in business, read that UPS was in search of volunteers, and he offered to assist long distance, from Phoenix. In a letter to UPS cofounder John Wilcock, Forcade warned of the creeping capitalism that threatened to corrupt the fast-growing underground industry. "The vultures are already circling and swooping, even feeding," he wrote, before yielding to a hopeful prediction of karmic righteousness. "The obvious and natural solution is that those publications which demonstrate their primary concern with commercialism will patently be unable to cooperate among themselves and will find no one among the hardcore junkie-freelancers Movement who will supply them with material or cooperate with them." He sent dummy pages from his not-yet-published magazine *Orpheus*—a kind of *Reader's Digest* anthology of articles from the underground press—and waited for a response. After some voting and vetting, the UPS committee accepted him into the fold.

Forcade had thrown himself into the job with the help of a revolving door of local longhairs. The *Orpheus* crew assembled booklets advising fellow publishers on how to use printing presses, founded a distributing agency, solicited national advertising, offered a clipping service for record companies, and—recognizing that authorities often used obscenity charges to repress political newspapers—drafted and circulated an amicus curiae brief to help member papers defend themselves against overzealous police departments.

Forcade's fellow UPS editors soon voted to move the bulk of the organization's administrative work to him in Arizona. For the next two years, Forcade and the *Orpheus* staff ran UPS operations from downtown Phoenix, in a five-bedroom white-brick house fortified with deadlocked doors and barbed wire across every window. And they continued to distribute *Orpheus*—along with various illicit and profit-yielding substances—via Forcade's roving 1946 Chevrolet school bus. If police pulled the bus over, Forcade, wearing a priest's collar, would produce a copy of *Orpheus*, a peace-sign-flashing Jesus on its cover, and lead the other passengers in singing a hymn, a ruse that was usually convincing enough to get off with a warning. (Any authority figure who actually looked at the pages inside might have been alarmed, or maybe confused, because the writings embraced a variety of political philosophies in rapid succession, from anarchist to libertarian to pacifist to Marxist.)

The *Orpheus* announcement of plans for the lawless Colorado River "liberated zone" was just one of many signs of increasing radicalism. The credo became: Don't compromise, don't be complicit, opt out. "If you want to be part of the solution, I say start acting and thinking *pure love, right now*," Forcade exhorted readers. "Turn in your draft card. Turn in *all* your cards. Turn in your clothes. Turn in your degree. Turn in your W-2 forms. Turn in your driver's license. Turn in your car, unless it was made in Sweden or a similar sane society. Turn it *all* in, and turn it *all* off."

By 1969, Forcade was warning against conservatives and liberals alike. "Don't trust anybody but a radical, because only a radical has got the guts to stand up on his hind legs and say where he's at. Turn off the supply of evil crap to your head—the media. Read only the underground press. The underground press does not attempt to 'give the other side.' That's crap. The underground press is to put forth good."

During the week of the *Orpheus* drug bust, Forcade welcomed a journalist named John Burks who wanted to interview him for a splashy *Rolling Stone* article on the underground press. Burks made no mention of the drug bust, although the article alluded to the house's strange lack of furniture: nothing but desk chairs and a table for the phonograph that played Cream and Dylan and free jazz records. Burks also noted that wire mesh had been placed over the windows.

"We make a fetish of being un-paranoid," Forcade told him, but the paranoia was immediately palpable when he reprimanded his assistant for not securing the door.

"Benny, we've got to keep it barred," Forcade said. "You're going to keep it barred, aren't you? It's something we've got to do, Benny."

"We've also got a fully developed plan of self-defense," Forcade assured Burks. "We don't talk about it, and we don't seek confrontation, but we're prepared."

Forcade maintained his rule about not having his face photographed. ("When they start rounding people up, I don't want to make it easy for them. It's just a preoccupation that I never have my picture taken if I can help it.") Nor would he reveal his age. "Time doesn't exist here the way it does other places," he explained.

But as they sat under the living room air conditioner, drinking beer and eating chili that Benny prepared, Forcade opened up more about his background to Burks than he had to even some of the people who worked for him. In a soft drawl he revealed he'd graduated from the University of Utah and worked in advertising, and that he'd even served in the military.

He was also, he said, a preacher at the Church of Life—its name was painted on the side of the school bus out back—and eager to bring Christ into the dialogues of the underground.

"We'll continue doing articles on the underground scene," he said, "but we'll quote Jesus where we want to make a point. It should appeal to a wider set of people. Most people are conditioned to a Christian way of thinking.

"I think there's a lot of Movement people who secretly want to go back to nonviolence," Forcade continued. "And there's no reason we can't do it. Just create a new synthesis within the Movement—and do it. I think the Movement has reached the point of diminishing returns with the techniques of shock and separatism."

And yet he beamed when Burks told him that John Sinclair of the militant White Panthers had called the underground press "a great bunch of motherfuckers." The White Panthers' battle cry for a "total assault on the culture by any means necessary, including rock and roll, dope, and fucking in the streets," may have seemed the antithesis of the Christian life, but "I really think Sinclair has genius," he said. "A deeply poetic vision of the revolution. I wish I could be more like him."

Later, Forcade showed off the modifications he'd made to the bus, freshly hosed off and gleaming in the hundred-degree-plus Phoenix sun. Seats had been removed, replaced by mattresses and equipment for assembling *Orpheus* on the road while traveling between Berkeley, Denver, Chicago, and New York. This also allowed them to spread the word and raise the profile of the Underground Press Syndicate, "to sustain the myth of a finely honed media institution that's going to roll over the whole land," as he put it. "I think the day will come when we'll have a daily underground paper in every city and a weekly in every town."

At the end of the visit, Forcade submitted to posing for some pictures outdoors, on the condition that his face remain concealed. Burks photographed him from above so that the brim of his hat protected his identity.

Three weeks later, on July 6, Forcade got in the *Orpheus* bus and left Phoenix. "We're going to New York for a few months," he wrote. "We've had it with small town mentalities."

First, though, they were headed to Michigan. The national conference of the Underground Press Syndicate awaited.

The travelers logged nearly two thousand miles in four days. From the Grand Canyon State, they sped through Tucumcari, up Route 54 to Wichita, and west through Kansas City. Sweltering heat and police hassles made it hard to breathe. Along the way, they liberally handed out copies of their psychedelically colored magazine, *Orpheus*, which charmed some of the Midwesterners and flummoxed others. The bus cruised northward day and night, blurring past motels and gas stations, blasting the AM radio soundtrack shuck of an Aquarian dream that was already fading: "Atlantis," "In the Year 2525," "Good Morning Starshine."

At 4:00 a.m. on the morning of Thursday, July 10, the bus eased into a parking lot near the edge of the University of Michigan campus in Ann Arbor. A floodlight illuminated the adjacent lawn.

The lamps and stereo at 1510 Hill Street were still on when the *Orpheus* bus emptied out, led by Forcade. They followed the sound of distant music, climbed the porch, and knocked on the mansion door. A purple and white flag, hanging above, remained still as the door opened.

This was the home base of Trans-Love Energies, the community founded by John and Leni Sinclair, and which also included the militantly anti-racist White Panther Party. They were having a fraught summer. John Sinclair—who'd drafted that platform of "rock and roll, dope, and fucking in the streets"—was at the forefront of marijuana legalization efforts and currently awaiting sentencing for possession after giving two joints to an undercover cop. Adding salt to the wound was the departure of the White Panthers' longtime house band, the MC5, whose members were now pursuing dreams of rock-and-roll stardom. The MC5 had been a key component of Sinclair's goal of creating synergy between cultural and political movements: a young listener might send fan mail to the MC5, asking for an autographed photo, and in response receive White Panther literature that included instructions for revolution.*

Greeting the visitors, the hosts lamented that the first delegates to arrive in town—representatives of the *Chicago Seed*—had themselves been pulled over and detained for possession of marijuana. The *Orpheus* travelers retrieved their sleeping bags from the bus and, before they crashed to sleep on the wooden floors, looked over the pamphlets they'd been handed:

> This conference marks the turning point in the revolutionary media. This is the year—1969—that the revolutionary youth media will reach beyond the hip artistic and political enclaves in Amerika out into the bowels of this society—to all our young brothers out there in

---

* "The White Panther Party is working toward obtaining control of large masses of young people for the primary purpose of causing revolution in this country," a Michigan state police detective would later testify before the Senate subcommittee. "The methods used to recruit these people is based upon a complete dropout of our society and the adoption of a system involving 'rock' music and the free use of drugs and sex in a setting of commune living. It is apparent that every attempt is being made to break down the moral relationship between the youth and his or her parents along with a complete disregard for law and order."

television land, in the suburbs, the school-jails, the factories and pool halls to turn our people on to the truth about the problem—and to the solution to that problem. This is the year we will transform our movement from an "underground press syndicate" to a functioning revolutionary brotherhood.

Forcade particularly admired two leaders in the political-countercultural world. One was John Sinclair, in whose home he was sleeping. The other was Abbie Hoffman, whom Forcade would finally meet this weekend. Hoffman had been a volunteer for the Student Nonviolent Coordinating Committee, a racially integrated civil rights group. When the SNCC purged its white members in the wake of the Black Power movement, Hoffman felt disillusioned—until LSD gave him the epiphany that he could politicize hippies. With a half dozen other pranksters who called themselves "Yippies," Hoffman threw himself into guerilla theater; at the New York Stock Exchange, for instance, they ate, threw, and burned dollar bills in a protest of materialism.

As the early morning sky lightened, Forcade closed his eyes. This weekend, he was to assume full leadership of the Underground Press Syndicate, making him an important player in the same movement circles, securing his place among the leaders. The underground papers now boasted a combined weekly readership of a hundred million.

Hours later, the *Orpheus* bus loaded up with groggy passengers and Forcade drove east, over a bridge, and onto Pontiac Trail. After a few miles, it reached a driveway surrounded by trees. Just past a dented piece of tin on which someone had painted a peace sign stood a White Panther member with a loaded 12-gauge shotgun, guarding the gate.

Ann Arbor was especially tense that weekend because there was a serial killer on the loose. Six young women between the ages of thirteen and twenty-three had been murdered and mutilated in the past twenty-three months, and days before the radical media conference, a seventh woman was killed.

"I've told my men to forget about traffic, forget about routine, and get out into the boondocks and search," Washtenaw County sheriff Doug Harvey told the *Times-News*. "We patrol the back roads, the lover's lanes, any place that's lonely. We stop anybody and everybody." There were still no leads on the serial killer, whom newspapers had dubbed the "Michigan Murderer."

Skip Taube, a prominent member of the White Panthers, had been passing around petitions for Harvey's recall, mocking the failed efforts to solve the serial killings. "He couldn't find eggs in a hen house," Taube sneered to a reporter.

Still, patterns had begun to emerge: Several of the bodies had been found in abandoned farmhouses. A psychiatrist at the university, noting that two killings occurred around Independence Day, sensed an "antigovernment message" being sent. Another psychiatrist, at the Ypsilanti State Hospital, had narrowed the killer's age range to eighteen to thirty. And a cab driver who claimed to hear "a lot of things" told reporters that "one of these hippie kids" was the murderer. The latest police theory was that the culprit was a political radical who was trying to humiliate the authorities.

Sheriff Harvey already disliked hippies. He publicly criticized their "animal conduct" and loud music. "The decent people of this area have a few rights, too," he said, "like not putting up with hopheads, sex nuts, and public drunks." They'd caused more and more trouble the past few years, he thought, culminating with a three-day riot the month before, at a music fest that ended with a melee of rocks and batons. That had caught the attention of FBI director J. Edgar Hoover, who ordered surveillance and disruption of the White Panther Party.

The guards at the driveway gate checked Forcade's credentials, and the bus crawled three hundred yards up a winding dirt road. The grassy hilltop had a panoramic view overlooking the city and countryside, perfect for lookouts. On a patch of mowed land stood the brick farmhouse owned by a former outrider with the Detroit Highwaymen motorcycle gang and members of a group he managed, the Tate Blues Band. Outside the house, visitors frolicked in the nude, some of them running around and spraying water on one another.

Skip Taube, the petition-circulating thorn in Sheriff Harvey's side, was also the White Panther's minister of education. Tall and gaunt, with glasses and fuzzy facial hair, he emerged to warn the arriving congregation that police harassment had intensified in recent weeks.

"We're going to set up a command post," Taube announced. "In the meantime, be very careful. Don't go anywhere by yourself—if you do, tell a friend so we'll know whether you're back in time. The pigs are watching the Hill Street houses, but they ain't going to get anywhere near here without getting their heads blown off. That's all. We just want people to know there's a lot of tension in the community."

The White Panthers' minister of defense, a high school track-star-turned-greaser-turned-union-organizer-turned-revolutionary named Pun Plamondon, sat on a bench with his wife, Genie—the minister of communications—and watched the road. They wore jeans. She held a can of beer. He held a shotgun.

B y the afternoon, more than two hundred representatives had gathered. They'd driven, hitchhiked, and forged youth-fare airline cards to descend from the Lower East Side, Vancouver, Houston, Bloomington, San Francisco, Atlanta, Seattle, and even Jackson, Mississippi. (A few visitors from the so-called establishment press were eager to see what this was all about. But the *Detroit Free Press* reporter was quickly ousted, and even a *Village Voice* columnist who'd traveled from New York got the cold shoulder.)

Art Johnston, a former Michigander who'd moved to California to write for the *Berkeley Barb*, began the proceedings. Johnston had a bushy mustache and hair that swirled over his eyes. He preached about a "youth culture revolution."

"We have to get out to TV land, to the suburbs where the people are," he said. Since "kids learn from B-movies," he reasoned that the language of biker movies, hot-rod culture, surfing, and other outlets of adolescent rebellion would resonate with middle-class white teenagers.

"It came to me in an acid flash," Johnston beamed.

Attendees floated from one workshop to another. Bill Schanen, the decidedly nonradical fifty-four-year-old owner of a Milwaukee printing business, had weathered costly boycotts, FBI visits, and lost friendships because of his willingness to print the underground *Kaleidoscope*; here, he gave a seminar on offset printing, his short white hair and deep tan conspicuous in the sea of wild-looking kids. Elsewhere, editors delivered instructional lectures on using ham radios, telexes, bulk mail, and street-corner distribution. Tents were assembled, wine was poured, and although much of Michigan was suffering a marijuana drought, joints were rolled.

Equipped with Bolex cameras and a Nagra recorder, Forcade and the *Orpheus* team began filming. Protestations arose—people wanted to speak freely, without worrying about incriminating themselves. Why did there need to be a document?

Forcade said he was working on a documentary, to be called *The Underground Press Loves You.* "If you don't want to be in the film," he suggested, "just stay out of camera range."

"Aren't we overdoing the paranoia business?" pleaded one publisher, as Forcade's camera trained on his face. "First, we bar the establishment press, and now we say we can't even cover the meeting ourselves?"

With this endorsement, Forcade darted around the grounds, conducting more interviews until shadows grew long. It wasn't hard to figure the reasons for all the paranoia. The editor of Vancouver's *Georgia Straight*—the first newspaper to be charged with "criminal libel" since 1938—told Forcade about paper confiscations, obscenity busts, and, after the publication of an article about planting seeds, a "counseling to cultivate marijuana" indictment.

Forcade also interviewed Abbie Hoffman, whose activism had been an inspiration to him. Hoffman had seen firsthand the ruptures in the anti-war movement. That spring he, along with a cross section of other well-known activists who'd soon be known as the Chicago Eight, had been indicted on conspiracy charges for the riots at the previous summer's Democratic National Convention. And only weeks before coming to Ann Arbor, he'd attended the final, acrimonious convention of the Students for a Democratic Society, in which the largest anti-war group in the country splintered before his eyes.

Hoffman gave Forcade a candid and concise description of Yippie tactics.

> The trick in manipulating the media is to get them to promote an event before it happens…get them to make an advertisement for an event—an advertisement for revolution—the same way you would advertise soap.…We got them hooked. As a result of Chicago, they just can't ignore what we're doing.…When the cops hear I'm going to speak at a university or in a small town, they'll bring in tons of cops.

They'll do the whole Chicago trip, bringing in the armed forces shit. And when they've got the cops there and all over the fuckin' place, that becomes the theater of the thing, and what you're talking about to the audience becomes very real. You're not talking about something abstract. There's a tension, a new kind of theater.

"Do you think the cops know you're here today in Ann Arbor?"

"Sure," Abbie said. "I have to write the US district attorney every time I leave New York City. I have to write him where I'm going, who I'm going to see, what I'm going to do, and when I'm coming back."

After everyone feasted on barbecued chicken and watermelon, the *Orpheus* bus led a line of cars down to a coffeehouse on the University of Michigan campus to hear the Tate Blues Band. The singer, Terry Tate—who, in the words of one observer, howled "like a panther in a bear trap"—had been jailed only a few weeks before for tearing off, piece by piece, his outfit sewn from an American flag. Undercover police, who'd caught the drug-induced performance on 8mm film, arrested him for indecent exposure, set his bail at $5,000, and banned further park concerts. The police had shorn Tate's long, kinky hair, but tonight his eyes looked as crazed as ever. Watching all the hooting, jumping, and shouting, even one of the attendant radicals commented, "These Trans-Love people are laying it on pretty thick."

Exhausted, they caravanned back to the hill in the late hours and slept outdoors or in barns.

It wasn't long before the conference encountered a manifestation of the very forces of suppression the papers were established to fight. While members of the underground cooked communal breakfast for three hundred over open fires, a phone call came in for Art Johnston. It was from Cheryl McCall, the nineteen-year-old editor of *South End*, the Wayne State University student paper that Johnston himself had radicalized only two years ago. The president of the university had just banned the paper, canceling staff salaries and refusing to print the latest issue—an extra-thick edition devoted to cultural revolution. He'd locked the pages in his personal safe.

Forcade bused a contingent of delegates to a press conference McCall was holding at the *South End* offices, where Art Johnston took the microphone and threatened a further "invasion of weirdos, dope-fiends, acid-heads, and motorcycle freaks." McCall, for her part, invited the Wayne State president to "sit down and smoke some dope with us." He declined.

The group departed for the Ann Arbor *Argus* offices and got to work re-creating the student paper. Staffers from Detroit's *Fifth Estate* soon joined them, hauling along their own equipment and materials. By Monday, a revolving crew of nonstudents would reset and print thirty thousand copies of the now-contraband *South End*.

Back on the hilltop, Michael Forman, whose Pennsylvania-based Concert Hall agency had been hired by Forcade to act as the advertising representative for UPS, stood up to debrief everyone about the current crisis with record labels. A few months earlier, Columbia Records had suddenly pulled all its advertising from the underground press—a major loss, because those contracts provided about $100,000 a year for the papers. An inside source at the label alleged that government pressure had been applied to Columbia's parent company CBS, a claim made even more plausible when the other television network-owned labels, ABC Records and NBC's RCA Records, also withdrew ads from underground papers.

Forman warned that *Rolling Stone* editor Jan Wenner—a "junior Hearst, co-opting our culture and betraying the revolution"—had contacted other Concert Hall clients to tell them they were wasting their money with the underground papers. One Wenner letter to national advertisers even asked why they would support publications that stood in opposition to capitalism.

Upon hearing Forman's speech, editors began to debate a boycott of Columbia releases, even those of New Left icon Bob Dylan. Abbie Hoffman demanded punishment for "ripping off the people's music."

Maybe all the revolution in the air was rubbing off on the businessman Forman. "Money is irrelevant," he declared, belying his buttoned-down appearance. "Our purpose...is to get the word out." Forget about Columbia: if the papers could stabilize their relationships with local advertisers, he said, they wouldn't have to rely on record ads or sex-soliciting classifieds. "You have to make your papers a permanent media."

The editors decided to write an open letter appealing for musicians to use their leverage to pressure Columbia. If that didn't work, well, maybe the label's records would have to be "liberated" from stores or its offices occupied.

Rock festivals were another matter of concern. The Palm Springs Pop Festival and others had already been scenes of militarized police action, riots, and killings. Promoters, looking for a quick buck, neglected details like sufficient PA systems, toilets, and water. The underground papers had to acknowledge that they'd been complicit in their support of these co-opting money grabs.

But Michael Forman told everyone that the Woodstock Music and Arts Festival, a month away, might be different. Forman and his partner at Concert Hall were themselves involved in the promotion, which was going to need the help of the underground papers to get the word out—and Concert Hall was even publishing the program that would be distributed on the festival grounds. (Forman did not mention that Concert Hall had bluffed its way into a $10,000 contract to finesse a hip image for Woodstock promoters, furnishing a midtown Manhattan office with black lights, cloudlike fabric hanging from the ceilings, and, in lieu of sofas or chairs, seating on wall-to-wall chartreuse carpet.)

As Abbie Hoffman listened, wheels began turning in his head. "I realized something of the magnitude of Chicago was in the making," he later remembered, "a huge rock concert lasting a few days presented an opportunity to reach masses of young people in a setting where they felt part of something bigger." What if rock concert promoters didn't just make money off the culture—what if they gave something back? What if some of the profits went toward movement goals? What if radical politics were given a voice at the concert? He made a mental note to visit the Woodstock offices as soon as he returned to New York.

Forcade's Ann Arbor coronation as the leader of the Underground Press Syndicate, replacing its five-man coordinating committee, was a smooth affair—no one else seemed to want the job. The conversation about the Liberation News Service, however, was a little bumpier. Whereas UPS concerned itself with the nuts and bolts of underground publishing—printing, advertising, distribution, and sharing of content—LNS acted as a more traditional news service, providing articles and photographs that could be run in member papers. The two were independent of one another but hardly competitors; most of the larger papers paid dues to both organizations.

In Ann Arbor, LNS drew criticism for its dogmatic stances on issues, often written with a Marxist bent. But the attending LNS representatives pushed back. "Hey," one of its editors shouted, "what are we, anyway—fucking journalists?" Everyone trailed off into grumbles. It would be only the first of the weekend's many internecine battles.

After the interruption of an evening rainstorm, the filmmaking cooperative Newsreel projected footage it had shot the previous summer: footage of draft resistance organizing in Boston; of Oleo Strut, a GI coffeehouse at Fort Hood, Texas; of *Rat* and Newsreel's takeover of a New York public television station; of the streets of Chicago during the Democratic National Convention police riot. Providing a running commentary throughout the screening was Newsreel's own Melvin Margulis, who only stopped shouting occasionally to swat violently at the mosquitoes attacking his nude body.

On Saturday, one speaker in particular—decked out in a "Free Huey" sweatshirt, tan pants, black boots, and sunglasses—commanded the conference's attention. Elbert Howard, better known as "Big Man," was the Black Panthers' deputy minister of information as well as editor of its newspaper, the *Black Panther Party Community News Service.*

He was in Ann Arbor to give his pitch for the United Front Against Fascism, an attempt to establish an alliance with white and Chicano radicals, leftists, and liberals.

Big Man urged last-minute press coverage for the United Front's upcoming conference, scheduled for the following weekend in Oakland. This was a momentous event—despite Huey Newton's calls for aid from white "mother country radicals," the New Left had mostly grouped according to skin color since the expulsion of white members from the SNCC in 1966. The upcoming meeting could be a chance to come together again, even if certain conditions applied to the alliance. The Black Panthers enjoyed near worship from the most radical elements of the counterculture, partly a mix of machismo envy, white guilt, and the awareness that, unlike some of themselves, the Panthers were committed to their mission out of necessity and not middle-class adventurism.

But Big Man was interrupted by some of the women at the conference, who accused the Panthers of chauvinism. Indeed, just four weeks earlier, at the Students for a Democratic Society (SDS) conference in

Chicago, one Panther leader extolled the charms of "pussy power," and then another took the microphone and explained, "The brother was only trying to say to you sisters that you have a strategic position in the revolution: prone."

Now, the women in Ann Arbor widened the sexism charge to all the papers, offering as evidence their back-pages pornographic advertisements. Those ads were a big part of what alienated the *Berkeley Barb* staff from its publisher, Max Scherr. (The other part was the discovery that he was pocketing four grand a week while they worked for low wages.) In just the past week, a group of departed *Barb* workers had decided to publish their own competing paper, the *Berkeley Tribe*; one of them even flew to Ann Arbor to show off the premiere issue, hot off the presses. The underground representatives took a vote and overwhelmingly decided to back the *Tribe* over the *Barb*.

Big Man, frustrated by the hijacking of his lecture, pointed out that his paper didn't even run ads. "We're not capitalists; we're against capitalism," he said; and accepting advertisements was "just perpetuating it." After counterprotests by some of the freakier men—say, wasn't puritanism the enemy here, man, and not the *freedom* of nude bodies?—resolutions were quickly drafted by an LNS editor:

1. *That male supremacy and chauvinism be eliminated from the contents of the underground papers. For example, papers should stop accepting commercial advertising that uses women's bodies to sell records and other products, and advertisements for sex, since the use of sex as a commodity specially oppresses women in this country. Also, women's bodies should not be exploited in the papers for the purpose of increasing circulation.*
2. *That papers make a particular effort to publish material on women's oppression and liberation with the entire contents of the paper.*
3. *That women have a full role in all the functions of the staffs of underground papers.*

These lines of debate exhausted, it was finally time for some of the delegates to gather in the shade of the *Orpheus* bus to tackle a proposal that Jeff Shero, the New-Yorker-by-way-of-Texas editor of *The Rat*, had been considering for the past few months: the formation of a Revolutionary

Press Movement. RPM member papers would dedicate themselves to promoting radical politics and even coordinating actions. "Revolutionaries first, journalists second" was the motto; the Ann Arbor *Argus, Berkeley Tribe, Black Panther, Fifth Estate,* and *Chicago Seed* were all on board. ("Get some cat who's really into ecology," Shero suggested as an example, "and guarantee him three million readers as payment for an outta sight series of articles.") Tom Forcade volunteered the UPS staff for the effort as well.

Abbie Hoffman was especially excited about what this plan could mean for the defense effort of the Chicago Eight. He believed that most editors and publishers had failed to make the sacrifices that he and the other defendants did and that it was time for them to put themselves on the line. The RPM papers, he said, should work to publicize the upcoming "National Action" in Chicago, which had been proposed by SDS at that same tumultuous conference that included the incendiary remarks about women. Set for October, the demonstration promised to "Bring the War Home," to show that white radicals would fight in a revolutionary alliance alongside the Black Panthers and the Young Lords.

As they plotted, a few of them noticed, in the distance, the two Ann Arbor officers who'd appeared at the perimeter of the property.

Pun and Genie Plamondon, armed with rifles, asked them what they wanted. One of the *Chicago Seed* people who'd been arrested for marijuana possession Wednesday night and released on bail had apparently disappeared. "He's not here," Pun told them, proud of his disciplined manner, "and you can't look without a warrant." The police promptly turned their car around and drove away. Up on the hill, Art Johnston was ready for a real revolution. "We have to develop contingency plans to go underground," he insisted. The law enforcement hassles were getting to be too much.

Pun and Skip Taube returned to grilling chicken for the next meal.

And then, ten minutes later, a frightened voice called out.

"Pigs!"

Dozens of Ann Arbor and Washtenaw County policemen were storming the property, flowing from the neighboring grounds. They climbed from bushes, armed with M1s, shotguns, and even submachine guns. There, in the middle field...was that a paratrooper landing on the lawn?

"We better sing 'We Shall Overcome' or stand up!" Hoffman announced. He jumped up but froze when he saw a shotgun pointed at him from only a few feet away. The deputy held the stock of his 12-gauge against his crotch, caressed it, and flashed an icy, daring smile.

Adrenaline racing, the troops encircled the hilltop and marched from the surrounding woods to search for the missing *Chicago Seed* person. The sounds of unclicking safeties bounced around the yard.

Plamondon ran from the barbecue pit, leaving the chicken to burn. Arriving at the farmhouse, he yelled for everyone to come outside, assemble in the front yard, and remain calm.

Out in the driveway, John Sinclair and a *Washington Free Press* editor confronted the sheriff as he emerged from his car. When the sheriff walked past them, they turned and followed, continuing to shout after him.

Helmeted deputies in bulletproof vests were running up the front road—their vehicles blocked the driveway—with guns drawn. Two teenage White Panthers had headed for the tall grass and dropped; now they were attempting a low crawl down the hill. When, after a few hundred yards, they jumped up to run, several cops raised their rifles before an officer called them off.

Police moved toward the farmhouse and lined up all the women—some of them still stoned, many of them topless—on the front lawn. They checked IDs, snatched cameras, took down license plates, and then smashed the locks on the doors to the house. Dazed onlookers hypothesized about their possible imminent deaths—a premeditated slaughter of hippies made to look like a shoot-out? "One wrong move," Ken Kelley wrote afterward, "and tomorrow there'd be a mass demonstration for the Ann Arbor martyrs, and 250 fewer underground papers in the world."

Meanwhile, Plamondon rushed into the farmhouse to give a tour—nothing to see here, sirs, just a Harley-Davidson parked in the kitchen, with transmission on the table and cylinder heads in the sink. An under-construction Marshall amp, atop an antique oak table, dominated the dining room; a six-foot-long papier-mâché shark, a drum kit, and two keyboards filled the living room.

When the cops found the house stash of thousands of underground papers, they settled in for a few minutes, turning to the back pages, taking in the sex ads, and eventually seizing them for evidence.

After half an hour, they headed for their cars. One of the police flashed a peace sign as he walked down the driveway. Boos rang out, car doors slammed, and the caravan departed.

When the sounds died, everyone gravitated to the barbecue pits, where the chicken had been abandoned. As dinner was salvaged, a discussion about self-defense began. Clearly, the movement was not yet prepared for an armed rebellion. Shero's plan for a Revolutionary Press Movement—*many fingers joining together to form a fist*—seemed more urgent than ever. Protests against the war were slowing, and the authorities were cracking down on the Black Panthers. In October, in Chicago, it would be time to take a stand.

In the quiet night, Abbie Hoffman lay in the grass and gazed upward. "It's a beautiful warm night," he wrote, "filled with a starry blue sky waiting for the astronauts to violate its silence. Lying on your back you can look up and repeat all the old hippie clichés to yourself about dropping out heading for the country. Why not?" He kept thinking this as he returned to his binoculars, surveying the road below, "ready to wake everyone up Paul Revere–style with shouts of 'The Pigs are coming.'"

In which of the trees around him, he wondered, lurked FBI cameras?

There were about thirty people on patrol in the Michigan darkness, armed with weapons and a memorized escape plan. In the house sat the nude mosquito-swatter Melvin Margulis, monitoring police calls with a UHF modifier and, with the help of a code-filled card, translating numbers into words.

"Don't know what the fuck I'd do if they came back," Hoffman would later remember thinking. "It would be as good a place as any and as good a reason as any to blast my first Pig."

Twelve hours later, the only trace of the conference was the matted-down grass where vehicles had been parked. Carpools had taken attendees in every direction, ready to seed the country with the latest calls for revolution.

Forcade stuck around for several more days, rapping with Sinclair and the rest of the Trans-Love group while they scrambled to raise travel expenses to bring a California psychic to Ann Arbor, hoping that he could solve the spate of co-ed murders where local police had failed. Finally, the *Orpheus* bus, with several conference attendees in tow, headed east to New York City to find space for the new offices of the Underground Press Syndicate.

Two weeks later, John Sinclair was convicted and sentenced to "a minimum term of not less than nine and a half nor more than ten years" for marijuana possession—a decade in a state penitentiary for two joints.

Police tore him from the arms of Leni, pregnant with their second child, and led him away.

On the way to New York, the *Orpheus* bus stopped at Concert Hall's offices in Glenside, Pennsylvania, at the home of Michael Forman's partner Bert Cohen. A motley group of young people worked side by side in an enclosed porch to produce the Woodstock booklet. But one glance at the driveway would clear up any misconceptions about bohemia: Cohen drove a Lotus Elan, and Forman had a Vincent Black Lightning.

Forcade immediately took notice of Concert Hall's secretary, a petite young lady with a pixie haircut. Cindy Ornsteen had grown up in the old-money Main Line town of Gladwyne. Her father was a doctor who'd served as a captain in the Korean War and chaired the Goldwater Committee in Montgomery County. Her mother was an inveterate letter writer, her witty barbs against New Frontier Democrats published in *Time, Newsweek,* and the *New York Times.* In 1965, when sentiment turned against the Vietnam War, Cindy's parents reached Lt. Gen. Westmoreland with an idea to boost morale, and before long, Operation Mail Call Vietnam was delivering letters of support to troops by the ton.

Cindy wasn't part of Mail Call Vietnam, because she had shipped off to college in Colorado, where she joined the Young Republicans, posing for a yearbook photo with a Goldwater bumper sticker. But by 1969, she'd shed her parents' politics and was living in a cheap pad near Villanova, working at the front desk of Concert Hall, writing copy and working with printers.

"She was very bright," remembered a colleague. "She kept a line between the creative guys and management. She was on the inside track and was careful not to let the creative people know any more than we needed to."

Cindy's first interaction with Forcade had been an angry phone call from him, after he'd sent a book manuscript via air freight that never arrived at Concert Hall. He blamed Cindy for losing the package and started yelling.

"You idiot, you're crazy!" she shouted. "I don't run Emory Air Freight!" She hung up on him.

But her interest was piqued. The balls on this guy, she thought, to chew out a stranger like that. When she finally met him, she was even more intrigued. "The first thing I thought was, 'This guy can't have an orgasm.' I thought, *this* would be amazing."

As it happened, Forcade's relationship with his previous girlfriend had ended after John Sinclair's sentencing. "My lady left me tonight," Forcade wrote, "saying that Sinclair deserved to go to jail because he had advocated guns. Then she threw a book on Vedantic religion at me, said 'That's where it's at,' slugged me a few times and left, raving about pacifism and condemning violence as she slapped me. Another victim of this screwed-up world, this time from the lunatic psychedelic fringe. Me, I'm tired of being a saint."

Forcade, now shuttling back and forth between Philadelphia and New York, started spending more time with Cindy on his trips to Pennsylvania, sending long-stemmed roses and notes signed "Love, Thomas King Forcade."

After Cindy introduced him to her mother, Mrs. Ornsteen was puzzled by his black preacher's outfit and his long hair shooting down from a black-brimmed hat he never removed.

"It looks like he has fake hair sewn into the hat," she said to her daughter after he left. "Is he an agent?"

CHAPTER 2

Two weeks before the Woodstock festival, it was time to put on the squeeze. "Everyone was ready for the pressure treatment," Abbie Hoffman recalled with relish, "jamming switchboards, blocking their offices, press conferences announcing that the crazy communists who ripped up Chicago were hoping the town board members of Bethel would give Woodstock Ventures a permit so we could come up and screw all their daughters." Aided by the use of theater-prop chains and attack dogs, Hoffman, Forcade, and about a dozen others burst into the Woodstock Ventures offices and demanded a meeting. Eventually, they shook down the promoters for about ten thousand dollars, to be divided among the Yippies, SDS, Alternative University, the Crazies, the Motherfuckers, NY Women's Liberation, Newsreel, and *The Rat*. They procured an area at the festival for distributing political literature—they'd call the space "Movement City"—and bought a $1,500 printing press to publish a daily paper from the fairgrounds.

"The potential of the situation is enormous," Forcade swooned in an essay written for Woodstock attendees. "More people can be turned on together, more people can have a good time together, more people can be reached with liberation message of rock and roll music than ever before." He also used the space to remind attendees of the plight of John Sinclair. "Take a sum of money equal to what you're spending on the Woodstock caper," he advised, "put it in an envelope, and send it to Magdalene [Leni] Sinclair."

Forcade's essay wasn't included in the program. Perhaps his best attempt at good vibes didn't quite make the cut. "Make violence and guns your very last alternative, after everything else is exhausted. I mean, after everything. But don't sweat your brothers who are into violence. White Panther leader Pun Plamondon and his lady Genie, universally acceded to be two of the finest, most beautiful people on the planet, are into guns."

Woodstock would go down in history as a moment of triumph for the counterculture, but the organizers squelched overt politicization. Amid the ocean of hippies, the organizers conceded to allowing just thirty square yards of plywood booth space to "Movement City"—and that area was separated from the main space by a forest. "They were able to co-opt those parts that were commercial, and the parts that were radical they were able to reject quite easily," said Abbie Hoffman. "They were able to turn a historic civil clash in our society into a fad, then the fad could be sold." Hoffman took the stage and attempted to rally the crowd in support of John Sinclair's defense; he was about to announce that Woodstock Ventures had agreed to donate 10 percent of profits to Sinclair's defense (it had not) when the microphone cut out. Then he tried again as the Who took the stage, but guitarist Pete Townshend walloped him in the back of the head with his guitar.

Concert Hall fared no better at the festival. Michael Forman's brother, Randy, was pulled over on the way to the festival, and thousands of full-color program books, printed beautifully on card stock, were confiscated.

Ten thousand more programs arrived via tractor trailer with Bert Cohen late on Sunday afternoon, just as everyone was leaving town.

The White Panther contingent, which had driven down for the celebration, had a bad trip, too. On their way back to Michigan from the festival, three White Panther leaders—Leni Sinclair and Pun and Genie Plamondon—were busted for marijuana in New Jersey.

The new Underground Press Syndicate office was in a large loft at 11 E. 17th Street, half a block from Union Square. A maze of ceiling-to-floor bales of underground papers and stacks of bullet-ridden issues of *Orpheus* hid marijuana stashes; psychedelic rock posters covered the walls. Forcade's quarters were in the back, in a tent fashioned from paisley bedspreads, next to a rack of clothes, a radio, and books.

"He slept in a pine box that was painted as an American flag, with pillows inside," recalled Michael Forman, who signed the lease and fronted the first two months' rent. "It was all very high theater. He would go to a supermarket and steal food and cook steaks until they were burnt to a crisp. He was just a very strange dude."

Running the UPS office was a middle-aged woman named Lillian Rouda, who'd owned a Connecticut computer company with her husband until the Mob ran them out of business. The couple moved into Greenwich Village's Hotel Albert, already infamous for its populace of musicians, partiers, and freaks.

"I was living in California at the time," remembered their oldest daughter, Sue, "so it was kind of this confusing moment where my parents were sending me all these letters as they're dropping acid. It seemed like they were having so much more fun than me." Sue's sisters, twins Diana and Nancy, had been forced to leave college when their parents could no longer pay tuition, and they joined a kibbutz in Israel. But soon all three Rouda daughters came and stayed on the floor of their parents' Hotel Albert room, where as many as fifteen people might be crashing at once.

Lillian was about to take a job at Al Goldstein's *Screw* magazine when her brother, who had a photography studio in the same building as UPS, introduced her to Forcade. He persuaded her to come to work with him instead.

"Forcade and my mother were good friends, so he was over a lot. And the apartment my mother had was kind of like a flea market for pot; people would come by and show their wares.... There were also a lot of musicians coming and going and lots of jamming, so it was a fun place to be, a happening spot. My mother was clear that there were to be no hard drugs. For a while there, we started selling speed because we didn't realize it was also a hard drug, so that kind of changed the whole nature of everything for a while until they got a grip on that."

The three teenage daughters soon joined their mother in working at UPS. Lillian handled the phones and office business in the front, while Nancy and Diane sold advertising; Sue's main job was to sort and photograph the underground newspapers in the back of the loft.

Forcade had negotiated a deal with Bell & Howell for reproduction rights to UPS publications, which brought in more income than the papers had seen before. The arrangement, though, raised some suspicions, even within UPS.

"Now who the hell would microfilm them but the CIA?" wondered Sue Rouda. "I mean, I didn't care—they were paying me. And it gave us a chance to put out these newsletters, which I thought were really important, you know? So it's like, fine, you know, it's all public record, it's not like we're...selling anybody anything that isn't known."

Then there were the clicking phone lines. "People would come to the office to make international calls all the time because—this was the other reason we thought Tom was a cop—everybody knew the phone was tapped, but it was also a free phone to wherever. Every month UPS would get a bill, and my mother would call the phone company and say, 'Oh, we didn't make these calls.' And they would say, 'Okay, Mrs. Rouda. Thank you very much.'"

Some of their time was spent counterfeiting press passes for various media outlets. "We would go out to eat as critics or, you know, take helicopter rides around the city to review it for this magazine or that. We'd say we were doing an article for *Time* or *Newsweek*...articles about 'fun things to do in New York.' Of course, the phone numbers went back to my mother, who would then say, 'Yes, of course. They work for me.' There were always ten bazillion scams of that kind."

But the experience was, at times, unsettling. "He'd never really look anybody in the eyes," Rouda said. "There was something really...off. He was out of his mind. Like, kind of pathologically so."

Just one month after Abbie Hoffman was denied the opportunity to rally for John Sinclair at the Woodstock festival, Hoffman's own trial—as a part of the Chicago Eight, charged with conspiracy to incite riots at the 1968 DNC Convention—began. Concert Hall sent out a full-page ad for UPS papers to run, soliciting contributions for the defense fund. The ad was also sent to *Rolling Stone*, as well; the magazine refused to run it.

But politics and the counterculture lifestyle couldn't be so easily extricated. That same week, President Richard Nixon announced the anti-marijuana initiative Operation Intercept, a near shutdown of the Mexican border. At thirty-one crossing points across the border, thousands of travelers were stuck waiting for up to six hours in miles-long lines for customs checks. It was the biggest crackdown in United States history, aimed at cutting down importation and raising the price of weed.

But prescient observers knew that such methods would soon be obsolete. "Because of the lack of proper equipment," the *New York Times* noted, "no one knows how much contraband may be coming into the country aboard fast, low-flying planes using the dozen or so air corridors long used by smugglers."

What Operation Intercept did accomplish was driving marijuana users to other drugs—among those affected by the marijuana shortage, use of hashish, alcohol, LSD, and opiates increased. Others turned to domestically produced marijuana. The cannabis weed had stubbornly continued to grow in the Midwest, where mills had once legally produced hemp. Now "hempleggers" with no previous criminal background went to work throughout the country.

"In the years to come the television dramas and movies will be making a big thing of the dope dealer of the Sixties," Timothy Leary wrote in an article published in the *East Village Other* the week that Operation Intercept commenced. "He is going to be the Robin Hood, spiritual guerrilla, mysterious agent who will take the place of the cowboy hero or the cops-and-robbers hero. The paradox of the dealer is that he must be pure. He must be straight and he must be radiant. . . . You can't be doing it for the money or the power and you can't do it on your own."

A few weeks later, Sinclair—already beginning his ten-year sentence for marijuana possession—and two other White Panthers, Jack Forrest and Pun Plamondon, were indicted for the bombing of Ann Arbor's CIA recruitment office a year earlier. (The surprising charge was the result of testimony by onetime White Panther David Valler, a former altar boy who'd gobbled too much acid while working on a Ford assembly line. Valler had become a hippie and run for president, but his peace and love trip ended when a motorcycle group raided the communal house he lived in, and he began a campaign of bombing parked police cars until he was busted.) Even though there were contradictions in Valler's testimony, the FBI came down quickly on the White Panthers.

Sinclair heard about the new charges on the radio while sitting in Marquette Prison. The radio report reached the White Panther commune, too, and Plamondon managed to go underground, with $200, some clothes, a loaded .38, and a copy of Mao's *Little Red Book*. Forrest wasn't so lucky. Secret Service agents dragged him out of bed while he was recovering from a broken pelvic bone.

On the very next day, the Chicago demonstration that had been hyped at the Ann Arbor conference turned into a bloody, disorganized fiasco. The "Days of Rage," as they were called, marked the beginning of the decline of the anti-war movement and started the SDS offshoot known as Weatherman on a road to violence and extinction.

A mere four doors down from UPS was the building that housed the New York headquarters of the Student Mobilization Committee and the Fifth Avenue Peace Parade Committee, which were busy organizing for half a million people to march in Washington in November 1969. It would be the largest march in the nation's history.

Forcade would be on the other side of the country by then, though. He flew back to Phoenix to face the June LSD charges, which were promptly dismissed for lack of sufficient evidence, and then he immediately wrote a column for the *East Village Other* that placed the charges in the context of a national campaign by the authorities at federal, state, and local levels against dissenting journalism. "Our case in Phoenix putting out *Orpheus* was a classic example. Over a period of a year, they systematically busted nearly every person on our staff, forcing people to quit to earn money for lawyers and making potential new staffers afraid to join us. In my own case, a narc worked for us for six months trying to get something on us. Finally, in desperation, they set us up. We got off, but it cost us almost $2,000 in legal fees to do it."

Because "overt political repression will not be entertained by the courts," Forcade wrote, the governmental war on the underground newspapers was being fought indirectly but no less fiercely. "With obscenity busts they get your money, with drug busts they get your people, with intimidation they get your printer, with bombings they get your office, and if you still manage to somehow get out a sheet, their distribution monopolies and rousts keep it from ever getting to the people."

For example, he wrote, "the *San Diego Free Press* has about two sellers busted each week on trumped up charges." Then he got on a plane to San Diego.

He'd been invited to speak at the annual convention of the national journalism society Sigma Delta Chi (SDX), which had recently voted to include the underground press in its ranks. At last, Forcade and his cohort were provided an opportunity to appeal to the most established journalists and editors in America. (David Hilliard of the Black Panthers declined the invitation on the grounds that ultraconservative San Diego "was not the healthiest place" for him to be.)*

There were two UPS member weeklies in San Diego: the radical Left communally produced *San Diego Free Press*, and the more culturally (i.e., music/sex/drugs) focused *San Diego Free Door*. Rather than ingratiating themselves with the mainstream journalists, the two papers decided to join forces in greeting the SDX convention with a protest against "the lies and distortions fed to us by the establishment press."

And so, on the morning of his panel, the ever contrarian Forcade was outside San Diego's El Cortez Hotel picketing the very gathering in which he was about to participate.

Forcade and the *Free Door* publisher—a former trailer-park owner in his late fifties who'd jumped into the underground press business after reading a story in the *Wall Street Journal*—stood near the front of the building, handing out signs.

---

* On November 22—nine days after the SDX convention—the San Diego Black Panther Party office was raided; all seven Panthers present were arrested. This, along with an FBI-stoked war between the Panthers and the Black Power group US, effectively marked the end of the Black Panther presence in San Diego.

CONVENTION OF
PROSTITUTES
OF THE PRESS

BEWARE OF
FANCY WRITERS!
THEY SCREW YOU

THE ESTABLISHMENT
JOURNALISTS
IN GERMANY
BACKED HITLER

About 10:30 a.m., Forcade went to the publisher's truck, which was parked a few blocks away, to grab more signs. As he walked back to the protest, two San Diego patrolmen addressed him by name, asked to see identification, and noticed that he had credit cards bearing someone else's name. They handcuffed him, hauled him to jail, and, upon discovering part of an American flag rolled up in the brim of his hat, added a charge of flag desecration.

Four hours later, in the Caribbean Room of the El Cortez, the moderator of the underground press panel was finishing his introduction when Tom Forcade—sans hat, which had been seized as evidence—stormed in and stomped onstage. Forcade grabbed a water glass from the panel table and hurled it toward the back of the room, where it narrowly missed eighty-one-year-old *Editor & Publisher* columnist Luther Huston. Then, shaking with anger, he picked up the microphone.

"The slogan for SDX in 1969 is 'A fair press is a free press.' The slogan for UPS in 1969 is 'It takes just five seconds to decide whether you're part of the problem or part of the solution.'"

He railed against the wire-service correspondents in Vietnam, accusing them of doing their reporting from the comfort of Saigon bars. "You call yourselves journalists. While people are being beaten, starved, and killed, you fill the pages of your rags with the news of bake sales and debutante balls.

"There's repression everywhere and you ignore it. If this situation were only in San Diego, I could get on a plane and get away from it, but it's common all over the US. How soon are you people going to stop being hypocrites?

"The cops called me by my name—they *knew* who I was. Somebody set me up. You people don't follow any ethics, you go out for the almighty buck," he charged, before segueing into a request for bail-expense contributions and passing around an empty water pitcher.

The rattled SDX president took the rostrum, denied any setup, and reminded Forcade that Sigma Delta Chi had *invited* Forcade and other members of the panel. The managing editor of the local daily, the *San Diego Tribune*, had personally spent four hours and $315 springing Forcade from jail.

While Forcade seethed, the other panelists spoke.

Art Kunkin, the publisher of the *Los Angeles Free Press*, was facing a $15 million invasion of privacy lawsuit for printing the names and addresses of LAPD undercover narcotics officers. He challenged SDX to condemn the LAPD for refusing to grant credentials to undergrounds. Lowell Bergman, a cofounder of the *San Diego Free Press*, which had been blacklisted by local printers after digging too far into municipal politics, echoed Forcade's tone: "You people were all over the South a few years ago, talking to people in rags, and shooting pictures of ramshackle houses, but you didn't follow up. If your editor says you can't print the truth, tell him to fuck off!"*

During a question-and-answer session, Forcade apologized to his hosts for the accusation of a setup. But the truce was short-lived. Merriman Smith, the veteran UPI journalist who six years earlier had broken the story of President Kennedy's assassination, tore into Forcade.

---

* The *Free Press* had been investigating influential San Diego businessman C. Arnholt Smith—a friend of Richard Nixon—and *San Diego Tribune* owner James Copley. Within weeks of the convention, the San Diego undergrounds were under more pressure than ever. The *Free Press*'s landlord was arrested and threatened, its offices were shot up and broken into, and 2,500 copies of the paper were thrown into the San Diego Bay. Its printing equipment was destroyed, and a staffer's car was firebombed. The *Free Door* got off relatively easy: its truck's tires were slashed, office windows shattered, and subscription list stolen.

The *San Diego Tribune* managing editor who bailed Forcade out of jail was later a source for a *Penthouse* feature that alleged that Copley allowed the FBI to place editorials in his news service and use journalists as intelligence sources.

"Do you know how many reporters, photographers, newsreel cameramen have been killed covering the war? A great many young people, and people of all ages, want the 'establishment' press to be very specific... but there is an equal obligation on your part and their part to 'tell it like it is.'"

"Do you know how many war protesters have been killed in the United States?" Forcade countered.

"How many?"

"You tell me how many reporters were killed in Vietnam, and I'll tell you how many protesters have been killed here."

"You say there's no freedom of press for underground newspapers," Smith said. "I can assure you there is no underground press whatsoever in Russia."

"Oh, there sure is," said Forcade. "And we are in touch with them."

"When are you going to stop being hypocrites?" Forcade asked the delegates, and then demanded a show of hands from those who had never tried marijuana.

The journalists, exhausted, raised their hands.

The next morning Forcade accompanied *San Diego Door* publisher Dale Herschler to a local TV station for an interview. But by the time of Forcade's Monday-morning arraignment, he'd left town, forfeiting the bail money.*

Forcade tried to spin the encounter as a win. "Although the glass did not break," he told the *Liberation News Service*, "this mild act became a subject of controversy among journalists who don't flinch at 500 Vietnamese villagers being slaughtered, not to mention police rousts.

"The only problem was a lot of young Sigma Delta Chi members trying to score dope off me. I didn't have any."

Though his powers of persuasion may have been questionable, Forcade's critique of Vietnam coverage was well timed. The day of the SDX conference, the Dispatch News Service, which was independently operated by a twenty-three-year-old working out of a spare bedroom in a DC house, sent journalist Seymour Hersh's explosive scoop about the

---

* Forcade was eventually granted a March 6 hearing, at which the judge granted the motion to suppress the flag as evidence, ruling that the arresting officers did not know that it was a flag wrapped around Forcade's hat until after they had taken him down to the jail for questioning.

US Army's internal investigation of a 1968 massacre in My Lai to thirty newspapers around the country. Hersh had sold the article to DNS only after several establishment publications had passed on it; now they were lining up to license it.

On November 14, the *Arizona Republic* ran an article it had been sitting on before the Hersh story broke: Phoenix veteran Ron Ridenhour, six months younger than Forcade, was the one who had prompted the army's investigation. Ridenhour had heard stories of the massacre from army buddies and had been collecting stories for more than a year, then sending letters to legislators from his shift at a popsicle factory in Phoenix.

Also in that edition of Forcade's hometown paper were two smaller items:

One announced that the LSD possession charges against Forcade had been dropped at the request of the county attorney's office. The other was an Associated Press story about arrests made for a four-month series of bombings of Manhattan skyscrapers, banks, and federal buildings—"a trail of explosive terror unrivaled in the city." One of five people charged by the FBI was Jane Alpert, a twenty-two-year-old Swarthmore graduate who worked at the UPS paper *The Rat*.

In early December, a phalanx of radical superstars convened at the UPS loft to discuss the establishment of a new Youth International Party, a superconsortium that would combine "revolutionary culture, militant internationalism, and anti-capitalism in a single organization." The national umbrella group would replace the now-fractured SDS.

Only months earlier, Forcade mentioned in a column that he'd attended a dinner with Abbie Hoffman, Jerry Rubin, Paul Krassner, and other Yippies, but he struck a humble tone. "I doubt they remember, for I was in no position to say anything." Now he was at the center of the action.

Hoffman and Rubin, on a weekend break from their Chicago defense trial, were there, as was Jane Alpert of *The Rat*, out on bail after her bombing arrest. Also in attendance were representatives from the White Panthers, the Committee to Defend the Black Panthers, the Gay Liberation Front, and WITCH (the Women's International Terrorist Conspiracy from Hell) and even the notorious militants known as the Crazies.

Yippie Nancy Kurshan suggested a springtime march from Woodstock to Washington and a smoke-in at the Washington Monument. Leni Sinclair took photographs of the assembled group that could be sent out to underground papers with announcements of the burgeoning confederation.

But unification wasn't so easy. Sharon Krebs, of the Movement Speakers Bureau, wasn't having any of it. "I've been to this meeting before. Everybody has a great rap, but when it comes to work nobody shows up! Then it's the same people who have to do everything."

"Forcade finally got together all the people he wanted, and he didn't know what to do with them, exactly," remembered White Panther Ken Kelley. "No one else knew either."

John Sinclair, behind bars, thought *he* knew what to do about the umbrella organization. He'd remained busy, writing letters at a furious pace; looking for publishing contacts, he'd stayed in touch with Forcade, who suggested that Sinclair sell newsletters-from-prison subscriptions and record an LP of his poems. "If you need anything, do not hesitate to ask," Forcade wrote. "I'm no Eldridge Cleaver, but I do what I say I'm going to do."

In letters to Leni and other White Panthers, who kept him updated on the follow-up meetings between the various groups, John Sinclair elaborated on his ideas for what he envisioned as a "Woodstock Nation," with "a political governing and/or negotiating body" for which he hoped to appropriate the name Youth International Party (the White Panther Party name was no good, he'd decided, because "white racists and Blacks both have a tendency to look at the White Panthers as a white racist organization"). He was discouraged by Jerry and Abbie's lack of commitment to a merger but hoped they would sign on for the value of their name recognition while other people did the actual work. "They might as well make use of the possibilities that exist and go to prison as bona fide political prisoners/prisoners of war," he wrote, "instead of as just a bunch of freaked-out individuals."

The new YIP, Sinclair figured, should consist of a Central Committee of Ministers. Forcade would lead the Communications Ministry, and UPS would print YIP propaganda supplements with the party platform, news of the merger, articles on the Conspiracy Trial, and messages from Sinclair, Jerry, and Abbie. Students for a Democratic Society, Liberation

News Service, and the women's liberation groups would maintain their individual structures while YIP continued setting up. (Sinclair was pushing for prominent personalities in cabinet positions so that the group could have better access to publicity: "It can't really be a wholly 'democratic' structure, because that's impossible in the circumstances under which we have to work.") For now, the negotiations for unification were under wraps, even from underground news services. "This isn't just another little thing, another movement news story, this is the birth of the revolutionary party in America if it's done right, and that's much more important than a release on the events of a meeting."

But the time to develop any kind of idealized "Woodstock Nation" was running out. On the very weekend of that first meeting at the UPS loft, Chicago police assassinated Black Panther Fred Hampton; at an Altamont Speedway concert in Northern California, pushed as a West Coast follow-up to Woodstock, the Hells Angels killed a man; and in Los Angeles, Charles Manson and five of his followers were indicted for the murders of seven people.

The next week, even the famously disciplined nonviolent organizers down the block from UPS, the Student Mobilization Committee and the Fifth Avenue Peace Parade, were finding it hard to keep control. A demonstration they led outside a Nixon speech at the Waldorf Astoria escalated, with bricks through windows of stores filled with Christmas shoppers, and ended with sixty-two arrests and brawls that sent both protesters and police to the hospital.

At the end of December, Leni Sinclair and four carloads of White Panthers drove west to Flint, Michigan, to check out the SDS's National Council Meeting, and what they saw put an end to ideas about forming an alliance with Weatherman. Inside a dilapidated ballroom, people laid on mattresses, clothes and trash scattered around, toilets out of order. The meeting had been renamed the National War Council.

"Dig it!" Bernardine Dohrn, a leader of Weatherman, exclaimed, enthusing about the Manson killings. "First they killed those pigs, then they ate dinner in the same room with them. They even shoved a fork into the victim's stomach! Wild!"

The White Panthers were horrified. "I think maybe it would be better not to say anything about them publicly, than either to put them down or praise them," Leni wrote to John Sinclair. "We should just try to get the real revolutionary party together as soon and as tight as possible and we'll attract all the kids who are now Weathermen for want of having anything better to join right now.

"The trouble is that, because this is such a violent country, they're copping the headlines because that's the kind of stuff people like to hear and that's the kind of action pigs love. Well, I really don't think that it's necessary for us to make a public statement and add to the confusion."

E ven as the anti-war movement was fracturing at the dawn of the 1970s, Forcade found that he still enjoyed pushing against order wherever he could find it. In mid-January 1970, Forcade once again used his membership in an establishment institution as an opportunity to stir things up. This time it was at the midwinter conference of the American Library Association, held in Chicago. Like everyone else, librarians were grappling with the speed of progress and factionalism.

Forcade interrupted the chair of the ALA's Intellectual Freedom Committee with the suggestion that everyone hop on a train and relocate the conference to the suburbs, in protest of Chicago mayor Richard J. Daley. (The chair ruled the motion "out of order"; Forcade was not a member of the committee.) "No one can deny that the effect of such a walkout would have been dramatic enough to rate nationwide coverage," reflected the *Library Journal*, "but it was clear that no one wanted any part of the proposal. This extreme case reinforced the growing impression that the Intellectual Freedom Committee, the Office for Intellectual Freedom, and the ALA itself have turned their backs on the possibility of engaging in any direct action for intellectual freedom."

As the committee heatedly debated doing away with requiring librarians to take a "loyalty oath" to the Constitution, Forcade stood up on a tabletop, shouted, "Let's go!" and led about thirty librarians out of the Sherman House Hotel and toward the courthouse, where the Chicago Conspiracy Trial was being held. They gathered across the street from the courthouse, holding signs in the cold. The *Library Journal* put the protesting librarians on its cover.

Throughout the Chicago trial, Abbie Hoffman continued hustling. He was writing the screenplay for an MGM adaptation of his book *Revolution for the Hell of It*, and he made plans to star as himself in another film, by *Rebel Without a Cause* director Nicholas Ray. Still, Hoffman had an eye on the "new nation": he told the *Quicksilver Times* (Washington, DC) that he was hoping to find "organizers and energy centers around the country who are interested in organizing and politicizing the hip community"—tying artists, publishers, and even dope dealers "into some sort of cohesive identity, rather than just creating a kind of consciousness."

But in Ann Arbor, preparations for the CIA bombing case, as well as various other charges against other members, were depleting the energy of the White Panthers. Upon returning from a trip to California, Genie Plamondon sent out a letter to branch chapters complaining "that the work concerning yourselves has not been taken care of properly from National Headquarters. You have not been receiving the information that you should from us, nor has the information we have been receiving from you been filed properly." Worse, she said, "the pigs follow us around in town and bust us whenever they can for anything they can think of."

The FBI was briefly relieved by the fissures of the Left. "Attempts by New Left leaders to unite these underground papers into some type of network have been unsuccessful to date," announced an internal memo, "since there are no concrete political philosophies agreeable to all."

The comfort wouldn't last. Minutes before noon on March 6, a nail bomb exploded in a Greenwich Village townhouse just six blocks from the UPS offices. The building had been occupied by a Weatherman cell that was planning a lethal attack on an officers' dance at Fort Dix in New Jersey. That same day, following an informant's tip, undetonated devices were discovered at two Detroit police buildings.

Just after 1:00 a.m. on March 12, a 911 call warned of bombs set to go off within the hour: in the Socony-Mobil Building, the IBM building, and the General Telephone & Electronics building in New York. Over the next twenty-four hours, as three hundred bomb threats flooded into New York City, authorities evacuated fifteen buildings, including the courthouses at Foley Square in Manhattan and Cadman Plaza in Brooklyn.

Meanwhile, in Washington, DC, as Congress heard testimony about recent revelations that the US Army had conducted domestic surveillance on citizens, Nixon aide Tom Huston delivered a memo about "Revolutionary Violence." That evening, the prominent conservative intellectual Irving Kristol went to the White House and told Nixon that the current crop of young white radicals reminded him of the aristocrats' children who had assassinated the reformist Russian czar Alexander II in 1881.

Kristol also warned that political kidnappings—the kind that had recently plagued Latin American countries—might be next.

At UPS, Forcade, ever the businessman, was more worried that nobody was paying enough attention to selling the advertising. "A curious thing began to happen," he wrote. "The people at Concert Hall began to really get into reading the papers. Soon, at least a half-dozen Concert Hall people dropped out of business: Mike Forman started hanging around with Abbie Hoffman and worked two months in Chicago at the Conspiracy office. [A] New York White Panther rep. was hired to sell ads, but instead drifted off into a world of politics and drugs."

Hoping to put pressure on Concert Hall, Forcade offered free space in the UPS loft for a young ad seller named Robert England to set up a new outfit called Media A. Months earlier, while working at a company called Campus Media, England had handled some national campaigns in the underground press, but Concert Hall had threatened to sue, insisting they had exclusive arrangements with the papers.

Concert Hall did not, in fact, have exclusivity, but the threat of competition from Media A did nothing to focus the company's attention on advertising. On the contrary, Forman, Bert Cohen, and Forcade started discussions with Warner Brothers–Seven Arts about publishing a competitor to *Rolling Stone*, a kind of national extension of *Orpheus*'s underground digest concept. And they got into the rock concert business.

Forman and Cohen figured that the half million spring breakers who flooded the sunny beaches of Florida would flock to a three-day rock festival, to be called Winter's End. Philadelphia club owner Shelley Kaplan persuaded a local psychologist to invest, and with this money Concert Hall paid advances to the highest-profile groups on a roster that included the Grateful Dead, Sly & the Family Stone, the Allman Brothers, and Ike & Tina Turner. Concert Hall recruited the publicist, sound man, ticketing service, and stage designers behind Woodstock. An additional five grand went to two Woodstock producers, in hopes of securing The Band and Jimi Hendrix.

Using the Woodstock model again, Concert Hall hoped to clear at least $40,000 in advance ticket sales, enough to cover final expenses. The Underground Press Syndicate, of course, would once again run the national advertising.

In February, Forcade and Concert Hall arranged bail money for two members of the Hog Farm commune who'd been arrested on marijuana possession charges; in exchange, the Hog Farm agreed to run the Winter's End kitchens and medical facilities. Forcade pulled in the White Panthers as well, to put out a festival newsletter and run an information center on the fairgrounds.

But the post-Woodstock festival world was tricky, especially in conservative Florida. "All the people involved, including myself, made one bad mistake," said Jerry Powers, the editor of the Miami underground newspaper the *Daily Planet*, who was in charge of selling all advance tickets in Florida. "We weren't really aware of the amount of repression we'd run into." After one venue fell through, and then another, Concert Hall leased the Hollywood Speedway in Broward County. Florida's Department of Transportation swiftly announced plans to dig up the access road to look for "lost calverts," and the speedway owner bowed out. Three more counties immediately issued anti–rock festival ordinances.

Even the underground press began to turn against Winter's End. In a scathing editorial, the *Quicksilver Times* railed against the "eight groups of three to four people traveling and doing promo work all over the east coast in fucking Cadillacs" and criticized the Hog Farm and White Panthers for allowing themselves to be co-opted. "The fact that the promoters have long hair, wear hip clothes, and gush forth with shitloads of hip talk," the paper declared, "does not make them any different from narcs." Promoters agreed to donate 3 percent of profits to "the community."

Amid whispers that, in the tradition of Woodstock, people would get in for free, advance tickets sales were slow. Concert Hall was running out of funds, and a new promoter—a hulking, long-haired Philadelphian named Steve Mishory—was brought in. He quickly arranged a loan of $30,000.

Finally, someone found a site: fifteen miles east of Orlando, over the border to Orange County, was a 110-acre dude ranch, riding stable, and bar complex. Mishory signed a lease with the Econ Ranch on Tuesday night and, sauntering into the Colonial Motor Inn with a black bag of cash, paid for twenty rooms.

Forman and Cohen arrived Wednesday morning. That night, the first fourteen portable toilets were delivered to the site.

Less than forty-eight hours remained to construct a stage, fences, sound and lighting systems, and sanitary facilities.

But Orange County had other plans. At noon on Thursday, a circuit judge issued a temporary injunction banning the festival.

Early Thursday afternoon, Forman was poolside at the Colonial when he saw uniformed men in the parking lot pointing in his direction.

"You the law?" he asked as he walked across the parking lot.

"District 1 Constable. I'm here to serve papers of injunction against your promotion."

"Man, I don't want to talk with *you*." As they moved closer, Forman walked away, toward a motel corridor. "You people won't talk with *me*." He sped up.

A few young guys standing around made whistling sounds and muttered about "pigs."

As the uniforms hurried behind, Forman shouted "Fuck you!" and gave them the finger. He headed back toward the swimming pool, leading everyone on a lap or two around before he made a dash for his room.

By the time the police broke down the door, Forman had assumed a yoga position, face down and silent. Cohen hid in the bathroom while Forman's wife, Pam, screamed at the cops. She wasn't the only one yelling. The room was filled with reporters, cameramen, and various associates as the constable read the injunction.

It was then that a man in an electric blue jumpsuit entered the room. It was Concert Hall's lawyer, Martin Blitstein.

"Get out!" he told everyone.

Blitstein, who was scheduled to appeal the injunction in a federal court, was promptly escorted to a patrol car, where he sat until his wife obtained an order from the federal judge.

"It was an ultraconservative community," said Blitstein. "For a bunch of hippies to get together to listen to music and smoke dope was absolutely off the charts. You would have been better off burning down the city. The DA and cops were fucking apeshit. It was visceral hatred. Every hippie was somebody who should die."

Meanwhile, back at the ranch, police had blocked the site entrance, causing confusion for the drivers trying to deliver truckloads of food and water. When the entrance reopened Thursday night, Jerry Powers— who owed money for the local print ads and radio commercials he'd arranged—grabbed a friend to stand at the gate and ask for money from people driving in. "Once we hit the amount that they owed us, we left."

Relieving Powers at the gate was the psychologist investor, desperate to salvage his own stake. He hired two men to guard the money in a nearby house.

Steve Mishory, meanwhile, gave orders from atop a white horse he'd borrowed from the stable. Walkie-talkie in hand, he told everyone that he was in charge.

At this point, the headlights of an arriving biker gang cut through the darkness.

Concert Hall, barred from hiring off-duty police for security, recruited a Fort Lauderdale–based motorcycle club in exchange for a fifth of the gate proceeds. Rumored to have ties to the Dixie Mafia, the Brethren covered the Econ Ranch on motorcycles, horseback, and foot and carried knives in their ankle holsters. "If there's any trouble, we've got some funny toys to take care of things," promised one leader, nicknamed "The Viper."

Concert Hall discouraged the Brethren from selling narcotics, but other drugs were everywhere. One dealer pushed around an ice cream cart filled with kilos of weed, while others used the stage microphone to facilitate buying and selling. Citrus, rumored to be juiced with LSD, and tabs of MDA circulated freely. Some of the acid was laced with strychnine; the Hog Farmers kept busy trying to cool out the poor souls in the bad-trip tent.

Tom Forcade arrived Friday morning and identified himself as the Director of Communications. He delivered a koan: "Legalities," he declared at the Colonial, "are nonentities."

But the real nonentities were water, food, medical supplies, lights, and music. Only four of the national acts had shown up, and none of them had been paid. There were, instead, nude and tripping young women, undercover police, 140 portable toilets, Hare Krishna chanters, and dried mud, all within a barbed-wire perimeter. Some attendees helped build a stage, while others scavenged fenceposts to use as firewood and camped on the adjoining dragstrip.

There was still no music Friday evening, but the crowd swelled overnight anyway.

On Saturday, as helicopters hovered above, rumors spread that the promoters might be re-arrested on charges of *conspiring* to violate a county ordinance. Jim McDonald, a local who'd been hired for security coordination, counseled them not to worry as long as they paid vendors. "No one is going to be arrested," Forcade assured reporters, while Forman declared that they were now "political prisoners."

The Hog Farm, at least, held up their end of the deal and served thousands of pounds of free food. And when the Winter's End soundman demanded a $1,200 advance before lifting a finger, a Harley-riding Hog Farmer snatched back some of the cash that state tax commissioners had impounded and delivered it straight to the mixing board.

The stage was finished, the amplifiers were cranked, and... out came a parade of local bands, for the next seven hours.

Finally, at 10:00 p.m. Saturday, the Allman Brothers took the stage, playing an embryonic rendition of "In Memory of Elizabeth Reed" and "Mountain Jam," their sprawling, ever-expanding instrumental cover of Donovan's "There Is a Mountain." Johnny Winter, whose own band had refused to play without cash up front, strapped on a guitar and joined the Allmans.

"Johnny Winter sent one of his roadies into the audience, and they came back with 50 or 60 doses of acid," recalled a crew member. "Johnny picked about 20 of them, washed them down with a beer, and said, 'I'll be ready in a couple minutes.' Then he came onstage and played for eight hours."

After the Allmans exhausted their own setlist, Johnny Winter's bandmates had a change of heart and backed their still-tripping leader.

The next morning, erstwhile security head Jim McDonald gathered all the promoters, their lawyer, and the ranch owner for a meeting in his hotel room. Half an hour later, sheriff's deputies entered the room and arrested them all on the charge of "conspiracy to violate a county ordinance."

McDonald, it emerged, secretly worked for the state tax department.

"It's better this way, boys," he assured the handcuffed promoters as he walked them outside to waiting police cars, and then he made a deal with the Brethren leaders to collect the money for the state.

Florida governor Claude Kirk, who'd threatened to call in the National Guard, was eager to speak to reporters. "That these dirty little dope pushers would choose Easter Sunday—a traditional day of love and peace—to peddle their junk is revolting," he thundered. "On a day when hundreds of millions of people pay tribute to the greatest disciple of peace, a handful of disciples of depravity take advantage of this religious holiday to corrupt our youth." He couldn't be more pleased, he added, that the promoters had lost hundreds of thousands of dollars.

Forcade tried to place the promoters in the grand tradition of radical activism: "Free the Rock and Roll Six!" They were held in a meeting room of the Orange County Jail, where they took turns making phone calls, playing penny football, and arguing. Bert Cohen wrote poems and Michael Forman resigned from Concert Hall. Forcade, posing as a lawyer, talked his way into the jail but was unable to convince anyone to release the prisoners on their own recognizance.

Eventually, they were bailed out. Most of them adjourned to their motel rooms to sleep it off. Bert Cohen, however, needed to sign papers in New York the next morning to pay off the debts in time. Forcade, now hallucinating from lack of sleep, drove Cohen the 235 miles to Miami Airport, and then back.

Upon his return to Orlando on Monday morning, Forcade found the promoters still at the Colonial—with company. Some of the seed money, it turned out, had come from a lieutenant in the Philadelphia Mob, and John Simone's Bruno Family emissaries had arrived.

"The people who had loaned Stephen Mishory the $30,000 were very uptight, and had sent down several representatives, who were saying who could and couldn't leave the motel," Forcade wrote later. "As I was hanging around the motel waiting for a phone call, suddenly a woman burst into the room yelling, 'The cops are back, and they've got warrants for everybody.' There was a fellow sitting at the bureau calmly cleaning an ounce of grass and he never looked up. The several people sitting on the bed seemed only mildly interested. I bolted in terror. Outside, there was this incredible scene of people running out of their motel rooms and roaring away in their cars, like some Holiday Inn LeMans start. The cops were just standing there, incredulous. Everyone was yelling, 'Run, Stephen, run.' Stephen was the only one of the six promoters still around. They got him."

Forcade removed the Winter's End insignia from his car and "went back to a secret rendezvous, picked up Michael Forman, and drove him across the state line into Georgia, weaving down the road with exhaustion, trying to be inconspicuous in our bright red Ford, chain smoking joints that wouldn't get us high. We took a plane out of Savannah."

The sudden disintegration of Concert Hall caused an immediate crisis of faith among Underground Press Syndicate papers. A replacement ad salesman was brought in, but the transition was messy, and editors swiftly expressed their frustration and confusion to Forcade. "Sure wish you all would get together & straighten out this ad mess," wrote one. "We don't know what the hell's going on but we do know that if we depended on national ads for revenue we'd have been bankrupt long ago."

Forcade, seemingly undaunted, announced bigger plans for the syndicate, including a cooperative newspaper in New York City. He signed a contract with Ace Books to edit an underground press anthology and declared that UPS would publish a "superdaily" newspaper, produced by the staffs of various New York undergrounds on a rotating basis—"*East Village Other* on Monday, *Rat* on Tuesday, *Corpus* on Wednesday, *WIN* on Thursday, *NY High School Free Press* on Friday, *The Young Lords* on alternate Fridays, *The Black Panther* on Saturday, and everybody on Sunday, with *Gothic Blimp Comics* as the comic section."

Forcade also, for the first time, began to cultivate a public image. He submitted to an interview with *Newsday*, which identified him as a "cultural guerilla, liberating America from the hang-ups of affluence and rigid morality." He even posed for a photograph in the UPS loft, staring straight at the camera. (Not that he'd given up mythmaking: the article identified him as thirty years old, even though he hadn't yet turned twenty-five.)

"Things like money, fancy apartments, marriage—they're basically unnatural," he said. "They keep people apart, orient them toward power instead of each other. What we're seeing now is millions of young people starting to realize this and trying to build a new society on more workable values." Underground papers, he insisted, spread the gospel of revolutionary ideology to the masses. "They give kids a look at an alternative way of living. Part of it is dope, rock 'n' roll, free sex. But also it's about communalism, personal freedom, a whole new way for people to look at themselves.... Ultimately, it's just a question of who owns the means of production. It's our whole money culture that's going to change."

But that dope part, Forcade said, was crucial. "Grass breaks down your social conditioning, makes you introspective," Forcade said. "Your mind loosens up and you start seeing the cracks in the system. Like: you pay them money to educate you to do what they want. You start on dope and you realize, 'Why should I do this, anyway?'

"Mao says a guerilla moves like a fish in the water of the people," he said. "Dope makes the water better... creates a more sympathetic populace. Any dope smoker is a potential friend. Maybe 99 of 100 will never become dropouts themselves. But they'll be more sympathetic to people who are."

That week, the first national action on marijuana legalization was announced in UPS papers all across the country. MAY DAY IS J-DAY! screamed the full-page ad, with a YIP flag surrounded by the phrases "Grass for the Masses," "A Joint in Every Mailbox," and "Pot in Every Public Place." It announced the "First Annual Marijuana Mail-In and Cross-Country Toke-Down," for which "dealers and heads all over the U.S." would roll up "at least one pound of weed each," tear random pages from phone books, and send joints to every listed name, along with letters of instruction on how to smoke. "Every policeman, mayor, senator, housewife, factory worker, and businessman will finally learn how to start the day right: with a little bit of reefer."

"Amerika," the announcement promised, "will break out in one huge smile as everyone will be stoned, high, fucked up, jacked out of shape, mellow, blasted."

A round this time, Forcade sat down and composed a poem:

Revolution for My Friends
by Tom Forcade on April 14, 1970, 5 a.m., acid.

I
do not
write
poetry,
this thing I have
to write comes

hard from me.
See, I was only kidding,
I AM a revolutionary, of God,
not volunteering, drafted in a blaze of light
on a hillside
just like in the Bible.
I am a bundle of emotions,
I, always, take a
hard,
sharp,
steel,
knife-
blade,
and in front of my friends,
I scrape it sideways,
down along my own EGO,
defenses, compensations,
pretensions, high motives,
virtues, tenderness,
scrape it,
scrape it, hard,
right down to the barebone of the basest motive,
the barebone of the last word, real, dirt, ID. But,
I AM HUMAN
and I love, too.

All I ever wanted and still want
is a dark-haired girl, a strand of her raven
hair falling across her lips, and money, of course.

But I know, that what we are dealing with here
is a highly powerful world machine of powerful business mother-
    fuckers.
I should know.
and it's either Them
or Us,
and the sides have already been chosen

and all my friends, whether they accept it or not
are on this side with me,
and we're going to use U.P.S., etc.
to drive a steel wedge
into the base of the motherfucker and start a fatal fracture
that will
eventually,
yes, in our lifetimes or not at all,
bring the whole motherfucker down.

and it's going to take some
heavy
Stalinist
games
to drive those wedges.

It's either Them, or Us,
and I've gotta drive those wedges
and please just remember that
I am human
and I love, too.

CHAPTER 3

IN MID-APRIL, THE *NEW YORK TIMES* REPORTED THAT, IN THE WAKE OF the Weatherman townhouse bombing and other attacks, the White House had concluded that political radicals would never accept compromise, or reason, and must be treated as hardened criminals. The administration was preparing to ramp up surveillance of left-wing radicals, utilizing informers, undercover agents, and wiretaps; it considered pouring federal funds to police departments for battling subversives at the local level.

"We need better trained people in metropolitan police departments," an anonymous Nixon aide told the paper, "so they can distinguish between a guy with a beard and a subversive."

Three days later, two Weatherman leaders, Linda Evans and Diane Donghi, were arrested in New York City, fingered by the sole FBI agent who'd penetrated their inner circle. ("You're right, I am a pig," the agent had admitted during an LSD initiation by fellow Weathermen, only for his confession to be interpreted as a metaphorical pronouncement.) But the bureau narrowly missed its chance to grab the more prominent Mark Rudd, who'd gotten spooked right before he was supposed to meet Donghi for lunch at a diner. And in the FBI's rush to make arrests, it now had no one on the inside.

But it was becoming apparent that few places were safe for revolutionaries during the spring of 1970.

In upstate New York, an SDS regional organizer nicknamed Tommy the Traveler drove his Mustang from campus to campus distributing underground papers and pamphlets and films by the Newsreel collective. He'd previously recruited students for the Days of Rage; now he stoked internal disputes within the local chapters. At a dozen colleges he shared his plans for a "terror squad" against the Right, showed undergraduates how to handle an M1 carbine, and scoffed that nonviolence was "an Establishment trick to maintain the status quo." He built explosives and taunted students for not being sufficiently "revolutionary" to use them. He encouraged arson, floated the idea of grenade-tossing as "guerilla theater," and suggested the kidnapping of a congressman. Eventually, he was able to persuade protégés to bomb an ROTC office located in a student dormitory building. Only then was it learned that Tommy the Traveler was on the payroll of a local sheriff, who'd hired him at the recommendation of a "higher agency" in the government that the sheriff refused to name.

"In a few instances, security informants in the New Left got carried away during a demonstration, assaulted police, etc.," the FBI admitted in an internal report, but this was a gross understatement. FBI-supervised informants in Seattle also built bombs and provided them to anti-war activists. An undergraduate informant at the University of Alabama spelled out four-letter words with lighter fluid in a dorm carpet and led fellow students in throwing rocks at Tuscaloosa policemen. "I did burn a few buildings," the informant later admitted.

It wasn't just college kids who were targeted by provocateurs. In April, a convict at the Lewisburg federal penitentiary in Pennsylvania, at the instruction of the FBI, befriended the activist priest Rev. Philip Berrigan, imprisoned for burning draft cards, and volunteered to become his letter courier. Thus insinuated into the Catholic Left, the convict offered Sister Elizabeth McAlister a gun with which to kidnap Henry Kissinger, and provided explosives manuals to another activist.

It seemed like everyone was playing dress-up. At Washington, DC's Uptown College, a long-haired ringleader used a bullhorn to lead four hundred protesters in a chant of "Burn, burn, burn it down!" The crowd threw bricks at the police, seized administration buildings, and shouted, "Ho Ho Ho Chi Minh," before fifty of them were arrested over the course of half an hour. But it was all make-believe—Uptown College was itself fictitious, a part of the "Operation Tone-Up" drill for the DC police's Civil Disturbance Unit.

In the midst of all this, army intelligence whistleblowers came forward with the revelation that the Pentagon was monitoring domestic "leftwing activities." One revealed that he'd set up a division to monitor the New Left. Another worked with a computerized file with thousands of names that included everyone from folk singers to physicians to underground newspaper editors; he also briefed the CIA on underground newspaper staffs. These officers later testified that the government had authorized purchases of marijuana and liquor to infiltrate a "Yippie commune."

And yet there were those in the government who worried that their hands were still too tied by legal strictures. At a special meeting called in the White House, Nixon aides wondered "whether—because of the escalating violence—something within the government further needed to be done." They would ask the president to meet with the directors of four different agencies to facilitate better domestic intelligence sharing.*

On May 1, for the "May Day is J-Day" event, one hundred demonstrators flooded the floor of the Michigan Senate. The governor and nearly the entire state legislature had received in the mail what state

---

* At the same time, John E. Ingersoll, director of the Bureau of Narcotics and Dangerous Drugs, solicited the help of the National Security Agency in an unprecedented domestic-intelligence strategy.

police lab tests would reveal to be "above average quality" joints, courtesy of the White Panther Party. "Smoke at least two of these every day, for one year," the letters read. "The method can't fail."

Tom Forcade drove up to Connecticut that day, for the unfurling of the new YIP flag—black, with a red star and a marijuana leaf—and the circulating of the new YIP manifesto. A May Day rally had been organized at Yale University, to protest a Black Panther trial held in New Haven. One of the defendants was Bobby Seale, and the rally prompted a reunion of sorts for Seale's fellow veterans of the Chicago Conspiracy Trial, who traveled to New Haven as a show of solidarity. It may have seemed to Forcade that the battle for legalization appeared to be taking its place alongside the civil rights, anti-war, and free speech movements. But the turbulence of May 1970 was about to change everything.

The night before, on Thursday, April 30, Nixon appeared on television to announce the bombing of Cambodia, a neutral neighbor of Vietnam. A flood of campus protests around the country erupted on Friday, which dominated the nightly news and accompanied tumultuous developments on the radical scene. The May Day rally expanded into a protest against the Cambodian bombing as well. The *Village Voice* described the Chicago Seven* defendants, each of whom appeared at the podium, as sounding angrier than ever before.

Tom Hayden urged campus strikes for the remainder of the semester, and students from Brandeis University, about two hours to the northeast, launched a project called the National Strike Information Center, which would help to coordinate the many student actions across the country. Editors of nearly a dozen college newspapers on the East Coast prepared a joint editorial calling for strikes.

At Kent State, the Ohio governor dispatched the National Guard; an ROTC building was set on fire. Shortly after noon on Monday, National Guard soldiers shot and killed four students.

That night, several Yippies—Hoffman, Rubin, Ed Sanders, Krassner—showed up for a Greenwich Village fundraiser for Timothy Leary, residing since March 20 in a San Luis Obispo prison. Things turned dark when Hoffman took the stage and called for armed revolution and for

---

* The Chicago Eight had lost one of its number after the judge severed Bobby Seale's case from that of his codefendants.

tearing down the walls of Leary's prison. Abbie started to beat the microphone with his fists; when Allen Ginsberg tried to calm him down, Abbie called him a "CIA pig."

And on the following day, May 5, the FBI made White Panther Pun Plamondon the first leftist radical to appear on its Ten Most Wanted Fugitives list, seven months after he'd gone on the run. Plamondon, who'd just slipped back from visiting the exiled Black Panther Eldridge Cleaver in Algeria, was now being hunted by all fifty-five continental bureau offices, including a special four-man team of agents in Chicago.

On Thursday, May 7, the FBI raided the former offices of the *Quicksilver Times*, where three weeks earlier, a hardline faction of contributors to the paper, criticized by their editors for their "berating of people new to the movement who don't match up to a revolutionary ideal," had seized the building, renamed themselves *Voice from the Mother Country*, and printed their own newspaper. Federal agents, staking out from the second floor of a Toyota dealership across the street, arrested two men as they left the office and charged them with illegal possession of four rifles, a shotgun, and a pistol. They procured a warrant to search for Weatherman fugitive Cathy Wilkerson and instead found four hundred rounds of ammunition. Outside, three hundred witnesses gathered, beginning a four-hour confrontation with authorities.

On May 8, two thousand helmeted construction workers, some of them armed with tools, confronted anti-war protesters in Lower Manhattan. There were seventy injuries recorded and only a handful of arrests. "The construction workers are organized brown shirts," Abbie Hoffman fumed. "They carved up people with meat hooks and chains and other devices—brutal devices—and the police stood by, watched, did nothing."

On Saturday, May 9, nationwide protests culminated with one hundred thousand demonstrators converging in Washington, DC's Lafayette Park, behind the White House. Chicago Conspiracy alumnus David Dellinger, now leading the New Mobilization Committee to End the War in Vietnam, was in charge of the action. He had to walk the line between "endlessly repeated marches and rallies, on the one hand, or mindless, counterproductive violence, on the other." He insisted that "such activities as work stoppages, draft-board disruptions, and other organized attempts to paralyze the war machine add power and variety to the movement's assortment of tactics."

Some feared that the organization's direct-action tactics were too chaotic. Abbie Hoffman, on the other hand, was one of those who now thought that protests didn't go far enough. "People should have circled the White House. There should have been two or three thousand arrests," he said. "Young people should be training themselves to be armed fighters, prepared for the prospect of 'being rounded up and shipped to concentration camps.'" He predicted that he and Jerry Rubin had "less than two months to stay alive and out of prison," and he called for "a national organization that's willing to support a growing military underground in America. There is a military underground and it is happening. It needs funds and it needs recruits and it needs equipment."

On May 13, 1970, a stretch limousine painted with the red, blue, and gold Viet Cong flag pulled into Washington, DC. Its passengers— one in costume as a reverend, another as a nun, and another as a member of the Puerto Rican activist group the Young Lords—piled out and made their way toward the New Senate Office Building on Capitol Hill.

The man dressed as a preacher was Tom Forcade, scheduled to speak at a presidential commission on obscenity. Joining him were the three daughters of UPS secretary Lillian Rouda—Nancy, Diane, and Sue— and a hash dealer from Marseille that the daughters had met on a kibbutz.

Their drive had been made memorable after a U-turn at a tollbooth— and, possibly, the Viet Cong flag—got them pulled over.

"The cop that stopped us, first he found all of the oregano and the cigarette papers," remembered Sue. "Because we were going to roll these red, white, and blue joints to hand out. And who can afford all that pot? And we had a few cases of *Guns & Ammo* magazine that we were going to hand out as examples of pornography, and we also had a very phallic empty anti-aircraft shell that was probably about twelve inches long. The idea was that Tom, dressed as a priest, would wear that in his pants, strapped to his leg, and pull it out and say, '*This* is obscene!'" The sisters immediately offered the officer some of the brownies that Lillian had thoughtfully sent along with them, which were of course baked with marijuana. "Here is this poor cop who finds all these whacked-out people with *Guns & Ammo* magazines, what he thinks is tons of pot—because he didn't know the difference—and an anti-aircraft shell. And the more he's panicking, the more he was just chewing on those brownies. So he told us to follow him because he was arresting us all, so we followed him for a little while until he kind of just ran off the road, and we kept going."

When they arrived on Capitol Hill, "We were walking down the street, and the cops converged on us," said Diane Rouda. "They didn't stop us, just followed us right to the building, looked through our gear, found this mortar shell, and said, 'Okay, go on in.'"

Once they entered the hearing room, the entourage, with the cooperation of a few local radicals, broke out a cardboard box and passed sample copies of newspapers to attendees. When Forcade was called to address the commission, he lowered his wide-brimmed black hat and read a thousand-word statement about the underground press:

> The Underground Press Syndicate has repeatedly encountered your brand of political repression in the thin but transparent guise of obscenity, despite the obvious fact that the primary content of Underground Press Syndicate papers is political and social writing....A study of daily newspapers found that 70 per cent of the readership did not believe the papers they read. They thought they were lying. In the past 20 years, over 400 establishment dailies have died, while in the past four years, UPS has gone from nothing to over 6 million readers. A journalism professor in California made a study of his class of 45 students, and found that 42 read the local underground paper, only 1 read the establishment propaganda organ.... We are the solution to America's problems. We are revolution, these papers are our lives, and nobody shall take our lives away with your goddamned laws. We are tomorrow, not you. We are the working model of tomorrow's paleocybernetic culture.... There can be no free country without a free press, and if there be no free country, then there will be no country. There is no difference and no separation between what is happening to the underground press and what is happening to the Black Panthers or any other group which opposes America's last crazed epilepsy.

Forcade punctuated his speech with a periodic refrain of "Fuck off, and fuck censorship!" During a momentary silence, the three-year-old pigtailed daughter of one participating radical couple repeated the phrase and punched the air with her closed fist. As nervous laughter subsided, Forcade cued a cassette recording of Bob Dylan's "Ballad of a Thin Man" and recited a list of papers victimized by censorship. But the song outlasted the list.

"Do you have anything more to say?" the chair of the commission asked over the strains of Dylan, but Forcade insisted that the music was part of his testimony. Only when Otto Larsen, a member of the commission, interjected and challenged Forcade's charges of "McCarthyesque witch hunts and inquisitional hearings" did the costumed priest approach the rostrum.

"I think I have the material in my box to explain that," he said. Reaching inside, underneath a pile of papers, he produced a cottage cheese pie, which he hurled into the face of Larsen as cameras flashed.

Forcade's pie-hurling made front-page headlines across the country.

OBSCENITY COMMISSION GETS CREAMED

THE PIE THROWER—RATED X

SMUT PROBER GETS PIE IN FACE

There was one detail that stuck in the minds of people around Forcade. Lawrence Leamer, who'd been working on a book about the underground press, was in attendance at the hearing and was surprised to see the group depart without incident. "I was nervous about it, because they could get their heads busted. And nothing happened; they just walked out."

"It just didn't make sense," said Sue Rouda. "Why weren't we arrested? It was too weird, their response. I would be surprised if Tom wasn't an agent. My mother was just convinced of it."

Shortly after returning from the DC trip, UPS threw a benefit to raise money for John Sinclair's defense fund. By now, Forcade was referring to UPS volunteers as the "Free Ranger Tribe," just as he had used "Orpheus" to refer to the amorphous collective in Phoenix.

John Sinclair wrote Forcade a long letter from prison. His wife Leni had passed along Forcade's idea that the Free Ranger Tribe might act as the New York branch of the White Panther Party. Sinclair wrote that this was fine, as far as they were concerned, but they'd have to get approval from the WPP Central Committee, and "there are some people on there who have funny feelings about you personally."

All I know is that they have some residual fear that you are a CIA agent or some kind of agent, although when asked about it they can't really come right out and say that. It's just a feeling is what they say most often, and that's not enough for me, especially since I know your work—and you personally too—and respect what you've accomplished so much that I would really be happy to have you work with us formally, and organize the New York Branch of the Party.

Sinclair encouraged Forcade to talk things out with the other White Panthers ("either you say these people are crazy and I won't have anything to do with them, or...you realize that they misunderstand you and try to straighten them out through revolutionary criticism and discussion"). Then he quickly pivoted to praising the DC pieing ("That knocked me right on my ass, I was laughing and carrying on for 15 minutes when I saw that"), the quality of recent UPS newsletters, and *Countdown* ("it's the best magazine/book to come out in a long time...like *Orpheus* translated into a mass-market publication"). He suggested that Forcade take over the White Panther News Service. "It would really be beautiful if you people could lead the way in New York City," Sinclair wrote, "because I really respect your work more than almost anyone else in that awful place."

Then he broke the news that the YIP–White Panther alliance was finally dead. "We have separated the White Panther Party from the Youth International Party and will develop our organization and program and policies along their highest and purest lines and hope that the Yippies develop to the point where they can see the necessity of moving in an organized, disciplined, democratic-centralized fashion to organize the youth colony into the Woodstock Nation and move to serve the people and build self-determination."

In mid-June, Forcade was one of a few thousand representatives of underground press and radio, film, and video attending an Alternative Media Conference at Goddard College in Vermont. As FM disc jockeys and groupies mixed with the radicals, there was a creeping sense that commercial interests and stoned rubberneckers had started to dilute the movement in insidious ways. "The Capitalist Rip-Off and the Dionysian Dope Freak circuits buzzed separately and frenetically for four days and four nights," a Liberation News Service reporter wrote, after lodging a feminist critique about a video collective's staging of a "fuck-in."

Forcade, of course, was happy to exacerbate conflict.

A reporter from the *Detroit News* observed him in action, his "scowl broken occasionally by a mirthless laugh," intimidating audiences in workshops. "What we're trying to do is create a revolutionary media in a situation where a revolution doesn't fully exist." He urged people to withdraw from establishment systems to create radical systems of distribution. "If people had courage," he complained, "they wouldn't even think twice about becoming outlaws. They already would be."

"People talk about peace. I'm into love, I'm not into peace. I don't want peace, I want life. I associate peace with graveyards. I associate peace with stagnation."

He'd brought parts of the sound system he was in the process of building. Called "King Kong," it included 550-watt quad-drive speakers that he claimed were able to push music out over a five-mile range. He'd acquired them, somehow, from an intercontinental ballistic missile site; their original purpose was for broadcasting warning sirens.

"I was playing the MC5 at about half-volume while I tried to get the mix right, when some ecology types accosted me," Forcade later wrote. "They told me that the sound system was *knocking leaves off trees and killing birds in the forest*, and I should shut it off. I refused. They played their ultimate ace—some Black guys nearby didn't like it. I went over and asked them. They didn't care. I left it on."

In an even more combative action, Forcade claimed that he stole $500 from the purse of Nancy Kurshan, Jerry Rubin's partner. "*I* took your $500, Jerry," he wrote. "I took those crisp green bills out into the woods and burned them, just like you told us to. YIPPIE!"

Shortly afterward, given a tab of LSD by a member of Andy Warhol's entourage, Forcade said he experienced a semi-epiphany. "I climbed out of the car, melted into the door, and slid down the side in a psychedelic blob. Somewhere, there was a great lesson to be learned from this conference." There were, he decided as the sky turned into millions of diamonds, three ways that people were experiencing the event. One was as a "Little Woodstock," a "friendly kind of disaster" in which "the people were swarming over the tiny site like Day-Glo ants, and there was a feeling in the air of 'we're all in this together, and we've got to stick together, no matter how much we hate each other'...the media itself had become the event." Another vantage point was that the various groups were "the alternative life-style equivalent of Roy Rogers roast beef parlors, Colonel Sanders Kentucky Fried Chicken parlors, Jack LaLane gyms.... One can open a Yippie office, a White Panther office, a Gay Lib collective, a Women's Lib collective, an underground newspaper, or one can even steal a credit card, buy a used school bus, and get a Hog Farm franchise. The people are all there to look over and compare the various 'franchises.'" The third was perhaps the most mercenary. "Other people were calling this a hippie Apalachin, a long-haired reenactment of the Mafia summit meeting of 1957.... All kinds of heavies and self-imagined heavies were dragging their weight around, demanding to be heard, demanding to be accepted. Each of them had built himself up into a heavy by taking some cause or some media or some angle and pushing it until enough people accepted it. These alternative culture chieftains and their lieutenants were there to carve up the tremendous pie that the straight power structure handed us, a pie consisting of millions of kids dropping out of the straight world, looking for something to plug into. At this conference, quietly, in back rooms, was being determined who got to control whom, and how much, and what the alliances were going to be."

"We were all looking for a way out and up," Forcade wrote, never saying which of the three points of view he subscribed to.

CHAPTER 4

THE ANTI-CAPITALIST LOWER EAST SIDE POLITICAL GROUP RYP/OFF FIRST struck at an April press conference at the old-school showbiz restaurant Sardi's, where a pair of music promoters promised that the upcoming Mountaindale festival would be an improvement on Woodstock. They'd purchased seven hundred acres in the Catskill Mountains, plus houses and cottages. Fences were already being built, and only a carefully limited number of tickets would be sold for the summer shows.

The RYP/Off members peppered them with challenges:

"Is this one more array of high-paid, manager-controlled superstars?"

"What about the people's bands, the bands that represent our communities?"

"What percentage will go to the Conspiracy defense?"

After hearing unsatisfactory, hedging responses from the promoters, the RYPsters vowed to hold a competing "Festival of Thieves" at the periphery of the festival. A follow-up letter demanded control of services and facilities, input into the Mountaindale lineup, ten thousand free tickets, copy of film, and bail funds for two of the New York Panther 21. "If you find these demands discomforting to your profit motivations, dig on the fact that Woodstock became a mythic event only insofar as it was supported enthusiastically in the underground press.... If our demands are not met, we will publicize... the manner in which you are trying to exploit our free culture."

There was some reason to fear the threats. When Warner Brothers had refused to contribute profits from *Woodstock* toward a Panther bail fund, RYP/Off organized a boycott and "total assault" on *Woodstock*. At the film's Los Angeles premiere, more than one hundred Yippies protested and deterred audiences from the Fox Wilshire; some of them set a fire outside the theater.

But before the promoters even had a chance to respond to RYP demands, they ran into complaints from the promoters of the upcoming New York Pop Festival, who'd already exclusively contracted several of the same acts. The Mountaindale festival fell apart.

So RYP/Off simply set its sights on the New York Pop Festival, scheduled for July. This time, Forcade would be on the side of the revolutionaries.

"The Woodstock movie was a huge provocation to people, they saw it as a complete heist of the culture," said Leslie Bacon, who arrived in New York that summer from California. At eighteen years of age, but with ten cross-country trips already under her belt, she'd accompanied friends who wanted to sell copies of their poetry magazine in New York. They needed a place to stay, and one of them had gotten Forcade's number from their journalism professor—Robert Glessing, who'd been on the Sigma Delta Chi panel in San Diego.

"We got there, and I don't think Tom knew anything about us. I think they might have called ten minutes before, or we just banged on the door. Tom said, yeah sure fine, they can stay. When they were going to leave, I was going to find my way out in the big city. Tom said, 'You want to work here?' I said sure. I'd only gone to college for one semester, but I had hung out at the *Oracle* office in San Francisco. After talking to me, Forcade said, here, you do this: editing newsletters, choosing articles to be shared." Now a member of the Free Ranger Tribe, she clipped, copied, and mailed newspapers and got pulled into Forcade's latest scheme: to join RYP/Off in extorting the New York Pop Festival promoters for money to be "returned to the community."

Promoters Don Friedman and Bob Gardiner, who'd been around long enough to bring Billie Holiday and Chet Baker to Carnegie Hall, had formed Brave New World, Inc., and secured Downing Stadium on Randall's Island, a part of East Harlem.*

On the afternoon of June 18, about two dozen white radicals descended upon Brave New World's midtown offices and presented a list of demands:

- Bail money for one of the Panther 21
- Bail money for all arrests incurred at the New York Pop Festival
- 10,000 free tickets for members of the community who could not afford the $21 price
- $5,000 plus expenses for each of ten "community bands" they would choose to play at the festival
- A videotape copy of the festival, which was being filmed for a movie
- Establishment of a "movement information and education center" at the festival grounds

In return, RYP Collective (which now included representatives from the White Panther Party, the Gay Liberation Front, the Committee to Defend the New York Panther 21, the Youth International Party, and the Underground Press Syndicate) would agree to promote the festival in the underground press and provide security.

They were thrown out of the building.

---

* The Mountaindale promoters responded to Brave New World by naming their company the equally dystopian Orwell Productions, and they promised to bring Grateful Dead, Van Morrison, The Kinks, and Richie Havens to the Catskills. Mountaindale would eventually be nixed by a local court order, but twelve thousand young people flooded the Catskills town of South Fallsburg anyway.

But Brave New World soon noticed that ticket sales were slow. And the NYPD, upon receipt of RYP's list of demands, was troubled by the possibility of Yippies set loose in El Barrio. Worried about a permit revocation, Brave New World agreed to negotiate.

Brave New World had a surprise bit of weird leverage: its third partner was a Black promoter named Teddy Powell, who'd suffered decades of discrimination and been abandoned by Black artists once they'd reached the limelight. He'd nurtured artists on the Chitlin' Circuit, only to see white businessmen and promoters whisk them away once their careers were taking off. He'd run the Randall's Island jazz festival for the past three years, and Brave New World had needed his community connections to get the lease for Randall's Island. So this, finally, was forty-three-year-old Powell's first chance to work within the pop music market.

"I'd like to see Teddy Powell's face when these white middle-class kids tell him he's got to give his money to them to help the Black community," one of the Brave New Worlders told Ron Rosenbaum of the *Village Voice*, who had come to witness the negotiations. And sure enough, after an amicable discussion between RYP and Brave New World about bail money, a surprise guest arrived: a Black associate of Powell's. A feature documentary called *Free* included a dramatic reenactment of the scene:

"You people are talking about *my* money. I don't know what is coming down, but I smell game, game, game. You people are talking about taking *my* money, putting it into my community, and *you* are gonna decide how to do it. Where you all from anyway—Great Neck?"

All eyes were cast downward.

"Anybody here from Harlem?"

More silence.

"Every day I leave my house, I see nothin' but Black people. The Panthers live a few blocks from me. I know where to find them, and they know where to find me—and we don't need no white liberal punks telling us how to spend our money. What you think, 'cause you got long hair, that's gonna make you some kinda *white nigger*? You try goin' Black skin next time! Don't start no shit with me! You jive ass crackers telling me what to do...don't you fuckin' a show us how to do nothin', you just leave us the fuck alone! You wanna build a better America, is that what you wanna do? I tell you what the fuck to do—you go back to where you live, kill your daddies, and fuck your mothers!"

The radicals were, as expected, stunned into near silence for half an hour. "Members of the collective admitted they hadn't been prepared to deal with a Black man as capitalist in the same way they could deal with white hip capitalists," Rosenbaum wrote. "But they talked about it and realized they had to avoid the trap of being unable to criticize any one Black. If Teddy Powell was Black he was still a Black *capitalist*."

More meetings followed amid a general uneasiness. "At one point, one of the promoters threatened to throw me through a plate-glass window," Forcade later wrote. "At another point, they threatened to bring thugs with baseball bats. In return, we threatened to hire a skywriter to advertise the festival as being free, and to spread the word that it was to be a free festival for the benefit of the Black Panthers. Never mind asking how a free festival could benefit the Black Panthers—it was a convenient means of combining the two things the promoters feared most."

Brave New World finally made concessions: bands "from the community" could play before the out-of-town bands, and two hours of political speeches from the stage would kick off the festival. Whatever seats weren't sold would be granted for free, and bail money . . . well, that remained vague.

On street corners, longhairs began handing out flyers touting Brave New World's credibility: "The New York Pop festival's decision to honor the people by re-routing proceeds to rock-community causes may turn out to be one of the most impressive precedents in popular-music history!"

But back at RYP meetings, paranoia prevented open discussion of the terms of the agreement.

"There's a pig in this room," cautioned RYP cofounder Jim Retherford. "Somebody here has been telling [rock show promoter] Bill Graham everything that goes on. Graham has been trying to undermine this whole thing."*

---

* Retherford, the former editor of an Indiana underground paper called *The Spectator*, had met Forcade back in 1968 when the *Orpheus* bus came rumbling through Bloomington. "I was put off by something about Forcade," Retherford told author John McMillian years later. "I got the sense he was a self-conscious high priest of cool on a pilgrimage, seeking supplicants." Retherford's suspicions of Forcade continued during the RYP/Brave New World negotiations. "We found out later, that we had this faction that included Tom Forcade . . . working together behind our backs to make deals with the promoters—and undercutting us."

When that was deemed unsatisfactory, Retherford advised, "Listen. Capitalists will *always* try to co-opt you. You have to be able to co-opt *them*! You have to be able to carry the thing one step further."

Forcade told Rosenbaum that the promoters of festivals in New Jersey and Connecticut had become "so desperate they are preparing steel walls, barbed wire, police dogs, ex-Marine colonels, and guns."

Rosenbaum's *Voice* article credited Forcade with the logistical plans. "Tom Forcade, who founded the Free Ranger Tribe, described the arrangement as just his people stepping in to save a dying festival and to prevent all of the money from being drained off by bands, booking agents, road managers, and promoters. Forcade doesn't like any festivals which charge money for people to hear music. But he talks about festivals as 'a reality you have to deal with,' and sees the possibility—if Randall's Island works—of a new kind of festival serving the community 'where you try to let people know it's hip to pay.'"

Just when it seemed like every tactic had been exhausted, another group caught wind of the concert plans. East Harlem, where Randall's Island was located, was the New York base of the Young Lords, a sort of Puerto Rican equivalent of the Black Panthers. "We were notified that a bunch of hippies were going to bring bedrolls and backpacks, sleeping in the streets in El Barrio," said Denise Oliver, who was the Minister of Finance for the Young Lords. "This was not a good idea—it would bring police into the neighborhood, and all hell would break loose." Forcade invited the Young Lords to meet at the UPS loft to figure out a plan.

Oliver arrived at the loft with her security detail. "There were eight or nine people there calling themselves the RYP Collective, and Forcade, this really skinny guy with long straight hair, who was odd and very intense. He said, 'We have to jack them up for money, make them hire people from the community to work security concessions, and pressure them into making commitments to local groups.' It was kind of a surprise that they were even considering that there was a problem with this festival, and supportive, and open to suggestions." They agreed that the festival would not happen without changes made.

Randall's Island was where the Puerto Ricans gathered for picnics and ballgames. If their space was being taken away, the Young Lords wanted money for bail funds and breakfast and lunch programs.

Denise Oliver visited the Brave New World offices shortly afterward. "I took two or three brothers in the defense ministry who were really tough. I was very gracious. One of the brothers behind me took out a Bowie knife and started picking his teeth, looking like he was going to rip out their eyeballs. They ended up saying, 'We'll give you ten thousand dollars.'"

The Young Lords returned to the UPS loft for a final press conference four days before the festival began. "Brave New World Productions has agreed to pay money for community services, and to have artists appear that represent the Puerto Rican community," announced Oliver. "Whereas before it was a money-making affair it is now a people's affair without the usual exploitation by rock festivals of people, culture, and land." A Brave New World representative gamely agreed that "this is the only way that large music festivals can go on."

Richard Nixon had better luck with his own music festival. On June 4, Nixon's friends Bob Hope and Billy Graham announced an "Honor America" rally to be held in Washington, DC, on the Fourth of July. The idea had come from the president of *Reader's Digest* and the head of the Marriott Corporation, and the planned entertainment was to be just as cutting-edge, from Dinah Shore to Pat Boone.

Unsurprisingly, news of the July 4 smoke-in in the Capitol now attracted the attention of the government. "Yippies' plans hinge on attracting as large a crowd as possible," the FBI warned. "[Abbie] Hoffman is willing to offer the psychedelic group, the Jimi Hendrix Experience, up to $70,000 to appear. In addition, Hoffman is demanding $500,000 in his negotiations with the Warner Brothers Studio for exclusive rights to films taken of the demonstration. . . .

"If a large crowd attends the 'smoke-in,'" the FBI concluded, "Yippies plan massive violence and destruction in the Washington, D.C., area."

"YIP-WP allegedly financed by donations," advised a memo from the Detroit office, "but possibly aided by illicit drug traffic."

They were apparently unaware that the YIP-WP alliance had failed. There had been disagreement between the parties about whether the anti-war and marijuana issues should be combined, but there were bigger issues.

Jerry Rubin spent June serving a month's sentence in the Cook County Prison, but not before—to the dismay of fellow radicals—visiting Charles Manson behind bars in Los Angeles ("I fell in love with

Charlie Manson the first time I saw his cherub face and sparkling eyes on national TV," he wrote). Abbie Hoffman was now, according to the FBI's own intelligence, interested in relocating YIP from the East Village, away from the "street people," and hoping to "utilize the YIP for publishing and filmmaking purposes."

The White Panthers' Pun Plamondon, interviewed while hiding underground, had no use for either. Although he praised the Weathermen as a great inspiration for "a higher level of revolutionary violence" and hoped that more people, inspired by these "new heroes," would pick up weapons, he said Rubin and Hoffman had become too complacent, lacking concrete agendas, and detached from the streets. "A while ago I found that they don't even live in communes, and here are two brothers who are supposedly representing our revolutionary culture, and yet they're still living just like a lot of pigs we know," he scoffed. "They mobilized a lot of people and they raised people's consciousness to another whole level, because the white brothers and sisters got a firsthand taste of fascism in Amerika. But what's too bad, is that the people moved ahead, and the 'leaders' didn't move ahead."

After the springtime wave of bombings and explosions, Nixon pointed to protests on college campuses—which, of course, had been kicked off by his decision to invade Cambodia and exacerbated by the killings at Kent State and Jackson State in Mississippi—as further justification for greater latitude in gathering domestic intelligence. In June, the secret new Interagency Committee on Intelligence—represented by heads of the FBI, CIA, DIA, and NSA—convened to formulate plans to strengthen surveillance on "subversives." After receiving the superagency's forty-three-page report, the president agreed with the recommendation from aide Tom Huston that nearly all the restraints on intelligence collection that it addressed—including covert mail coverage, surreptitious entry, more campus informants, and wiretapping—should be relaxed or altogether removed.

Weatherman and the Black Panther Party were the agencies' top priorities, but other radicals were hardly off the radar. On the day the Interagency Committee on Intelligence was formed, an FBI letter to the president reported that

Hoffman has announced that the Yippies will become a more "gutsy" organization in response to the May 9, 1970, demonstration in

D. C., which he described as a fiasco led by a "decaying dinosaur," the New Mobilization Committee to End the War in Vietnam. A source has advised that the Yippies will adopt a more radical mantle which will enable them to attract a greater following. Hoffman visualizes the new Yippies image as similar to that of the Black Panthers and plans call for the wearing of red berets and taking over a leading role in community-based "radical action." One individual is coming to the capital to help organize Yippies into small "community defense groups" of approximately six people, hoping that this tactic will make mass arrests, raids, and police infiltration more difficult.

Also that day, a CIA situation report carried a concise quote from a Hoffman interview in the *Quicksilver Times*:

"We're gonna declare war on Amerika."

"Amerika is a death machine," proclaimed the new YIP manifesto, a practically posthumous document that was only distributed after the alliance had run its course. "It is run on and for money whose power determines a society based on war, racism, sexism, and the destruction of the planet. Our life-energy is the greatest threat to the machine.... They cut our hair, ban our music festivals, put cops and narcs in the schools, put 200,000 of us in jail for smoking flowers, induct us, housewife us, Easy-Rider murder us."

Out of caution, news of the July 4th Smoke-In had been spread only by word of mouth and stories in UPS papers, which meant that there was no leadership for the government to infiltrate or serve with injunctions, but it also meant that no one was sure if the event had been effectively orphaned by fears and disagreements.

"1,000,000—ONE MILLION—JOINTS ARE GOING TO BE DISTRIBUTED," trumpeted the *East Village Other*. "This writer personally knows several people who swear they are bringing a pound each," proclaimed a *Quicksilver Times* contributor.

By the end of June, though, the FBI reported that YIP, not wanting to "attract kids to a likely arrest," was backing away from the smoke-in. Rennie Davis, one of Hoffman's and Rubin's fellow Chicago Conspiracy defendants, announced an "Emergency Committee to Prevent a July 4 Fistfight," expressing concern that the event might turn into "America's most massive red-white-and-blue bloodbath." Davis said he would discourage youths from coming to the capital. "There might be some conflict if they try to smoke dope in the middle of a right-wing rally. We want to talk to the Honor America Day people about how to avoid conflict." Newspapers, though, swept aside the intention behind these comments and reported them as though they were incitements. HONOR AMERICA DAY BLOODBATH THREATENED BY CHICAGO 7 GROUP, read a typical headline.

Longhairs did indeed turn up in the capital on the Fourth of July, some of them camping out in sleeping bags, rolling joints in red-white-and-blue rolling papers, and raising a few Woodstock Nation flags. They pushed a searchlight truck into the Lincoln Memorial Reflecting Pool, wading and frolicking half-naked, "moving through the water towards the slightly larger crowd on the steps like an invasion force storming the beach," as Liberation News Service reported.

"Smoke dope, get high, all the pigs are gonna die," some shouted.

Tear gas and batons were met with rocks and soda cans.

The AT&T- and Standard Oil–sponsored official entertainment vied for attention with chants of "Fuck Miss America," "Free Bobby Seale," "Fuck Bob Hope," and "Ho Ho Ho Chi Minh, Acid Heads are Going to Win!"

Marijuana smoke floated all the way to the stage. "Before this is over," Bob Hope admitted from the stage, "I may need some of that stuff myself."

For better or worse, the chaos was mostly kept out of the news. "The national media mentioned the smoke-in as a minor incident," Liberation News Service reported, "and painted a rosy picture of 50,000 more citizens flooding Washington in patriotic fervor."

The opening night of the New York Pop Festival began with two hours of speeches, as promised. "We talked to the pigs and told the pigs to get out of here," Denise Oliver announced. "Politics don't end when you listen to music. We are the people—all of us, except for the undercover pigs. If you dig on any undercover pigs and if you check out any pigs walking around, you tell us about it."

Someone took a bolt cutter to the padlocks on the twenty-six gates, and the ad hoc community security teams let thousands come in without tickets. Some locked gates were opened by someone with a pass key; other gates were just torn down. So many tickets were stolen from the box office that they were being unloaded for fifty cents apiece.

"We're also here, white revolutionaries, cultural revolutionaries from the RYP Collective in NYC," Retherford read into the microphone. "The White Panther Party in New York City. Youth International Party, as well as the Weathermen. We are one arm of a worldwide revolution."

A recording of Bernardine Dohrn's voice came over the PA system, delivering a Weatherman dispatch: "Within the next fourteen days we will attack a symbol or institution of Amerikan injustice." Provocative, but an old tape—and the attack had already happened a month earlier, when the NYPD Headquarters Building was bombed. It was almost like the recording was played back just for thrills.

As Jethro Tull's performance was transmitted to giant television screens before twenty thousand people strewn about the concrete-surrounded grass, the NYPD's Tactical Patrol Force was outside turning away late arrivals from the front gate, insisting that the clearly audible concert had finished. A street gang pushed a parked car over an embankment. Forcade took the stage and found himself in the unusual position of pleading that people buy tickets.

At 4:00 a.m., Grand Funk had finished, and the Jimi Hendrix Experience was about to go on. A reporter from *Rolling Stone* was onstage trying to get an interview with Don Friedman when she was "heaved out the stage door and down the steps by a Randall's Island heavy." She wrote that Forcade, having "emerged as a kind of radical non-leader" during the negotiations, "had now somehow become head of the Randall's Island Collective, and decided he was in charge of clearing the stage."

By Saturday, most of the big names—Joe Cocker, Richie Havens, Eric Clapton, Miles Davis—had heard about money troubles, and canceled. A mayor's aide had the lights shut off while Ten Years After finished its set, and the dissatisfied audience set the field ablaze and fed the fire with trash barrels and police barricades. As the NYPD stormed into the stadium to remove Viet Cong flags that fans had raised on a flagpole, the crowd demolished the wooden fence blocking the stage. They directed a barrage of cans and bottles toward the stage, one knocking out a Woodstock producer.

On Sunday, the New York band Elephant's Memory and the New Orleans voodoo-costumed Dr. John played for free, but the bad vibes remained. Little Richard concluded his set by throwing his glass-bead-adorned jacket into the audience, and everyone who grabbed for it was rewarded with a bloody hand. Sly Stone's manager arrived to explain why Stone was a no-show and, when his limo was surrounded by Young Lords, insisted that he "gave up being the vice president of CBS to, uh, join the revolution."

There was no money for the bail fund.

Later, Forcade wrote an account that at once distanced and centered his own involvement. "There was almost no advance ticket sale and therefore no money, and we realized that if we wanted a festival at all, we would have to put it on, for the most part, ourselves. I called everybody I knew in the festival world, and they generously responded. Soon there was a double security fence around the stage, lights, sound, security people, stage crews, free food, an inflatable dome for bad-trip cases, and all the other by now standard accoutrements of a festival."

"The psychedelic sounds that turn on the white 'cultural nationalists' so much are merely distortions of Third World rhythm," the Young Lords asserted in their own underground newspaper, *Palante*. "Rip off the Festivals! An eye for an eye!"

But it would be hard to make the case that anyone got what they wanted out of New York Pop. "The white radicals said they wanted money for causes, but they were obviously more interested in the free ticket concept than in selling tickets to bring that money in," Carman Moore of the *Village Voice* wrote afterward. "Since bringing down capitalism in all its forms is one of their main credos, they stood to lose nothing either way."

The following week, the Manhattan District Attorney's Office began investigating six people—three from the RYP Collective and three from the Young Lords—on charges of conspiracy to commit extortion and grand larceny. The Young Lords told Liberation News Service that promoter Teddy Powell had financial connections to the Mafia, and that the loss of its profits had led to a $20,000 contract out on the life of Young Lords chairman Felipe Luciano. The *East Village Other* ran a notice informing readers that, although its already-typeset behind-the-scenes story about the festival "had some interesting things to say about 'the movement' and festivals," it was withholding publication for fear of indemnifying some of the participants.

Perhaps the legacy of Randall's Island was best articulated by one of its own promoters, in a moment of hype-free candor. "The love-peace thing of Woodstock is out," Don Friedman declared on Sunday night. "Anarchy. Complete and total anarchy. That's what replaced it."

On July 23, 1970, eighteen members of the Weatherman group were indicted by a federal grand jury in Detroit on charges of conspiring to commit assassinations and bombings in four cities.

That same day, Pun Plamondon—who'd now been underground for nine months—and fellow White Panthers Skip Taube and Jack Forrest were on their way to their Michigan safehouse, carelessly tossing beer cans out of the window of their Volkswagen van. A state trooper pulled them over, but Plamondon's fake-name license worked, and they were let off after they picked up their litter.

And then the trooper realized his mistake. Three hours later, in the upper peninsula of the state, a county sheriff's car pulled into traffic and followed the van.

"Do we shoot it out? Do we shoot it out?" Plamondon screamed as the sheriff's car wove through traffic behind them. He had a .38 Derringer with him. Taube had an M1 carbine with a thirty-round clip. "Should we shoot the son of a bitch?"

The deputy turned on his car's lights and siren.

"No shooting!" Forrest yelled.

The Volkswagen pulled over. Forrest went back to talk to the deputy and was quickly cuffed, and a revolver was put to his head.

A state police car sped in from the other direction, and Plamondon and Taube surrendered.

The following day, the White Panther Party invited the press to their Detroit office. "This kangaroo trial is going to be revenged," vowed Abbie Hoffman. He'd flown in from New York to join Genie Plamondon and Ken Kelley at the press conference, for one last show of solidarity between the Yippies and the White Panthers. "Within the next week, we plan an act of revenge."

But Hoffman was still exhausted from his own yearlong trial, and he instead headed west with his wife Anita, visiting the Grand Canyon and Las Vegas, while he gathered material for his next project, *Steal This Book*.

Forcade, too, was feeling burned out. After the Randall's Island escapade, he complained in a letter to John Sinclair that the New York scene was uptight and paranoid, filled with rat-racers trying to climb the social ladder of the radical community. The Randall's Island speeches had been turnoffs, he said, failed opportunities to reach out to the younger kids who'd come for the music. Forcade thought that movement leaders should be reaching out to high schoolers in Brooklyn, Queens, Long Island, and outward to the suburbs, and grooming them for radical engagement.*

Sinclair replied to Forcade with a seven-page, single-spaced letter that began with another shot at the Yippie leadership: "The so-called 'radicals' are running around acting in movies in their heads, telling these suburban freeks to pick up the gun and start mowing down the policeman on the block," he complained. "They're still talking about 'co-optation,' while they're being co-opted by the FBI every day...acting like tough guys and woofing and waving inadequate rifles around in the air and scaring off the youth masses and the broad masses of the people in this country. Those guys have a lot of waking up to do before we can consider them seriously anymore."

The rest of the letter outlined Sinclair's plans for his vision of a self-determined subculture, keeping money out of "the piggy banks of the rock and roll imperialists" until the movement could "unite and build revolutionary consciousness and move to abolish the paid society altogether."

Sinclair felt that Forcade had the means and the mechanisms to recruit dedicated young revolutionaries. "The point now is to start building up our alternative social order so we can start moving, and as far as I can tell you are doing more of that than anyone else in New York City."

To this end he proposed a three-prong system of "unified media assaults." The most autonomous would be *Sun/Dance*, the White Panther Party's new color magazine. Next was the *White Panther National Supplement*, an eight-page biweekly "political information transmitter" that

---

* Forcade soon found the low-hanging fruit: teenagers who had already been working on an underground newspaper with the daringly appropriated name of the *New York Herald Tribune*. Many of these students even briefly formed an "underground high school" called the New World School.

would be sent out for inclusion in underground papers.* Finally, there was the White Panther News Service, through which "our pieces would merge into the context of the other papers and would then be seen as having been endorsed completely by the papers." By exciting readers at the grassroots level, Sinclair reasoned, the party could establish local chapters under one central policy and a national governing body.

All of that would have to wait. Michael Forman, now living in Los Angeles and occupying some nebulous but apparently powerful position with Warner Brothers—the word "troubleshooter" was tossed around—had called Forcade two weeks before to offer him a vacation of sorts: an invitation to join the Medicine Ball Caravan.

The caravan was an attempt by Warner Brothers to make the *Woodstock* lightning strike twice. This time, though, the studio could control everything from the beginning. It would pack the musical roster with its own acts—most notably, the Grateful Dead—and recruit the on-screen audience the way it'd cast any other movie. In exchange for signing a release, each of the 150 participants would have all expenses paid for a cross-country adventure. If they stuck it out to the end, they'd get a free trip to the Isle of Wight festival. A French film crew would film twenty vehicles' worth of musicians, dealers, hustlers, and just plain zonked-out stoners on their three-week patchouli-scented reality show as they traveled east. It was a vision of the Aquarian Age, carefully filtered through the lenses of Madison Avenue.

But who was using who? The people in front of the cameras—for instance, the Hog Farm—were sure that they were manipulating the studio into conveying their own message of radical love. There were wheels within wheels within the caravan.

Michael Forman figured that this contrived depiction of the hippie lifestyle might be a little bit too sterile and that it could use someone like Tom Forcade to keep everybody honest. Forman even suggested that

---

* "I think we can make it without advertising, but I'd like to pick up some extra money that way and also take some money on our endorsements of certain high-energy products. I mean, I would run free ads for Bobby Seale's book, or for a record by Tony Williams or Miles Davis or Pharaoh Sanders or some of the Detroit bands, you dig, but it would be very much nicer to get the money for running those ads and use it to support the paper. But…it isn't worth the money to run an ad for the Hypes, or the Creeps, or the latest greatest horseshit churned out by Capitol records, you dig?"

Forcade bring along David Peel, the doggerel-shouting troubadour of Washington Square Park, as a kind of traveling heckler.

And so, in late July, still reeling from Randall's Island madness, Forcade went shopping for his big road trip. In Newark he bought a 1965 Cadillac limousine that seated nine. Elsewhere he tracked down a $200 plexiglass dome, a bubble machine, and spray paint and got to work.

On the way to meet the caravan, Forcade had one important stop: that summer's UPS conference was hosted by the Milwaukee *Kaleidoscope*, on a farm in Ozaukee County, Wisconsin. A pink flyer promised "three days of meetings to bring us together, from outspread fingers into one mighty fist!"

Even before the meeting began, though, *Kaleidoscope* staffers were concerned about a growing feeling against the way UPS was being run.* Several of the more ideologically pure papers were burning out, as the endeavor of managing business ran up against anti-capitalist and nonhierarchical values. Concert Hall's dissolution—and its subsequent $300,000 lawsuit against Media A over advertising exclusivity—had left editors nervous about revenue streams. And there were also qualms about the Bell & Howell arrangement, which gave Forcade a sizable chunk of earnings.

When Forcade's Cadillac rolled up to the farm, jaws dropped. On the roof of the car—painted olive drab with Army stars—Forcade had welded a stage constructed from steel and marine plywood, twenty feet long and six feet wide. Atop the stage, which would eventually provide a platform for David Peel's performances, Forcade had mounted his Minuteman missile-site speakers and the plexiglass dome that would serve as a sound-mixing booth.

It was hardly a modest entrance to begin with, and *Kaleidoscope*'s ad manager was less than thrilled when he saw that Forcade had also brought guns.** But Forcade was quickly chastened by a flurry of complaints about UPS, and receded into the background.

---

* Less than three weeks later, the Milwaukee *Kaleidoscope*'s sister paper, the Madison *Kaleidoscope,* would come under police scrutiny when it gave space to a group that claimed credit for bombing Sterling Hall at the University of Wisconsin.

** The Cadillac was well stocked with squirt guns and cap pistols, so it's possible the ad manager mistook them for real firearms.

For all of Forcade's back-and-forth with Sinclair about elevating the White Panther agenda, in the end it was Ken Kelley, the editor of the *Argus*, who delivered the party's talking points. Kelley proposed a co-op advertising plan for papers and drummed up editor interest in joining the White Panther Community Information Services.

Overall, the mood of the conference, conducted on bales of hay between the farmhouse and the barn, was dark. There were no cameras allowed, and the security detail kept its firearms concealed. Late arrivals and early departures abounded, while disengaged attendees wandered out to score hot dogs and donuts at the local supermarket rather than settle for the brown rice and vegetables served by the hosts. After a group discussion about whether forty-two dollars in collected funds should go to grass or acid, one woman stepped up with the idea of putting it toward bail for Milwaukee Black Panthers.

"*No way*," the hordes shouted back. "We gotta have dope!"

Stragglers were still arriving on the last day of the conference, as Forcade beat a retreat from Milwaukee. The Medicine Ball Caravan had set out from San Francisco, and he would try to catch up with it in the Southwest. On his way out of Wisconsin, he misjudged a highway clearance and the top half of his Lucite dome was sheared off, but after a quick glance at the detritus in the rearview mirror, he kept his foot on the gas and raced south. He picked up a pair of hitchhiking German tourists who handled the wheel down to Texas and then west to Albuquerque.

Finally, they caught up to the Caravan in the parking lot of an Albuquerque Holiday Inn, their arrival heralded by a blaring tape deck. Just over a year ago, the *Orpheus* bus had pulled into the Radical Conference in Ann Arbor; now a new Forcade—dressed in a World War I general's uniform, driving a 7,800-pound mud-caked behemoth with an Army star on the side—faced a wholly new scene.

Forcade later wrote that the first thing that happened—after someone asked that he *please* turn down the Hendrix—was that people from the Caravan, already tired of living their lives under the close watch of the cameras on the buses, tried to line up rides in his car.

Forcade described the Star Car with relish:

Inside the Caddy there were enough amplifiers to drive the big speakers and other assorted speakers to the point of crumbling walls. Also built in was a tiny Tiger-Mite generator capable of powering all the electric apparatus. In the trunk were boxes of firecracker smoke bombs, flares, skyrockets, Roman candles, picket signs, Magic Markers, White Panther leaflets, underground newspapers, paintbrushes, spray cans, paint, and two telephones with the bootleg induction apparatus to call from the car. A few special items, such as a baby-blue Rudy Vallee megaphone for impersonating the director, a Mack Sennett clapboard for running out in the middle of scenes and yelling "Cut!" and a Lawrence Welk bubble machine for producing clouds of bubbles for the rock and roll music. And to get it all down, a 16-mm Bolex and a typewriter.

Forcade introduced himself to Tom Donahue, the 350-pound underground-FM radio DJ from San Francisco who had helped to hatch the idea of the Caravan. Donahue, who bridged the corporate and turned-on worlds, had seemed the likeliest target for another monetary shakedown, but the DJ was aloof. Forcade would have to pick another time to make his pitch. With that stymied encounter, and to the consternation of the proximate hippie travelers, the Cadillac peeled out of the Holiday Inn amid a hail of exploding firecrackers and smoke bombs.

They stopped for a night at the New Mexico headquarters of the Hog Farm. Despite Forcade's growing militancy, he was still fond of its clownlike leader, Wavy Gravy, although he'd started to see Wavy's disarming sweetness as a good-vibes weaponization, a calculated strategy to defang everyone around him. Ever the psychic strategist, Forcade tried to scratch at the surface, wondering what kind of fissures might exist within the Hog Farm collective. He couldn't find any, and it nagged at him. How could they all get along so well? He couldn't reconcile his simultaneous admiration for the peaceable Hog Farm and the fierce Weather organization. "It was a syndrome of insanity that resulted from working too long at UPS," he wrote, "where I had confronted among the papers a spectrum of beliefs as wide and varied as the world itself."

Arriving in Boulder, Forcade reunited with Michael Forman, who a week earlier had started his own trip with a bang. On the morning that the Caravan set out from San Francisco, Forman spotted superagent Freddie Fields, a producer on the film, in the back of a chauffeured limousine. "Watch this," he chuckled to Donahue, hopped into his station wagon, and slammed backward into the limo before pulling away and into the fog.

"Forman, a showman of the first order, was playing so many different roles that nobody was quite sure how powerful he was in the hierarchy," Forcade wrote. "Some thought he was the producer, others thought he was a spy from Warner Brothers, others thought he was just one of the folk. Even Warner Brothers and the Caravan management weren't quite sure what to make of Forman. Without qualification, Forman is a genius, but no one has ever been sure what he is a genius at." For his part, Forcade was counting on Forman to help him extract some donations from Donahue and the Caravan for radical causes.

Before the Boulder concert began, Forcade drafted Forman's lawyer, George Goldstein, and a former Hog Farmer named Butch to help him track down a local dealer. With Warner Brothers' money, they made a wholesale purchase of peyote buttons, to be delivered to the concert site. With that out of the way, Forcade swallowed a mystery pill from a Caravanner and waited for the music.

The Grateful Dead had dropped out at the last minute, so it was the non-superstars of the Warner Brothers roster, including white funk group Cold Blood, Cajun fiddler Doug Kershaw, and a newly formed rock band named Stoneground, who were providing the entertainment. As the pill started to take hold, Forcade couldn't decide which side of the stage to watch from, so he kept walking behind the stage where, bathed in floodlights, he began constructing a paranoid fantasy: *The audience members were moths being drawn to hidden cameras that captured every moment, each to soon be manipulated by Hollywood.* He stumbled from one side to the other, back and forth, eyes glazing over, making wide detours to stay out of the floodlights and in the shadows.

Naturally, he decided that this would be a good time to go visit Tom Donahue and have a talk.

He found Donahue ensconced in his Winnebago, surrounded by women tending to his every need. After some small talk, Forcade asked why he hadn't seen any political engagement on the Caravan.

"This could be more than just a 'good vibe' trip across America, you know? You're in San Francisco, you know radicals. Why aren't they here?

How can you promote dope and ignore people like Sinclair, who are in jail because of it? You can't separate the political element from the rest of the culture—it contains the analysis that holds the culture together, protects it from the old culture, builds the future. Politics is nothing more, or less, than taking control of one's own life, and without it, there's no liberation, no freedom, and ultimately, no good times."

Donahue nodded.

"Look," Forcade continued, "the further east you go, the more opposition you're going to find to this escapist attitude." He recited the negotiations with the promoters of Woodstock, of Winter's End, of Randall's Island and worried aloud that some of the weirdo politicos he knew might get into a little festival-trashing if profits *from* the culture didn't go back *into* the culture. A nice Caravan; sure would be a shame if anything happened to it.

Donahue nodded again. "Uh-huh. How much do you think the Caravan should give back to 'the culture'?"

"Fifty thousand is a nice figure. That's about five percent of the budget."

"Okay, man, if you're really concerned about it, you can go onstage and talk about it. I'll put you on every fucking night. We'll give you the microphone and you can close the show."

Forcade sensed a trap—he'd be framed as a "bad vibes" rogue, an outside agitator who could be relegated to the sidelines, cut out of the film.

"I don't want just a few of us to have heavy politics in opposition to an anti-political majority. It would have much more impact if we all had a little politics. I want little things, really. I'd like to see a few buttons and stickers, like hippies normally have."

"Look, man, I think you're fucking it up," Donahue said. "If you want to make it with them, you've got to make them *love* you so they'll listen to you. And instead you think you can sit over there in your Star Car and figure everybody's going to beat a path over to you to meet this great representative of the White Panthers."

Donahue seemed unmoved, so Forcade turned up the dial a little bit.

"I think you're being used as a pawn of Warner Brothers," he cautioned. "You are adrift among powerful forces." He sprinkled in some insinuations about secret connections between the Kinney Corporation (owner of Warner Brothers), the Mob, the Hog Farm, and Michael Forman. "Do you think it's an accident that all these people are on the

Caravan? How do you think I was able to assemble such an expensive counter-Caravan so quickly?"

Donahue advised Forcade to loosen up.

As if on cue, a member of Donahue's entourage took out a mirror, assembled two lines of mescaline in crystal form, cotton-candy pink, and passed it around.

Forcade, persuaded, concluded the meeting with a convivial mescaline snort, and he wandered back out to hear a set by the Youngbloods. "Everybody get together," they sang, "try to love one another, right now."

Making his way through the crowd, Forcade told anyone who would listen that if they needed free food or advice on bad trips, they should head back to that Winnebago over there.

"Tom Forcade has hardly opened his bag of tricks," wrote John Grissim, covering the Caravan for *Rolling Stone*, "but already a vague Star Car paranoia is sweeping the ranks, feeding not upon the fear of disruption but rather upon an uneasy feeling that this whole operation may be an artificial setup for a Hollywood hippie flick after all."

As the Caravan moved from town to town, no one could quite figure out Forcade's agenda—most of the Caravan just knew they disliked his negative energy. Why was this creep, this would-be saboteur, sticking around?

B y the time they reached Nebraska, the Star Car had assembled a team of regulars.

Butch, the exiled Hog Farmer (the commune deemed him too outrageous even for them), was a former Marine seemingly fueled by Southern Comfort and weed. What Neal Cassady had been to the Merry Pranksters, Butch was to the Star Car, driving the limousine a steady hundred miles an hour (although it was hard to know for sure, after Forcade disconnected the speedometer). Whenever they feared the vehicle might be searched, everyone gave their contraband to Butch, who could ingest it all and remain operational. As operational as possible with all that weight, anyway. The bottom of the car's frame scraped along the interstate; it would suffer eleven tire blowouts on the journey.

In Kearney, Nebraska, the car picked up Ron Rosenbaum, who'd been invited by Michael Forman to cover the Caravan for the *Village Voice*. Rosenbaum was twenty-three, a Yale graduate, and the paper's rising star. With his long red hair, beard, denim, and tennis shoes, he practically melted into the background.

When Rosenbaum had first met Forcade, while covering RYP negotiations for the *Voice*, Forcade was dressed in all black, like Lee Van Cleef in *The Good, the Bad, and the Ugly*. But Rosenbaum couldn't shake the feeling that, for all of his angry rhetoric, Forcade was repressing a smirk, like it was all a prank. Rosenbaum liked him. And when he saw that Forcade's UPS stationery reproduced the "muted post horn" symbol from the Thomas Pynchon novel *The Crying of Lot 49*—about an underground, seditious communications network—he liked him even more. "Forcade is one of the few people in the left who has enough skills and intelligence to outwit the hip capitalists at their own media games, and enough sense of purpose to avoid getting lost for its own sake," he wrote in the *Voice*. "He knows about the half-hidden webs which connect the underground with the above-ground— he's part of some of them—but he knows which side he's on."

Another former Hog Farmer, Andy Romanoff, had heard about the Caravan, and was hitchhiking west from Chicago to try to find it. Serendipitously, shortly after starting his travels, Romanoff looked across the highway and spotted a Caravan bus driving in the opposite direction. He persuaded his ride to turn around and pursue the bus, which they successfully flagged down.

But when he learned that his old friend Butch was traveling with Forcade, Romanoff—who'd originally left the Hog Farm because they'd strayed from the Merry Prankster legacy of a traveling, Dionysian party and who was currently carrying a lot of drugs with him—switched to the Star Car. He quickly found another familiar face in Forman, whom he'd met when the Hog Farm crashed at his Philadelphia home and partied with a tank of nitrous oxide.

The passengers of the Star Car quickly realized that they shared an interest in Terry Southern's novel *The Magic Christian*, in which billionaire protagonist Guy Grand uses his fortune for mischief. Grand's stunts include filling a vat of excrement and entrails with money to tempt passersby and offering a police officer $6,000 to eat the parking ticket he's just issued. As Grand tells one hapless victim, "I was just curious to see if you had your price."

Before long, the Star Car crew decided to make little movies of its own as they traveled. Butch, Forman, and Romanoff made business cards identifying themselves ("Butchoff, Formanoff, and Romanoff") as members of something called the "Grand Corporation." Armed with a camera, slate board, and megaphone, they'd stop at Stuckey's restaurants (home of the "pecan roll") along the highway and offer patrons and waitresses three dollars each if they would agree to be filmed getting a pie in the face.

There was an element of class privilege to the *Magic Christian* trickery that was missing in the early Yippie pranks—Guy Grand wasn't just giving money away; he required a kind of submission or debasement in return, pushing people into discomfort for amusement. Still, the idea that "everyone has a price" resonated with their protestations against the Caravan, where every morning the film's participants lined up at the back of a station wagon to trade expenditure receipts for cash payouts from Warner Brothers accountants.

The singer David Peel arrived at the Omaha airport on the evening of August 17, greeted by signs (OMAHA CHAPTER DAVID PEEL FAN CLUB WELCOMES HIM!), cameras, and a cheerleader with a megaphone. Then someone walked up to him and dumped a whipped cream and cherry pie on him.

Peel's reception had been coordinated by Michael Forman and the Star Car, with whom he would now be traveling, and whose antagonism he would channel into song. Peel had the voice of an angry deaf man, fearless against the rules of pitch and pronunciation, and hoarsened from years of appearances at Washington Square Park demonstrations.

In a strange twist of fate—or was it?—Warner Brothers had acquired David Peel's label, Elektra Records, only a few weeks earlier. Now he would use the Star Car roof stage to badger its production, chanting menacingly at every Caravan campsite stop:

"Rip off! Hippies! Hippie Ripoff! Rip off hippies!"

They covered eight hundred miles in two days, picking up Peel's guitarist and drummer along the way. Peel convinced the Star Car travelers that they should henceforth be known as the Caravan of Pirates—convenient since he had skull-and-crossbones flags and buttons with him, promotional material for his latest album, *American Revolution*. (Peel's insistence on wearing and waving the symbol had, in fact, recently driven the White Panthers to exile him from their Ann Arbor headquarters, complaining that the Jolly Roger was "a death trip, reactionary, provocateur kind of thing.")

The limo announced itself to the Caravan campsite in Yellow Springs, Ohio, with more firecrackers and cherry bombs, earning a quick rebuke. They alighted to nearby Antioch College, and Forcade drove the car up to the front of the largest dormitory on the campus.

"Hello, we're from Warner Brothers and we're here to make some Looney Toons," announced Peel from the rooftop stage.

But to the Antioch students, who were already waiting to confront Warner Brothers for its exploitation of the counterculture, the limousine—covered in hand-painted slogans that said FREE JOHN SINCLAIR and FREE BOBBY SEALE and FREE TIM LEARY and even FREE EVERYBODY—looked like nothing less than a Hollywood movie prop.

"A hip capitalist is a capitalist pig!" they shouted, and

"Hip pigs!" and

"Go Back to Hollywood!" and

"Fuck Warner Brothers!" and

"If the White Panthers hear about this, they'll rip you all off, pigs!"

That was too much for even journalist Rosenbaum. "Listen, you cretin, this guy"—he gestured at Forcade—"is *with* the White Panthers."

"Bullshit, bullshit, if the White Panthers were here, they'd get rid of this bullshit. Warner Brothers pigs!"

Some students began deliberating about whether to smash any cameras they might find in the car, while others added taunts like "oink" and "rip-off" to the limousine graffiti. They painted on the windshield and let air out of the tires before finally considering that the Warner Brothers caravan might be elsewhere. The Star Car team offered to take them to find the *real* pigs, and half a classroom's worth of them piled in, ready for blood.

At that moment, Chan Laughlin showed up. Laughlin was Tom Donahue's number two on the Caravan, a former Special Forces Marine who'd been a player in the early San Francisco hippie club scene. Laughlin, unhappy to hear his project being maligned, jumped up onto the stage and got into it with Peel.

"You haven't got the balls to go out in the world and do something worth filming!" Laughlin taunted. "While you're all whining about Warner Brothers in your little rooms, we've been living.... We've got them making our own movie for us with their money."

"You're just a money slave for Warner Brothers," Peel shouted.

"I'll take money from anyone who gives it to me," Laughlin said, "if they let me use it the way I want."

Now Forcade chimed in. "From Nixon?"

"From Nixon, from anyone, if they pay my way to somewhere I want to go."

Taking money from Nixon? The crowd wasn't so sure about that. Laughlin told them to take their car and get out of there.

"Who do you think you are, giving orders?" replied an indignant Peel. "What am I, a Jew for you Hitlers at Warner Brothers?"

That was too much. Laughlin produced a hunting knife from his belt and lunged at the singer. He grabbed at Peel's vest, but Peel slipped from his grasp, jumped from the stage, and hit the ground running. Laughlin jumped off, too, and chased Peel around the Cadillac.

The crowd was screaming now.

Peel tripped on a turn, and Laughlin jumped on top of him. Forcade, a pair of drumsticks in hand, jumped on Laughlin. The knife was pried from Laughlin's hand.

"It's all right, I'm cool," Laughlin said.

That night, the French film director went up to Forcade. "Now I have a movie!" he exclaimed, and a Warner Brothers worker appeared to ask Forcade to sign a release.

Later, *Medicine Ball Caravan* producer Fred Weintraub told Ron Rosenbaum that Warner Brothers had in fact hired Forcade to stage the knifing scene. Forcade's response was coy: "That's so far out I have to stop and think about it for a second, reexamine my premises, to make sure there's not some reality warp happening.

"No, I'm sure that's not true. It was all too *reel*."

David Peel returned to New York the next day, while Forcade and the rest of the Star Car carried on to Washington, DC, for the final concert of the cross-country trip. It was in the capital, Forcade later wrote, that he'd started to question whether there were forces even greater than Warner Brothers pulling the Caravan's strings.

When one of the Caravan lawyers asked Forcade for a ride to the passport office—to prepare for the Caravan's trip to London—he saw the lawyer easily procure passports for individuals with criminal convictions on their records. Even more suspicious, he said, was a listing for the concert in the *Washington Post*, which offhandedly included a sentence ("the United States Information Agency is supplying some of the money for the film") that seemed to implicate the Caravan in official propaganda efforts.

"I told several Caravaneers about the article," Forcade recalled, "but no one seemed interested. 'Groovy. Far out. We're ripping off the government,' was the general response."

The *Quicksilver Times* followed up with a feature that painted the Hog Farmers as "Zen bodyguards" serving Warner Brothers and the United States Information Agency (USIA): "Since literally millions of kids in this country have become outlaws, smoking marijuana, fucking each other, blowing up police stations, and dodging the draft, propaganda about 'our nation's youth' has become a very sensitive area for the country's image-makers; a well-screened film of kids passively getting their cakes off behind a government-sanctioned rock concert could be most useful in presenting the false image of a united country to people elsewhere in the world."

Forcade distributed firecrackers and smoke bombs to attendees of the concert, where Warner Brothers' commitment to apolitical entertainment was such that the filmmakers were instructed not to film any raised fists.

The next morning, as Forcade departed for New York City, Michael Forman rammed his T-Bird into the side of the Cadillac. The Caravan had finally ended its tour of the United States.

"Coming off the trip, we had to admit that virtually all of the people we met in America were helpful and friendly to us above and beyond the call of duty, despite our outrageous appearance," Forcade wrote. "Repeatedly, people with right-wing type stickers on their car would go out of their way to help us get back on the road when we broke down. In 1965, hippies were the most tolerant people in America. In 1970, we found them to be the least tolerant."

Forcade went to London to see the final Caravan show, which included performances by Pink Floyd and Rod Stewart, and then, he claimed, headed to Paris to meet with the North Vietnamese about staging a rock festival in the demilitarized zone. ("The Vietnamese were polite, but skeptical.")

When he returned to the States in mid-September, there was one last adventure for the year. Forcade and Ron Rosenbaum reunited with David Peel and the Lower East Side for a trip in the Cadillac up to America's Cup in Newport. There, they joined Hunter S. Thompson and his illustrator partner Ralph Steadman, who were on a magazine assignment.

The troublemakers chartered a yacht, raised the Jolly Roger flag, and planned to charge into the race, alongside the American defender ship *Intrepid* and the Australian challenger *Gretel*. Thompson, wearing an upside-down navy hat and a patchwork-quilt coat, dug into his hearty supply of hallucinogenic pills, while Steadman manned the bongos and joined the Lower East Side in its repertoire of songs like "Oink, Oink," "I Want to Get High," "I Want to Kill You," and "The Pope Smokes Dope." On the first night at sea, the Coast Guard boarded the ship and arrested Forcade—who had brought along his Minuteman speaker system and tapes of the MC5—for disturbing the peace. David Peel poured orange dye from a distress kit into the race waters. Before the plan to intrude on the race could be executed, the harbor police escorted their boat to the dock.

Eventually, Thompson and Steadman sneaked by dinghy into the shipyard to spray-paint FUCK THE POPE on the *Gretel*. Upon discovery, they fled, and in their drugged mania launched flares that ignited small fires on surrounding boats.

Steadman called their Newport adventure "a dress rehearsal for *Fear and Loathing in Las Vegas*," referring to the 1971 book that would come to define gonzo journalism. Forcade and his crew had not seen the escapade through to the end, however—Hunter S. Thompson had thrown them off the boat for "being too outrageous."

CHAPTER 5

IN THE MIDDLE OF ONE LATE-AUGUST NIGHT, RADICALS BOMBED THE Army Math Research Center on the University of Wisconsin's Madison campus, in protest of the center's work for the Department of Defense. The blast killed a research scientist who was in his laboratory to catch up on work before a vacation.

In a letter published by the Madison underground newspaper *Kaleidoscope*, a group calling itself the "New Year's Gang" took credit for the bombing and demanded the abolition of ROTC, as well as the release of three Vietnam veterans who'd bombed the power substation of a nearby army training base. "If these demands are not met by October 30th," the letter read, "open warfare, kidnapping of important officials, and even assassination will not be ruled out."

In an extraordinary action by a federal prosecutor, *Kaleidoscope* editor Mark Knops was jailed for six months for refusing to answer questions before a federal grand jury. But although authorities thought they knew the identities of the four bombers within hours, they could not locate them, and the suspects' names joined fellow radicals H. Rap Brown and Angela Davis on the FBI's Ten Most Wanted Fugitives list.* When Angela Davis was captured, Weatherman's Bernardine Dohrn moved onto the list within hours.

Bombs were exploding at least weekly—in Chicago, in Marin County, in Seattle, in Santa Barbara, in Long Island City, in Orlando. And radical actions were moving into other areas of adventurism. Members of Weatherman helped Timothy Leary escape from prison in San Luis Obispo. Two women who'd worked for the National Strike Information Center at Brandeis—coordinating campus protests immediately following Kent State—took part in a Boston bank robbery that left a police officer dead. They, too, went underground, and joined the most wanted list.

The FBI stepped up its wiretapping and black-bag jobs in its dragnet for radicals, effectively enacting the proposals of the formally rejected Huston Plan of months earlier. To get access to on-campus intelligence, it even lowered the minimum acceptable age for recruiting informants.

But it was mostly coming up empty-handed.

---

* The day after the bombing, the New Year's Gang borrowed a 1961 Plymouth and raced out of town. Their first stop was the White Panthers' headquarters in Ann Arbor. They figured that Pun Plamondon's group must have an underground network in place that they could use. The White Panthers told them to go away.

"Face it," a Justice Department veteran said, "we're in what amounts to a guerrilla war with the kids. And so far, the kids are winning."

Still, a thirty-three-page FBI report shared information from a confidential source that Youth International Party activities were "minimal" and that "the possibility exists that unless the non-leaders of the organization start planning activities, the organization will collapse." YIP had no formal membership and no bank account. The same week, Abbie Hoffman ducked out of a San Francisco fundraiser only minutes before he was scheduled to speak, leaving his attorney Michael Kennedy to pass along to the booing crowd Hoffman's complaint of "a lack of leadership in San Francisco for a revolutionary movement." An FBI source had an alternate explanation: Hoffman had been up on amphetamines for four days straight, they said, and "really freaked out."

The movement backlash against the Yippies, now perceived to be ego-tripping celebrities, had begun. "It is tough being a leader when the movement has no leaders," chided one San Francisco underground paper.*

The FBI, naturally, was happy to help escalate any internecine conflicts. Soon afterward, a memo recommended that its New York office anonymously mail a fake leaflet to "selected new left activists designed to broaden the gap between Abbott Howard Hoffman and Jerry Clyde Rubin... to fragmentize the organization and hopefully lead to its complete disintegration":

ABBIE OINK HOFFMAN

WANTED

WANTED

FOR RIPPING OFF THE STREET PEOPLE,

FOR PISSING ON THE REVOLUTION,

FOR FUCKING JERRY RUBIN AND YIP

The government struck a more sober tone when it warned that "several anarchistic groups" were planning to "blow up Federal Government operations and to kidnap government officials." In Michigan, a sergeant for the state police testified that the White Panthers wanted to kidnap

---

* Jerry Rubin had gone to visit Timothy Leary and Eldridge Cleaver in Algeria.

multiple congressmen to exchange for John Sinclair and other political prisoners. "Gerald Ford might be good for trading for Black Panther party leaders such as Huey Newton and Bobby Seale," the detective said, and added that the vice president, Spiro Agnew, was also considered a target.

Underground newspapers, once again, came under fire. In an October speech in Phoenix, Vice President Agnew castigated the *Quicksilver Times* by name and claimed that those who sold it "may be contributing to the maiming or death of other human beings." In New York, a man claiming to work for the government arrived at the UPS office and confided that the authorities "decided that the underground press was the main network causing all the trouble" and "had decided to wipe it out"—UPS in particular.

The FBI visited the old Concert Hall offices in Philadelphia—and not for the first time. They'd come before to look for White Panther Pun Plamondon, who they claimed had received money from Concert Hall, and again after Concert Hall printed Abbie Hoffman's *Woodstock Nation*. Now, they said, they had information that Weatherman leader Bernadine Dohrn had been involved with the Winter's End festival.

The actual existence of such leads is, in retrospect, debatable. A memo from the Philadelphia FBI office at the time indicated a consensus that "more interviews with those subjects and hangers-on are in order for plenty of reasons, chief of which are it will enhance the paranoia endemic in these circles." The federal government was intensifying its campaign of intimidation against underground newspapers and leftist groups.

"Law and order" as a political slogan had been popularized by Arizona conservative Barry Goldwater in his 1964 campaign for president of the United States. The Phoenix lawyer who'd suggested the strategy to Goldwater, Richard Kleindienst, had then gone on to work for Richard Nixon's 1968 campaign, and after Nixon won the election Kleindienst was rewarded with the position of deputy attorney general. He quickly earned the nickname "Mr. Tough" and a reputation as something of a hatchet man. One nationally syndicated column described Kleindienst as "boisterous," a "Phi Beta Kappa from Harvard" who "often hides a brilliant mind with discourtesy bordering on crudeness." In the early months of the administration, Kleindienst caused a stir when an interviewer quoted him as saying "people who demonstrate in a manner to interfere with others should be rounded up and put in a detention camp."

With the ear of his boss, Attorney General John Mitchell, Kleindienst immediately recommended the hiring of two fellow members of the so-called Arizona Mafia who had worked for Barry Goldwater. "One of you Arizona cowboys is enough in the Department of Justice," Mitchell told Kleindienst.

But Mitchell relented, and William Rehnquist, a Phoenix lawyer whose long sideburns, pink shirts, and loud ties belied his right-wing ideology, was put in charge of the Office of Legal Counsel. Within months, Rehnquist made headlines for giving a speech in which he warned that the "barbarians of the New Left" posed "a threat to the notion of a government of law which is every bit as serious as the 'crime wave' in our cities." If force was required to extinguish that threat, Rehnquist said, so be it. "Disobedience cannot be tolerated, whether it be violent or nonviolent disobedience."

Kleindienst also successfully recommended his best friend, Robert Mardian, for the position of General Counsel of Health, Education, and Welfare. As the most conservative person in the department, Mardian—"an absolutely cold-blooded political operator," in the words of one colleague—quickly gained fame for easing desegregation deadlines in Southern states. His steel-rimmed glasses and balding head enhanced his generally on-edge vibe. "There are two kinds of people in the world—winners and losers," he once told a reporter. "I knew a loser once and he was a queer."

In the fall of 1970, the Nixon administration made a series of moves designed to vanquish dissent. First, Mitchell and Kleindienst prepared to revive the nearly dormant Internal Security Division of the Justice Department. Only now, instead of combating communists, the ISD would pursue radical groups of the New Left. Kleindienst once again made a recommendation for his carpool partner Mardian, who stepped into the role as assistant attorney general in charge of the division.

In mid-October, Nixon signed the 1970 Organized Crime Control Act. Among other measures, the act allowed the government to invert the grand jury system. Grand juries, originally designed as a check on overzealous prosecutions, were held in secret to protect identities of both witnesses and falsely accused individuals. Questioning was done without lawyers present because witness immunity was guaranteed. But the Organized Crime Control Act authorized the misleadingly named "use immunity." Held as unconstitutional since the nineteenth century, use immunity meant that the witness could still be indicted for the very crimes investigated by the grand jury, provided the crimes could be "independently" corroborated—but, because of that pretense of "immunity," the witness was not allowed to exercise the Fifth Amendment. They could be jailed for contempt at the first moment they refused to answer a question. The government could commence grand juries anywhere in the country, at any time, for up to eighteen months, and renewable after that. If a witness refused to testify, the court could jail them for those same eighteen-month terms. Even if a grand jury didn't prove a crime, it could tie up both the movement leaders and the lawyers who defended them.

By November, young left-wing radicals accounted for the bulk of the FBI's list of most wanted fugitives. The ISD's staff of lawyers, which had withered from ninety-six to forty-two, built back up, and suddenly Mardian found himself the third most powerful man in the Department of Justice.

Attorney General John Mitchell then seized on the White Panther Party to help him provide a judicial imprimatur for the crusade against the radical Left. The number three man in the FBI had recently warned, in a public speech, that the White Panthers had "suggested the possibility of kidnapping high government officials and United States ambassadors, demanding freedom for White Panthers now in prison in exchange for release of the officials."

Mitchell filed an affidavit in *United States v. Sinclair*—the case charging White Panthers John Sinclair, Pun Plamondon, and Jack Forrest with conspiring to bomb a CIA building—that admitted that the government had picked up Plamondon's conversations when it was conducting warrantless wiretaps. Then, reviving an argument that he'd made during the Chicago Seven case, the attorney general claimed that the president of the United States had inherent constitutional power to authorize such surveillance in the name of national security.

Shortly after the America's Cup adventure in Newport, Forcade returned to the Alternate U, the site of the Randall's Island RYP-Off meetings, to introduce himself to Alan Jules Weberman, a friend of

David Peel who was teaching a class entirely dedicated to the study of Bob Dylan.

"I dig what you're doing to Dylan," Forcade said. "Can I take you out to supper?"

When they sat down to eat, Forcade told Weberman that he was a part of Weatherman and had participated in bombings. Weberman had no reason to doubt him—who would make up something like that?—but wondered if Forcade was a little too trusting with sharing information.

Forcade had adopted an ever more militant stance—for instance, hosting a benefit for the Black Panthers Defense Fund—even as he increasingly engaged with institutions of capitalism and establishment politics.* Both tendencies were evident when he invited Charles Baker, the director of an anti-extremist group called the Institute for American Democracy, to interview him at the UPS office.

Baker couldn't figure out how seriously to take Forcade. He'd contacted the University of Utah, which checked records back to 1965 but couldn't find evidence of a degree for Forcade. He found the UPS office décor suspicious, too. "From the rickety furniture by the windows ('Liberated,' I was told, from a defunct brokerage office) to the hanging paisley towels marking out the living space at the rear to the leather jacketed costume of the speaker, everything about the cavernous office had the appearance of a put-on," Baker wrote. "But you got the impression he meant every word of it."

"In general, I think most of us would approve of the latest bombing at the University of Wisconsin," Forcade told Baker, carefully measuring the interviewer's reaction. "We're sorry about the fellow who got killed. But compare that to all the people getting killed as a result of the kind of research going on there.... The straight press keeps trying to make a martyr out of one man—one man, mind you—and we are concerned with the many." Forcade told Baker that he was a proud member of the White Panthers but insisted that the group had nothing to do with the 1968 bombing of the CIA facility in Ann Arbor.

"Behind that fierce handlebar mustache," Baker observed, "lurks a thin-shouldered intellectual who runs a business which, he concedes,

---

* Michael Forman's brother Randy visited the UPS loft during this time and remembered seeing "a ping pong table, automatic weapons and a bunch of pot in the corner...a whole pile of bricks, like Christmas without a tree."

takes in and dispenses about a quarter of a million dollars annually." Baker's article pointed out that the Free Ranger Tribe worked without wages, despite advertising revenue from record companies and the UPS microfilming project for Bell & Howell, which brought in another $25,000.*

Forcade was also now venturing into book publishing. Abbie Hoffman had crowdsourced for a compendium of ways to rip off the Man. A "handbook for survival and warfare," an anthology of secrets, it would be packed with information on hitchhiking, drug dealing, street fighting, bomb construction, and shoplifting and, of course, legal advice. But Random House rejected *Steal This Book*, and then thirty other publishers passed as well.** So Michael Forman suggested that Hoffman bring it to Forcade, who had experience with packaging and distribution.

"Forcade's idea," said Gerald Lefcourt, Hoffman's lawyer, "was to use head shops all over the country and a syndicate of marijuana dealers to distribute *Steal This Book*—developing another alternative distribution system for books." They agreed that Forcade would edit the manuscript and distribute the book.

But disagreements started almost immediately, beginning with the proposed three-dollar cover price for something that would only cost about 25 cents to print. "I urged Hoffman to publish the book and give it out for free," Forcade said, "and offered to put up a third of the cost and find others who would pay for other parts. Hoffman stated that the People had money, and they should pay.

"It seems to me," Forcade countered, "you don't advocate ripping off the system on the one hand and then charge $3 to find out how to do it."

Forcade also complained that Hoffman only wanted to meet about financial arrangements, not the editorial content, and was rushing to publish *Steal This Book* before Jerry Rubin published his next book. But after some haggling, they agreed that Forcade would receive a flat fee of

---

* Forcade had only just begun to send out royalty checks, as mentioned in an October 21, 1970, UPS letter: "Enclosed is first in what we hope will be a long line of microfilm royalty payments, resulting from the sale of microfilm copies of your newspaper. As soon as we can, we will send you your microfilm copy for your own files."

** *Steal This Book* would be published in April 1971, only three months after William Powell's *The Anarchist Cookbook*, which also included information on making bombs.

$5,000. In December, Hoffman handed off the manuscript and went to serve thirteen days in a Chicago jail for writing FUCK on his forehead.

Forcade later said Hoffman's original manuscript for *Steal This Book* was "too fucking academic. It was bullshit. It didn't even sound like Abbie." The further he got into the book, he said, "the more disturbed I became about the casual way in which people were urged to do things which were patently unworkable. Bomb diagrams were included which were self-destructive or inoperable. Statements were made without qualifications. I was worried for the safety of the reader." Hoffman didn't know "which bombs blew up where," he said.

Two weeks later, Forcade delivered his edits and a bill for $5,000. Hoffman, claiming to be unsatisfied with his efforts, offered $1,500. "I don't work for hippie wages," Forcade responded. While Forcade waited for his contract to arrive, though, Grove Press expressed an interest in distributing the book. "As soon as Lefcourt found out," Forcade said, "they went directly to Grove, thus immediately betraying our contract." *Steal This Book* would be published without Forcade's participation after all.

Still, Forcade continued to tout the importance of alternative distribution systems. "There is a strong case to be made for movement people flatly refusing to give books to any establishment publisher," he wrote in a column that was printed in multiple UPS papers. "Capitalist publishing and distribution of books is like the Grand Canyon and radical books are like water being poured in there making that Canyon deeper. Use your own channels. Yes, I know that if you publish your own book you reach only thousands and when you sell it to them you reach millions, but it ain't quantity that counts, it's quality…mimeograph it, Xerox it, make carbons, or pass it around to your friends, but don't sell it down that Colorado River to become a fucking product, like a frozen TV dinner."

And yet despite his stated stance against corporate publishing, Forcade himself accepted $10,000 to write about his adventures on the Medicine Ball Caravan for New American Library, a division of the giant Times-Mirror Co. He also signed on as the coeditor of two paperback collections of articles that had run in UPS newspapers: *The Underground Reader* for New American Library, and *The Underground Press Anthology* for Ace Books.

"Perhaps you are wondering why I am having my current books done by establishment publishers," he wrote in a column. His justification was weak. "The answer is that I have already sold these. I did take the one unsold book back from Random House. But my next book will be FREE! (and remember, folks, you get what you pay for)."

Ironically, Forcade's notoriety as an anti-establishment crusader, and his inside knowledge of underground newspapers, now brought him further into the mainstream. At the end of 1970, the Twentieth Century Fund, a New York–based research foundation, invited him to participate on a Task Force on Press Freedoms, charged with investigating the US government's assaults on the free press.

Even the establishment media was under siege by now. Reports surfaced about federal courts serving subpoenas to the *New York Times, Time, Life, Newsweek*, and other outlets to demand notes, tape recordings, and even testimony from journalists; the corporate owners often complied with these demands. In New York, Detroit, Albuquerque, and Washington, DC, intelligence and law enforcement agents were caught posing as journalists or photographers. The *Chicago Tribune* reported that the army had videotaped rallies from a truck emblazoned with the name "Midwest News."

Upon joining the committee, which included such old-guard luminaries as Mike Wallace and George Reedy, Forcade traded in his all-black suit for an all-white one, although he looked not so much like Tom Wolfe as he did the ghost of a riverboat gambler. He wrote to friends that he was going to learn "the ways in which the media has been fucked over by the government."

Over the next several months, Forcade's public profile was virtually nonexistent as he worked on his books and shuttled back and forth between New York and the District of Columbia, where he set up a three-person UPS news bureau and applied for a White House press pass. For the first time, he vowed, the radical media would cover the president.

At the end of 1970, FBI director J. Edgar Hoover had appeared before a Senate appropriations subcommittee to ask for $14 million for a thousand new field agents. Then, despite advisement from the Internal Security Division (and others) that there was insufficient evidence, Hoover announced that he had information about a threat from a group made up of priests, nuns, students, and teachers. He claimed that the group was planning to explode electrical conduits and steam pipes in DC and to kidnap a White House official as ransom for the end of bombing in Asia and the release of political prisoners.

Hoover's bombastic speech, which he subsequently leaked to the press, ensured that the Internal Security Division had no choice but to indict the group, soon to be known as the Harrisburg Seven. The ISD's first major case would be a weak one. "There's goddamn no telling what we would have if Hoover hadn't talked," Robert Mardian said later. "We depended on informants, and they shut up after he testified." One of the witnesses called, a fifty-two-year-old nun, refused to appear. "The evidence on the basis of which I have been named as an unindicted co-conspirator, subpoenaed to testify and asked questions, was secured by illegal wiretaps," she said. She was jailed.

That same day, in Detroit, the district court hearing *United States v. Sinclair* rejected the reasoning behind the John Mitchell affidavit that claimed a president's constitutional power for warrantless wiretapping. "An idea which seems to permeate much of the government's argument is that a dissident domestic organization is akin to an unfriendly foreign power and must be dealt with in the same fashion," Judge Damon Keith wrote in his ruling. "In our democracy all men are to receive equal justice regardless of their political beliefs or persuasions." After extensive meetings between Mitchell and Mardian, the Justice Department decided to file a mandamus appeal, bringing Keith's ruling on the wiretap issue before the Sixth Circuit.*

Meanwhile, more information about the surveillance of American citizens came to light when a group of former army intelligence agents testified before a Senate subcommittee. Beginning in the late 1960s, the US Army's Counterintelligence Analysis Branch had received information "from approximately fifty agencies within the U.S. intelligence community," cross-referenced files, and sometimes passed it on to other agencies. One of the agents in the CIAB, Ralph Stein, was nicknamed "Mr. Radical" and specialized in the New Left and the underground press. He testified that he'd also been ordered to share his findings with men from the

---

* As Jeff Hale explained in his 1995 dissertation, "Wiretapping and National Security: Nixon, the Mitchell Doctrine, and the White Panthers," there is reason to suspect that the government had calculated exactly this outcome and had in fact invoked the Mitchell Doctrine expecting that Keith would reject it. By making a mandamus appeal on Keith's order, the DOJ fast-tracked the wiretapping issue to the Sixth Circuit, where it could be put to the test in a higher court immediately, even as the Sinclair case itself carried on.

Central Intelligence Agency, who, he later said, were especially interested in learning more about the editors and writers, asking "a lot of questions that indicated that they had already examined some of the underground publications in question" and seeming to have already "investigated the personalities." Of the names in the army's files, Stein testified, "the overwhelming percentage are of people who did nothing more than exercise basic constitutional rights and civil liberties, and who are anonymous Americans." And a former army captain revealed that an Interdivisional Intelligence Unit in the Department of Justice had since supplanted the army's counterintelligence branch, maintaining a "political computer" that "can produce a rundown on almost any past or coming demonstration of size, which will include all stored information on the membership, ideology, and plans of the sponsors."

And shortly after that shocking testimony, the *Washington Post* reported that an anonymous group calling itself the Citizen's Committee to Investigate the FBI had—in response to the Harrisburg Seven indictments—burglarized files from the bureau's offices in Media, Pennsylvania. (It later emerged that UPS was among those suspected of the break-in.) Among the sensational contents of these files, which the *Post* quoted from, were descriptions of FBI policy on hiring student informers; a memo in which Hoover ordered surveillance on student groups that "organized to project the demands of Black students"; plans to develop informant networks in "ghetto areas"; and stern reminders to informants that they weren't supposed to assault policemen. The stolen documents also revealed that the aims of the bureau went beyond law enforcement and into the realm of psychology. The agency was determined, as one memo put it, "to get the point across there is an FBI agent behind every mailbox." Eventually, the files were determined to be part of a widespread counterintelligence program called COINTELPRO. Its mission was not only to thwart leftist activities but also to sow suspicion among dissenters.*

---

* Robert Wall, a disillusioned former FBI agent, was the first to name COINTELPRO in the media in his article "Special Agent for the FBI," which appeared in the *New York Review of Books*, January 27, 1972. He had earlier read the article at a Committee for Public Justice conference at Princeton University at the end of October 1971.

Even as John Mitchell urged publications not to disclose the information from the FBI files, the United States government's legislative branch began making new claims about spying. Rep. Hale Boggs, the House Democratic leader, claimed to have proof that the FBI, using "the tactics of the Soviet Union and Hitler's Gestapo," was surveilling members of the House and Senate. "Mitchell is obsessed with tapping wires," Boggs said, and he demanded Hoover's resignation. Then the chair of the House Judiciary Committee, Rep. Emanuel Celler, called for an investigation of surveillance activities. "We're certainly heading toward a police state," he warned.

On the eve of two hundred thousand demonstrators gathering for the May Day action at the Capitol, Mitchell gave a speech to rally support for the warrantless wiretapping policy. "We need intelligence on the movements of suspected conspirators, not formal evidence on which to convict them," he said, and touted the value of the hundreds of wiretaps he'd authorized. "In order for a national security wiretap to do any good, it should come near the beginning of the investigation." Chalking accusations up to "tapanoia—the belief that your telephone is being tapped," Mitchell said another senator had "twisted the facts" about the FBI's surveillance of Earth Day rallies.

"This is not a police state," Nixon insisted at a press conference, but on the same day Richard Kleindienst cooked up a plan for the Bureau of Narcotics and Dangerous Drugs to monitor and record drug use among May Day activists as a pretense for canceling park protests. "Their plan is now to bust the demonstrators Sunday morning, and probably move in with narcotics agents to arrest as many as they can," wrote White House chief of staff H. R. Haldeman in his diary that day. "Thus they think we'll bust up their plans and make it hard for them to do their traffic-stopping exercise on Monday."

The May Day demonstrations in DC resulted in the largest mass arrest in US history, with more than twelve thousand people detained. When local precincts were stretched to capacity, thousands were crowded into a Washington Redskins practice field surrounded by cyclone fencing or into the exercise yard of a jail and then bused into the Washington Coliseum. A quarter of those were swept up during a protest outside the Justice Department; Kleindienst and Mardian joined John Mitchell on his office balcony to gaze down at the roundup. While Mitchell puffed on his pipe, Mardian snapped photos of the masses below.

Tom Forcade was absent from the May Day action, but one former member of the Free Ranger Tribe was right in the middle of it. Leslie Bacon had left UPS and moved to Boston before coming down to the Capitol, where in early 1971 she worked with a variety of Yippie and White Panther alumni to put out a Mayday newspaper. She also worked on booking bands to play at a concert the weekend of the demonstrations.

On March 1, when a bomb exploded in a Capitol building bathroom, the Weather organization—now calling itself the Weather Underground—had quickly claimed credit. But Bacon was taken into custody, and, following her release, she was reported on by multiple infiltrators within the movement.

On the morning of April 27, as a stoned Leslie Bacon prepared to take a shower at the communal house, she heard a woman's voice downstairs yelling, "You're gonna pay for this!" Someone had ripped down the front door.

The next thing she heard was one of her housemates bounding up the stairs, running to the bathroom.

"Leslie, get the fuck out of here, the FBI's here!"

The screaming downstairs continued, now joined by the sounds of crying from her housemates' small children. Bacon threw on a sweater and skirt, dashed up to the attic, and pulled herself up through a skylight onto the roof. Then she climbed down to the house next door, and the neighbors called a lawyer while she finished her shower, smoked some more weed, and listened to some music. When the lawyer arrived, he told her what he'd learned: the Justice Department had come to subpoena her as a witness for a grand jury in Seattle, to ask about the March 1 Capitol bombing. They were not looking to indict her. Did she know anything about the bombing? No, she told the lawyer.

Then there's no reason not to talk to them, he said. Will you go to the grand jury if you're not arrested? Yes, she said, and he told her he'd speak with the lead prosecutor of major crimes at the Justice Department.

Later that day, though, the FBI came back to the house, grabbed her, and brought her down to a waiting car. One of them got on a walkie-talkie.

"We picked up that object we were looking for," he reported, and they headed to the airport.

Leslie Bacon became an overnight celebrity within the movement. Year-old pictures of her at the UPS offices, smiling for the camera, circulated in newspapers across the country. The Free Ranger Tribe got its name in the *New York Times*. The whole time, she was in custody, forced to answer questions.

A line of questioning from the Internal Security Division's chief litigator, Guy Goodwin, would begin something like this:

> Tell the grand jury every place you went after you returned to your apartment from Cuba, every city you visited, with whom and by what means of transportation you traveled and who you visited at all of the places you went during the times of your travels after you left your apartment in Ann Arbor, Michigan, in May of 1970.
>
> I want you to describe for the grand jury every occasion during the year 1970, when you have been in contact with, attended meetings which were conducted by, or attended by, or been any place when any individual spoke whom you knew to be associated with or affiliated with Students for a Democratic Society, the Weatherman, the Communist Party or any other organization advocating revolutionary overthrow of the United States, describing for the grand jury when these incidents occurred, where they occurred, who was present and what was said by all persons there and what you did at the time that you were in these meetings, groups, associations or conversations.

"Goodwin just has totally evil vibes," Bacon said of the slick, impeccably coiffed witchfinder.

In the next few years, the Internal Security Division would conduct more than one hundred grand juries in eighty cities. It would subpoena thousands of witnesses, in some cases forcing them to travel from one part of the country to another without the presence of lawyers. The grand juries would be used not only to gather new information but also, by steering scared witnesses to confirm what had previously been learned illegally by FBI surveillance or black-bag jobs, to launder information for prosecutions. Goodwin often offered immunity and then threatened contempt sentences if witnesses didn't testify against associates.

Investigations of radicals that had previously been conducted independently by the FBI, Secret Service, and Treasury were now coordinated under the aegis of the ISD, which used the Interdivisional Information Unit's computer system to consolidate thousands of dossiers. Goodwin crossed the country, connecting the cases together like they were one grand conspiracy.

Many of the subpoenas that resulted from Leslie Bacon's testimony were for people who'd associated with Forcade: in New York, three Yippies and two members of RYP-Off; in Detroit, two members of the White Panther Party. Forcade had attended a May Day postmortem conference in Indiana along with a few of those people only days before the subpoenas were issued, but he was untouched.

He had largely remained out of the spotlight, and indeed away from the movement, as he focused on his plans to report on the White House for UPS.

Ironically, Forcade arrived in Washington just as the establishment media was exposing government malfeasance with an independence previously seen only in the underground press.

In the same week that Forcade covered Tricia Nixon's wedding (from outside the White House grounds) for UPS, the *Washington Post*, developing leads from the Media break-in, reported that the Internal Security Division maintained an index with the names of thousands of potential subversives to be rounded up in the event of a "security emergency." (Forcade was on the list, but not named in the article.)

Three days later, the *New York Times* published the first of the leaked documents known as the Pentagon Papers. The Nixon administration, in its most flagrant attempt at media suppression, attempted to muzzle further reports.

But if Forcade expected anything like an esprit de corps to accompany his quest for press credentials, such optimism was short-lived.* He learned that membership in the Congressional Press Galleries was a prerequisite for a White House pass, and when that body's standing

---

* That summer, Forcade made a rare radio appearance in which he described the tenor of the meetings: "I said to them, 'I read a lot of news stories in the straight press about communist troops attacking Allied forces, but I never read anything about communist troops attacking capitalist forces. One side's defined in terms of ideology, but the other side is defined in terms of some kind of weird solidarity.' And at this point one of the guys started screaming and got up and left the room. It was a very emotional kind of meeting. People were getting up and screaming, threatening me, and, you know, back and forth."

committee presented him with arcane admission requirements—insisting, for example, that UPS possess a telegraphic service, file stories on a daily basis, and get prior State Department approval for foreign member papers—Forcade lashed out at what he called "a group of puppet journalists of the fascist U.S. government."

In a press release, Forcade attempted to use the Pentagon Papers case as a fulcrum against his colleagues. "On the same day when everyone was weeping and crying about the repression of the *New York Times*, they were actively carrying out the same repression—preventing access to news—upon the underground press.... The so-called Standing Committee can put progress off, but they cannot stop it. The day will come when I, as Washington correspondent of the Underground Press Syndicate, will achieve equal access to the news, as it should be, and all the rights that are mine."

Then he added a page entitled "Credentials? These Are My Credentials!" "It is true that for many years I have usually been content to remain in the background of the Movement," he wrote. "But with the underground press now being trampled upon more than ever, it is necessary to come out of the shadows and stand up and fight openly. If credentials as a radical journalist are necessary, let the press speak for itself." Following this was a long list of quotes about him, taken from various press clippings in the past two years.

CHAPTER 6

IN THE SIX YEARS SINCE AN ACID-SOAKED LISTENING SESSION TO *BRINGing It All Back Home* awakened one A. J. Weberman to the genius of Bob Dylan, he'd dedicated himself to pioneering the science of Dylanology. Weberman, whose frizzy hair telegraphed his excitability, had been working on a massive book that would crack Dylan's lyrical codes, and, in service of that goal, he developed a computerized concordance to the singer's collected works. He said that he'd gotten so dizzy poring over every music magazine at the Lincoln Center Performance Arts Library, looking for Dylan references, that he'd developed a Dramamine habit. More recently, he'd upped his game a notch and begun picking through the garbage outside of the singer's MacDougal Street home, hunting for clues. When Weberman and David Peel decided that Dylan had abandoned politically conscious songwriting—and convinced themselves that Dylan had become a heroin addict—they had announced the establishment of a Dylan Liberation Front. They made up buttons that read "Free Bob Dylan."

For Dylan's thirtieth birthday, Weberman threw a block party outside of Dylan's townhouse. Abbie Hoffman, Jerry Rubin, and five hundred other people showed up. Weberman unveiled a birthday cake with hypodermic needles in place of candles, while David Peel shouted into a microphone: *"Happy Birthday, Bobby junkie motherfucker!"* Bob Dylan, who was visiting Israel at the time, was so alarmed that he cut his trip short and flew home.

A few weeks later, when John Lennon and Yoko Ono arrived in New York City for an extended visit, fellow celebrity Jerry Rubin took them to see David Peel perform in Washington Square Park. Within days, Lennon was on the cover of the *New York Post* wearing a "Free Bob Dylan" button given to him by A. J. Weberman.

Suddenly, it seemed, Abbie and Jerry were recharged.

"Abbie called and said we were going to put Yippie back on the map again," said A. J. Weberman, who headed to DC, where the Yippies issued a statement promoting another July Fourth smoke-in. This time, they'd connect the issue of marijuana prohibition with a congressional report and newspaper articles that contended that heroin was being transported via the CIA's own Air America airline and that 10 to 15 percent of American troops—between thirty thousand and forty-five thousand men—were themselves using high-grade heroin.

Forcade appeared on the Capitol steps with a disclaimer. "I come here strictly as a reporter for the UPS, breaking a news story to other reporters," he said. "I am not an organizer of the Smoke-In and Anti-Heroin March, although I am fully supporting it.

"On July 4, 1971, there will be the largest number of people in history gathered in one place to rally for new governmental drug policies. Last year, 25,000 people showed up, despite the Honor America/Billy Graham/Bob Hope fiasco. This year, as a result of intensive underground publicity, I expect at least 50,000 people to gather at the base of the Washington Monument to listen to rock bands sing songs that are banned from the airwaves, and to march to the Capitol to return their hypodermic needles to the government."

Two days after that announcement, Yippies gathered outside the federal court building where the Nixon administration was hoping to have an injunction ordered against the *Times* for publishing the Pentagon Papers. Weberman and David Peel joined Abbie, Jerry, and two dozen others in mock-protesting the "soft" treatment of the *New York Times* compared with the likely jail sentences that would have been handed down to underground newspapers.

Forcade wrote approvingly to John Sinclair that "the old-time Yippies (Rubin-Hoffman-Albert) have sublet part of the UPS office in NYC, and it is like old times, except that they all have new 'girlfriends,' with the exception of Abbie, who is married. Something good might come of it. The New Yippies seem much more together, however, and much less into $. They are going all out on the Smoke-In and the Peace Treaty. The UPS office in NY is run entirely by women, by the way, which should be healthy."

But by the time of the July 4th Smoke-In, Jerry and Abbie had withdrawn their names. "Jerry and Abbie definitely do not want to take a conspiracy rap for a demonstration they are just attending," read a UPS press release. "There are no organizers."

This was not quite true. Much of the behind-the-scenes organizing was done by one of those so-called New Yippies, although he'd been in and out of the scene for half a decade. Dana Beal was an old friend of A. J. Weberman and David Peel, and back in 1967, he'd identified as a member of the pre-Yippie consortium known as the New York Provos, which had sponsored the pioneering smoke-ins in Tompkins Square Park. That summer, an undercover cop arrested—and beat—Beal for LSD possession, touching off a series of demonstrations, including one in which jazz musician Charles Mingus was arrested.

Out on bail, Beal skipped town, and he'd been on the run ever since, operating under various aliases. After a stint in Mexico, he found his way to Vancouver, until another pot bust required that he pull up stakes again. Next he darted around the Midwest, helping to organize a White Panther chapter in Milwaukee and writing for an underground there, under pseudonyms. He was still remembered by his fellow Lower East Side radicals—in fact, shortly after the 1968 Chicago convention, Abbie Hoffman cited Beal's tactical expertise. ("I had remembered Dana Beal's brilliant advice," he wrote. "'When the shit hits the fan, the safest place is in the middle of the crowd.'")

"He was a very intense, nervous person," said one Wisconsinite. "Two years' running had done a lot to him." The editor of the Milwaukee *Kaleidoscope* called him "very high energy, almost to the point that it bothered you," and that "all he did was talk politics." A teenage Milwaukee activist named Patrick Small experienced that intensity firsthand. One late night in 1969, Small got a visit from a friend who'd met Beal on the University of Wisconsin campus. Beal needed a place to stay. But the next morning, one of Small's unsuspecting housemates put Beal's paper bags of possessions out to the trash, which was picked up early that day. Beal's typewriter, his in-progress manifesto about culture wars, his clothing, and his stash were gone. Beal tracked Small down at his high school, got the principal to summon him from class, and berated Small right there in the principal's office.

The following year Beal was arrested again, during a police raid of a Yippie house in Milwaukee, but he made bail and hit the road before authorities figured out that he was a fugitive. Still, Beal managed to move freely around the country. He was credited with stepping in and saving the 1970 smoke-in in DC after other organizers backed out, and he was back again for the follow-up.

The Second Annual July 4th Smoke-In was, in many ways, a repeat of the first. Again there were showdowns between hippies and horse- and motorcycle-riding cops in the Reflecting Pool. But this year, with no Honor America crowd to act as a buffer, the escalations began before noon. Police, dodging firecrackers, chased longhairs around the perimeter of the Monument grounds.

This time, the hippies found another crowd to infiltrate. Nearby on the Mall, the Smithsonian Folk Life Festival—including gospel acts and canoe-carving Indians—was entertaining an audience of fifty thousand. By the early afternoon, as Yippie and National Liberation Front flags and clouds of marijuana smoke popped up on the green, David Peel and the Lower East Side had crashed the main stage. An American flag burned while David Peel shouted his version of the "Pledge of Allegiance"

("...to the bag / of marijuana made in Mexico..."). But between songs, Peel let his guard down and was replaced onstage by a string band. Then the police stormed the stage.

"Four cops on horseback and one squad car tried to cut right through the crowd towards the stage, but the Yippies began to throw stuff at them," reported the Liberation News Service. "They lit fireworks under the horses and a few minutes later the cops retreated."

Around seven, the Yippies began their stoned march to the Capitol, the permit procurer having forgotten to convey that the permit didn't start until nine. Finally, the crowd chanted about "CIA heroin" for TV cameras. Then, in homage to the anti-war Vietnam veterans who'd recently flung their medals onto the steps, several of them threw hypodermic syringes.

Ten days later, Dana Beal was hitchhiking north on Interstate 94 with Kathy, his girlfriend, when a blue station wagon carrying four men pulled up. As the hitchhikers settled into the car, they noticed that the men were carrying guns. While Beal exited the car and ran, Kathy tried to hold two of the men down, but it was hopeless. One of the men caught Beal, broke his rib, and brought him back to the car.

There were warrants out on Beal for a hashish sale to a Madison informant, the four-year-old LSD charges from his Lower East Side days, and bail-jumping. The pair was also charged for the possession of the dozens of bags of marijuana in their suitcase. Kathy was charged with assault and aiding the escape of a federal fugitive. Because she was only sixteen years old, Kathy was released into the custody of her parents.

Beal headed to the Dane County Jail, where he posed for a photograph with a clenched fist. He remained defiant. "I am convinced that the reason I'm sitting in jail now is not because of any drug sales, and not even because I organized demonstrations to legalize. The reason they assigned a four-man team to track me down was that at the July 4th Smoke-In we also had an anti-heroin march, which came very close to exposing the conspiracy within the present government to flood the Black and youth communities with smack."

That didn't mean he didn't have regrets of his own. The first duty of a revolutionary was to get away with it. "I should have taken the bus," he lamented to a reporter, "but it was such a beautiful day—I let my guard down."

In New York, Forcade got to work on Beal's case. He helped arrange for prominent attorney William Kunstler to take Beal's case and began drumming up media attention. Laurence Leamer, who was working on a book about the underground press, had a front-row seat to see the machinations. "Tom calls this reporter at the *New York Times*, and he tells him, 'My friend was arrested on this trumped-up drug charge. Nobody knows this, but he was the intellectual genius of our entire movement. All our ideas come from him. And the government knows this, and they're trying to get rid of him, but he's our great leader.'

"The reporter says, 'My God! What a great story, are you sure?'

"'Yeah, he doesn't want anybody to know this, but he's the genius.'

"The reporter says, 'But I've got to have a second source for this, Tom.'

"Tom says, 'Well, of course you need a second source. Would Abbie Hoffman make a good second source?' 'Yeah, Abbie Hoffman would be great!'

"Tom gives him Abbie's number and hangs up. He calls Abbie Hoffman and tells him what to say when the reporter calls."

The story appeared in the *New York Times* the next day, with the headline A MAJOR YIPPIE THEORIST SEIZED ON DRUG CHARGES and a photo of Beal. It described Beal as "a founder of several radical youth groups, including the Yippies," a "behind-the-scenes leader," and "one of the first movement writers to argue for a merger of political radicalism and the psychedelic lifestyle." Abbie Hoffman told the reporter that Beal's writings "are far more important and impressive than people like me and Jerry Rubin." For his part, Rubin said that Beal's manifestos "were a strong force in helping us understand who we are" and claimed that local and federal agencies targeted Beal because he was an important symbol.

Still, some were suspicious about Beal's sudden notoriety. The Associated Press noticed that "very few members of the establishment—and some say, very few in the subculture either—ever heard of Beal before Hoffman and Kunstler called attention to him."

"It has the ingredients of a perfect Yippie hoax," wrote a reporter for the *Milwaukee Journal*. "Dana Beal is busted for drugs in Madison. Almost immediately he is identified by Abbie Hoffman and Jerry Rubin, no less, as a famous underground organizer and theoretician, protected in his ceaseless travels across the country, including a stay in Milwaukee, by fanciful aliases—Leon Yipsky, Paul Yippie, George Metefsky of the White Panther Party.

"Attorney William Kunstler, whose clients are the leaders of a political movement that could use a few heroes, flies to Madison to lead Beal's defense, converting the mystifying claims of his importance into a genuine cause. Kunstler indicated that he would use the Beal case to test the constitutionality of the marijuana laws, which he contends are being used to suppress the youth culture."

"It's all going to be cool," Forcade assured Beal in a letter, informing him about smoke-in benefits that were being scheduled for fall in Madison and Milwaukee. One of Beal's manifestos, Forcade added, was "going to be slid into the *East Village Other* when politics permit; e.g. A.J. has to twist [the editor's] arm, probably. We will also send it out to other key papers, such as the *Barb*, the *Freep*, *Straight*, etc., who are likely to run it."

The biggest news, though, was a single sentence that foreshadowed Forcade's bigger plans. "We are planning an invitation-only YIP meeting in December," he wrote, "to implement a new party structure."

For months, Forcade had been hounding Abbie Hoffman for payment for his work on *Steal This Book*. What had seemed at the time to be a minor disagreement would eventually make the two men into bitter enemies, push Abbie Hoffman away from movement politics, and turn Tom Forcade against many of his former allies.

"He was acting very belligerently, and doing off the wall things," Hoffman's lawyer, Gerald Lefcourt, said. "He came into my office one day in his white suit, so fancy looking, demanding to see all of Abbie's files that I ever had. He was just not being reasonable. The FBI was distributing leaflets that said the very thing Tom was saying—that Abbie is ripping off the movement, living in a penthouse, which was totally false. Tom could have been buying what the FBI was putting out." Some suspected worse intentions.

Forcade filed a lawsuit against Hoffman. In another letter to Dana Beal, Forcade pushed back at the idea of a truce with the founding Yippie.

"I am not cooling things out with Abbie on any level," Forcade wrote. "I consider Abbie to be utterly corrupt. His response to [Beal's girlfriend's] request for help should be proof enough. He refused even to give her phone numbers of lawyers, or his many media contacts, and of course, money. As the enclosed article notes, Abbie dodged collective responsibility by trumpeting anarchy, outflanked criticism from other organizations by claiming all youth culture as their constituency."

Then Forcade moved in for the kill. "Either Abbie and Jerry must be utterly destroyed in the media as Yippie leaders, or a new organization must be created. Since I would rather put my energy into creation rather than destruction, I, of course, favor the latter course. You understand so many other things. Why can't you see that? The Yippies are dead. DEAD."

In August, Bob Dylan performed at the Concert for Bangladesh, an all-star benefit for Bengali refugees. A. J. Weberman and David Peel, certain that the Dylan Liberation Front had successfully prodded the singer's conscience, expanded their scope. Now calling themselves the *Rock* Liberation Front, they vowed to strike against more sellouts and anti-revolutionaries.

To stage a mock funeral for Paul McCartney, the RLF drove up Fifth Avenue in a hearse and, outside of the midtown Manhattan home of the ex-Beatle's in-laws, produced a satin-lined cardboard coffin with copies of the *Ram* and *McCartney* albums. Peel sang his songs, and Weberman, wearing a sandwich board, delivered a eulogy. When the PAUL IS DEAD protest signs elicited anger from a gathering crowd of teenage Beatles fans, the RLF hoisted up another sign: MCCARTNEY GROUPIES ARE NECROPHILIACS.

From there they immediately proceeded to the New York offices of *Rolling Stone* magazine, where they shoved their way through the main doors and stole advertising files, setting off a series of fistfights.

When someone grabbed Forcade, who was near the center of the melee, Weberman threatened to hit them over the head with a chair unless they released him. "Abbie Hoffman has first dibs!" Weberman explained.

Before the battle between Forcade and Hoffman came to blows, Rex Weiner, an *East Village Other* writer, convinced them that there might be another way for them to settle their differences.

"It's a family matter, so we decided to settle it within the family," he told the Associated Press. "Here we are saying we distrust the courts for some things but not for others, when in fact they're untrustworthy all the way. I said we're an alternate culture so why not have an alternate form of justice? Why not have a People's Arbitration Panel?"

A jury of three peers was assembled: Dr. Howard Levy, who'd been court-martialed for refusing to train Green Berets; Meyer Vishner of War Resistance League; and Craig Karpel, an *Esquire* editor who'd written about "hip capitalism" (and commissioned A. J. Weberman to do an article on garbology). Weiner served as the bailiff. On September 1, they met at the Washington Square United Methodist Church in Greenwich Village for a closed-door trial, with national press asking questions on the church steps outside.

They were each allotted two hours to make their cases, with depositions and witnesses. Hoffman refused to be in the room at the same time as Forcade. Forcade agreed, telling a reporter that if the two were together, "it would just turn into a screaming match."

"What we're trying to do," Vishner told the *New York Times* just before the tribunal began hearing the witnesses, "is to go back to the roots of what legal systems were about at the start. Now they primarily serve the interests of the state and they forget about the people they're dealing with. Everything is done to accommodate the judges and lawyers."

The emotional crux of Forcade's testimony was that he was the latest in a long line of underappreciated workers who handled the money for movements. "The guy who was the business manager of the French revolution was taken out and beheaded for having counter-revolutionary ideas," he said. "What happened after the Russian revolution? They ripped off the people who put up the money. What happened in Cuba? Che Guevara was the economic minister and they put him under house arrest, and they wouldn't even give him money to have a revolution in Bolivia. They decided he had fucked-up ideas. My own experience in the movement is that every time you handle money, especially in the quantities that I've been handling it, someone calls you a rip-off."

What other movement organization has an auditor come in and check their books? A movement auditor at that? From a completely other town, doesn't even know us, they never found any money missing, and yet people still have this image in their mind that anybody handling a quarter million dollars must be doing something shady. During the Randall's Island thing, I took my rolodex to the Brave New World offices, which, we were using part of their office to do our thing, and some of these idiots from the RYP-Off Collective copped the rolodex. Why? "Well, man, Tom Forcade is a hip capitalist." Why, because Tom Forcade's rolodex is filled with names of dozens and dozens of people like Freddy Weintraub and Jac Holzman and Ahmet Ertegun and people like that? Where did they think all this money materialized anyway?...I don't expect people to like it, or want to get into it, but the least they could do is understand it. Historically, anybody working with business or money is considered a rip-off per se, and it's been a drag for me.

TRIBUNAL: But that's what your talents are—

FORCADE: In ripping off, or running businesses?

TRIBUNAL: Well, both.

FORCADE: True! But the question is, what happened to the money? Even the money we rip off, except for the dope dealing money, is all audited. The dope dealing money, there's no way to audit it. Who's gonna keep records? *I'm* not.

Forcade needed to carefully thread the needle in his argument: he wanted to highlight his skill at operating within the capitalist system while at the same time illustrate his integrity and dedication to righteous causes. Just by picking up the phone, he claimed, he could "get people to hire me for $2,000 a week as a consultant." Companies were desperate for information about the youth market, he said, and "If I wanted, I could put through Madison Avenue about three times and walk away with a couple hundred thou, but like, I don't want to do it, 'cause I don't want to be their whore, and tell them how to rip us off. I do things that, they think they're getting the best of *me* but I know I'm getting the best of *them*. Every festival they ever hired me for, I ended up turning into a freak festival, and pouring the money back in the movement."

The judges were not overly impressed with either Hoffman or Forcade. "We found each man's notion of the karma of the situation to be a little out of whack," they concluded. In a prescription for "karma alignment," they ruled that Forcade be awarded $1,000 in cash—a fraction of the original $5,000 fee—but gave him the option to buy up to ten thousand copies of *Steal This Book* at cost, which he could then turn around and use to demonstrate his ability to distribute through the underground channels originally discussed.

Although it was not the outcome either party had wished for, the mainstream outlets portrayed it as a finding against Abbie Hoffman. "They assumed since Tom was awarded any money at all that he had won and I had lost," lamented Hoffman, the man once revered as a master media manipulator. By the end of September, finished with what he called "my second most famous trial," Hoffman had left for St. Thomas, in the Virgin Islands. He was tired of hearing his three-room, $150/month Lower East Side apartment referred to as a penthouse, angry that nobody mentioned that profits from his books had gone to Black Panthers' bail funds, John Sinclair's legal expenses, and his own conspiracy trial and May Day arrest defenses. He didn't answer his phone anymore, and he'd stopped using the phrase "brothers and sisters." "I stay away from 'movement' people these days, partly out of a security problem," he wrote in a letter to the War Resister League's magazine *WIN*. "It's hard to go to meetings when you pick up *Newsweek* and read that there is a federal agent whose only job is to go to meetings and hear references to Rennie Davis and Abbie Hoffman, or read the government brief signed by Richard Kleindienst himself explaining the government's right to wire-tap all my phones since I'm a 'national security hazard.'"

Forcade, on the other hand, had secured a decisive victory on another front.

Among those who'd objected to Forcade's seeking of congressional press credentials was Luther Huston, a reporter from *Editor & Publisher* who'd had his own encounter with Forcade's provocations. Huston still hadn't forgotten the 1969 Sigma Delta Chi convention in San Diego, at which a water glass Forcade hurled from the panelists' table had smashed near Huston's head.

So it was with some bitterness that Huston now found himself reporting that, "by a 3 to 2 vote, after weeks of controversy, the Standing Committee of Correspondents has admitted to membership in the Senate press galleries a newsman who once threw a pie in the face of a member of the U.S. Commission on Obscenity and Pornography."

Tom Forcade had finally become the first self-described radical journalist to gain access to the Congress.

He expected to get his White House credentials in a matter of weeks. "I'm just gonna play it straight for a while," he confided to the *Steal This*

Book panel. "I'm getting together with some creative movement people to talk about what can be done in front of a live press conference that won't get me shot down immediately in a hail of Secret Service bullets. The worst thing I can do for Nixon is not some bullshit like a pie or something in Nixon's face; it's to report what really is going on. There's some heavy things, like, they hand out the body counts about Vietnam, and the guys snort as they hand them out. Where does that ever make the *New York Times*, the whole corruption of media working hand in hand with PR flacks? That's what I want to get into. That's my official identity."

In Madison, two thousand people attended a September 25 smoke-in, held to coincide with the beginning of Dana Beal's trial.

Forcade did not attend. "I have yet to hear any concrete explanation of what my value would be once I got there," he'd written to Beal, somewhat impatiently. "The evidence of the publicity and legal recruiting would seem to indicate that I am having more effect here. . . . I think bringing me in at this time would be a substitute to strengthening [the new iteration of] Y.I.P., because they are certainly not going to develop any self-reliance by bringing in me to do work."

Beal's superstar attorney, William Kunstler, couldn't make it either; when the Attica riots had broken out two weeks earlier, he'd been called in by the inmates as a negotiator and was still consumed by its aftermath.

But A. J. Weberman spoke at the rally about Beal's history within the movement, and David Peel performed old classics like "Up Against the Wall, Motherfuckers" alongside new songs like "The Pope Smokes Dope" and "The Ballad of A. J. Weberman." A group called WERM, the Wild-Eyed Revolutionary Movement, provided weed-laced brownies, and the crowd marched to the Wisconsin State Capitol, chanting, "We smoke pot and we like it a lot!" Then they headed for the jail, shouting, "Free Dana Beal!"

Among the marchers were about thirty undercover members of Madison's brand-new "Affinity Squad," formed to infiltrate protest groups.

"Our men were in the middle of them," Inspector Herman Thomas boasted afterward. "There was nobody sick and nobody high. The smoke smell from the Brittingham shelter house was nothing but the smell of dead elm wood burned in the fireplace."

Law enforcement was especially concerned about Dana Beal, even though he was still behind bars. The US Secret Service had contacted the FBI in Milwaukee after hearing from a source that Beal and Morales were plotting to assassinate Nixon.

About a week later, Forcade did finally fly to Wisconsin for YIP conference planning in Milwaukee. He made an instant impression. "He was very high-energy, like a human dynamo," said John Mattes, a student who'd procured the Madison smoke-in permit and relayed information between Beal and the outside world. "Wisconsin is just a bunch of students; you don't see many guys wearing black suits and hats. He got our attention, and he got people to do what he wanted them to do."

In mid-November 1971, Forcade received a call from Fred Graham, the *New York Times* journalist leading the Task Force on Press Freedoms. Graham told him that the Secret Service had now denied Forcade's application for a White House press pass. He was unable to get further information. The Secret Service agent assigned to Forcade's case wouldn't return calls, and a spokesman for the department would only say that its decision was "on the basis of certain information."*

Graham got the story into the next day's edition of the *Times*, under the headline WHITE HOUSE BARS A RADICAL REPORTER. Upon reading it, a secretary for the American Civil Liberties Union wrote a letter inviting Forcade to join Robert Sherrill, a *Nation* journalist who'd once socked a Johnson administration press secretary in the jaw in pursuit of access rights.

The timing of the story couldn't have been more perfect: a few days later, at a posh Upper East Side townhouse, the task force on which Forcade served delivered its final report, which included an argument for the validity of the underground press. When asked by reporters about his fight for a press pass, an unchastened Forcade announced a plan to park a van across the street from the White House and monitor activity at the mansion with binoculars. "I don't know what's going on in the White House that they don't want to let me in," he said. "It must be terrible."

---

* It was around this time that the assigned agent, Alfred Wong, nominated the firm of future Watergate burglar James McCord to provide security for the 1972 Republican National Convention in Miami. Wong himself would later install the recording system in Nixon's Oval Office.

He also proudly told a writer from the *Washington Post* that he was a former Weatherman and White Panther—and that he owned "two guns, like any other American."

Back in DC, Forcade filed mischievous reports from the Senate Gallery, for publication in UPS member papers. He wrote about pilfering Senate stationery, placing underground papers in press gallery reading rooms, and introducing himself to children visiting on field trips as "the Senator from Woodstock Nation." Forcade painted a picture of a thoroughly paranoid press corps, resigned to the idea that their office phones were tapped and subject to midnight visits from the FBI, who would check in on stories in progress. "A reporter told me how one time he remained standing a moment too long," Forcade wrote, "and was firmly planted in his seat by Secret Service goons."

And then there was the paranoia that Forcade himself seemed to be trying to cultivate. In one column, brazen with allusions to the Weather Underground's March bombing, he wrote: "I spent one Friday at the Capitol building, familiarizing myself with the layout. I walked up and down the corridors, my hair down to my shoulders, with a large 'Free Leslie Bacon' button on my chest. Leslie Bacon started her movement career at the Underground Press Syndicate. Every time I encountered a guard at the Capitol, I would ask him where the private restrooms were. In every case, the guard would helpfully point the way. Despite the Capitol restroom bombing, there is no paranoia.

"The Capitol building is wide open for another bombing."

While Forcade was lurking in the halls of Congress, Jerry Rubin was excited about the prospect of celebrity allies. Specifically, he was hoping to persuade Bob Dylan to team up with John Lennon for a series of benefit concerts leading up to the protests at the 1972 Republican National Convention in San Diego. Dylan and Allen Ginsberg had, after all, already recorded a ditty called "Come to San Diego." So when Dylan showed up at Rubin's house and complained about A. J. Weberman, Rubin acted swiftly.

Lennon, who'd been photographed wearing a Free Bob Dylan pin in the *New York Post*, had been deeply entertained by Weberman's antics. He'd even called Paul McCartney to needle him when the Rock Liberation Front had staged its "Paul Is Dead" demonstration. "I hope they're not after me," Lennon said. "I think it's funny as shit." But Rubin convinced him that Weberman was a menace. And then he delivered a humiliating blow. A scathing open letter to Weberman, printed in the *Village Voice*, demanded that he apologize to Dylan. It was signed, "The Rock Liberation Front—David Peel, Jerry Rubin, Yoko Ono, John Lennon."

"I thought that when Dylan saw he was free of A. J.," Rubin said later, "he'd be so appreciative that he would agree to tour the country with John and Yoko, raising money for political causes and rallying people to go to San Diego."

Yoko Ono ensured Weberman's apology when she dangled before him an offer to help get Dana Beal out of jail. The following week, another letter appeared in the *Voice*.

Dear People,
Please accept my apologies for past untrue statements and also the harass-
ment of Bob Dylan and his family. From now on I'll leave them alone.
If any nasty articles come out about him I'm sorry. I wrote them long ago
and I'm doing my best to have them killed.

Sincerely
A. J. Weberman
Minister of Defense
Rock Liberation Front

A few days after Weberman's letter of contrition was published, John Lennon, in the throes of revolutionary fever and inspired by David Peel's quick-turnaround troubadour style, wrote a song about John Sinclair ("in the stir for breathin' air"). It even managed to include a mention of CIA heroin. Next came the announcement that Lennon and Ono would be headlining a long-planned "Free John Sinclair" rally at the Crisler Arena in Ann Arbor. Fifteen thousand three-dollar tickets sold out in a day.

Many of the usual conspiracy suspects were there. Bobby Seale, Rennie Davis, and David Dellinger spoke; a taped message from William Kunstler opened the proceedings. After performances by Bob Seger, Phil Ochs, Archie Shepp, and Stevie Wonder, David Peel took the stage at 3:00 a.m. to a generally hostile crowd that was eager to see Lennon. Lurking at the rear of the stage, Tom Forcade threw firecrackers at the band's feet.

But Lennon remained Peel's number one fan. He stepped to the microphone for his first performance on US soil since the Beatles played

Candlestick Park in 1966. Then he shouted Peel's catchphrase, "The Pope Smokes Dope!" into the microphone and sang the song he'd written about Sinclair. Backing John and Yoko were a radical-hootenanny crew of Leslie Bacon on guitar, *East Village Other* writer Lennox Raphael on tambourine, and Jerry Rubin on congas.

As Lennon tuned, Rubin spoke. "All the prison doors should be open, and all the people should be free, and all the judges who sentence Black people to prison, they should go to jail for two days to see what it's like." There was pause while Lennon began the next song and then, as if Rubin remembered one last talking point, he added: "Also, we gotta destroy capitalism."

Three days later, the Michigan Supreme Court ruled that the ten-year sentence John Sinclair was serving for the possession of two joints qualified as "cruel and unusual" punishment. He was released from prison.

Afterward, when John and Leni Sinclair visited with Jerry Rubin and the Lennons in New York, they talked excitedly about plans for the big political tour. "We've been planning to do a tour for some time," Lennon told Sinclair. "Your needs got us out earlier than we anticipated.... Now we have a taste of playing again, and we can't wait to do more. We want to go around from town to town, doing a concert every other night for a month, at least. We'll pick up local bands along the way in each town." They wanted to have "bands playing outside of the arenas on the streets, on the nights of the concerts. We'll play for the halls and the people will pay to get in, but we'll leave our share of the money in the town where it can do the most good."

Sinclair thought the Ann Arbor concert had opened the Lennons' eyes to new possibilities. The dream of bridging culture and politics now had the endorsement of a Beatle. "I'm ready to build a motherfucker socialist music empire in this country," Sinclair beamed.

Forcade, who'd maintained good relations with David Peel even amid the Rubin–Lennon fallout with A. J. Weberman, helped Peel get out of his record contract with Elektra so Peel could release his next album, produced by John Lennon, on Apple Records. Forcade also remodeled and partitioned the old UPS loft space, installed recording equipment, and lent it to the proto-glam band Teenage Lust, formed by former members of the Lower East Side, for use as a practice space. Finally, Forcade prepared to launch his own record label, New Morning Records, from offices in the loft. (*New Morning* was the name of a Bob Dylan album, but more recently it had been the name of the Weather communique in which the militant group allowed that armed struggle was not "the only real revolutionary struggle" and endorsed "grass and organic consciousness-expanding drugs" as "weapons of the revolution.")

The duties of UPS itself were now carried out in new, smaller offices on West 10th Street in Greenwich Village. When Forcade was spending more time in DC, he'd made the de rigueur decision to temporarily let the syndicate offices fall out of hierarchical and patriarchal rule. "Women took over the Underground Press Syndicate," an author of counterinsurgency reports testified before Congress. "They say in some of their latest material they will never again let a man be a full-time staff member of UPS. They have a man running an office down here [in Washington, DC], but the main office is run by women." Forcade had told Sinclair that the arrangement was "healthy," but he was proven very wrong. Over the summer of 1971, rogue staffers at UPS had carried off files, tried to sell back to the airlines plane tickets that Forcade had scammed, attempted to loot the Bell & Howell royalties, and threatened to turn in then-fugitive Dana Beal to the police.

Now that Forcade was back, he was in charge again. But the new offices were broken into, a typewriter stolen, and only one telephone line functioned. "Our staff is small, no more than five people," he reported. "There is a lot more to do, but it will have to wait for better times. The staff is currently funding the expenses of UPS (which are considerable) out of their own meager pockets. Winter is making it cold in New York, but UPS and Free Ranger Tribe are doing o.k., thank you."

Forcade's biggest plans, though, had almost nothing to do with newspapers. A notice in the UPS newsletter announced "a convention for the purpose of planning youth-freak strategy for '72" to be held in Madison in January. Sponsored by the "remnants of Yippie and White Panther party structure throughout the country," the convention would endeavor to "make youth culture and radical politics an inescapable factor in the '72 elections."

During the second weekend of 1972, about three dozen people—from Philadelphia, NYC, DC, Miami, Ann Arbor, Chicago, Boston, Boulder, and elsewhere—arrived in Madison and assembled in a dimly lit church basement. Forcade accused Jerry Rubin and Abbie Hoffman—neither of whom were present—of setting themselves on a pedestal and lording their "discriminative elitism" over others. New and dynamic leadership was needed, he insisted, complaining that Rubin and Hoffman had retreated to, respectively, yoga and the Virgin Islands. Weberman even said Rubin had asked for $200 plus airfare to give a speech on Beal's behalf.

The conference attendees agreed to revoke Youth International Party membership from Rubin and Hoffman. In the words of an FBI report based on observations from a confidential informant, "neither of these zany protest victims was present at the meetings to defend himself against the charges of falling victim to his own publicity and of lording himself over others."

The time had come for a new movement: the Zeitgeist International Party. "To confuse 'the establishment' and its monitoring of YIP events," the report continued, "YIPs will also refer to themselves as 'Zippies.'"

While most of the activists were concentrating on the August Republican National Convention in San Diego, the Zippies set their sights on July's Democratic convention in Miami. "The Republicans don't care about the youth vote, but the Democrats have to. We have to stand up and make sure the youth vote is not co-opted. We will have leverage in Miami that couldn't be bought in San Diego."

The Zippies would increase their focus on marijuana legalization protests and prepare to confront any nonradical candidate. They unveiled their official banner for the convention demonstrations, which showed a youth clenching a rock in his hand, over the caption "Cast Your Vote." (The FBI informant also advised that Tom Forcade was the only conference attendee "who was not in agreement that there should be no violence in Miami for the Democratic National Convention.")

A brand-new underground, the *New York Ace*, would publicize the convention plans in every issue. And, Forcade said, they had another ace up their sleeve. David Peel had recently taped an episode of *The David Frost Show*, performing with John Lennon and Yoko Ono, which was scheduled for broadcast the following week. Soon a national television audience would be hearing all about the Zippies in Miami.

The following Monday, at the State Capitol, twenty of these newly christened Zippies held a press conference. They whisked a Zippie flag from a pedestal at the rotunda, revealing their presidential candidate: a fifteen-pound rock resting on a pillow. The rock could not speak, they explained, as it was "stoned."

"Every state will bring a rock to Miami, and two rocks will be chosen as the YIP-ZIP slate for office."

"Hippies are gone and Yippies are passe," one delegate said, "so we're calling ourselves Zippies, because we've got lots of zip."

Once again, they set May 1 as "J-Day," on which Zippies would protest marijuana prohibition laws in various state capitals. A Zippie "tribal council" would be conducted in Washington, DC, July 1–4, 1972, during which another marijuana smoke-in would be held to further protest anti-marijuana legislation.

And they unveiled plans for a five-day "Zippie Party Freek Circus," a sideshow aimed at attracting young people to Miami.

Super slide: twenty greased feet into a plastic pool filled with jello!

Kissing booth: Male & female, gay & straight. Upon special request there will be dogs, sheep & turkeys!

Pie time: 500 whipped cream pies & a yen for revenge!

"This will be no ordinary party," they promised. "It will require commitment and dedication. Only the most serious partiers should plan to attend."

The 1972 Zippie political slogan was "Don't Take Youth For Granite."

There was a kind of handbook for the Zippies, too, a reading that Forcade required of every one of them. *Agent of Chaos* was a 1967 science-fiction novel by Norman Spinrad, in which the Hegemony (the establishment) and the Democratic League (the opposition) are locked into stasis, an unstoppable object and an immovable force. A third force, the Brotherhood of Assassins, comes along to break this dialectic, assassinating members of both the Hegemony and the Democratic League.

"Confusion reigns supreme, predictability is shattered, and both the dogmatic movement and the totalitarian government are rendered helplessly bewildered," Forcade beamed, describing the book. "A social system based on freedom and anarchy sweeps in."

That's what we're gonna do, he told the Zippies.

Forcade returned to New York just in time for the airing of the *David Frost Show* episode featuring David Peel. On-screen with John Lennon, Yoko Ono, and Peel was Jerry Rubin, hitting a woodblock for Lennon's "John Sinclair" and Peel's "New York City Hippie" and shouting along: "I'm proud to live in a garbage can." Peel introduced a song from his forthcoming album on Apple Records. But there was no mention of the Zippies, nor of Miami.

That same day, the FBI announced that it had matched fingerprints to connect the placing of bombs in nine banks in San Francisco, Chicago, and New York City to a Yippie. Ronald Kaufman was an army veteran, an alumnus of University of Wisconsin at Madison, and had traveled to Mississippi with Abbie Hoffman for the Freedom Summer campaign in 1964. During the fateful 1968 Democratic National Convention, Hoffman had even stayed at Kaufman's Chicago apartment.

"He was like Captain Gentle—very easygoing," Forcade told the Associated Press reporter who called for a comment. "He disappeared more or less. Everyone asked Abbie about him but even he didn't know. There used to be a lot of Ron Kaufman jokes, but then suddenly they stopped when he disappeared. He became a Yippie nonperson."

But now Forcade, too, was under close scrutiny from the FBI. Days earlier, on the way back from Madison, he'd stopped in Detroit to meet with an accountant who was doing financial work for the Underground Press Syndicate. The accountant, though, appears to have been the FBI informant who reported to his handler that Forcade had told him that

> He was trying to obtain a White House press pass and if he is allowed to enter the White House, he will conceal a gun in his camera and shoot the President. _____ added that the subject has been dealing in the sale of marijuana and is an extremely unstable person.

The FBI took a look at the recent UPS column in which Forcade declared that "the Capitol building is wide open for another bombing" and decided that it had better put him under heavy surveillance.

Forcade went down to DC the following week, press credentials in hand, to cover the 1972 State of the Union Address from the press gallery of the House.

"Our cities are no longer engulfed by civil disorders," Nixon proclaimed. "Our colleges and universities have again become places of learning instead of battlegrounds."

During the speech, Forcade thought he'd test the feeling that he was being monitored. He walked up to the top seats in the gallery and squatted down. Sure enough, a Secret Service agent who'd been standing several rows down walked to the top of the stairs until Forcade was again within his field of vision.

"They had at least four of them watching me at all times," Forcade wrote later. He'd needed to show his pass every ten feet, he said, but "strangely, I was never searched."

Forcade's report for UPS read like a taunt:

> I was sitting above Nixon and behind him, about 50 feet away, when he gave his speech to the joint session of Congress. In front of me, all within 100 feet, were the entire Supreme Court, the entire Cabinet, the Joint Chiefs of Staff, the Senators, the members of the House, and most of the Ambassadors. . . . As I stand listening to Nixon's jive, I can't help thinking that one good bomb would wipe out the entire military, executive, legislative, and judicial hierarchy, and that if that bomb went off, I would go too. Even with wall-to-wall Secret Servicemen, I felt a little unsafe.

Three days after the speech, the NYPD pulled Forcade over, booked him for altering his license plate, photographed him, and released him.

The White House was taking no chances. A week later, on January 31, Nixon's deputy press secretary sent a confidential memo to his staff about Forcade: "Under no circumstances should the above be admitted to the White House on a temporary basis."

The Zippies hardly depicted themselves as threats. In his column in the *New York Ace*, A. J. Weberman wrote about a benefit concert Zippies had put together for Dana Beal, with performances by David Peel, Teenage Lust, and, playing its first official gig, a band called the New York Dolls. "Unfortunately, not too much money was raised since the hardcore freaks who came to the thing were stoned poor and no superstars were on the bill to attract the teeny-boppers. . . . Anyway, Teenage Lust played some great rock and roll while the lead singer of Dolls just blew everyone out. I got drunk for a change—I'm a confirmed pothead—and cooled my head out completely."

A story in the *Miami News*, picked up by the Associated Press, identified the Zippies as the only group planning protests ("deeply political moves . . . like filling up swimming pools with Jello and things like that") at the Democratic convention. "It is not known how serious the Zippies' intentions are," the story concluded.

Nonetheless, when Forcade went down to St. Petersburg, Florida, to set up another benefit concert and drum up Zippie interest, G-men filed reports, even recording that he'd signed into a motel registry that he was driving a Silver Cloud Rolls-Royce with Welsh tags. It was just a little joke on Forcade's part, but the FBI knew that he was really driving a black four-door Cadillac Fleetwood.

In Washington, DC, the Secret Service, armed with Forcade's recent mug shot photos, asked around and learned that he'd vacated his DC apartment in November. He was now working out of 10th Street in the West Village of Manhattan, they were told. FBI agents then visited that building's superintendent, who with some hostility told them that Forcade did not work there but that an underground paper called *Other Scenes* occupied the basement apartment, which had a separate entrance. No one's usually there during the day, the super said, but sometimes people come by at night. Voila! A phone number for *Other Scenes* matched one that the Secret Service had provided. The basement was put under surveillance.

Around that time, the Secret Service heard from the police department in Madison, Wisconsin, which was conducting its own investigation of Forcade and some of the Zippies there. Could the Secret Service send an agent out to Madison to interview one of their police department's informants? The Madison police had already traced calls that Forcade had made the last time he was in town. Now those phone numbers were turned over to the Secret Service.

The feds were also keeping tabs on Chicago-area Zippies, who picketed the local ABC-TV news offices for their failure to cover the Zippie candidate for president. "Let the Rock Speak!" shouted a dozen Zippies, carrying signs that read FREE HOWARD HUGHES and YOUTH CAN'T BE TAKEN FOR GRANITE as FBI agents looked on from a distance. Their report read, in part:

On gaining any interest from a passerby, demonstrators would call one of the demonstration participants who carried a red, white and blue towel, with white stars on it, draped on a pillow on which a rock was placed. The demonstrators would tell the passerby that the rock was their candidate. The demonstration participants all appeared to be good-natured and the entire affair was conducted in a carnival manner. The demonstrators were frequently heard telling people to be "happy."

It appeared, then, that the Zeitgeist International Party was "at most a mass confusion without substance, a membership or even an identity supported by any element of society." But, the report warned, the party "could fan an incident into a nasty affair and claim credit for disruption as the result of an imagined or an actual grievance of the masses. Such occurrences are absolutely essential for the perpetuation of the megalomania of such proclaimed leadership and people of this nature will be alert for incidents to utilize for their own personal notoriety."

As surveillance on Zippies continued, the Department of Justice was fighting tooth and nail to win the ruling on warrantless wiretapping. In late February 1972, *United States v. United States District Court*—its challenge against Judge Keith's disclosure order in the White Panther case—went to the Supreme Court. The decision would have a major impact on other radical trials, including the revived Chicago Seven trial, known as *Dellinger et al.*

Arthur Kinoy, a former law partner of William Kunstler, had finished arguing *Dellinger et al.* only days earlier, and now he was in DC to argue this case for the defense. Observing from chairs in the back of the chamber were John and Leni Sinclair, in their purple White Panther Party T-shirts.

To their surprise, the head of the Internal Security Division appeared in the courtroom, in traditional morning dress. Robert Mardian himself would argue for the prosecution.

While Mardian prepared his opening remarks, his fellow Arizona Mafia appointee, William Rehnquist, stepped out of the courtroom. As the head of the Office of Legal Counsel, Rehnquist had authored the administration's position on wiretapping. Now, as a recently appointed Supreme Court justice, Rehnquist recused himself at the last moment.

Mardian's argument was nothing less than a power grab for unchecked presidential power. The privacy of the American citizen, Mardian said, was better protected if the authority to wiretap was in the hands of only one man, Richard Nixon. "This Court must, as a coordinate branch of government, rely almost entirely on the integrity of the Executive Branch," he insisted.

Kinoy would call this "one of the most dangerous moments in the long history of the Supreme Court" in his memoirs. "It was one of those rare moments when for an instant the outer wrappings of rationalization are peeled off and, like a flash, the truth is revealed. Without hesitation or apology, Mardian demanded from the Court judicial approval for a course of conduct that would place in the President, in Nixon, the un-reviewable and absolute power to suspend the provisions of the written Constitution, the fundamental law of the land."

Only weeks earlier, Nixon aide H. R. Haldeman had accused opponents of Nixon's Vietnam policy as "aiding and abetting the enemy." Would these critics, Kinoy asked, be included in the scope of domestic intelligence?

Now the matter would await the decision of the court.*

In the meantime, Robert Mardian and his boss, Attorney General John Mitchell, left the Department of Justice to work for the Committee for the Re-Election of the President.

By February of 1972, John Lennon still hadn't committed to plans for a fundraising political tour. A. J. Weberman, who had procured a prom-ise that some of the funds would go to Dana Beal's defense, blamed Len-non's manager, Allen Klein. He took notice when a *New York Magazine* article accused Klein of pocketing proceeds from the soundtrack album for the Concert for Bangladesh benefit. And when he learned that Klein was holding a press conference to announce a $150 million defamation suit, he revived and mobilized the Rock Liberation Front.

Zippies Weberman, Ann Duncan, and Frank Rose showed up to the event with two photographers, taking their places on the plush office car-pet with the rest of the press. Klein—whose office, only weeks earlier, had announced David Peel's signing to Apple Records—held court from a regal swivel chair behind a horseshoe-shaped antique desk.

As Klein recited bookkeeping numbers and defended his business practices, a surprise guest appeared: the producer of the album, Phil Spec-tor, looking like he'd shotgunned a pot of coffee, entered with a string of profanities. He didn't like how Klein was handling the interrogators.

"Hold it!" Klein demanded. "Hold it!"

"You've had four fucking months to get the figures."

* Attorney General Richard Kleindienst wrote in his memoir that, in regard to wiretap-ping, the issue of national security "had been handled as a hot potato by each succeed-ing attorney general. Sooner or later the potato had to be tossed into the hands of the Supreme Court." Kleindienst then chose curious language to describe the Keith case: "A Black federal district judge in Michigan, in dealing with the situation of another Black [sic] by the name of Plamondon, made the critical toss."

"Phil, please. Let me finish."

Duncan asked why they should take their word that they hadn't prof-
ited on the album. Spector came up to her and began stepping on her.

"You swine!" she shouted.

Spector recoiled. "Did you hear what she called me?" he asked the
assembled press corps, and then turned his attention to Weberman: "Go
back to the garbage can!"

"Go back to the 50s, Spector!"

"Why don't you sell some more hot dogs in front of Dylan's house,
Weberman?"

While Spector and Weberman were going at it, one of Klein's
men handed him a flyer they'd confiscated announcing an upcoming
"celebration."

MUSIC EXECS FREE FOOD PROGRAM

The Rock Liberation Front, who brought you Bob Dylan's 30th
Birthday Party and Paul McCartney's Funeral, now begin a free
lunch program for starving music execs—starting with Beatle
manager, Allen Klein of ABKCO Industries

DINE WITH KLEIN

SO COME WITH US WHEN THE ROCK LIBERATION FRONT PRESENTS

LOVABLE ALLEN KLEIN WITH HIS FIRST FREE MEAL:
ROAST SUCKLING PIG WITH A ROTTEN APPLE IN ITS
MOUTH & A PIE WITH A FINGER IN IT FOR DESSERT!

BE THERE!

THURSDAY, MARCH 2, 11 A.M.
ABKCO OFFICES, 1700 B'DWAY—55TH
ZIPPIES & ROCK LIBERATION FRONT
477-6243

"I think it's time to show Mr. Weberman out," Klein said, and two security men quickly appeared to grab the garbologist. Weberman broke free and sent one of them across the room; Klein clutched his desk. But then Spector took a hostage.

"Call your man off," Spector told Duncan as he held her by the throat against a wall. "Call him off or else I'll karate chop you in the throat! I know karate!"

Weberman grabbed Spector by his collar and slapped him in the face. "The next time I hit you," he yelled, "it'll be a punch in the nose! And you'll never snort coke again!"

A giant hand yanked Weberman out of the room, and more security appeared in the hallway. With that, the RLF was thrown into an elevator and ejected onto the street.

They were still outside ten minutes later when Spector emerged from the building. "Let's be friends," Weberman said to the producer.

"Fuck you," said Spector.

Through Ron Rosenbaum's connections, Frank Rose placed a story on the dustup in the *Village Voice*. NBC carried the footage of the Spector–Klein fiasco, and *Rolling Stone* wrote about it, too.

Three days later, as promised, twenty Zippies returned to midtown. They were armed with picket signs and baskets of rotten tomatoes, lettuce, and apples; someone carried an apple pie with a fake finger sticking up from the middle.

"*Klein come clean! Where's the buck-fourteen?*"

"*You'll wonder where the money went, when Klein runs a charity event!*"

"*Bengalis will die for the $3 million lie!*"

At 1700 Broadway, Forcade and Weberman sneaked past the lobby guards. Blocking the entrance to the elevator, though, was Allen Klein himself.

"You're not going up!"

"Yes, we are!" yelled Forcade, and they started to tussle.

"Let me out," said an innocent bystander trapped in the elevator behind Klein. Klein told the man to shut up.

Forcade decided that the lobby guards might be of help now. "He assaulted me!" he shouted, pointing at Klein. "He assaulted me! Arrest this man! He assaulted me!"

No soap. The guards told Forcade and Weberman to leave.

But outside a sympathetic building manager told them that they could return if they discarded their signs. They raced back inside.

Up on the forty-first floor, the new chant was "Free Allen Klein!"

A building employee put his hand on Forcade's shoulder, and Weberman went ballistic, arms flying.

"Let him go! We need him for Miami!"

A truce was called, and everyone took a deep breath.

Modifying their behavior, one said, politely, "We'd like to see Mr. Klein."

"I'm sorry, he's not here right now. Why do you want to see Mr. Klein?"

"We came to pick up the three million dollars," Forcade said.

"What are you going to do with it?"

"What's Klein going to do with it?" Forcade said.

"We're gonna give it to UNICEF," Weberman said.

Apple Records' publicity director stormed in. "What about the mothers of the children who'll die," he asked, "because you're discouraging people from buying this album?"

"You're the one," Weberman retorted, "helping to steal the money by . . ." and here he turned to exchange smiles with Forcade.

"Duck!" two Zippies shouted to Weberman, who turned back just in time to dodge the PR man's fist.

It was time to leave.

John Lennon, who'd been in the studio with Phil Spector on the day of the second RLF action—working on an album that would include the song "John Sinclair" and another song with a line about David Peel—was impressed enough by the demonstration that he invited Weberman to visit with him at his Bank Street apartment.

That week, a carload of Madison activists set out for New York, at Forcade's invitation—he wanted to bring them into the convention plans and introduce them around. "We'd heard that John and Yoko wanted to help us," said Jane Hopper. The activists also hoped to get support for Karl Armstrong, one of the four who'd bombed the Army Math Research Center two years earlier. Armstrong had been captured in Canada the previous month, and now he was awaiting extradition hearings.

Julie Maynard, a Madison activist who was working on the Karl Armstrong defense campaign, arranged to pick up a driveaway car and bring Hopper, John Mattes, the student who'd secured the park permit for the last Madison smoke-in, and Dana's girlfriend, Kathy Morales. Ironically, the driveaway was a former police car.

Arriving in Manhattan at 3:00 a.m. Friday, they crashed at Weberman's place on Bleecker Street. A. J. rounded up Forcade and Frank Rose, and they all braved the sleeting rain to drive out to Long Island to drum up Zippie support at a meeting of college radicals at Stony Brook.

The next day, Rex hosted a party at the *New York Ace* headquarters; beforehand, the Madison group made a stop at the apartment Forcade shared with Frank Rose. One of them, Julie Maynard, was actually an informant for the Madison police. She recorded the following:

> He lives in a real dump at 209 East 5th Street. His office is at 204 West 10th street (basement). He has no legitimate phone. To call out he taps into a Hungarian person's phone. There is a girl there named Linda who acts as a servant for Tom and Frank. Linda's parrot interjects "Right On" whenever the conversation gets rousing. Tom is trying to train it to say "eat shit" whenever he argues with anyone, but the bird now says it to him whenever he sees him. The cage is surrounded by small objects that Tom has thrown in response.
>
> From there Hopper went to the party. She was introduced to the elite of the radical left. Jerry Rubin rushed up to Jane and begged her to let him be a Zippie. She said we would have to iron out a few differences first and she agreed to meet with him the next day. Jane left with Forcade for a while so John, AJ and his girl Ann mingled for a while. Frank was acting as a chauffeur dressed up in a fancy uniform. Jane got quite drunk and Jerry began to give her trouble about it.

Hopper returned to A. J.'s, where everyone was finalizing plans for more upcoming smoke-ins. Madison and Albany were next, but they were thinking big: twenty US states, plus England, the Netherlands, France, Germany, and New Zealand.

From there, they headed to Jerry Rubin's apartment on Prince Street.

Stew Albert was there. Jerry told us that the bad press we were giving him had hurt him badly politically. He said he would be finished in politics unless we patched things up. They replied that they thought he was an asshole. He said that Abbie was coming back next month and that he wouldn't let us kick him around. They told him that they would meet Abby at the airport and throw him out of the party also. He laid down on the floor close to tears. Stew said they were being too rough on him, so they chewed him up in like fashion. Jerry asked us to negotiate with him and we agreed to it. We listed our bitches.

1. *His superstar ego which enables him to appear to lead us while he does none of the work yet gets the credit;*
2. *Financial deals that have netted him money in the past that he made in the name of Yippie but then used for himself;*
3. *His b.o. and other bad habits;*
4. *His feud with Tom and other Zip people.*

He said that he would do anything, and we should just tell him what we wanted. They told him they wanted money and they told him that they wanted him to get signatures for the Armstrong petition. They also told him that we would stop bad-rapping him in accordance with how well he performs his assignments. We will make no interferences in his affairs political or otherwise as long as he didn't claim leadership in Zip or Yip. He will have no decision-making powers, if he or Abbie want responsibilities in the new party, they will have to earn them like everyone else. The fact that they are superstars and can get coverage of events does not impress us at all. They are a liability within the movement. They have turned too many people off. John and Hopper left for Madison. The only trouble they had on the way home was an incident in Pennsylvania. Their car was identified as having been involved in a burglary. They were stopped for about an hour and then released. They were somewhere around Sharon and Mercer, Pennsylvania.

Jane and John seemed to think that Jerry was losing the friendship of John Lennon. John had thought that he was the center of radical politics and by throwing him out we let the thought enter Lennon's head that perhaps Jerry was washed up. Lennon had a message delivered to us at Stonybrook that he would do an Armstrong benefit if we didn't let it out that he was coming. In other words, it had to be happening on its own terms before he would come. He will also come to the conventions. If they are peaceful, under the same terms.

Julie Maynard's recollection was forwarded to the FBI and included in John Lennon's file. On Monday, the US Immigration and Naturalization Service agency canceled Lennon's and Ono's visas. ("Jerry couldn't keep his damn mouth shut," Lennon said years later. "He was already on the press, blabbing off. Jerry told *Rolling Stone* there was going to be a San Diego concert with John and Yoko and their friends. Even though we had no plan of going to San Diego, the Right must have been looking and said, 'Anyone who seems to be powerful enough to be used by these crazy radicals is dangerous, so therefore, why have them here? They are foreigners. We don't need any more freaks. We got enough of our own.'")

Years later, John Mattes recalled the absurdity of the return drive to Madison. "We are being driven physically in a police car by an FBI informant. And then we get stopped on the way back. We're just sitting in the back seat while the FBI informant is talking to the police officer."

The FBI also learned of a plot by a Zippie contingent—the Emma Goldman Brigade—to infiltrate the Women's National Republican Club luncheon at the Waldorf Astoria, which would kick off Nixon's re-election campaign in New York. The Zippie plan, according to an informant, was to release live rats onto the floor of the Grand Ballroom to the horror of First Lady Patricia Nixon, John and Martha Mitchell, Governor Rockefeller, and 1,800 others. The Red Squad of the NYPD refunded fifteen-dollar tickets at the ballroom door, claiming that the event was at capacity. Three rats were quietly released in the lobby.

But three of the ten Zippies made it through, and as an award was being presented for "Distinguished Service to the Party," one of the infiltrators stood up.

"We have got to get the men to end the war!" she yelled. "It's immoral, it's illegal. Please, do something to stop it!" She marched out.

From the podium came assurances that this disruptor was "nobody's daughter." And then, "Let us pray." Everyone bowed their heads.

"I took the opportunity to shake the two rats out of my purse," wrote Gabrielle Schang, one of the two remaining gatecrashers. "The first shriek came halfway thru 'God Bless America.' My accomplice on the left gulped. She still had two rats in her purse and this was the finale.

"'Kathie,' I whispered, 'Here they come.' Kathie jumped on her chair screaming 'Mice! Mice!' And we had two escorts from the Red Squad on each arm. While the police dived under the table for rats, the freaked honkies at our table repeated all our screams."

Ladies clutched their white napkins in the ensuing stampede. A general manager kicked at a woman as she ran through the lobby screaming, "There are rats in the lobby, there are rats in the rooms!"

Gabrielle and Kathie were taken downstairs to a security office, where they overheard someone say that rats had been found in a phone booth.

No charges were pressed. "The only thing we were asked," Schang wrote, "was to please keep this out of the news."

Gabrielle Schang had been kicking against rules ever since she was snitched on for smoking a joint while president of the Convent of the Sacred Heart's Class of 1969. She grew up surrounded by high culture of another sort—her grandfather was a cofounder of the Columbia Artists Management agency, guiding the careers of Paul Robeson, the Von Trapp Singers, and Enrico Caruso. But the counterculture found its way to her via her father, an intellectual who read Eldridge Cleaver and took her to the Electric Circus to see rock bands. Following the Kent State shootings, she'd dropped out of Briarcliff College and moved to San Francisco for a year, but when her father died, she moved back to New York and met Tom Forcade. With his now-signature black hat, his periwinkle eyes, and his Cadillac—the horn now geared to play "Here Comes the Bride"—he made an instant impression on Schang. "I felt like I had been in a tower for a long time," she later said, "and I needed a fix on the real world." She soon went to work at UPS, filing the latest underground papers. He gave her science-fiction books; they dropped acid and went to see *Diamonds Are Forever*. Their relationship didn't turn romantic immediately, and when it did, it wasn't serious. She was also seeing the head of the Hells Angels, Sandy Alexander. "I think Tom was a little jealous of him," she said, "but I just didn't have strong feelings about either one of them. It was just fascinating, the life that opened up." Schang knew about Cindy Ornsteen, who, as she saw it, was Forcade's "real" girlfriend. "I liked to pal around with him. It wasn't really romantic in my mind, what we were doing." That would change.

At a *New York Ace* fundraising party at the Café Au Go Go, Jerry Rubin assured Forcade that he'd be essentially inactive during the 1972 campaign, even though he'd already held a press conference in Miami, promising "10,000 naked Yippies marching down the avenue." Forcade advised Rubin that the Zippies in Madison were against him and that they wouldn't welcome him at the upcoming smoke-in there, but the two agreed that they had nothing to gain by attacking one another. They promised to keep lines of communication open and hash out their differences in private. Eventually, they'd agree that Hoffman and Rubin would keep using the name "Yippie," and the Zippies would get to use Youth International Party.

The rest of the world would have a harder time keeping track of the names. At the party that very night, during an intermission, the master of ceremonies got up to lead a cheer.

"Yippies, on to Miami!"

The crowd groaned its correction: "*Zippies!*"

The emcee shrugged.

"Forcade doesn't like Abbie that much," Weberman told an interviewer. "I have nothing against Abbie, I think he's right on, and he'd be with us, but Jerry... Anyway, Abbie quit, and Jerry we don't want."

Forcade would later tell Beal that "Jerry had this super-paranoid fear" that the Zippies were building their platform on tearing down Rubin and Hoffman; Forcade said it was probably a guilty conscience. He told Beal:

He had been backstabbing me and you and AJ and probably others involved in Zip–YIP for years... and couldn't imagine that we had a higher purpose than getting even—that we seriously wanted to create a revolutionary youth party to replace the terrible vacuum left by the factional demise of SDS, and didn't consider him important just a possible obstacle, since he had in the past had the greatest capability to define the public through the straight media what YIP was—e.g. anarchistic, rather than an organized ongoing party capable of calling national actions without the cooperation of the straight press. The last point becomes particularly relevant in the current situation, as the media has extended in Smoke-In type blackout to pre-coverage of Miami—which is really hurting any effectiveness Abbie and Jerry might have had as publicity agents.

"What may be the epic event of the '70s," Forcade worried, "is being mostly blacked out."

Forcade was also upset about what he saw as a lack of recognition for the work of UPS papers, a slight that was nowhere more apparent than in San Diego. The local undergrounds, first the *Street Journal* and then the *Door*, had spent nearly three years attacking the corruption within San Diego leadership, which included close friends of President Nixon. In return, they were faced with drive-by shootings and explosions and infiltrated by both police and vigilante terrorists. "I wish there was a way to bomb them clear to the other side of the Coronadoes," San Diego business titan Arnholt Smith told stockholders.

Because James Copley, who owned both of San Diego's daily newspapers, was near the center of the San Diego power circles, mainstream local coverage was kept to a minimum. The San Diego police chief refused to give the *Door* press access, and when the *Door* appealed to Sigma Delta Chi—the same journalism fraternity whose conference Forcade had disrupted three years earlier—they learned that Copley employees ran the Sigma Delta Chi decision-making board. It would not help the *Door* in its fight.

But in early 1972 the *Door* teased out the connections between (1) the $400,000 that International Telephone & Telegraph had pledged toward San Diego's bid to host the upcoming Republican National Convention and (2) the Department of Justice's dismissal of an antitrust suit against IT&T.

Weeks later, syndicated reporter Jack Anderson received a leaked IT&T memo that explicitly tied the $400,000 to the suit dismissal. Anderson also reported that Richard Kleindienst—Nixon's pick to replace John Mitchell as attorney general—had been personally involved in secret meetings about and with IT&T. Kleindienst was quickly called to testify before the Senate Judiciary Committee, and his nomination stalled for nearly four months.

Suddenly, the president's cozy relations with San Diego business leaders warranted a cover story in *Life*. The magazine charged that the administration had "taken steps to neutralize and frustrate its own law enforcement officials" to protect Nixon's San Diego friends, interfering with investigations into 1968 campaign funds and with the bribery trial of the San Diego mayor, all "to keep San Diego's law-abiding veneer from being washed away." After so much negative publicity, word started to circulate that the GOP might even take its convention out of San Diego.

Meanwhile, several writers for the *Door* were also, under the name San Diego Convention Coalition (SDCC), organizing activists in preparation for the summer. SDCC members' tires were slashed, brake lines cut, and doors ripped down. One person found tear gas crystals on their car door handle. In late April, a car belonging to someone who worked for the *Door* and SDCC was firebombed.

Heightening paranoia was the emergence of Louis Tackwood, an LAPD informer who told an explosive story about being recruited for something called "Squad 19," an alleged FBI plan in which agents provocateurs at the convention would time explosives to coincide with riots in the streets. Among the possible contingencies of the plan were delegate fatalities, martial law, and canceled elections. Underground reporters in California broke the story, followed by front-page coverage in the *Los Angeles Times* and the *Washington Post*.

But the IT&T–San Diego scandal remained the political bombshell of early 1972, and Forcade believed that the underground press deserved more credit for its suffering. When brand-name mainstream journalists, from Nora Ephron to Pete Hamill to Gloria Steinem to Tom Wolfe, gathered in New York for a "counter-convention" to the annual American Newspaper Publishers Association, a group of Zippies deposited four boxes of undergrounds on the stage, taped smoke-in flyers to the panelists' table, and handed out leaflets:

FUCKED AGAIN

The Underground Press has once again been ignored by a back-patting sock hop of New Journaloids whose Creative Writing III skills and high fees enable them to appropriate the landmark innovations of genuinely alternative journalism. While Talese-Wolfe-Anderson-Halberstam-Lukas-Steinem-Hamill-Breslin-Newfield have a place on the platform, having these discussions without the underground press is like the cocktail without the Molotov.

... The LA Free Press, Berkeley Barb, Chicago Seed, Great Speckled Bird, Fifth Estate, and hundreds more you never bothered to find out about were exposing the Vietnam War while Tom Wolfe was at the Paramount with Baby Jane Holzer. The Pentagon Papers were old copy to our readers. The *San Diego Door* exposed the San Diego scandal months before Jack Anderson lucked onto a wastebasket at the end of a rainbow....

The new journalism will only be new when its highly paid scribes move to control their own press. This is a central principle of the Underground Press, to

TAKE OVER

At 8:30pm on Monday, underground press people attending this conference will seize the microphones and give their own awards for underground press excellence. In the meantime, we want this conference stopped immediately until the assembled multitudes put an underground press person on every panel! It's up to you.

—*Ad Hoc Liebling Committee of the Underground Press Syndicate and the New York Ace*

Surprisingly, their demands were met immediately. On Sunday afternoon, Forcade was added to a panel called "Covering the Campaign." Dressed head-to-toe in white, with dark sunglasses and his mustache grown to Fu Manchu length—or was it fake? He kept touching it, as though to keep it in place—Forcade sat next to Dan Rather. Ignoring the stated topic of the panel, Forcade used his time to boast about his White House ban.

That evening, Forcade made an unannounced appearance on another panel. Celebrity subjects Gore Vidal, Tony Randall, Otto Preminger, and Abbie Hoffman had convened to discuss "How They Cover Me." After Hoffman, who'd insisted that he was *not* a millionaire, passed out copies of his tax returns, Forcade, Cindy Ornsteen, and Jerry Rubin (who was wearing a blue netted shirt) took to the stage to promote the Zippie plans for Miami.

"Z comes after Y, as in Yippie—this is the natural progression," Forcade told the confused audience. But to Forcade's surprise, Rubin and Hoffman took over the microphone for an additional message: in the name of Zippie, they were endorsing George McGovern for president.

Four years after nominating a pig for president, Rubin and Hoffman were wading into conventional politics—sort of. "If the Democrats are stupid enough to nominate Hubert Humphrey or Ed Muskie," Rubin announced, "we'll throw them into the ocean like we're going to do to the Republicans." The McGovern-leaning crowd, the *Washington Post* reported, answered with "shouts of applause and cries of despair."

Perhaps predictably, McGovern's political rivals immediately used the Hoffman and Rubin endorsement against him. "Apparently the people who tried to wreck the Democratic Convention from the outside in 1968 want to do it from the inside in 1972," sneered the hawkish Democratic candidate Henry "Scoop" Jackson. "It is perfectly fair to ask why these two hate-America leftist extremists, who have been in the forefront of violent demonstrations, should find Sen. McGovern's candidacy congenial to their own problems." That "Hoffman, Jerry Rubin, Angela Davis, among others, support McGovern should be widely publicized and used at every point," Richard Nixon wrote to John Mitchell, stressing that "nailing him to his left-wing supporters" should be a "top priority objective."

The endorsement, Forcade wrote to Dana Beal, was "just another example of the impossibility of working with such irresponsible 'spokesmen.' It was the equivalent of Rubin's previous statement that 10,000 Yippies would march before the convention hall. This sort of rhetoric was totally inappropriate to the mood and political climate."

B ut there was also plenty of rhetoric blowing through the Zippie ranks. Dana Beal, recently christened in a *Washington Post* headline as "The Yippies' Karl Marx," was out of jail—briefly—while he awaited sentencing. Beal dazzled a Madison smoke-in with his plans to buy pot from the Viet Cong ("reparations") with money confiscated from US corporations and give it away to citizens for free.

The smoke-in doubled as a rally in support of Karl Armstrong, the Madison bomber who was still awaiting extradition from Canada. With banners that read UNCLE KARL SEZ GET A BANG OUT OF LIFE and FREE THE WEED, the rally sent the message that armed revolution and marijuana legalization might come hand in hand.

"Karleton Armstrong has put out the word to strike a blow against imperialism," Jane Hopper told a Madison newspaper, "and the best way to stop imperialism is through the culture. With the refoliation project, pot will literally be within the reach of everyone."

By now, the Zippie smoke-ins had started to accrue traditions: the twenty-two-foot-long papier-mâché joint they carried around; the podium demands for free pot ("We want a guaranteed minimum stash for every man, woman and child in the USA!"); the pot-leaf Yippie flags; the howling songs of David Peel.

Beal was also excited about a guest star at the Madison smoke-in: Jerry Rubin. Forcade had warned Jerry Rubin that the Madison YIPs didn't want him there, but Beal's invitation implied otherwise. While Rubin was in Madison, he told the local UPS paper *Take Over* that he and Abbie were looking forward to working with the Zippies in Miami.

"We're Yippies & we're Zippies too. We'd certainly like to be Zippies. . . . What is the difference really when you get right down to it?

"We should unite against a common foe, and not fight amongst ourselves over bones of the Movement because all we would be fighting over is the bones."

But by the time the interview was printed, the YIP-ZIP war had escalated.* Privately, Rubin was telling people that Forcade was a "hip capitalist" and not a true YIP. Forcade was furious with Beal for making what he termed "entirely secret negotiations and invitations" to bring Rubin to Madison. He felt "ripped off and sold out," he told Beal, and "had to seriously question the discipline and political sense of intersections."

When Rubin returned from Madison, Forcade and a few other Zippies showed up at his apartment. Rubin refused to open the door. Minutes later, a bottle came crashing through his front window.

The word got out to dozens of people that night: Forcade had turned violent.

On May 5, 1972, the Republican Party finally decided to move its convention from San Diego to Miami. Now the city would be hosting both parties: the Democrats in July and the Republicans in August. And

---

* "Some New York Yip/Zips have already trashed Rubin's front window & sped away in their Cadillac as well as denounce him as an 'aging publicity hound,'" read the introduction to the *Take Over* article.

the Zippies, who'd been focused on Miami all along, hoped to attract even greater numbers. The next day, at the Albany smoke-in, the Zippies handed out a broadside that celebrated the convention relocation and commemorated the unexpected death that week of FBI director J. Edgar Hoover, who'd led the bureau since its founding. The handout also condemned Rubin's appearance in Madison and the McGovern endorsement. "It's bullshit," the screed read. "Rubin and his pals have absolutely nothing to do with Zippie and never have. We consider Rubin a publicity hound seeking material for another book to add to his wealth. A movement parasite. The FBI had Hoover for life. Will youth culture have Rubin?"

Back in Madison, anti-war demonstrations had escalated following the sealing of North Vietnam ports with mines. On campus, protesters erected flaming barricades and smashed windows; downtown, rock throwers and tear-gassers faced off. The tensions climaxed on May 11 with a shoot-out between members of the Madison police's undercover Affinity Squad and radicals at a house occupied by the Wild-Eyed Radical Movement, the group that had provided weed for the Zippie smoke-in.

The use of affinity groups was "creating an incredible paranoia among the street people," Inspector Herman Thomas boasted. "They don't know whom to trust."

"Perhaps the highlight of our affinity operations was reached during the evening hours of May 10 and the early morning hours of May 11, 1972," Thomas wrote in an article that ran as a cover story in the *FBI Law Enforcement Bulletin*. "The affinity detail accounted for 14 of 18 arrests of mob hoodlums. Five of those arrested were charged with serious felonies. Police undercover intelligence was able to report on the afternoon of May 11, 1972, that attempts at further disruptions in Madison had been canceled by a united front of organizers that had been staging them. This group decided it was simply too risky to protest violently because the police were too effectively organized." Strangely, the Thomas article made no mention of the shootings.

The night after the Madison shoot-out, John Lennon appeared on the *Dick Cavett Show* and put an end to John Sinclair and Jerry Rubin's dream of attracting throngs of young people to the convention with a superstar music festival. "They think we're going to San Diego or Miami or wherever it is," he said. "We ain't going. There'll be no big jam with us and Dylan, because there's too much going on. We never said we're going, that's it."

But Lennon's friend David Peel, and camera crews, showed up for a Zippie press conference about Miami that week. At the midtown Diplomat Hotel, Zippies in bizarre regalia addressed the nightly news audiences with slogans like "Make sandcastles, not war" and "Bring the boys to the beaches."

"We are going to stress nonviolence," announced Rex Weiner, wearing an open vest and aviator sunglasses. "Miami Beach is too nice a place to have to go running around in—"

"Too hot," someone chimed in.

"And no place to hide," added Forcade, dressed in a black suit and gigantically brimmed hat and round sunglasses.

A. J. Weberman bounced a beach ball. He was wearing short shorts, a Rock Liberation Front T-shirt, and a buckled football helmet with "Eat the Rich" written on the side. Next to him was a young woman in a bikini. Frank Rose towered behind them all.

David Peel promised a new national anthem for their candidate.

"Speaking of candidates, who is your candidate for president?" one of the newsmen asked.

The Zippies looked at each other. That was their signal. "The rock! The rock! The rock!" they chanted, suppressing laughter.

Weiner kept his deadpan. "The rock is the candidate for the highest office because, ah, it's the most stoned."

After Rubin and Albert headed to Miami for their own press conference, Weiner went down and negotiated a "YIP congress" that would include eight Yippie names and eight Zippie names. But it was hardly a ceasefire, and one of the Yippies was Gabrielle Schang. A self-described Pollyanna, she'd realized that she identified more with the sunnier gestalt of the Yippies, who welcomed her into their group, than with the caustic Zippie attitude.

"The Yippies called me in New York to declare 'war,'" Forcade recounted in a letter to Beal. "Personally, I did not wish to continue if the struggle was going to be on that petty level. I was tripping on what I thought was acid but later turned out to be STP at the time I got the war declaration." He took immediate action. He hailed a taxi.

CHAPTER 7

JERRY GORDE WAS A TWENTY-ONE-YEAR-OLD FORMER STUDENT ACTIVIST when he was recruited by Abbie Hoffman and former *Rat* editor Jeff Shero to help coordinate Miami plans for the Yippies. Gorde lined up Yippie living quarters at the Albion Hotel, but until the rooms were available everyone was crashing in a Miami apartment. So Gorde was driving back and forth from the airport, picking up Yippies and transporting them to the apartment: Hoffman and then Rubin, followed by Allen Ginsberg, Ed Sanders, Leslie Bacon, and Gabrielle Schang.

On the first night that everyone was gathered, a yellow New York City taxicab pulled up outside the apartment. The driver appeared at the door and announced that his client, "Mr. Tom Forcade," wished to speak with "Gabbie."

Gorde looked out and, sure enough, there was Forcade sitting in the back of the cab.

"I was in a room with Jerry, Abbie, Ed, Kathy, everybody," Schang remembered. "I was mortified. They *hated* him, they were suspicious of him. He'd been arguing with Abbie about *Steal This Book*—there were all these splitting hairs about politics, but I think it was mostly about the book. I didn't know what to do. I just let them take care of it."

The Yippies huddled and decided that Gorde should tell Forcade to *fuck off.*

He walked out to the cab and approached the rear window. "Forcade was dressed all in black—it reminded me of the *Spy vs. Spy* character in *Mad* magazine. I told him, 'Gabbie doesn't want to see you.'"

Forcade, still high on STP, was firm. "I'm not going to leave until Gabbie comes out."

Gorde went back inside.

Hours later, the cabbie knocked on the door again.

"Look," he pleaded to Gorde, "the meter is running, and it's good money, but I'm Jewish. I observe Sabbath, and I can't be here past sundown."

"If you leave the meter running, and Tom in the back seat, can I drive you to shul, and I'll pick you up at sundown on Saturday and bring you back?"

"If he's willing to pay the additional twenty-four hours," the cabbie said.

Forcade agreed to the terms. He paid the cabbie and remained in the back seat until the following day.

In the meantime, security agents had begun appearing outside the house. A "landscaping crew" came from the university and cut the hedges. They wore suits and sunglasses.

Shortly after arriving in Miami, Forcade and Zippie Patrick Small and the Vietnam Veterans Against the War (VVAW) met in the office of Miami police chief Rocky Pomerance. Forcade introduced himself as a former Weatherman but proclaimed that "the American public is tired of violence" before laying out the Zippie plans for a smoke-in. After the meeting, Forcade and Small held a press conference from the police headquarters, calling the talks "satisfying" and the police "eminently reasonable," and announcing that they'd be demonstrating in favor of withdrawing from Vietnam, legalization of marijuana, repealing of abortion laws, and repealing laws that discriminated against gay people.

Forcade rented a sprawling house with an overgrown yard on Mary Street in Coconut Grove, which would serve as Zippie headquarters. They were quickly infiltrated; among their new ranks were a pair named Carl and Doug. "I recognized them immediately as undercover cops when they first came to one of our meetings," says Pat Small. "Tom said, 'Yeah, yeah, yeah. That's okay. They've offered to drive us places, they've offered to help us... let's let them do it.' Already we were spending a lot of money getting around. For the next few months, these guys were our taxi service. They could be counted on short notice to take us to the printer, or to a press conference, or whatever."

As the date of the YIP Congress approached, the FBI was internally reporting rumors that militant anti-communist Cubans were planning to "launch an attack against a meeting of the YIP scheduled to be held at the Center for Dialogue, Miami." There was talk of bombs, tear gas, gun caches, and "attacks upon those persons subsequently emerging from the building."

Whether such a plan would have been carried out will never be known, because the YIP Congress idea was scrapped. Instead, a "YIP conclave" was held at the Zippie house in Coconut Grove. Saturday afternoon, about forty Zippies and Yippies gathered, ostensibly an attempt to iron out differences and, possibly, to merge. But the Yippies had planned an ambush on Forcade. When Hoffman and Rubin arrived, they branded him as an agitator who was trying to split the movement. Now the Yippies took a vote to expel *him* from *their* ranks—and won 32 to 3, with four abstentions.

Forcade took the news poorly. Trembling, he picked up a pair of scissors, carved up some wood paneling on the wall, and stalked out of the house alone. Rubin and Hoffman embraced.

According to an FBI informant's report, that evening Forcade headed up to Gainesville to attend a meeting of the Vietnam Veterans Against the War.

That weekend, the VVAW was planning for the conventions in the Gainesville attic of Scott Camil, the group's Southeast regional coordinator. The vets were sufficiently anxious to dispatch a team of walkie-talkie-carrying guards to the edges of the property. A pair of Miami members—nicknamed Salt & Pepper because one was white and one was Black—had passed along word that the police planned to turn Cubans loose on hippies, so Camil agreed to work things out with the Cuban groups. Then the attendees moved on to the horror stories they'd heard about law enforcement plots for the conventions—like cutting off exits from Miami Beach to the mainland and slaughtering demonstrators.

The vets transitioned to a demonstration of weapons they might need if police unleashed violence: fishline bolos, firebombs, hand grenades. One of them fired a crossbow, and someone sent smoke-bomb slingshots at a building across the street that housed the conservative group Young Americans for Freedom. At one point, according to later testimony, Camil suddenly produced a Derringer from his sock and fired into a stack of papers that a Zippie had brought that weekend. (Although there is no account of Forcade's participation at the meeting, an issue of the Zippie publication *Yipster Times* briefly mentioned an unnamed Zippie in attendance in Gainesville.)

On Sunday, one of the veterans, Bill Lemmer, even proposed the formation of a security team—code-named "Weathervets," a play on "Weathermen"—and suggested they wear chest guards with lightning-bolt emblems and carry eight-foot staffs with nooses on the ends that could remove mounted police from horses. By the time he floated the idea that they bring automatic weapons into the hall and "bag some Republicans," the other vets were quiet.

After the meeting broke up, Lemmer, in a fit of conscience, asked to speak privately to Camil and another veteran.

"I'm a pig," Lemmer told him.

Lemmer was a double agent working for the FBI. The bureau, he said, was going to try to set them up on drug charges. But, Lemmer quickly insisted, if they would trust him, he'd try to protect them.* Camil thought about this and decided they could still use Lemmer in the organization. After all, he had a car, and it'd be good to have a witness when he talked to the Cubans.

The next day, Camil and Lemmer drove down to Hialeah to sort things out with the Cubans. Along with some other vets, they met up with Manuel Mayan, a member of the activist group Abdala, in front of a drugstore, but when Mayan warned that other militant exiles might try to blow up one of the vets' meeting sites, the peace talks quickly moved into a conversation about possible weapons purchases. "If you need help," Mayan offered, "I can get machine guns." Camil asked if they knew where to buy carbines. Mayan said he could get plastic explosives and Claymore mines.

Mayan's real name was Pablo Fernandez, and he was wearing a wire.** He'd been busy. Earlier that month, he was part of a ten-person "vigilante squad" recruited by the White House's Special Investigations Unit to travel to Washington, DC, and attack demonstrators. The group included Eugenio Martinez, Bernard Barker, Virgilio Gonzalez, and Frank Sturgis, all of whom would soon be arrested in the Watergate Hotel burglary. After the DC trip, Martinez offered Fernandez $700 a week to pose as a hippie protester in Miami, part of a gang that would descend on McGovern headquarters, throw rocks, break windows, and defecate and urinate in public, all "to give the voters a bad impression of the people supporting

---

* On the way to the Gainesville meeting, Lemmer told a passenger that Weathervets were already training on farms throughout the Southeast, in preparation for convention disturbances. In the event of a riot, he said, New Left leaders would either be shot or captured and taken to Mexico City.

** Only a week earlier, Fernandez had given his own name to a reporter, who identified him as an activist for the Cuban Revolutionary Party. "If they want violence, they're going to get it from us," Fernandez said of Abbie Hoffman and Jerry Rubin, and promised that twenty thousand "well-trained Cuban Freedom Fighters" would meet anti-war demonstrators.

McGovern." Fernandez declined that assignment, but he did volunteer to work with the Miami Police Department to infiltrate the VVAW.

The reports filled out by Fernandez and the reports filled out by informant William Lemmer were delivered to Eugenio Martinez's boss, James McCord, who was the head of security for Nixon's reelection campaign. McCord, too, would soon be arrested at the Watergate.

Upon Forcade's return to Miami, the Underground News Service immediately warned of a new threat. "The biggest problems on the horizon are the right-wing Cubans, the government and factionalism," the UPS newsletter reported on Thursday, June 1. "The right-wing Cuban organizations can be considered an extension of the CIA that can be used against demonstrators without Nixon getting the blame in the media. All reports indicate that the Cubans are planning heavy response to organizers and demonstrators, but ultimately they will do what the government decides is expeditious for them to do."

Soon after, Zippies Cindy Ornsteen and Frank Rose visited Rocky Pomerance for a UPS News interview.

"What about the Cuban problem?" Ornsteen asked.

"I don't know that it's a problem," said Chief Pomerance. "I know that you've referred to it several times..."

"We've gotten phone threats, nasty letters," Ornsteen said. "People have been saying they're just waiting for the Conventions to beat up on long-haired people. We heard that at least 250 are in training for riot control for the government."

"Let me squelch that," Pomerance said. "I know of no governmental entity that's involved in anything even remotely approaching this kind of situation."

As far as overzealous policing, Pomerance assured them that there would be no tear-gassing. "We have a sort of calm, rational approach to this."

The Zippies, however, were not so calm and rational. Upon his return to Miami, Forcade continued his role as an antagonist. After one ejection from the Yippie office, other Zippies had to drag him onto an elevator as he screamed, "Come out and fight!" Afterward, some Yippies went down to see if the coast was clear. They found Forcade stalking around the building with a gasoline can.

On Monday, June 19, by a unanimous 8–0 decision, the Supreme Court finally upheld Judge Keith's ruling, effectively outlawing most of the "national security" wiretaps on "domestic subversives."

The close proximity in time between the June 19 ruling and another momentous incident, two nights earlier, is intriguing. Attorneys for the defense later theorized that there was an advance leak from somewhere in the court that the government was going to lose its case that Monday, and this was why five men had broken into the offices of the Democratic National Committee at the Watergate Hotel on Saturday, June 17—they were sent in to remove previous taps.

"If the case had been won [by the government]," wrote Arthur Kinoy, "and the Watergate wiretapping was later accidentally exposed, the Attorney General, acting for the President, could openly acknowledge his authorization, and the entire affair would be covered with the mantle of legality. But if the case had been lost, and the wiretapping was subsequently exposed or discovered, there would be no explanation at all available to the administration."

L. Patrick Gray, acting director of the FBI, moved quickly to have other devices removed. "I knew from my earlier domestic intelligence briefing with [FBI agents] Ed Miller and Mark [Felt] that we had several such warrantless domestic taps and microphones in place, so I told Mark to meet with Dick Kleindienst and then to get written instructions on which ones to cancel. I also told Mark to brief Dick on the status of the Watergate investigation.... At his meeting with Mark that afternoon in Washington, Dick ordered that four telephone taps and two hidden microphones be removed from the Black Panther and Weather Underground targets but to leave in place the one directed at the Communist Party, USA."

"You could probably count them on the fingers of both hands," Kleindienst, just confirmed as attorney general, told *Time* the day after the ruling. "We only used them where we thought there was a threat of violence. I had just authorized a couple more last week, but I'm not going to talk about any individual taps. If I say anything, they [defendants and suspects] will come in and ask for transcripts of everything we took." Wouldn't it be proper, *Time*'s reporter asked Kleindienst, for the Department of Justice to notify anyone who had been illegally overheard? "Hell, no," said Kleindienst. "Our duty is to prosecute persons who commit crimes. We don't have to confess our sins anywhere, like some bleeding heart. We were acting in good faith."

The fallout from the Keith decision was enormous. In the coming months, the government, much of its evidence now firmly ruled illegal, was in jeopardy of losing longstanding conspiracy cases involving the Weather Underground, the Black Panthers, and the Pentagon Papers.

None of this, alas, helped the Zippies in securing a campsite in Miami. After authorities expressed concerns that camping protesters would ruin the grass, Pat Small held a press conference to disclose that a Cessna from the "Zippie Air Force" had secretly made three nighttime passes to seed a local golf course with thirty pounds of Jamaican marijuana. ("Depending on the rains, the pot should flower just in time for the July 9th toke-down.")

Weeks later, when it came time for the city council to take a vote, they were still battling. "In 1938 Chamberlain appeased the Germans, and you know what the result was," one councilman said. "And I don't intend to appease the hippies, the Yippies, or the schmippies."

With nearly five hundred in attendance, each speaker was allotted only a few minutes. Patrick Small managed to fit in a few different strategies: "It's too late to tell people not to come to Miami," he reasoned, before advising that the upcoming solar eclipse was sure to cause "strange behavioral reactions."

"Tom Forcade is coming here to cover the convention for underground newspapers," Small finally warned the council. "If there's no campsite, he'll just have to invite everybody to his hotel room."

But the campsite proposal was defeated.

At the end of the meeting, Small, who'd been standing in the press area, walked up to City Councilman Rosen, a butterscotch pie in hand.

"You're going to throw that pie at me," Rosen said and lunged at Small, who lost his balance. The pie twirled in the air and fell a foot short of its intended target, glancing both men.

Rosen, a six-foot-two ex-boxer, hit Small in the jaw, kicked him in the groin, and punched him in the stomach. Other city officials pulled at his hair, trying to bang his head against a table.

The Miami Beach police booked Small.

Small was thrilled by the media coverage, which included a twenty-four-paragraph story in the *Los Angeles Times*. But the Yippies came out against Small immediately. "We think this attack on councilman Rosen was an act of an agent provocateur or madman," said Jeff Nightbyrd, the former editor of the New York *Rat*. "We want to completely disassociate from it. It obscures the real issue, which is campsites."

Even the *Daily Planet*, a UPS member paper in Miami, gave a decidedly thumbs-down review to the performance: "Throwing a pie is a purely visual event. To be effective one must first be seen to create viewer expectation. The process must then be distinctly carried out in order to maintain the tension of continuity and finally, the ultimate effect of the thrown pie must be made perfectly clear."

The Miami Convention Coordinating Committee—an alliance comprising the former San Diego Convention Coalition, various Florida groups, and Rennie Davis of the Chicago Seven—was already unhappy about Zippie plans for "Che Guevara Day," which seemed almost designed to provoke the three hundred thousand Cuban exiles living in Miami. The Zippies relented and called it off, "in order to avoid any repercussions from the CIA front group of Cuban refugees." Their sarcastic June 28 press release, delivered in Spanish ("¡LBJ Si! ¡Ché No!"), promised to instead celebrate Lyndon B. Johnson and to "construct a symbolic monument of his importance."

Before the convention had even begun, such disparate groups as the National Welfare Rights Organization, the Southern Christian Leadership Conference, the VVAW, the People's Coalition for Peace and Justice, the Yippies, and just about every coalition and committee were in agreement on one thing: nobody wanted anything to do with the Zippies. At the end of one contentious meeting, as Forcade screamed demands for public apologies for accusing Small of being a police provocateur, Allen Ginsberg urged everyone to stop arguing and instead chant, "Om."

In early July, Forcade's "Childhood's End" appeared on the front page of *Daily Planet*, Miami's UPS paper. The essay was a curious blend of cynicism and optimism, positing that the leaders of "Amerika" (who were merely stand-ins for the "superpower oligarchy") were being "whipped to a frenzy over which brand, vanilla or strawberry, will be fed to Amerika for the next four years." Even if George McGovern was elected, he'd just be "locked into a historically inevitable role of trying to hold the empire together."

And yet, there was reason to be hopeful, Forcade argued, because thanks to technology and media—from planes and highways to records and magazines—"we are all now connected in an organic web." And on the heels of a lot of people getting very high, the global village was coming soon.

As the media interconnects our intellects into a true collective consciousness...as the pervasive influence of the incredibly powerful drug LSD-25, its super companion, STP, and that specific antidote to capitalism, marijuana, spreads through the control centers like wildfire (everyone from Hyman Rickover to Henry Luce has taken LSD), we come to a point of crossing over a consciousness boundary.

The real value of the conventions is as a choice to convert their diversionary spectacle into *our* spectacle, to advertise for global awareness. The world is watching us, and they want to know what's different about us. This is our chance to extend the web-without-a-center.

When you repress a political movement, it becomes a cultural movement. When you repress a cultural movement, it becomes a religion. That is what we have now, a Religion. Have you heard the word, sister, the word of the Movement? Have you read the good book of Mao? Have you renounced your capitalist sins? Would you like some literature? Would you like to come to the Meeting?

Rolling, heaving Amerika, I love you very much. You're going to live through it and it'll do you good.

Telephone service at the Zippies' house on Mary Street was erratic. The phone often didn't ring; most afternoons it was completely out of order, and when it was working, there was sometimes whispering on the line. Once Forcade called the house and, instead of a ringback tone, he heard a click and then the sound of everything that was going on in the house. No one had picked up, but he could hear the stereo playing and conversations loud enough to recognize the voices. He listened until there was another click and it was gone. Another time, Cindy picked up the phone to make a call and heard a man's voice say, "Shh, they're on the line." No one else was in the house.

On July 7, New York Police Department's Special Investigation Services—better known as the Red Squad—filed a report about Forcade that mentioned his presence in Florida and his alleged threat to the president. On the same day, Forcade's press pass for the Convention Hall was revoked. It didn't thwart the Zippies, though, who simply printed bootleg laminates bearing the logos of *Time*, *Newsweek*, ABC, and NBC. (They eventually gave away five thousand fake passes.)

Forcade and Ornsteen, scouting Convention Hall with Carl and Doug—whom they still suspected were undercover police—happened upon a catwalk where the Democrats had placed eight-foot-high murals of every Democratic president.

"We gotta get that," Forcade said, pointing to a portrait of Lyndon B. Johnson. It was the perfect thing for their upcoming LBJ Day celebration. The four of them quickly but quietly loaded the mural onto Carl and Doug's car and drove it back to Coconut Grove.

Forcade, appearing as a defense witness to Small's municipal court hearing on disorderly conduct charges, leveled a deadpan concern about the "lack of humor" at the council proceedings. "We heard that a councilman threw a pie at another councilman about a year ago," he said. "We thought that was the way they did things at Miami Beach. We had a few funny lines prepared. But Pat never got the chance to say them. How were we to know Rosen is a former boxer who works out every day?"

Small's defense attorney used a different tack: How about "any councilman or his agent can throw two pies at the defendant"?

Small was given a suspended sentence of ninety days in the Dade County Stockade.

Just before the convention began, the Miami Beach City Council finally approved a campsite for protesters. The City of Miami Beach had spent hundreds of thousands of federal grant dollars on crowd-control tools like plastic handcuffs, gas grenades, and night-vision binoculars. In the basement of the nearby Jackie Gleason Auditorium, protected by armed guards and cooled by a specially installed air-conditioning system, a massive intelligence center reeled in information from eleven different agencies' undercover operatives.

But the campsite arrangements were easy: it took only a simple chain-link fence to contain the amateur guitar strummers, wayward frisbees, and muddy tents in the thirty-six acres of Flamingo Park.

Inside the park was a public swimming pool and an open market for pills and LSD sugar cubes, but the center of commerce was under a giant banyan tree at the middle-north section of the park, where Zippies constructed a giant sign that read "People's Pot Party." From this home base they sold grass; customers would pay their money on the ground, and lids of Colombian would fall from the Zippie-peopled branches above. "It was the earliest version of a marijuana dispensary," said Keith Stroup, founder of the National Organization for the Reform of Marijuana Laws. "There was no age requirement or medical authorization required; just the courage to buy marijuana openly in front of hundreds of other protesters in the park."

"When I saw that huge crowd under the eucalyptus tree," Forcade recalled later, "I saw the politics of the '70s."

The Zippies engineered a six-hosed hookah, which all but guaranteed that things would move at a slightly slower speed in the immediate vicinity. It was almost enough to make one forget the sounds of helicopters and the riot squad outside.

The number of tents grew steadily, and on the Friday preceding the Democratic convention, several hundred nondelegates—and now, curious senior citizens from the neighborhood—started to mill about the thirty-six acres of the park.

Nearby, at the Vietnam Veterans Against the War encampment, the mood was far more serious. They'd figured out, with the help of a lawyer, a network journalist, and a Yippie, that Salt and Pepper of the VVAW were, in fact, Miami Public Safety Department agents. An announcement of the discovery went out over the Flamingo Park public address system that night. But the warning came too late. Hours earlier, thirty subpoenas went out for a federal grand jury to be convened in Tallahassee, at the behest of the Internal Security Division of the Justice Department. The VVAW was the latest victim of Guy Goodwin.

The Zippies rushed to converge on Florida by the time the convention officially began.

Up in Wisconsin, Dana Beal was released from Rock County Jail. The Milwaukee FBI office took down descriptions of the people who picked him up and informed the Miami office to be on the lookout for the Bel Air station wagon they drove.

Rex Weiner flew in from New York and headed for the Zippie house on Mary Street in Coconut Grove, where Forcade greeted him with the cryptic words, "I got LBJ on the roof."

Mark Gallagher thumbed rides from Key West and showed up at the Mary Street door. He impressed the Zippies when he said he'd been at the Days of Rage in '69, and they put him to work writing for *Beach Blanket News*.

Ron Lichty, who grew up on an Iowa farm and was raised in the Church of the Brethren, had been drawn into the Zippie orbit while in college. He came to Miami to write for the Underground Press Syndicate. (A former Republican, Lichty was profiled that summer by the Associated Press in an article along with a more steadfastly conservative young man who'd come to Miami, Paul Manafort.)

Tim Hughes, a seventeen-year-old self-described "Abbie Hoffman fan" who was eager to volunteer for the Yippies, had hitched from New York City. But, upon arrival, he was disappointed that they were staying in a hotel suite, and after he heard them complaining about the provocations of the Zippies, he switched sides. Hughes noted the bedroom drawer where Hoffman kept his marijuana stash and called the number of the Zippie house. "I've got Abbie's weed here; you guys want to pick me up?" Forcade drove over and picked him up.

Mike Roselle hitchhiked from Los Angeles. He was ushered to the back garden of the Zippie house, where a tangle of chicken wire was being shaped into a giant cylinder. He spent an afternoon applying layers of starch-soaked newspapers to the chicken wire, helping to create a thirty-foot-long papier-mâché joint.

Saturday afternoon, everyone piled into cars to set out for Flamingo Park. Forcade handed Weiner a bag of balloons, each bearing the words GET HIGH! FAREWELL DINOSAURS—ZIPPIE, before they hopped in his Cadillac, its odometer now reading 125,000 miles and the horn rigged to play "Here Comes the Bride." Forcade planned to set the car on fire when McGovern was nominated Wednesday.

Forcade carried a color TV into the park. He switched it on and added a sign that read THIS IS TO KEEP AN EYE ON THOSE DEMOCRATS.

A. J. Weberman was already at the banyan tree, smoking grass.

With the national press corps gawking at all the colorful pro-test groups, there were plenty of opportunities for the Zippies to hammer their talking points. They seized on the payment Hoffman, Rubin, and Sanders were receiving to write a paperback called *Vote!* and propagated the notion that the old-guard Yippies were living like air-conditioned, maid-serviced kings in the Albion Hotel, while the Zip-pies were sweating it out with the masses in Flamingo Park. ("We never viewed the revolution as crowded living conditions," pleaded Stew Albert.) In truth, there was nothing remarkable about the Albion, but the accusations started to gain traction in both the underground and mainstream media.

"They're under contract to write a book about the scene in Miami Beach and they've taken a $33,000 advance," Zippie Ron Lichty told a reporter in Flamingo Park. "But when a kid was arrested last night for selling lapel buttons without a permit, we called them to ask for some money to bail him out. They wouldn't help us. They're not interested in the welfare of the kids now they've tapped the big money."

The constant Zippie complaints that Hoffman and Rubin were aging celebrities, no longer of the people, got under Rubin's skin. "It's like the Zippies are two people and three or four hangers-on," Rubin complained. "Whenever I go to a college campus, 2,000 or 3,000 people show up." Two years earlier, Rubin had told a crowd they weren't prepared to change the country until they were prepared to kill their parents. Now, faced with Zippie attacks, he theorized instead that "age is in your head, not your body."

"There are times in history when revolutionaries must unite with the liberals," Rubin insisted. "It's not a cop-out. It's a matter of survival. We'll oppose McGovern one week after he takes office."

"They're just a satellite group that appeared from nowhere," Ed Sand-ers said of the Zippies. "We're the real Youth International Party, offi-cially registered.

"The advance money from the publisher we've already spent on arrangements in Miami Beach. As a matter of fact, Abbie is going to sleep in the park tonight."

Any publicity for the battle was a victory for Zippies. The New York *Daily News* described the Yippie offices as "a receptionist, pretty girls bustling around and plenty of easy chairs."

Allen Ginsberg summed up the rivalry in a letter to a fellow poet. "Dostoyevskian snit-hassles between vicious Zippies with young strength and tired Yippies wanting to write books."

Sunday morning, at the Zippie house, Rex Weiner woke to the sound of hovering helicopters.

"They found him," said Forcade.

"Found who?"

"They found LBJ."

Forcade led Weiner up a ladder to the roof and pointed out the eight-foot-high portrait of the thirty-sixth president of the United States that lay facing the sky. (Ultimately, Pat Small said, "The cops didn't bust anybody for stealing the mural, because they wouldn't want to admit that the car used to drive it away was a police vehicle.")

They rushed back to Flamingo Park for the smoke-in. "The smoke-in is actually more or less a continuous type of thing going on at Flamingo Park," the FBI had keenly observed, but Sunday was the big action, the *politicized* toking. The poster read:

LEGALIZE MARIJUANA!

STOP CIA HEROIN

ZIPPIE!
PRESENTS
3RD ANNUAL
INDEPENDENCE
SMOKE-IN
& SMACK ATTACK

MUSIC-THEATRE-RAPS
BRING YR OWN STASH

"Trying to bust us for pot," Beal crowed to a group of three hundred, "is like trying to bust the government for the Star-Spangled Banner, the flag, and Sunday morning sacraments."

The thirty-foot papier-mâché joint, slightly sticky from its recent coating in white housepaint, was paraded around and then smashed with a bat. Exploding from its belly were six pounds' worth of Madison-grown marijuana in individually plastic-bagged joints.

Forcade climbed up to the park's scoreboard and hoisted the LBJ portrait. He'd stenciled a brilliant yellow *Zippie!* logo in the upper-left-hand corner, just above the former president's hairline. A marijuana joint was drawn onto his lips.

"The anti-heroin march, after the smoke-in, to convention hall, was not only high on weed, but many of us were doing acid-ade," Forcade wrote in *Beach Blanket Struggle.* "In fact, while listening to Dana Beal rap about CIA smack evils and pot pleasures, those initial *hi-how-are-you?* rushes began entertaining my own body. It was a fabulous scenario. There were about 2,000 of us passing around joints 'just like kisses.' There was a helicopter hovering above our heads inspiring everyone to flip the old-fashioned bird in the air."

But the good vibes weren't shared by everyone. That evening, Nora Sayre, reporting for the *New Statesman,* watched as Miami Beach senior citizens mingled with Yippies and Zippies near the Flamingo Park baseball field. They'd embraced the protesters—most of them. "Several old people told me that they thought Forcade was a cop and that the zips were paid provocateurs," Sayre wrote. "One elderly woman said, 'Plants. I think I'm seeing plants. To discredit the youth movement.'" Forcade, the woman told Sayre, was "too-too."

After a tense Monday night, when five hundred demonstrators tore down a sixty-foot section of the perimeter fence, the week settled into more hijinks. Cindy Ornsteen roamed the convention hall with acid test invitations—engraved lettering on linen card stock—and attacked every possible surface with a rubber stamp that read:

THE UNDERGROUND
PRESS SYNDICATE
WAS HERE

—

WHY NOT
IN THE WHITE HOUSE?

Zippie activities were outlined in a special *Beach Blanket Struggle* one-sheet handout. Under the headline FUCK THE DEMOCRATS (spelled out in giant penis-shaped letters), the Zippies urged participation in the morning's "Know Your Candidate Parade":

The entire march route will consist of right turns to honor George McGovern's recent backpedaling on the issues of 1972, such as pot, abortion, military spending and Donald Duck. At the Convention Hall, there will be a Laugh-In for Muskie, a Yawn-In for Wilbur Mills, a Toke-In for Chisholm, and an Egg-In for Humpty Dumpty.

The Zippies will also call for the total integration of the US prison system and its several million population back into the mainstream of American society. Our solution to that problem is simple: declare all of Amerika a jail.

That afternoon, Forcade and Ornsteen handed out hundreds of paper masks featuring the photocopied face of Arthur Bremer, the young man who'd recently attempted to assassinate the race-baiting Democratic candidate George Wallace. (Wallace was left paralyzed from the waist down.) Two Zippies loaded a George Wallace dummy into a wheelchair that Forcade had liberated from the Miami Amtrak station and began running toward the ocean. Chasing behind them, the legions of masked Artie Bremers chanted, "Free Arthur Bremer, give him a second chance!" Finally, at the water's edge, the Wallace dummy was thrown to the sharks. Then, after a moment's pause, they fished it out, strapped it back into the wheelchair and marched to Convention Hall, closely followed by a helicopter hanging low in the afternoon sun. Outside the Convention Hall fence, a Zippie produced a pistol and fired shots into the dummy.

"Give George back to the Democrats!" someone shouted, and the Wallace effigy was hurled over the fence.

They stopped at a moat near the Convention Complex and held a ceremony to rename it the "Mary Jo Kapechne Causeway," after the victim of Ted Kennedy's 1969 car accident. They launched into a chorus of "Bridge over Troubled Water," and then someone threw a "symbolic steering wheel" into the stream, and they returned to the park at last, all traces of good taste extinguished.

That evening, the big news was a McGovern statement that the candidate might leave residual troops near Vietnam until prisoners of war were free. This, Forcade responded, was "the straw that broke the camel's back."

"We're way beyond McGovern," he told a reporter that night, under the banyan tree. "We don't even recognize there is a government. In fact, I think it was very opportunistic of the Democrats to hold their convention down here at the same time we're holding our cultural festival."

Dana Beal began Wednesday by megaphoning in the park about the media's lack of interest in the Wheelchairs for Wallace demonstration. "We didn't come here just to party," he shouted over the sounds of a rock band. "Oh, we did smoke some dope. We had a smoke-in twice. But we've got to get moving now at a time when it is strategic to put pressure on McGovern."

The Zippies then wrested the Flamingo Park bandstand from the Jesus Freaks, who were chanting "God loves you!" The Zippies shouted back— *The pope smokes dope! The pope smokes dope! The pope smokes dope!*—as they crowded them from the stage.

"One or two announcements, and then we'll stop," Beal promised the booing crowd.

Their scheduled action of the day was at the Doral Hotel, where— along with a mutant version of the SDS—they were staging a sit-in to try to get George McGovern to talk to them. But the SDS beat them to the buses, and the Zippies were left to march there.

They showed up in the marble lobby of the hotel, a few of them hoisting the LBJ portrait, and began what would be a seven-hour wait. The lobby grew more and more pungent with the smells of weed smoke, suntan lotion, and sweat; increasingly irritated McGovern volunteers jostled them for the duration.

As long-shot negotiations with McGovern's people went through back channels, the Zippies chanted "Eat the rich." Doral employees boarded up the front desk and closed the hotel restaurant. Riot police assembled outside.

At last, around 8:00 p.m. McGovern made his way down the carpeted stairway that met the middle of the lobby. He stopped ten steps above the locked arms of Secret Service agents and spoke into a microphone that was connected by curlicue cord to a bullhorn.

But the SDS and the Zippies had their *own* bullhorns, and neither wanted to cede the floor to the other. As the networks struggled to assemble an audio feed and get a clear shot of McGovern, their cameras were drawn to a striking image to the right of the candidate.

Leaning up against the Doral wall was the Lyndon B. Johnson portrait, now with a "McGovern" sticker affixed to his forehead, in addition to the yellow Zippie logo and the spliff. Live national coverage was theirs at last.

The SDS tried to get McGovern to sign an anti-racism bill it had drafted, and there was some back-and-forth about points he disagreed with.

Chants drowned out that debate.

"Marijuana! Marijuana!"

McGovern addressed the crowd. "I do not believe," he announced, "in sending anybody to the penitentiary for the use of marijuana!"

A few cheers broke out.

"At the same time, I am not prepared to advocate for the complete legalization of marijua—"

Boos and screams.

Now Dana Beal had his shot. As Patrick Small hoisted him up, he raised his bullhorn and aimed it at McGovern. "Alfred McCoy recently made a speech to Congress where he talked about the involvement of the Central Intelligence Agency in opium trade between Laos, Saigon, and Thailand.... We've been researching this for two years! We have documented proof that the Nixon administration is actually doubling up on the major source of heroin in the world."

CBS briefly switched its feed to visuals of the floor at Convention Hall, where nothing was happening, as though trying to will other news into existence.

"Now, my mother sent you a letter," Beal continued, to laughter from the crowd, "how do you have credibility if you're going to—"

"I was the first and only member of the Senate that made a public charge that South Vietnamese were conniving in the heroin trade," McGovern said, "and I demanded an investigation."

"George!" Beal shouted. "There are thirty-four million people, according to *Life*, who smoke marijuana occasionally. How do we protect these people from hard time?" Marijuana should be sold over the counter, he argued, like alcohol, so that smokers wouldn't be exposed to harder drugs.

"I've always been told," McGovern began, "the use of marijuana was not a factor leading to the use of heroin or other hard drugs."

Now it was the SDS's turn to overpower speech with chanting.

Beal yelled for them to shut up, but McGovern shook his head. The moment was over. After a few short exchanges with SDS, the candidate and his Secret Service detail floated back up the stairs.

On CBS, a resigned correspondent, reporting to Walter Cronkite, shook his head. "Well, Walter, they have been standing here all day long and we pulled off our TV lights and pulled back our cameras, suspecting that maybe they would go away. But they stayed nonetheless."

The Zippies moved LBJ into the hotel ballroom, where a television was tuned to the nomination proceedings at Convention Hall, and McGovern workers were starting to file in.

"You are media vultures," a Pepsi-drinking McGovern volunteer railed at the Zippies. "You're ripping off a political movement built by the people of this country to really change the electoral process and make it viable so that democracy can be implemented through the ballot box," cried a McGovern kid.

"Eat shit," replied a reefer-exhaling Zippie.

George McGovern officially secured the Democratic nomination at midnight.

The Zippies started a collection to buy more weed for the evening, but they picked the wrong guy to buy it. He walked out to the Doral driveway and started shouting as he dumped the coins and bills into the fountain. Then he ran off, cackling, into the night.

With the nomination clinched, the city started to empty out, but Zippie actions continued. Forcade's Cadillac was impounded by the Florida Department of Law Enforcement. With no car to set afire, the Zippies gathered an audience of a few hundred outside Convention Hall, took lighter fluid and a match to the LBJ portrait, and hurled that over the fence.

It was an odd action to match the "Pledge to Non-Violence & Harmony" they circulated. "We have consistently emphasized the necessity for non-violence," it read. "The motto of the Zippies is 'We Mean Business.' And it is true that we are considered the militant pranksters of the movement. Therefore, we believe that there are many more creative and effective ways to make our points than with mass violence. . . . No one is going to push the Zippies of the Youth International Party into a riot."

Meanwhile, in Tallahassee, the grand jury voted to indict the six members of the VVAW on charges of conspiring to cause riots with fire-bombs, automatic weapons, and "slingshot-propelled fireworks." (A week later, the Dade County police would announce that they were launching an undercover investigation into allegations that the VVAW was being financed through illegal drug deals.)

On Friday, Forcade and Weberman took a contingent over to the Albion to surprise Jerry Rubin for his birthday. Brandishing a cake with thirty-four candles, "retirement certificates" for Abbie Hoffman and Ed Sanders, and fake gold watches, and waving $33,000 in Monopoly money, they yelled up for the Yippies to come down.

"Obviously, they had their swords drawn on each other, and this was not really an attempt to ameliorate anything," said Yippie Jerry Gorde. "But Abbie wanted to go down and fuck with Tom." Gorde, Hoffman, and a third Yippie went downstairs. Yippie no. 3 had a revolver tucked into his waistband, under a light jacket. At the appointed moment, said Gorde, Yippie no. 3 "opened the right side of his jacket and showed Tom the handle of his revolver. Tom took his eyes off Abbie, and Abbie cold-cocked Tom in the face. Tom fell backward, landed on the ground with the cake, and we walked back into the hotel and up to the rooms."

A camera crew asked Weberman about the fighting. "They called Pat Small a cop! 'Cause Pat Small threw a pie at this guy's face. They called Tom Forcade a cop. I know Tom is not a cop. I know Pat's not a cop. I would have been in jail a long time ago if they were cops. They know Pat in Wisconsin, he's a figure there, just as Forcade is in New York with Underground Press Syndicate. In fact, this guy just called me a cop today, one of the Yippies. . . . Anybody they don't like is a cop."

At the end of the week, UPS hosted an acid party to celebrate the end of the Democratic convention. Forcade had arranged to use a mansion belonging to a local Zippie sympathizer, but the owner hadn't been answering the phone.

"We drove up in the limousine," said Rick Namey, an Orlando concert promoter, "and the door was locked. Tom looked under the mat, and he said, 'That son of a bitch was supposed to leave us a key. There's no key.' Then he said, 'Oh, wait, I know where there's a key.' He goes back to the trunk of Cadillac, pulls out a tire iron, goes back and rips the door off the hinges. He said, 'I knew that key would work!'"

Throngs of establishment media representatives and hippie kids from the park filled cups from a formal silver punchbowl. "The acid was a special batch called Childhood's End," Forcade wrote, later, in *UPS News.* "The acid test just may have more impact, ultimately, than the convention."

Jim Fouratt, a former Yippie who was now part of the Gay Liberation Front, attended and did not like what he saw. "They gave all these kids acid and then deprogrammed and reprogrammed, in a classic sort of CIA way," he said. "I think they might have just misused Timothy Leary's ideas and adapted a sort of brainwashing technique."

The Zippies promised to return to Miami in force for the Republican convention. "Everywhere that the fascist pig Nixon shows his face, we will confront him, but not necessarily in a non-violent way," Dana Beal vowed. "This was a dress rehearsal for August. We will have a lot more people and be a lot more serious in August. We all hate Nixon. We are going to try to push him into the sea right here. We don't want trouble, but we are prepared for Nixon to react."

Beal's words aroused suspicion, even among the mainstream press. "It is almost as if the Republican National Committee had planted *agents provocateur* inside key groups of youthful protesters who gathered in Miami Beach during the Democratic convention," mused one nationally syndicated editorial. "How else to explain the threats...from assorted Yippies, Zippies and just plain hippies promising trouble when the Republicans roll into town?" Perhaps, the editorial allowed, "their minds are simply befuddled by pot."

David Dellinger and Rennie Davis, meanwhile, had just about had it with both the Yippies and the Zippies. "We won't be threatening the Republicans with 1,000 naked Yippies," Davis promised. "We are concerned with matters of life and death."

Forcade returned to Miami in mid-August. After the landlord evicted the Zippies from their Coconut Grove rental, they simply moved down the street and took over a house that the Hare Krishnas vacated after the DNC.

Once again, the local underground *Daily Planet* voiced concern about the Zippies. "Tom Forcade, depending on who you talk to, is either the grooviest revolutionary to come down the pike or a contemptible subversive who is wrecking the movement and is probably a police provocateur." The paper also recorded conflicts between Forcade and the VVAW, who were volunteering as security guards ("Red Star One this is Red Star Five; we have a redneck roaming around the Gay Lib area harassing people") and growing weary of the Zippies' apparent irrationality.

One VVAW national coordinator pleaded with Forcade to call off a Zippie "sleep-in" in defiance of city ordinances. "What we don't need here," he said, "is a bunch of people running around acting crazy."

"Who's acting?" replied Forcade.

The next day, at a council meeting, Forcade persisted in taunting Rennie Davis, who was in the middle of a hunger strike, with an empty box of butternut cookies.

Forcade also told the media that relations with authorities were straining. A local newspaper quoted him as saying, "Nobody was calling cops 'pigs' the last time, but they are now. There's a lot more energy ready to be released down here now than there was last month."

So unyielding was Forcade's antagonism that the Yippies circulated a handbill featuring his mug shot throughout Flamingo Park. "Tom Forcade dealt hard drugs and strung out a local organizer," the flyer read. "This man uses his ample money and drugs to control people. His actions have been disruptive and suspicious. It is wise to avoid him."

"Whenever you get three people gathered in the name of protest, you have government agents," one activist told a reporter. "But when you've got Thomas King Forcade around, you don't need agents. He's not called Mr. Bad Vibes for nothing."

The section of the park that the VVAW had marked off for themselves was, unfortunately, right next to the Zippies, who flew an American flag upside down on a nearby pole, just above a pair of pink panties.

"Forcade set off a firecracker behind the head of a guy who had been home from Vietnam for about a week and a half," said Ann Hirschman, a nurse who was working with the VVAW. "I intervened to make sure that the vet didn't actually tear off any of his limbs.

"He was like, 'I will kill you!' and I was like, 'Good luck.' He was not the most presupposing physical specimen on the planet. I got in his way whenever he was doing things that were going to bring the police down on our heads."

"We went over and we told Forcade that unless he wanted to die, he'd better never threaten one of our people again," said veteran John Musgrave. "He got a whole bunch of his little kids, his little jerk-off, cotton-brained people over there, smoking dope and all this. He got them to come: 'Let's go get the vets. They're all pigs. They're all FBI.' So they came over with Forcade in the background, urging them on, to take our campsite. There was a shitload of them, a hell of a lot more of them than there were of us. We just started punching out the first ones that came in. The rest of them said, 'Oh, no hassle, man.' They didn't want any problems."

"It's not that they're any more or less radical," another veteran said of the Zippies. "It's the fact that they're irrational. They're just plain crazy."

On August 18, an article in the *Washington Post* quoted the director of the Committee for the Re-Election of the President admitting that Nixon campaign funds "were used on the initiative of [Watergate defendant Gordon] Liddy for the purpose of determining what to do if the crazies made an attack" on Nixon at the Republican convention.*

The same day, a reporter for the *Saturday Review* noticed a man at Flamingo Park who identified himself as merely an "interested observer," smiling and watching the Zippies argue about "whether to fly the flag upside down or to burn it."

"This is a good bunch of kids, a good group," volunteered the genial man. "I came down on the bus to see what these young people are up to. I believe in getting out and talking to people."

That night, over drinks at the Fontainebleau, the man divulged that he was, in fact, a friend and longtime aide to Richard Nixon.

What was such an important figure "doing on a bus, when the closest you can get to Flamingo Park by bus entails an eight-block walk?" the reporter wondered later.

---

* Liddy was specifically trying to verify that convention plots were "being printed in underground newspapers," the chairman of the Committee for the Re-Election of the President would later testify. In fact, though, the underground papers were entirely focused on what Nixon and the authorities were going to try to do to *them*.

"I had a queasy feeling in the pit of my stomach when we finally said good night," he wrote about the aide, one of those "obscure yet important cogs in the great machine that grinds out power in this country."

During the weekend leading up to the convention, the population of Flamingo Park swelled from the hundreds to the thousands, but it hardly approached the turnout of demonstrations even a year before.

"When the war was the issue, there was a false impression created about the size of the movement," Forcade observed. "It was an easy issue to organize around. But there is an impression now that the war is over. The people who only turned out for Sunday marches aren't here now."

"I doubt if there was two thousand people," said one Miami police officer, years later. "And half the demonstrators were undercover people."

And yet the Zippies were still attracting new supporters.

Chip Berlet had come to Miami in July to report for Denver's *Straight Creek Journal*, but by August he'd been drawn into the Zippie orbit, even printing the successor to July's *Beach Blanket Struggle*. "We obtained 50,000 sheets of paper and started printing a little street sheet called the *Flamingo Park Gazette*, which was just a bunch of graph sheets stapled together." Cranking the mimeograph machine by hand at first, he got a boost from a Vietnam veteran in lineman boots who climbed a telephone pole and hacked into the electrical wiring of the park. The *Gazette* informed readers of which pharmaceuticals, considered "death drugs," were banned in the park ("reds, barbs, smack, speed, paint thinner or glue") and Zippie rules ("1. Don't hurt anyone. 2. Stay 'high'—meaning psychically and physically alert and aware of the world we live in. 3. Procure higher quality pot and derivatives.").

Kalif Beacon, twenty-eight, had arrived between conventions, along with two girlfriends, two dogs, and two babies. He made himself valuable as a dynamo fundraiser, silk-screening and selling Zippie T-shirts. (But he also made enemies at the house. Once, Tim Hughes opened a closet door to find a candle that Beacon had left burning next to a photo of a baby. "You can't blow that out," Beacon told Hughes. "It's for my dead cousin." Both Hughes and Pat Small worried that Beacon was "a Charlie Manson type.")

Shay Addams, twenty-six, had been a fugitive from justice since selling a thousand hits of Mr. Natural blotter acid to a Georgia narc six months earlier. He was selling cases of Budweiser in Flamingo Park when he met the Zippies during the Democratic convention.

Aron Kay, twenty-two, volunteering for a Los Angeles group called Green Power, which provided free sandwiches and brown rice and watermelon to the hungry hordes, also found himself drawn to the Zippie philosophies and actions. When he wasn't spreading peanut butter on white bread or rattling a large coffee can for Green Power donations, he was eagerly attending the farcical actions.

One of these events was the Second Coming.

Outside the Convention Center, Shay Addams dressed in pastel robes, nearly fainting from the heat and humidity and the weight of the large cross he was carrying, climbed up on a van and answered questions from Rex Weiner, who was calling himself "Mike Media from KZIP Radio."

"Yeah, I'm Jesus," Addams said, before rousing the crowd with riffs on Nixon, Vietnam, and marijuana.

Then they commenced with the ritual desecration of what they called "Honky Culture Items." It was the world's first piss-in.

Cindy Ornsteen held up a draft card.

"Piss on it!" the crowd screamed.

Cindy poured a glassful of orange-hued liquid onto the heap.

Then, in quick succession, she held up a bra, an issue of *Life* magazine, a Bible, and an American flag.

"Piss on it, piss on it!" they shouted for each item, which was dutifully christened.

Meanwhile, an NBC camera crew was moving in for the action. But by the time they got to the front, they were too conspicuous.

"Piss on them!" someone shouted, and a chant began. Cindy poured out the rest of the liquid on the camera crew, who yelled and ran away.

"Aw, it's only orange drink," Cindy said, innocently, just before the assembled mob started to unzip and pee on the pile of honky items.

It was still eighty-five degrees in the late afternoon heat when the Zippies returned to Flamingo Park from the piss-in, just in time to witness nineteen white-shirted Nazis on the makeshift stage of a flatbed truck and Vietnam veterans holding back the disgusted park denizens.

"Genocide is being practiced on white people by the Jews through busing and taxes," declared the Nazi leader.

"Let's tear them in half!" yelled a Zippie woman.

"White Power!" chanted the Nazis.

The VVAW tried to negotiate a peaceful but complete exit for the Nazis. Eventually, one of the vets told a Nazi to come down off the truck. The Nazi started to kick him, but the vet grabbed his other foot and whisked him down.

An instant melee erupted, filled with screams and shouts and bloody faces. Chunks of watermelon rained down on the Nazis, all of whom were soon pulled to the ground.

By the time they'd been ejected, the mood of the park had shifted. Forcade grew impatient that the evening's scheduled Vietnamese Cultural Program, presented by the Miami Convention Coalition, was delaying Zippie plans for…a rock-and-roll opera. "The MCC told me they'd be taking the stage for a couple of minutes," he complained to the crowd, "and they stayed for two hours."

Then the Zippie rock band took the stage, drowning out Jane Fonda, one of the MCC-arranged speakers.

Rick Namey, singing lead, had hastily assembled the group about a week before the convention, drawing mostly from local musicians in Orlando. Namey and Forcade provided the group with a small repertoire of their original songs and dangled promises of national press and television coverage. They set everything up like a bank heist—the guys didn't even know each other's last names.

The band, dressed in drag, were announced as "The Gooks." Jane Fonda spat in Namey's eye.

They kicked off with a "three-part rock opera" about sexism, racism, and imperialism. Then, after a quick costume change, there was "The Calley Stomp," in which Namey screamed "Calley, you shithead," while pantomiming the choking and dismembering of a doll representing William Calley, the court-martialed US Army lieutenant who'd overseen the My Lai massacre. "Free Artie Bremer" once again celebrated the George Wallace assailant ("Free Artie Bremer, won't you give him another chance / He should've shot him in the head / But he shot him in the pants"), and "Eat the Rich" ("She told them to eat cake / when the people had no bread / but the French had a plan / they chopped off her head / when there is no cake / you can eat the rich instead") was an attempt at an audience sing-along.

For the finale, a rendition of David Peel's "The Pope Smokes Dope," someone came out dressed as a pope while the band tossed dozens of joints into the crowd. They also threw out buttons that said "Gook," until people started getting jabbed with the pins.

The following day, the Miami Convention Coalition voted to ban amplified music from the park.

On Tuesday, Kalif Beacon led a group of more than two hundred Zippies down a blind alley near Convention Hall and into the arms of police. "Because one weirdo in tactical leadership incited people to ignore the rest of us, block traffic, and then burn some red-white & blue bunting on a streetlamp," a Zippie newsletter read, "our pitifully small march against Coca-Cola Imperialism became the first mass arrest of the week."

Police chief Rocky Pomerance accused the Zippies of roughing up delegates and beating on cars, smashing the windows of a bank and a burlesque theater, and "terrorizing" people sitting on their patios. An aide of Pomerance said they clubbed delegates. In fact, newspapers reported that it was SDS members who'd broken windows, that witnesses said there had been no violence against delegates, and that a check of local hospitals turned up no victims.

Regardless, there'd been a major lapse in discipline, and the Zippie bail fund was emptied out before the convention was over. Pat Small, furious, pushed for Beacon's expulsion.

Nixon's renomination was on Wednesday, August 23. After the long days in the miserable heat, the Flamingo Park crowd was increasingly irritable, and the City of Miami was increasingly on edge. If there was to be trouble, this was the day they expected it to happen. Business owners, bracing for violence, closed early and rolled hurricane shutters down over their storefront windows.

Thousands of officers reported for duty by noon. Inside the main entrance of Convention Hall stood more than 1,500 Miami and Miami Beach policemen and teams from the Florida Highway Patrol, the Secret Service, and the FBI. Two thousand National Guardsmen were ready at a nearby high school; twenty miles away, more than 2,500 Marines and paratroopers were on call. This was a show of force.

In a surprise move, the city lined up buses end to end along the perimeter of Convention Hall, creating a steel wall. The demonstrators, who'd been planning for highly visible and widely filmed nonviolent protests as the delegates entered the building—banking, really, on a photo-op set against the backdrop of riot guards—were stunned. Reconfiguring their strategy, they voted to march to the Doral Hotel, which housed Nixon's headquarters.

It was almost dusk when a Dade County motorcycle cop observed a 1½-ton stake truck slowly approaching on the wrong side of Lincoln Road, with dozens of kazoo-blowing demonstrators on the flatbed waving Zippie flags. The Gooks were also on board, playing their songs. Forcade, Cindy Ornsteen, and Blake, the group's equipment manager, were all squeezed into the cab.

The officer waved down the truck, and then parked in front of it. Forcade threw the truck in reverse, but this only ended up blocking traffic. The motorcycle cop approached and asked him for his license.

"It's in the glove compartment," Forcade said, but already more motorcycle police were converging.

"Please exit the vehicle, sir," the motorcycle cop said. "This truck is under arrest."

Forcade was put in the back of a police car. The cop noticed a can on the truck's seat that "looked like a rope wick or something coming out of the top. It appeared to have a wax substance it was sitting in." He put it on the curb and called in for a bomb expert.

Blake slid into the driver's seat. Now the police asked him for *his* license.

Meanwhile, as thirty Zippies ran off the truck and into the streets, officers seized a five-gallon can of gasoline.

In the passenger seat, Cindy was smoking a cigarette. She picked up a wax-filled tuna-fish can from the floor of the cab and ashed into it.

"What's this?" another officer asked her.

"It's a candle," she said, as he took it away from her. The officers seized two additional cans from the truck.

Blocks away, things had gotten weird. Without warning, police began flooding the area with mace grenades and tear gas cannisters and arresting protesters en masse. After they filled up all the paddy wagons, they started stuffing detainees into rented trucks. The streets were soon littered with the peeled backings from the Polaroids they used for mug shots.

Motorists tried to run down demonstrators; some demonstrators overturned parked cars, and others set garbage containers afire in the middle of the street.

Outside Convention Hall, protesters who hadn't gotten the change of plans were dressed as maimed Vietnamese peasants. The Republicans were shuffling delegates in through side entrances.

One group of Zippies calling themselves the "Godzilla Brigade" surrounded a bus carrying delegates from South Carolina. They slashed tires, cut an engine hose, yanked an ignition wire, stuffed a potato in the exhaust pipe. According to one Zippie, they'd already begun dousing the bus with gasoline when a VVAW marshal showed up and said, "Look, you can't barbecue the South Carolina delegation."

As two Miami motorcycle officers went to escort the delegates from the bus, two hundred demonstrators swarmed around, shouting, "Eat the rich!"

The Godzilla Brigade was on its way back to the park when the police caught up with them. Emerging from their cars with guns drawn, the cops handcuffed them and drove them back to the Convention Hall area, where a number of undercover police were waiting.

One of them was Carl, one of the guys who'd been hanging around the Mary Street Zippie house, offering rides and helping to procure the LBJ portrait.

"We always knew you were a fucking pig," sneered Godzilla Brigade member and Mary Street resident Mark Gallagher. Gallagher was promptly thrown into a car. He was charged with aggravated assault on a police officer, resisting arrest with violence, inciting to riot, sale of marijuana, and four counts of desecration of the American flag.

Gallagher later claimed in the *Yipster Times* that he was beaten "so badly that I had to be doused with water to bring me back to consciousness." Finally, he said, he "continued the struggle with the only means available": he vomited all over the officer and his car.

Inside the hall, the air-conditioning was turned off to keep the gas from leaking in. Richard Nixon, accepting the presidential nomination for reelection, spoke of his "all-out offensive against crime, against narcotics, against permissiveness in our country."

Five blocks away, on Lincoln Road, the tear gas was drifting in from the east. Forcade soon had company in the back of the squad car: Blake—the second person in the truck arrested for driving it without a license—and Steve Conliff, a Zippie from Ohio, arrested on a disorderly conduct and profanity charge.

"Tom was very, very manic," Conliff remembered. "The police radio was freaking out—'There's two thousand Zippies armed with rocks and bottles marching towards Collins Avenue'—and Tom says, 'Ah, that's the crowd that's coming to free me!'"

Later, at the police station, Forcade kept insisting that he was "T. K. Forcade, journalist," who had nothing to do with that other Forcade fellow.

"How much is my fine, officer?" he said, in the most upright-citizen voice he could muster. "And let me bail out my buddies here, too." Confusing matters further while they were transferred from one jail cell to another was the fact that he and Conliff both wore UPS press passes identifying them as Thomas Forcade.

"We don't want to be with those dirty demonstrators," Forcade pleaded. "We're just traffic violators!"

They were put in a holding cell. Briefly unattended, the slender Forcade attempted to reach through an opening to a nearby telephone. When the guard returned, he was stuck at the waist. She shoved him back in.

"I only wanted to order a pizza!" he cried.

From a window in the cell, they could see a command-center board showing police activity throughout the city. It was lit up like a Christmas tree.

By the time the delegates poured out of Convention Hall near midnight, the streets were quiet and empty, and the only traces of protest were the lingering smells of garbage and tear gas. Twelve hundred protesters had been arrested, two hundred of them Zippies.

Pat Small got a ride back to the Coconut Grove house, exhausted. Most of the residents—Dana Beal and Kathy Morales, A. J., and Cindy—were asleep. But Kalif Beacon was in the living room, with an entourage of teenagers.

When Small demanded that Beacon leave the house, Beacon first came at Small with a broom handle and then ran into the kitchen. Small followed.

Beacon opened a kitchen drawer and pulled out the biggest knife there. Small positioned himself on the other side of the kitchen island counter.

Small screamed out to Dana Beal, who was in another room, for help, just before one of Beacon's teenage followers came up behind Small and smashed a Coke bottle over his head. Small ran out a kitchen door to the outside of the house. Moments later, he heard a gunshot and screaming.

Beacon ran down the hallway to Forcade's bedroom and grabbed a shotgun Forcade had left leaning against the wall. Beal rushed him, and as they wrested for control, the shotgun blew a hole into the ceiling.

"At that point," Small said, "other people just jumped on Beacon and the other kid. I was still sitting in the backyard, stunned and bleeding. I came back in a couple minutes later and they were gone."

Then a phone rang, breaking the eerie silence.

A very agitated Cindy Ornsteen picked it up. "There was this huge fight with Pat and Kalif and Dana, and a gun, but they were gone now, thank God," she said, and hung up.

"Cindy," Pat said, "who did you just tell that story to?"

"Carl."

"Ohhh, Cindy, you shouldn't have told him that."

Small hid the shotgun in the rafters of a shed and started packing. A. J. had arranged rides for everyone back to New York; within hours, as soon as the cars showed up, they'd all get out of there.

Then he heard more screaming, from the living room.

Twenty narcotics officers and SWAT members, dressed in ninja black and armed with submachine guns, had burst through the door and pushed their way into the house. Carl and Doug were there, too, wearing Zippie T-shirts but now carrying guns. They had arrest warrants for Small and Cindy.

"Where's the weapon?" the SWAT members demanded, their submachine guns pointed at Small's head. He told them where he'd hidden the shotgun.

Salt and Pepper, the police who'd posed as Vietnam vets, interrogated Cindy.

Some of the police "proceeded to take Dana and beat him up, and charged him with possession of marijuana," Small said. "They took AJ into a room, they beat him up a little bit, but they didn't arrest him."

Small was taken downtown and, to his amazement, placed in the same cell holding Forcade. David Dellinger was in there too, now, weak from three weeks of fasting. Dellinger, who'd just turned fifty-seven years old, had recently endured a gall bladder operation, a ruptured appendix, peritonitis, a hernia, and torn knee ligaments. Now the pacifist leader was being made to suffer an angry harangue from Forcade.

"It was five in the morning, 100 degrees and humid, and we had all just gone through a night of hell," Small said. "Tom started to berate Dellinger—he would get angry and not let go of it. Finally, Dellinger said, 'Would you guys just let me sleep? I don't want to talk about any of this anymore!' We relented."

When the sun rose, there were still six hundred demonstrators in jail, most of them declaring solidarity, refusing to be bailed until everyone was freed, clogging the system and testing the capacity of the jails.

A. J., Dana, Kathy, and Pat finally got their ride back to New York.

"The Miami Convention Coalition's line was that the Zippies were apolitical, just dopers and probably CIA agents," said Conliff. "The MCC went around and told people that everyone's bail had been reduced and they could leave—except for thirteen leaders of the MCC, and 'A couple of people who were in there for drugs who we just can't do anything about.'"

Forcade hadn't been arrested for any drug offense; rather, the charge finally leveled against him and Cindy was grand larceny—for the theft of the Lyndon B. Johnson portrait.

On the following day, the Associated Press reported that Forcade and fellow Zippie Mark Gallagher—arrested for "aggravated assault on a policeman, resisting arrest with violence, inciting to riot, sale of marijuana and desecrating the American flag"—were two of only five people who remained in the Miami City Jail.

Once Forcade's bail was paid, he left town and disappeared.

The trials of Forcade, Ornsteen, and Pat Small were scheduled for October. Judge Ellen "Maximum" Morphonios had become Dade County's first female criminal court judge the previous year. She was a former beauty queen who maintained a conservative radio talk show, wore spiked heels, and carried an automatic pistol.

On the advice of attorneys, Pat Small pleaded guilty to his possession charge—sale charges were dropped. But almost immediately, it seemed like a mistake. "If this is the guy that threw the pie," Judge Morphonios warned, "he better not come in front of me. I'll hang him." He would eventually be sentenced to a year in jail.

Cindy showed up in court; Tom did not. Luckily for both of them, the Democratic National Committee witness also failed to show, and their grand larceny charges were dropped.

A week later, another Zippie was in trouble with the law. On Halloween night, Tom Hanifin, who'd been arrested for LSD-inspired nude cartwheeling during the Republican convention, walked into the Nixon campaign headquarters in Binghamton, New York, carrying a cloth-covered rifle and ordered workers out. Then he replaced a Nixon–Agnew banner with a Viet Cong flag, spray-painted "He murders children" on the wall, tossed a typewriter and a folding chair from a second-story window, and finally the gun, which turned out to be an M1 carbine BB air rifle. "Nixon paid me to do it," Hanifin said after surrendering. "I've got $3,000 in a secret bank account in Mexico."

Prominent journalists began digging into Forcade's background. The nationally syndicated columnist Mike Royko interviewed activists who alleged that Forcade had instigated fights and attempted to pose as a veteran, and he quoted Miami police who said they'd been told "at a high level" not to bust Forcade during the convention. They were convinced that the GOP had funded the Zippies. Said one anonymous source, "We don't even know if Tom Forcade was his real name."

Allen Katzman, the former *East Village Other* editor and Underground Press Syndicate cofounder who just four years earlier had agreed to have Forcade set up the UPS operations in Phoenix, piled on:

> When the coordinating committee for the eight radical groups planning the Miami Beach counter-conventions broached the problem of the Zippies with Rocky Pomerance, the chief of the Miami Beach police force told them in no uncertain terms that "his hands were tied by the Federal authorities who have a hands-off policy as far as Forcade was concerned."

It turns out Forcade is working for the FBI as a cooperative to avoid going to jail for transporting drugs across state lines with intent to sell. As far as Weberman, Weiner and the rest of the Zippies are concerned, they're dupes for Forcade.

Katzman then accused Forcade and the Zippies of turning "the streets of New York City into a political gang war," citing the vandalizing of Ed Sanders's Land Rover and Jerry Rubin's car and apartment. "Abbie Hoffman has been driven from the city by constant nighttime terror tactics against his wife and family," Katzman wrote, and "the Movement has turned into a Mafia Miracle play. People in this country are already getting used to the idea of four more years of Nixon. In the radical movement, it is no less different than four more years with the likes of Forcade."

Katzman even made the startling claim that "the only service the Underground Press Syndicate can talk about with any pride is that it has served as a complete record of information for the FBI."

David Dellinger, hardly known for espousing conspiracy theories, had his own stories. "During the Convention, the government tried to pacify the demonstrators by flooding them with Quaaludes," he wrote. "One of the chief middlemen who received the Quaaludes from the government and distributed them to demonstrators was a Zippie whom I knew.... Before the convention was over, the Zippie distributor of Quaaludes had been arrested for some particularly flagrant 'malicious destruction of public property,' and Rocky Pomerance, the Miami police chief, had sworn that he had the goods on him. But, given the distributor's connections with the government and what he could have brought out in a trial (or around it), the Justice Department forced the city to drop the charges, much to the displeasure of Pomerance."

After *Washington Post* journalists Bob Woodward and Carl Bernstein reported that operatives for President Nixon's reelection campaign had plotted to recruit and pay "radical, long-haired kids" to pose as demonstrators at the Republican National Convention, the Pulitzer-winning muckraker Jack Anderson followed up on the Forcade rumors. Anderson dug up government files showing that "Thomas King Forcade" was in fact Gary Goodson, born in California in 1945, and that he had served in the military in the mid-1960s. Goodson's Air National Guard records even included a 1969 psychiatric exam that had resulted in his discharge.

Anderson located Forcade in a Florida recording studio, where he and The Gooks (now renamed the slightly more palatable Dixie Outlaws) were working on a concept album called *Eat the Rich*. Forcade insisted to Anderson that the Zippies were funded by panhandling, money borrowed from friends, and a book advance. (Anderson also noted that Forcade "was known to have dabbled in drugs and acid.")*

"Forcade is known in the radical netherworld as a weird character with a black sense of humor who would undoubtedly have been tempted by the prospect of taking Republican money to harass Republicans," Anderson wrote, before ultimately concluding that there was "no evidence that the Republicans secretly financed" the Zippies.

The matter was soon dropped. Two days after Anderson's column was published, Richard Nixon, weathering the scandal of the Watergate break-in, was reelected in a landslide.

---

* Four days after reaching Forcade, Anderson shared an additional scoop: the publisher of Sanders, Rubin, and Hoffman's book *Vote!* had been "inundated with hate mail. One envelope contained human waste."

SEEDS,
1897–1969

CHAPTER 8

JOHN LATHAM GOODSON BECAME THE FIRST GOODSON TO SIGN THE
name Forcade, when, in 1897, he endorsed a check with the forged signature of his father-in-law and occasional cattle-business partner, Peter
Forcade. Then he attempted to do the same with the signature of his
brother-in-law. Found out and owing multiple debts, the twenty-four-
year-old Goodson immediately left his home in Maryville, Missouri,
leaving behind his wife, Grace, and two infant children. Speculation
around town was that he had headed for the Klondike.

"The crooked transactions of J.L. Goodson have at last reached the
point where publication of the facts in the case can no longer be with-
held," reported the *Graham Post*. "We have refrained from speaking of
the case before in hopes that the charges might be disproved, out of regard for the feelings of the wife and relatives of this very foolish young
man, who deeply feel the disgrace of his actions. It appears that Goodson had been planning for a long time to gather in as much money as
possible, and was not at all particular as to the way it was obtained. He
mortgaged his corn crop to three different persons, one of these being his
father-in-law, Peter Forcade. He also mortgaged his hogs, horses, wagon
and other articles, and, it is claimed, secured cash from all of them."

But John Goodson eventually returned to face the charges, and spent
a short time in jail. He and Grace then moved with their children to
Kansas, and then to Phoenix, where he quickly integrated into the community. John Goodson became a charter member of Montezuma Lodge
No. 35 and a member of the Odd Fellows and the Sciots and the First
Baptist church, and he was hired as engineer of the Federal Building
downtown. In 1913 he and his wife welcomed their eighth child, Kenneth F. Goodson. The *F* stood for Grace's family name, Forcade.

Back in Missouri, the Forcade family endured tragedy. Grace's
brother hanged himself in the granary of his farm. "It is thought here
that his mind had been affected for some time," relayed the *Beloit Gazette*, "caused by much brooding over the possibilities of his being forced
to return to the army life." Months later, her uncle James attempted suicide by carbolic acid. (Uncle James survived, but twelve years later he
shot himself in the right temple with a rifle.)

It might have seemed that such darkness would not follow the family to sunny Phoenix. But the following year, John and Grace's oldest son, John Jr., enlisted in the aviation division of the navy. Five weeks later, when he was given three days' leave, his father came out to California to visit. On the night of August 5, they went to a theater and then returned to their room at the Hotel Rosslyn.

Los Angeles Herald, August 6, 1918

SAILOR DREAMS HE IS FIGHTING GERMANS, AND SHOOTS SELF

Springs from Bed in Night and Turns Gun on Himself
Probably Will Die
Mother in Race Against Death Hurries to Bedside from Arizona

Dreaming that the Germans were attacking him and that he was fighting them off, John L. Goodson, Jr, a sailor from the naval reserve training station, shot himself, probably fatally, in his sleep early today.

The sailor boy was sleeping with his father at a downtown hotel at the time of the remarkable accident.

Apparently he sprang from the bed, in his sleep, turned a gun on himself and discharged it straight into his breast.

His father, wakened by the shot and feeling the bed shake, discovered that his son was not at his side. The room was in utter darkness and the boy made no answer to the father's cries.

JUMPS FROM BED

The father jumped from the bed and turned on the lights. They revealed the form of his son lying bleeding on the floor, partly under the bed.

Young Goodson was unconscious and for a moment his father feared he was dead. He lifted the boy to the bed and summoned help from the receiving hospital.

At the receiving hospital where the sailor was at once taken, it was found that the bullet had entered young Goodson's breast and taken an upward course, probably lodging somewhere near the spine.

FINALLY CONSCIOUS

It was several hours before the sailor was restored to partial consciousness and could explain that it was a dream which impelled him to shoot.

His conscious moments were still fraught with the influence of the dream, for he murmured, to his father and the surgeons:

"I think it was a Pro-German who shot me. But I'll get them yet, won't I, Dad?" And again he whispered, "I thought the Germans were coming at me and I tried to get my man."

The father, who is an engineer at Phoenix, Ariz., stated that his son had come to Los Angeles on July 9 and enlisted in the navy. He had written home glowing accounts of his experience, the father said, and seemed to be in a sound, wholesome condition of mind and body. The boy had chosen the navy because he had a brother in that branch of the service.

Grace was notified by telegram of the incident and rushed with two of her children to see her wounded son. But the boy, "conscious to the last," expired before they reached Los Angeles. The grieving family brought his body back to Phoenix, where Col. James H. McClintock, a former officer of Teddy Roosevelt's Rough Riders, delivered the eulogy. "There could be no happier death," he proclaimed, "than that of one who died for his country."

The surviving Goodson children were tough, carrying with them the scars of the family. Mel would become the youngest Speaker of the House in Arizona, but in his earlier days he led a neighborhood entourage known as the Goodson Gang, which struck fear into the heart of, among others, a young Barry Goldwater. "He was the roughest, toughest guy who ever hit this town," the future leader of the conservative movement told his biographer. "We called him 'Bull Goodson,' and when he came down the street we got on the other side."

The youngest of the Goodson brothers, Kenny, was nine years younger than Mel, only five years old when his oldest brother, John, had died for his country. Kenny became a running guard on the Arizona State football team, and then went to work as an engineer for the Arizona Highway Department. When he was twenty-four—the same age his father had been when he forged those checks—he met Laura Belle Parks, an

Arizona State student, at a dance in Flagstaff. They married and had a daughter named Judy and a son named Gary, who, when he himself was twenty-four, would invoke the Forcade name once again.

Laura Belle, like her new husband Kenny, had a family history marked by both illegality and violence. Her grandfather, Jasper Page, had been a city marshal in Tombstone and deputy sheriff in Cochise County. Two of her uncles, Leonard and Sid Page, were officers of the peace as well. Neither, however, remained on the right side of the law.

Late on the night of September 9, 1899, bandits held up the Southern Pacific's westbound No. 10 train at Cochise Station, eleven miles southwest of Willcox, Arizona. Masked men ordered the engineer to detach the rear passenger cars from the engine and luggage car, in which they chugged forth for about a mile. Then they dynamited the luggage car's iron safe, seized about $3,000 in cash and jewelry, and disappeared on horseback into the darkness.

The Cochise County sheriff sent out a posse that included Willcox constable Burt Alvord, his deputies Billy Stiles and Bill Downing, and Willcox night watchman Matt Burts—but the horse trail went dead.

About six weeks later, as the sun was setting in the nearby mining town of Pearce, a freshly shorn and shaven saloon owner named Chris Robertson was sitting on the front porch of his establishment when Sid Page, twenty-one-year-old deputy constable of Pearce, approached. After loud words were exchanged and five shots rang out, Robertson lay dead. Matt Burts, the Willcox night watchman who had seen the entire episode, collected both men's warm guns.

Sid Page waited at the scene until his superior, Pearce constable Bert Grover, arrived. He told Grover that Chris Robertson had confronted him about money. Page and Robertson had argued, and when Robertson reached for his gun, Page simply outdrew him. "I shot Robertson," Page told his boss, "but I had to do it."

Matt Burts handed the guns to Grover. Page was taken to the jail in Tombstone, the Cochise county seat.

"There was considerable talk last night about a lynching bee, and all they wanted was a leader," reported the *El Paso Herald*. "Up to 1:30 a.m. there were groups at every corner. The jail, however, was amply defended by cowboys who are friends of the murderer."

Sid Page's December trial ended with a hung jury.

While Sid Page awaited a retrial, another train was held up nearby, this time in Fairbank. One of the bandits was shot, and his partners left him behind. Before "Three Fingered Jack" expired, he spilled the beans on those partners, and it turned out that some of them were also involved in the unsolved September robbery at Cochise Station. In fact, under the leadership of Willcox constable Burt Alvord, they had led the unsuccessful search party to find... themselves.

Deputy Billy Stiles quickly agreed to turn the state's evidence against fellow lawmen Alvord, Bill Downing, and Matt Burts, who were soon captured. Then, in a shocking twist, Stiles, who was free because of his status as a government witness, went down to the Tombstone jail, shot the jailer, and freed Burt Alvord. Matt Burts and Bill Downing stayed behind.

At the end of June 1900, the *Tombstone Weekly Epitaph* noted the presence of Sid Page's family at his second trial: his mother embracing him, and his youngest brother crawling onto his lap. "Page is constantly attended by his father and brother, his father especially paying close attention to every stage of the proceedings and conferring with his son and with the attorneys for the defense."

But the key witness for Page's defense, Matt Burts, had just been indicted for the most sensational train robbery in recent memory. The witnesses for the prosecution swore that the shooting victim, Chris Robertson, was never armed. And Robertson's eighteen-year-old daughter—left to raise her four orphaned siblings—testified that her father had been murdered for knowing something about the Cochise robbery.

Once again, the jury was deadlocked.[*]

Sid Page was finally convicted at the end of his third trial. "One pathetic side of the case," reported the *Tombstone Epitaph*, "is the prostration of the prisoner's mother, who it is said is sorely stricken at the fate of her son. The mother has been quite ill and the verdict shattered a mother's clinging hope of her son's release, the news being a culmination of many months of anxiety."

---

[*] Only days after Sid Page's trial, his deputy sheriff father was summoned to a Willcox saloon when Warren Earp was shot and killed by John Boyett. J. C. Page brought the news of the shooting to Tucson—he commented to newspapers that "Boyett was always a peaceable man and put up with a great deal from Earp"—but even Earp's death did not produce the number of headlines that the trial of Page's own son had.

In the same week that Page was sentenced to twenty years in the territorial prison in Yuma, his key witness, the train robber Matt Burts, was sentenced to five. Two days after Christmas, guards escorted them to Yuma, with Burts's left arm chained to Page's right arm. When they stopped at a lunch counter, Burts made a dive for a guard's gun, was pushed backward, and tried for a second guard's gun. Finally, a third guard dragged the chained duo to an adjoining barroom, where Burts gave up. The fourth guard, standing by, was Page's own deputy sheriff father.

Burts was pardoned by Arizona governor Nathan Oakes Murphy four months later; Page was not.

"The result of this case is a forceful commentary on the pistol-carrying habit," wrote a correspondent in the *Cochise Review*. "There is no justification for men and boys going about with ten pounds of deadly iron and led strapped about their bodies." The paper predicted a protest movement that would cause "a discontinuance of the gun habit" in Arizona.

Owing to so much outlawry, Arizona ranchers, mine owners, railroad officials, and newspaper editors demanded better law enforcement, and Governor Murphy appointed a tax-funded special force modeled on the Texas Rangers. From a pool of 240 candidates, Sid Page's older brother Leonard was chosen to be one of the first four Arizona Rangers. Another was Bert Grover, the man to whom Sid Page had surrendered.

On August 16, 1902, Grover was arrested for instigating a post–poker game brawl with Bisbee police outside of the Orient Saloon. Later that day, Leonard Page took the jail keys from the jail and freed Grover, riding with him to his home in Tombstone Canyon. Police put out a warrant for Page.

Leonard Page turned himself in and left the Arizona Rangers. Thus ended the Page family's affair with Cochise County law enforcement.

Not long after her brothers' troubles with the law, Sid and Leonard Page's younger sister, Annie, met and married Harry Parks, the son of a cattle rancher. They moved into an adobe house in Willcox, operated a mercantile store, and bore witness as the new century transformed the area. In 1911, the year before Arizona was granted statehood, the *Vin Fiz Flyer* biplane, making the country's first transcontinental flight, touched down in Willcox and frightened Harry's hitch-racked horse. The town had been the largest cattle shipment point in the state, a destination along the Southern Pacific Railroad, but the new highway directed traffic away from Willcox, and its glory began to fade.

Harry and Annie raised two sons and a daughter, Laura Belle, in Willcox. Shortly after Laura Belle turned twenty, she met Kenny Goodson.

Kenny Goodson's work in highway construction took him to small cowboy towns.

"Just for the fun of it," a nephew remembered, "he would go to the bars, and after he would drink for a while he would say, 'Does anyone here think they can beat me up? I'd like to challenge anybody in the bar who thinks they can.'" On the job, he was known as a "pusher," responsible for getting road segments finished, jumping up on construction vehicles and threatening violence on drivers if they didn't perform to his standards.

"He had to kind of establish that he was the guy in charge, running the show," recalled Kenny's daughter Judy, who was born in 1941. "It was weird, but my mom seemed to think anything he did was great."

As the scope of Kenny's work expanded to bridges, pipelines, and highway systems, the young family moved often—to Alaska, Palo Alto, Okinawa, and Keflavik, Iceland, where NATO was constructing an air base.

Kenny and Laura Belle's second child, Gary Kenneth Goodson, was born into this itinerant life in Hayward, California, on September 11, 1945. In and out of schools, Gary's only consistent friendship was with his older sister.

"I wanted to make sure that he didn't have some of the same problems that I did with leaving three schools in one year," said Judy. "My mother said that I could help him with reading and arithmetic if I didn't push him too hard. And then I started noticing that he was way ahead of what I was doing, all kinds of things that I hadn't even showed him. My mother pulled me aside and she said, 'You need to realize that he's just very bright, and he's taken off on his own.' He just wasn't teachable, as it turned out. He taught himself."

The Goodsons returned to Arizona in 1955, moving into a three-bedroom brick house painted pink and turquoise. With a father interested in manly pursuits—he took Gary's cousins quail hunting, while Gary stayed home—and a protective mother who didn't want him riding his bicycle farther than the sidewalk in front of the home, Gary entertained himself with a huge electric train set that sprawled through the house's sunroom, when he wasn't stocking up at the local library.

He was shaped by the mythos of the American dream as much as any midcentury kid, intoxicated by tales of the limitless possibility of the Old West. The movie *Lust for Gold*, about a lost treasure buried in the nearby Superstition Mountains, stoked a lifelong dream of finding fortune.

Only two years after moving the family to Phoenix, Kenny Goodson accepted a job heading construction on a $200 million aluminum rolling mill for Kaiser, which would pull up the Goodson roots yet again. While the children finished the school year in Arizona, Kenny went out to Ravenswood, West Virginia, to begin work.

In the early morning of April 29, 1957, a group of Boy Scouts camping near Marietta, Ohio, heard a horrible eruption of crunching metal sounds. They left their tents and found that a car had plunged through the guardrail on Route 7 and overturned. Kenneth Goodson, forty-four, was dead.

News came to Laura Belle Goodson in Arizona with a 7:00 a.m. call. She rushed to the bedroom where her visiting parents were staying and told them the shocking news. But the ringing phone had also awakened Gary in the next bedroom down the hall, and he overheard the news of his father's demise. "He heard it second-hand. He was standing there with these big eyes, like, what are they talking about?" remembered Judy. "He was only eleven years old."

Questions about the high-speed single-car crash lingered, although they were not discussed openly in the family. Kenny Goodson's life had become complicated. When the family had returned from Okinawa, they sponsored their nanny, a woman named Kane, to come to Phoenix and attend nursing school. She became pregnant with Kenny's child, a son. Laura Belle found out about it; it's not clear if Gary ever knew he had a half-brother.

"Gary never really talked about his dad," recalled his cousin George, but his friend Chris Peebles remembered him expressing "significant pain about his dad's emotional distance."

Gary did keep a clipping of a *Popular Mechanics* ad for a US missile arsenal model kit. "Here is the ideal joint project," the copy read, "for every dad and boy." He entered a regional science fair sponsored by Arizona State and won a first-place prize in the junior division. He drafted mechanical plans, wrote a paper on Thomas Edison, joined a ham radio society. And he absorbed languages—Latin, ASL, and morse code—as if by osmosis.

"When he walked into somebody's house," said Judy Goodson, "he just sort of focused on information. He might also carry on a conversation, but if you had a magazine or a book out, he'd pick it up and start reading it."

He tore through espionage adventures, from T. E. Lawrence to James Bond. Even the science fiction he read sometimes dipped into double agentry: the hero of E. Everett Evans's *Man of Many Minds* joins the counterintelligence division of the Interstellar Corps to penetrate a conspiracy and must pretend to be disgracefully expelled from its ranks, "apparently an outcast, outwardly hating the Service for its harsh treatment."

Darker themes started to thread through his solitary pursuits. He drew axes, knives, robotic riflemen, and car crashes. "Unfortunately, I do not remember my happiest Christmas," he wrote in one essay for school, "because none of them have been outstanding or distinctive." The Christmas tree lights "scared me, with the frayed wires running hither and thither. It looked as if it would catch fire any second." At the end of a short story called "Santa and the Killer," a Christmas-tree robber named "Joe Corn Cobber"—short and blue-eyed, just like the Goodson men— escapes when the police arrest the wrong man.

A few short years later, another school essay tackled drug use. "Here I am taking a drink, nearly two years after Mr. Boetto told us of the serious consequences," Gary began. "I guess this all started when I was joking around with Bob and Jim over at Jim's house. It was there that Jim offered me a drink. I had never taken a drink but he chided me into it. Bob and I both liked it and soon went to Bob's house regularly.

Another friend of mine approached me with marijuana. This was much more satisfying than liquor, so I smoked it for a while until it too no longer gave satisfaction. I went to sniffing heroin. This I got at the liquor counter at El Rancho. One day after sniffing it I went to

El Rancho. The detectives noticed my strange actions, I saw him and ran. Before I knew it I had been sentenced to seven years.

This would be a good example of addiction if it were true. But I don't think things happen this way. In the first place I don't think a person can become an addict or alcoholic as the result of taking the "first drink." I believe that it is more deep-seated than this. A person must have a certain kind of personality resulting from background to become addicted. No matter how they act toward others it's what bothers them on the inside.

When Gary was fourteen, Judy went off to college, and his mother got a job at a pharmacy. Now he came home from school to an empty house.

"He was not one to ever say, 'I'm lonely,' or, 'I wish somebody was around,'" said Judy. "But that's when a lot of the depression started. I think it was not good for him to be by himself so much." He started to get in trouble at school and began seeing a psychiatrist.

"He was a weird kid," one classmate remembered, "always very suspicious of everybody."

The passion that sustained teenage Gary Goodson was one that he'd inherited from his departed father: a love of automobiles. Kenny, who'd raced cars in Alaska, left behind a coral-colored 1937 Cord sedan in the garage; Gary thrillingly showed it to his friends, sometimes sliding behind the wheel and pretending to drive on make-believe adventures. When Gary was sixteen, Laura Belle bought him a beat-up 1929 two-door Model A. Perversely, he refused to allow his mother to have it fixed up.

A letter from the Ford Motor Company warned him about the state of his Model A. "If you are going to drive on the highways," the letter read, "for goodness' sake, install hydraulic brakes and don't waste a minute doing it."

"In a way it was like a passive-aggressive acting out," said Chris Peebles, a high school friend. "He left it in a beat-up state. It looked like it shouldn't even be on the road. The battery to the car was on the floor and it would slide around as he would turn. He didn't want to waste his time putting it into the floorboards like you would normally do for a Model A. He wanted to enjoy people's reactions. Once we were driving along and he pulled up to give a hitchhiker a ride and the guy declined. So, that was the image it was giving off."

Peebles also had a Model A, and the two took cross-country off-road camping trips, traveled to Yuma with a recreational club, and toured the California side of the Colorado River, including a "lost island" that had been created when the Colorado changed its course, leaving a portion of Arizona land on the California side of the river. Authorities were eager for the legal status to be settled, fearing a criminal refuge. Goodson would later fantasize about moving there. They also regularly attended the Manzanita Speedway, a dirt track where supermodified cars raced; they built their own car, which crashed after several contests.

Peebles believed that Goodson's interest in automobiles was, in a sense, a way of connecting to his absent father, and maybe even living up to a kind of imagined standard. And so was an ambition to succeed financially. "His dad was interested in financial success, striving for that end, and Gary also took that on for himself. He was initially striving to succeed by his dad's standards. Eventually, this evolved into a motivational blend of rebellion and business drive."

"He was always going to be somebody who built something from scratch," said Judy Goodson. "He wasn't going to go work for somebody else."

In the eight years between the Goodsons' arrival in Phoenix and Gary's graduation from high school, the population of the city nearly quadrupled as people swarmed from the north and even from the west to newly constructed ranch houses. The federal funding that poured into Phoenix's infrastructure—railroads, mining enterprises, dams, and waterworks—brought large corporations and growing workforces. The desert was irrigated and air-conditioned, newly green lawns were broken up by swimming pools, and shopping center–bound traffic backed up on multiplying highways. The cactus and chaparral ceded to stone and glass and the bright plastic signs of fast-food restaurants and gas stations.

"We would be driving on the freeway through Phoenix," remembered Chris Peebles, "and Gary would look at a business complex or an industrial area, and see beauty and opportunity, and think about different ways that businesses could prosper and people could prosper."

But for now, Goodson's entrepreneurial spirit found a different outlet. According to his cousin, the freedom of mobility afforded by car ownership also facilitated lucrative pursuits.

"There were several drug sources. One of them was a place down at 51st and Southern called the Salt River Inn. If you had money, and they could see you above the bar, you could drink all you wanted, and usually, you could buy either hashish or pot. And then of course, at the Roadrunner Truck Stop on the Black Canyon Highway, you could get amphetamines of sorts, uppers, downers, things like that.

"He never used drugs that would allow him to get caught *selling* drugs. He always wanted to have everything at an arm's length. In fact, you could say that about most of his life—everything was at an arm's length."

G ary Goodson began business management studies at the University of Utah in the fall of 1963, a choice that may have had less to do with academics than with topography. Salt Lake City was convenient to the Bonneville Salt Flats, the perfect locale for car racing—the jet-propelled *Spirit of America* set the 400 mph land speed record on the month that Goodson arrived at school.

Goodson was an average student—he earned an A in Public Relations, Bs in Magazine Writing and American Folklore, and a C in Mental Health—but he was, in the words of one fellow student, "more purposeful than other nineteen-year-olds." Jim Collier met Goodson in their freshman year and remembered that he talked about one day "building an automobile company like Henry Ford."

Goodson also expressed admiration for Ayn Rand—who wrote about an auto manufacturer in her novel *Atlas Shrugged*—and Howard Hughes. These were icons of rugged American individualism, not so far in their philosophies from Phoenix's celebrated Barry Goldwater. In a spirited paper defending J. P. Morgan, Goodson suggested that, had Morgan improved his labor practices, purchased a newspaper, and publicized his philanthropic acts, the bolstering of his image might have been able to keep unions at bay and, ultimately, prevent passage of the Sherman Act and the Interstate Commerce Act. "I think more of myself than I do of any state or association," Goodson wrote for a management course assignment, "and any person who doesn't deserves to be subjective to the state....If one individual has his basic rights of life, liberty, and pursuit of happiness infringed, what good is the state?"

He drove a rebuilt 1959 Studebaker with modified suspension, the back seats pulled out, and salvaged airplane seatbelt harnesses in the front. He kept a chef's knife under the seat and a sledgehammer, body-work tools and black spray paint in the trunk, always prepared to cover up any accident he might have by the time police showed up. He liked to spin around curves on the cratered roads of the Utah hills, sometimes driving in the left lane for an extra challenge, and to see how fast he could fly through an intersection. The SLC police went to bed early, so for thrills he'd have to head west, remove his license plate to bait the Nevada cops, and then beat them back over the border into Utah. After one particular near-death exploit, he stopped the car, turned to his hostage-passenger and deadpanned, "Well, I guess I just pushed my ability out one more step."

Goodson's escapades were enough to eventually earn him the attention of the state of Utah. "It is possible," read an official letter, "that you have developed some driving habits which are not in the best interest of public safety."

"In his third year in school," said George Misso, "Gary disappeared for about a month and a half. He wouldn't tell any of us what he was doing during that time. I asked him why he'd done it, and he said, 'You know, I just got tired of everything. I just wanted to get away.'" A psychiatric report in his FBI files may provide an answer: "At age 20, he saw a psychiatrist in Utah at the recommendation of the school administration and saw the psychiatrist off and on for six months."

It was about this time that Gary met Jill Anderson through someone in his English class. She was a few years older, an editor for the college literary magazine, engaged to a young man who'd gone off to Vietnam. Jill hadn't totally shaken her straitlaced Mormon upbringing, but her interests in the arts and social justice had moved her politics to the left.

Later, she'd say she felt sorry for shy, skinny Gary, a loner who holed up in his engine-parts-littered apartment. She thought he seemed distressed and sad, but she was also a little bit frightened by the guy she called "scary Gary."

One night in March of 1966, when Jill was taking codeine for strep throat, he gave her shots of whiskey and suggested they get married. "You've got to keep me drunk, or I won't do it," she insisted. With another couple they set out for a drive to Pocatello, Idaho, and signed the license.

Two weeks later, to ensure that he wouldn't be called off to Vietnam, his uncle Mel helped him enlist with the Air National Guard of Arizona.

After graduation, he spent a month in basic training at Amarillo, Texas, and then was stationed at Sky Harbor Airport in Phoenix, where he'd continue to serve a couple weekends a month. Gary and Jill moved in with his mother, briefly, and then the couple found their own place in Phoenix.

CHAPTER 9

A YEAR OUT OF COLLEGE, GARY WAS HAVING A HARD TIME REALIZING his vague ambitions of becoming a mogul. Although he'd made up stationery for a company called "Wendre Motors," the old cars he was fixing up and reselling hardly put him in the league of Howard Hughes. In fact, the Hughes Aircraft Company had recently rejected his application for employment. So Goodson booked interviews to work as anything, from social worker to substitute teacher, and took a civil service exam.

In June 1967, cruising through downtown on a borrowed motorcycle, he swerved to avoid colliding with a black Cadillac at an intersection and instead hit the curb. It sent the handlebars flying off, his shoulder into a No Parking sign, and, when he landed, his head onto the pavement. The Caddy fled, and Goodson called the police, but the officer who showed up thought the motorcycle had been stolen and briefly detained him in the back of his cruiser. His day-press slacks, Arrow cum laude shirt, and French shiner shoes were all ruined by abrasions. The next morning, though having trouble focusing his right eye, he reported to a drill meeting at the Air National Guard, where he was serving on weekends as a reservist. The dispensary nurse told him to check out.

So he began the Summer of Love bedridden, taking Darvon to relieve nausea and pain in his head, legs, and right arm, unable to report to his temp job with a typesetting company, brainstorming for ways to make his mark. There was no question for him that most of the excitement was pointing in the direction of the burgeoning counterculture. On the days he scoured the classified ads, he also read reports of the cultural upheaval that was roiling America. Amid the escalations of recreational drug use and the Vietnam War, two anti-establishment forces—the hippies and the politicos—were grabbing headlines. The New Left was largely composed of doctrinaire, clean-cut college students who'd been galvanized by the Black protest movement and comprised the largest anti-war group in the country, Students for a Democratic Society (SDS). Less organized were the increasing numbers of longhairs united by drugs and music. Recently, the groups had been attempting to cross-pollinate at "be-ins" in San Francisco and New York, "a union of love and activism previously separated by categorical dogma and label mongering."

Of course, the Summer of Love didn't really apply to conservative Arizona, where even the handful of Phoenix teen dance clubs that existed were shut down by vice squads and neighbor complaints. Local newspapers picked up rumors, published in underground publications elsewhere, that a love-in would bring twenty to fifty thousand hippies to the Grand Canyon to commune with the Hopi Indians and channel collective energy. But the DMT-smoking California hippies who came to scout ahead alienated the tribe. ("We fucked up," admitted one of the hippies with contrition. "One couple was balling in the canyon, somebody else was teaching the kids Hare Krishna chants without permission of the elders...it was just a mess.") On the appointed day of the celebration, only two dozen people showed up, and they were put under police surveillance immediately.

Shortly afterward, some enterprising students planned a happening called "The Star-Spangled Parachute Test," complete with rock bands and the requisite LSD-simulating light effects...but this time only fifteen people showed up for the experience, and the young promoters packed up their psychedelic tents. The local police turned their attention back to the new shops that had opened with names like the Liquid Giraffe and the Acid Vat, which had so vexed the residents that they'd begun to arm themselves.

The *Arizona Republic* wondered whether the brand-new Phoenix-based state narcotics squad would be protection enough in the Age of Aquarius, "with Mexico so close and the hippie generation in an experimental mood," and later ran a call for volunteer undercover agents in its pages. Goodson clipped the article.

On the running list that Goodson kept of possible pursuits, he began to make room for hipper activities: *Harvard Business School* and *motorcycle lawsuit* gave way to *underground movies* and *article on drugs*. He wrote to the filmmaker and critic Jonas Mekas in New York, asking for information about the Filmmakers' Cooperative, which provided interested cineastes with the tools necessary to make their own movies. He bought a Bolex camera. And he sent a letter to friends asking for them to record their experiences with psychoactive drugs so he could write something he called "The Heads."

But what if Goodson could find another way to bring the energy of the counterculture to the desert? He spotted an opportunity when he saw an item about the Underground Press Syndicate, a fledgling consortium of independent papers throughout the country. The aim of UPS was to pool the resources of dozens of budget-crunched publications, to share content and revenue from national advertising deals. It was through this cooperation, in fact, that news of both the promise and the demise of the Grand Canyon Love-In had so quickly spread throughout the Southwest.

It was then that Goodson read that the UPS, currently being administered by the *East Village Other*, was looking for a volunteer to coordinate everything. He created the name Thomas King Forcade and dialed the *EVO* offices.

On August 15, Walter Bowart, editor of the *East Village Other* and the temporary de facto head of UPS, received a call from Thomas King Forcade, a twenty-two-year-old journalist with advertising and photography experience. In a calm, flat voice, Forcade—or Forçade, pronounced so that it sounded almost like "façade"—announced that he and his colleagues—spread across Phoenix, San Francisco, Los Angeles, and Salt Lake City—were about to publish a national magazine called *Orpheus*, which would be a sort of *Reader's Digest* for the counterculture, and that they would be happy to work for the UPS from Phoenix.

Gary Goodson wasn't the only one making overtures about what could be done with the underperforming UPS. A week later, another *East Village Other* cofounder, Allen Katzman, was approached with a proposition.

Marshall Bloom had been president of the college-newspaper group the United States Student Press Association until he was, as he put it, "summarily fired for being too radical." So he and his colleague Raymond Mungo were starting a "Liberation News Service," providing college and underground papers with packets of original news stories. The goal, they said, was to expose Americans to "news of people and places they are denied in the established press—news of Havana, Hanoi, Peking, South Africa, university insurgency, sexual freedom, serious psychedelic research." Bloom and Mungo wanted to merge this new service with the Underground Press Syndicate, and they wanted to hammer out the details in Washington, DC, on the weekend that tens of thousands of people were marching on the Lincoln Memorial.

The march promised to bring together disparate movements more than any event before it. The organizer was the National Mobilization Committee to End the War in Vietnam—the Mobe, for short—and its cochair David Dellinger said that the march would mark a shift in the anti-war movement, from simple dissent to active resistance. But something unexpected happened after Dellinger lured the Berkeley political activist Jerry Rubin to come east and participate in the planning: Rubin quickly became enamored and entangled with the prankster strategies of Abbie Hoffman, who'd made headlines burning money at the New York Stock Exchange. Pretty soon, the march on the Lincoln Memorial was expanded to include a march on the Pentagon. And Rubin, Hoffman, and a few of their New York friends promised that they were going to *exorcise and levitate* it. "Evil spirits will pour out," Hoffman promised, "and it will start to vibrate." ("I don't want to take a chance interpreting that," SNCC chairman H. Rap Brown told a reporter when asked about the raising of the Pentagon. "I'd say it's something that people who are high might understand." Brown was disinvited after he threatened to bring a bomb.) It was not just a political but a metaphysical event, and the disseminating power of the UPS and LNS would guarantee that the underground readership all around the country knew what was going down.

"You think that only angry Mothers and bearded students march," forewarned the inaugural LNS dispatch, "and that hippies stay in Haight-Ashbury and the East Village. Look out your window on Oct. 21 and freak out at what will be marching toward the Pentagon...mutter to yourself that hippies aren't supposed to be political."

By the time "Thomas King Forcade" mailed a mock-up of *Orpheus*—colorful, produced with offset printing, and saddle-stitched—to the people at the *East Village Other*, they were surely more focused on the excitement of working with LNS and the mischievous energy that their fellow New Yorkers Hoffman and Rubin were injecting into the protest. Still, Forcade received an invitation to the meeting in Washington.

"I doubt that I will be able to attend, due to various reasons," he coyly replied. "Perhaps I can send a representative."

But in late October, it was Forcade himself who stepped off the plane in DC, wearing a lime green shirt and slacks and carrying only an airline bag as luggage. Inside the bag was a change of underwear and a two-inch stack of accountants' predictions, legal opinions, public relations presentations, and various other statistics documents outlining his plans to organize the UPS library, initiate a filing system, and open a bank account.

Forcade had been seated on the plane behind another attendee, who offered him a place to sleep at the communal Liberation News Service brownstone. Now he was instantly in the center of the action. He hung out and listened to records in the bedroom of Ray Mungo, who'd just returned from meeting with the Viet Cong in Czechoslovakia. Wandering around the basement, he found Marshall Bloom and filmmaker Shirley Clarke discussing her plans to film the band the Fugs when they arrived in town.

The next day, three hundred representatives from college and underground newspapers packed into a nearby abandoned loft. The *East Village Other* contingent included cofounders Allen Katzman and Walter Bowart, plus Bob Rudnick, who'd been acting as UPS's default coordinator. Katzman and Bowart—wearing a Native American headdress—gave speeches about battling corporate consolidation of media. But when members of the *Washington Free Press* accused the *EVO* of misappropriating UPS funds, another *EVO* cofounder, John Wilcock, who'd become estranged from the paper, turned on his former colleagues and offered to take over UPS himself.

Meanwhile, the occultist-filmmaker Kenneth Anger railed against "Trotskyite fascists" and "rich Jewish liberals" and accused Shirley Clarke, who was filming the proceedings, of working for the cops. As fistfights broke out, Bob Rudnick, already discouraged by the hippie papers' disinterest in political news—"psychedelic recipes and pot poetry" was how *Newsweek* characterized most UPS content—retired to the back of the loft and got drunk on apricot brandy.

"Our glorious scheme of joining together the campus editors, the Communists, the Trots, the hippies, the astrology freaks, the pacifists, the SDS kids, the Black militants, the Mexican-American liberation fighters, and all their respective journals was reduced to ashes," Ray Mungo later wrote. "Our conception of LNS as a 'democratic organization,' owned by those it served, was clearly ridiculous; among those it served were, in fact, many whose very lives were devoted to the principle that no organization, no institution was desirable."

John Wilcock, on the other hand, was encouraged. "I loved the Washington UPS meeting, chaotic as it was," he later wrote to Forcade. "In fact, the chaos and lack of organization and complete disorder is one of the underground press' (and YIP's) greatest strengths."

Forcade, too, was encouraged. Now he could move in and be the one to unite the papers.

After returning to Phoenix, he wrote to Marshall Bloom: "Since your organization and *Orpheus* are the only two conducting regular correspondence with underground publications, it would seem there would be room for cooperation in some areas." And, maintaining good relations with the *East Village Other*, he offered to publish Bowart's and Katzman's speeches from the Washington gathering in *Orpheus*. Forcade also mailed Bowart a brochure from the League of Arizona Cities and Towns about the procedures for incorporating a town. "The ecology is very favorable in this area to dropping out," he noted. "If you like Arizona, be my guest any time."

The only catch was that *Orpheus* still did not exactly exist.

But Forcade quickly secured permissions to reprint material by Timothy Leary, Allen Ginsberg, Michael McClure, and William Burroughs. A local Arizona State student was recruited to do the artwork, and a local printer contracted to print the magazine. But the printer blanched when it saw the profane words. It would take twenty-five attempts to find a cooperative printer, and at least one lawsuit for jobs aborted partway through.

None of which stopped Forcade from soliciting advertisers or trying to drum up publicity. "*Orpheus* is a national magazine, printing and distributing 75,000 copies, selling 60,000 with luck," read one letter.

Can your business use the attention of 60,000 hip people and their friends? *Orpheus* wears funny clothes, turns on, marches for peace, sits in at the draft board, makes love, wears flowers, does a co-op thing, plays with 16mm, seeks god, and when necessary, will shit on the Pepsi Generation and its creators, even if Pepsi is an advertiser.

By the time the first issue of *Orpheus* finally did roll off the printing press, John Wilcock had successfully wrested control of the UPS from the *East Village Other*. "The whole operation has been thoroughly fucked up," Wilcock wrote. "Katzman got very angry about these allegations, said that most UPS papers owed EVO money and as for me, he'd see me run out of 'the underground' and buried six feet deep. 'You want a fight?' he said. 'Well, you've got one and you'll lose. We'll finish you off.'"

But Katzman finally threw up his hands and turned the increasingly abstract entity of UPS over to Wilcock; *Orpheus* would handle administrative work and mailings from the "western headquarters" of Phoenix, also becoming signers on the UPS bank account. Forcade's only request, he wrote, in a letter to UPS editors: "I would prefer to have absolutely no publicity whatsoever of any type regarding my work for UPS."

His lobbying had paid off, and he seized the opportunity. A press release laid out the various challenges facing UPS papers with printing, distribution, archival access, and journalism training and answered each of them with ambitious initiatives. *Orpheus* offered to supply UPS papers with names of printers and, if no local printer could be found, "print the publication [ourselves] on a high-speed newspaper web fed offset press." Because of the "virtual impossibility of getting underground material decently distributed regionally or nationally," the Underground Press Distributing Agency was established. A UPS library would keep on file "one permanent copy of every printed, recorded, or filmed piece of underground material," available to all. *Orpheus* also offered "to place any and all college journalism students, teachers, or straight journalists into a work-study program dealing with the underground press...we will do our best to see that every student gets a chance to be clubbed by the police, be insulted by everyone, be thrown out of meetings, write a story in jail, write a story at 4 a.m., have a number, and generally make love with the underground press."

He set up an office in the house downtown that his father's mother, Grace Forcade Goodson, had lived in, and longhairs began gravitating to what he called "The Wendre House."

He gained the invaluable help of a young local activist named Virginia Norton, who did the lion's share of administrative work; Benny Alvarez, who acted as a kind of aide-de-camp; and a revolving cast of volunteers who dropped by irregularly. He bought an old school bus and painted the *Orpheus* logo on the side.

Then Forcade began the work of building mystique.

Due to the fact that we like to stay close to the people and due to the fact that our type of work requires guerilla tactics, *Orpheus* Magazine will continue to be published from our roving 1946 Chevrolet school bus. As in the past, no itinerary will be announced.

Orpheus Magazine herewith announces its intention of moving its offices to a Free Zone, located on a delta of the Colorado River, midway between California, Arizona, and Mexico. Since the status of these deltas is ambiguous, we will declare it a Free, Liberated Zone, and inhabitants will not be obliged to follow any of the irrational laws now in force in unliberated zones. The liberated zone will have no laws regarding the draft, what you can put in your body, what you can do with your genitals, what you can read and see, where you can go, what kind of economic system there will be, or what preconceptions there shall be as to how people shall live together.... We are dead serious, and we will need several thousand hardy souls to help us secure this beautiful territory on the Colorado River, the only territory in the U.S. that they're unlikely to touch, because its sovereignty is ambiguous. Whites, Blacks, Indians, everyone claim this territory now with us!

"I teased him, 'Is this what you really believe?'" said his cousin George Misso. "Down in Winterhaven, where California, Mexico, and Arizona meet, that's where he was going to set up this place. Of course, about half of the land there was Indian land, so he was going to have to figure out a way of getting the Indians to agree with this. He said, 'It's not a matter of what I believe; it's a matter of what sells.' But I think his motivation was sincere. I think he was trying to find a utopia, or at least have people envisioning a utopia, that met some of his desires but all of *their* desires. In order to have followers, he had to be a symbol of something. And he could never quite decide what symbol he was going to be."

The *Orpheus* team sent letters and brochures inviting every Black, Chicano, Puerto Rican, and foreign underground newspaper to join UPS; as de facto press agents, they lobbied mainstream magazines to write about underground papers; they compiled lists of radio stations for an Underground Broadcasting Syndicate; they coordinated with traveling rock bands to stage benefits for papers in cities along their tour itineraries.

It wasn't without challenges. Underground papers weren't noted for their correspondence skills or fiscal responsibility, and the person *Orpheus* hired to handle the Underground Press Distributing Agency turned out to be a disaster, never setting up the printing press they'd purchased, failing to pay rent on the post office box, and absconding with Forcade's Bolex camera. Forcade was a bit of a self-admitted taskmaster, given to quoting a line from *The Last Tycoon* to volunteers: "If I order a limousine, I want that kind of car. And the fastest midget racer you ever saw wouldn't do." He also maintained a strict drug policy. "We smoke dope," Forcade wrote in a letter, "but we don't stash it on the property. You would think this would be simple enough and the reasons would be obvious (Phoenix, home of Barry Goldwater). But no, not so. Some people fail to understand, which means eventually I will probably go to jail under Arizona law for maintaining a house in violation of narcotics laws, not to mention the Underground Press Library which would be confiscated as 'evidence.'"

"It wasn't a big staff," said Ken McKechnie. "It was mostly Tom and [Virginia] doing most of the work. They had one or two other people who I hardly ever saw, who like me would show up and do things for a few hours, no set schedule, maybe come back the next night, or maybe a week later. I don't know how many original articles they did, but it's a given Tom wrote them all. Everybody just showed up, put in some hours, and then left."

But work continued through the annus horribilis of 1968, through the violent jolts of the Tet Offensive, the Orangeburg massacre of civil rights protesters at the hands of state troopers, and the twin assassinations of Martin Luther King Jr. and Robert F. Kennedy.

The second issue of the magazine was laid out so that there was about a square inch in the center of each page that was without text or images. After it was printed, about a hundred copies were packed together at a time and shot through with a rifle.

THIS MAGAZINE HAS BEEN SHOT WITH A COLT .45 AUTOMATIC, the cover read. "Ugly, Isn't It?"

The American Left, meanwhile, seemed to be dividing and redividing into smaller and smaller factions. Liberation News Service, the group that

had once been intended to partner with UPS, had broken into two ideo-
logical camps, their differences exacerbated by FBI infiltrators.* After the
majority of the LNS staff voted to transform into a Marxist collective, a
minority anarchist contingent—which included founders Marshall Bloom
and Raymond Mungo—absconded with the organization's equipment
and started a breakaway news service in rural Massachusetts. The Marxists
then retaliated with a violent midnight raid on the Massachusetts farm.

At the end of August 1968, Tom Forcade came to Chicago for the ill-
fated "Festival of Life" at the behest of Abbie Hoffman and Jerry Rubin, now declaring themselves part of a "Youth International Party." The
gathering was intended as a counter to the simultaneously held Democratic National Convention. "We demand the politics of ecstasy," read the
YIP announcement. "We are the delicate spoors of the new fierceness that
will change America. We will create our own reality; we are Free America.
And we will not accept the false theatre of the Death Convention." But the
DNC protests became a bloodbath at the hands of Chicago police, and
Hoffman and Rubin—along with Tom Hayden and Rennie Davis of SDS
and David Dellinger of the Mobe—soon found themselves called before
the House Committee on Un-American Activities. Rubin attended the
hearings wearing beads, bells, and no shirt, carrying a toy machine gun
and a bandolier of live ammunition. Hoffman carried a bullwhip.

On Thanksgiving weekend, during a recess of those hearings, Rubin came to Madison, Wisconsin, for the largest underground press conference yet. John Sinclair of the weeks-old White Panther Party, whose
manifesto included lines like "we are LSD-driven total maniacs" and
"we don't have guns yet—not all of us anyway," was there too. Sinclair
brought with him the rough mixes of the just-recorded debut album by
the MC5, the only band that had played the disastrous Festival of Life
in Chicago. Now they were the White Panthers' official "high-energy
guerilla band" poised to infiltrate popular culture and destroy "millions
of minds in the process." The music was, reported Lennox Raphael of the

---

* The October 1967 Pentagon march, held the weekend of the initial LNS meeting, was
a flashpoint for FBI surveillance on anti-war activists. Hundreds of new investigations
were opened on individuals who had taken part, and the names of those arrested were
forwarded to local FBI offices in individuals' hometowns.

East Village Other, the "sound of god reaching out to grab your mind, to make you see the temper of blood & visualize the promise of change, make you take action."

The conference, held less than a month after the election of Richard Nixon to the presidency, at times resembled a contest of militancy. Liberation News Service, now represented by its Marxist faction, had increasingly been making references to "pigs" in its packets. And Newsreel, the nascent documentary collective behind such recent films as *The Columbia Revolt* and *Off the Pig*, threatened to steal the show from all of the newspapers. "We in Newsreel see ourselves as the propaganda element of the most militant factions of the movement in the country today," Robert Kramer, who'd also been arrested at the Chicago demonstrations, boasted.

But Forcade was prepared. He'd enlisted two local Phoenicians, Patrick McCune and Monson Davis, to accompany him to Madison. McCune, the older brother of one of Goodson's high school classmates, had worked for Air Force intelligence at Alaska's Northeast Cape station, intercepting radio traffic from Russian fighters flying out of Siberia. He'd returned to Phoenix and adopted a hippie lifestyle, writing for *Gambit*, an underground magazine that Davis was putting together and that Forcade had agreed to help print and distribute.

Just before they headed to the conference, McCune informed Davis that they were going to "out-radicalize the radicals." Forcade provided them with an unloaded AR-15 and old Russian field rifle.

In Madison, "we went into an apartment where Jerry Rubin was," said Davis, "as little stage monkeys carrying these guns behind Forcade. Rubin took one look, and I could see it in his face, he thought something was very wrong and didn't want anything to do with us."

For the first time, Tom Forcade didn't stay in the background. He mixed with the luminaries, sharing joints and ideas with, among others, Sinclair and Rubin, both of whom would have a profound impact on his life. And now he, too, was sounding political, talking about the dozens of newspapers around the country that were facing repression from both local and federal authorities. UPS was compiling stories about grand jury indictments for obscenity, confiscated equipment, marijuana possession arrests, shot-out car windows, firebombings, surveillance, evictions, and, increasingly, undercover infiltrations.

On the return trip, police pulled over Davis's speeding car. Let me go talk to them, Forcade said, and headed back to converse with the officers.

"This was after they'd seen the two guns," Davis said. "And they let us go. I didn't even get a ticket."

"I really suspect that he was operating for the government," Davis said. "From the position of the Underground Press Syndicate, he could basically funnel to the government all of the voices that were out at that time opposing the Vietnam war, find out which ones were coherent and therefore dangerous, and which ones could be ignored."

Back in Phoenix, Tom Forcade still had to contend with the life of Gary Goodson. Shortly before the Madison conference, he'd signed the paperwork to finalize his divorce from Jill.

The Goodson family would later remember Jill as simply more conventional than Gary and say that he wanted the divorce, although they did remember her complaining about his "difficult" mood shifts.

But Jill, a student of mythology, thought of Gary as a coyote, in the Navajo sense—a trickster, making chaos out of order. He was like a solo shapeshifter, creating the illusion of an Orpheus community, worried that drugs would affect his own mental state but using them as a cover for his outbursts, watching other people take them and seeing where they were vulnerable.

Jill had come up with the name *Orpheus* in the first place, as an inside joke to herself, because she'd seen herself as Eurydice, and Gary Goodson as her captor Hades. By the end of 1968, she was freed.

In early 1969, the *Orpheus* bus returned from a trip to Los Angeles—where once again a printer turned them down—to find the window of their office forced open. Forcade's house had a broken window and had been ransacked. Around that time, Pat McCune and Monson Davis were arrested and jailed on drug charges.

"Events have always been a little weird here at UPS-Phoenix," Forcade wrote to Liberation News Service, "but instead of becoming paranoid, we have always laughed off things like the guy across the street who watches our office with binoculars and the paperboy with a walkie talkie, and the world's strangest telephone. Now, however, we don't know whether to laugh or split town." On top of that, the US Postal Service had refused to grant a third-class mail permit to UPS for its newsletter. "The Post Office," Forcade concluded, "is an active arm of the pig establishment."

Privately, though, Forcade was less brash. In a letter to a woman he'd met in Madison, he expressed ambivalence about the White Panthers' militant pose. "Even I am beginning to get a little bit intimidated, but I don't suppose I will pick up a gun unless they push me personally into it. So much shit is coming down, I can hardly blame people who do, but I really do not think that violence is the answer or that violence can produce peace.... I think we must live peace in order to have peace when we get in power...if you don't, well, what's the point of a revolution?"

> I think perhaps we could use some militancy now, some real commitment even more. A bunch of jerk-offs wearing berets and intimidating people who are trying to mind their own business is not where it's at, but some real commitment would be nice, and I truly appreciate people like Jerry Rubin and many more who stood up for me. My own thing is organizing, though, and I am too quiet and introverted to be a revolutionary (yet) or a Yippie, although we have a lot of fun and are not afraid of anyone, except the police, of whom I am terrified. And I must admit, I, too, have carried a gun for self-defense, once for about a year, and for a while in late '68 I carried an M16 machine gun in my car at all times. But you are almost the only person who knows that; it was not a part of my "image." It was just that the police were really worrying me.

On the next bus trip, the UPS reported, "we were stopped and searched 6 times, and taken to jail in Grants, N.M., despite our disguise as a traveling church group, hymn singing, six people quoting copiously from the Bible, and Rev. Tom Forcade with ten Bibles in his clerical garb. They hate crazies on Route 66. Be looking for a green and yellow bus with 'Jesus Saves' on the side."

Soon afterward, Gary Goodson borrowed his cousin George Misso's Chevy Nova and took a driving test to obtain a second license, this one issued under the name of Thomas King Forcade. "He was very convincing when he took his 'first drive,'" his cousin recalled. But three days before it was issued, according to FBI records, "Detective ___, Intelligence

Unit, Phoenix, Arizona, Police Department, advised that THOMAS KING FORCADE is an alias used by GARY KENNETH GOODSON."

"I worried about Gary because he wasn't worried about any of the things that you should be worried about," said Misso. "He thought absolutely nothing of getting a phony driver's license, making a phony birth certificate, signing up for social security. I always attributed it to the fact that he was so damn smart. He was truly the smartest person I ever knew.

"But when the Tate–LaBianca murders were here in California, one of the first things I thought was, 'Oh, my God, I hope Tom isn't going to go off the deep end like that.'"

It was the week after those murders, in fact—the weekend of the Woodstock festival—that Gary Goodson appeared in the office of a Phoenix doctor and underwent a psychological exam.

GOODSON, Airman Gary

This 23-year-old single Caucasian male was examined on this date at the request of _____ who is a reserve officer with the National Guard. Mr. Goodson is currently on active duty with the Air National Guard of Arizona. He has been noted to sit on the floor of a restroom with a bayonet pointed at his abdomen and then claim that he was cleaning his nails with the bayonet and he also has been noted to be carrying some sash cord in his pocket as well as other bizarre behavior which called him to the attention of the guard and _____.

Mental status examination reveals a slender young man of about five feet six inches who is overtly paranoid. He is well oriented as to place, month and year but does not know the day (Tuesday or Wednesday) nor the exact date (August 11 or 12). Marked difficulty in concentrating is noted as well as loosening of associations (constantly feels that people are staring at him, talking about him and trying to mess him up; this occurs both at work and in the guard). Mr. Goodson is of estimated bright normal intelligence. Affect is flat and inappropriate. He laughs at very inappropriate moments during the interview. Lately he has felt stared at and does not know why. He guessed that he just looks different. He feels that someone is following him and he feels that he has enemies. People want to hurt him because they are jealous and they are "uptight." He feels that people talk about him all the time and that a lot of people think that he is wrong or an evil person.

He denies hallucinations either auditory or visual but says "that it does not make any difference." He feels that people in his business are trying to manipulate him. Unreality to him is half his life. Half the time he feels that things cannot be real. Insight is totally lacking and judgment is markedly impaired. . . .

Brief background history reveals that Mr. Goodson's father allegedly died at age 42, twelve years ago in an automobile accident and the patient was not there at the time. His mother is 50 years of age and lives in Phoenix, Arizona. She is described as "weird" (laughs inappropriately just as the patient does). He says that she is obsessive about everything. . . .

Mr. Goodson allegedly graduated from the University of Utah with a degree in business administration. He joined the Air Force in April 1966 because he thought it would be the easiest service. His basic training was at Amarillo, Texas for one month and then he has been stationed at Phoenix, Sky Harbor Airport since that time. He allegedly lives in his own home and signed up for six years. He had no idea why he was brought here for a Psychiatric examination. Mr. Goodson states he first saw a psychiatrist at age 15 in Phoenix. At that time the school recommended treatment and he continued to see the Psychiatrist until he graduated from high school. He allegedly received no medication. At age 20 he saw a Psychiatrist in Utah at the recommendation of the school administration and saw the Psychiatrist off and on for six months. He terminated treatment after he graduated. Nine months ago he saw a psychiatrist in Phoenix and also saw another psychiatrist in Phoenix. He states that he got a divorce and his wife insisted that he see a psychiatrist. Mr. Goodson allegedly runs a publishing house here in Phoenix and states that "other people have taken over and I am just a figurehead. I have been coasting on my reputation."

He states that his appetite has been poor for a couple of years and that he has put on 100 pounds in the past week. Mr. Goodson's current thoughts are that everybody is out to get him and has been out to get him for the past 18 months. He feels that he was nice to people and they have been stabbing him in the back for the past 18 months because they are sick, really sick.

He states that he has a lot of business transactions and too many people are depending on him at the present time for him to be going into the hospital.

Finally, Mr. Goodson has been arrested in New York on an LSD charge and is awaiting the outcome of that charge. He feels too that the police in New York have been hassling him for some time and that they were out to get him.. . .

Diagnosis: Schizophrenia, Paranoid Type.

Recommendations:

In my opinion Mr. Goodson is not fit for active duty at this time and He should be sent to the Maricopa County Hospital to be observed to see whether or not commitment to the State is in order.

_____ has been informed of my opinion that _____ should be in the Maricopa County Hospital for observation and possible commitment to the State Hospital and I believe she will contact the Mental Health Bureau in order to see that the proper steps are taken.. . .

Gary Goodson's time in the Air National Guard came to an end.

A few weeks later, officers from the Pima County Sheriff's Department knocked on Laura Belle Goodson's door and asked to speak to Gary, who she told them no longer lived there.

The police explained that a dog had carried a human arm to a residence in nearby Pinal County, and deputies had located the body of a bearded man in his twenties in a nearby shack. He was carrying Gary Goodson's ID. She knew it wasn't him—the body was estimated to have been dead for months, and she'd seen her son a few days earlier.

After the police left, Laura Belle called Gary. He told her that he believed it was a hitchhiker he'd picked up while driving from New York; he'd let the passenger out in downtown Phoenix, he said, and he must have stolen the ID. He called the police.

"They sent two detectives out to talk to him," Laura Belle recalled years later. "Nice fellas. But no one knew who the kid was."

Three months later, in November 1969, Tom Forcade moved to New York City.

HARVEST,
1972–1974

CHAPTER 10

FOLLOWING THE MIAMI CONVENTIONS, TOM FORCADE AND CINDY Ornsteen had stayed in a farmhouse with Tim Hughes and Rick Namey and Namey's girlfriend in Sanford, Florida, north of Orlando, living off neighboring tomato gardens and cornfields and occasional trips to the A&W Drive-In, watching the Munich Olympics on TV. The Zippies might have seemed well-heeled in Miami, but Forcade was now truly broke. Cindy suggested they write a book about Miami; Tom was intent on producing an album. To scrape together a couple grand for the *Eat the Rich* record—which included such new originals as "Bozo Rebozo," "Starving on the Land," and "Celebration of Death"—he sold some of his precious electronic equipment and gave Namey some items he'd acquired from his old UPS pal Michael Forman: a Smith and Wesson .38-caliber revolver with short barrel, two boxes of ammunition, and a tan leather shoulder holster.

Despite their relative poverty, Cindy later said their stretch underground was the best time she and Tom had together. "The more animosity there was against him," she said, "the stronger he got. He was in a very good mood all summer."

A "good mood," however, was a subjective term. Tom still felt jilted by Gabrielle, and he and Hughes spent some time contemplating various revenge plots against her, such as administering her LSD and putting her in a hall of mirrors.

And Forcade fell into a depression as the grand larceny trial for the Lyndon B. Johnson portrait loomed. He informed Cindy that he was going to act insane in the courtroom; instead, he stayed in bed and did nitrous for three days while Cindy took care of pretrial motions.

Forcade returned to New York in October and immediately made a lasting contribution to Richard Nixon's legacy. Literary agent David Obst, who'd been struggling to sell a book called *All the President's Men*, visited A. J. Weberman's apartment to examine items Weberman had obtained from Henry Kissinger's garbage. Forcade spiked Obst's drink with acid, which was still kicking in the next morning as Obst was meeting with Woodward, Bernstein, and Dick Snyder of Simon & Schuster. That day's *Washington Post* carried a blundered story by Woodward and Bernstein that the White House had attacked, and Snyder passed on *All the President's Men*—until a tripping Obst began weeping. "I've never seen anyone care so much about a book," Snyder said. "I'll buy it." The presidential cosmos must have aligned for Forcade, because on that very same day, the grand larceny charges were dropped.

Forcade was writing a book, too. He started working with Rex Weiner on an outrageous comic novel called *Visions of Hitler*. The news was filled with rumors and sightings of Nazi leaders in South America, and so Forcade and Weiner figured they could sell a story about the Fuhrer reemerging from the rain forests of Brazil and joining forces with a nineteen-year-old rock-band groupie named Sunshine.

"Adolf Hitler was a super-villain whose vast deeds were so horrifying that the world is still fascinated," their proposal read. "This book is a surreal fantasy in the best tradition of black humor, creating a bizarre juxtaposition of history's evilest monster grown older and wiser, with today's pop counterculture."

The writing was in the sleazy, if erudite, tradition of 1960s men's magazines, shot through with black humor and inside jokes for counterculture readers:

> "I want to know," said Hitler patiently, "what organizations you are with."
>
> "Oh, I belong to a lot of organizations. Let's see, the Peace and Freedom Party, the Venice Ecology Project, SDS—I was balling Mark Rudd, the Yippies, Zippies, Scientology—but only for a little while; let's see, I was secretary of the Dave Clark Five Fan Club, ummmm, I was in Fair Play for Cuba Committee, the Rainbow People's Party, the Neo-American Church—I balled Art Kleps, he's the Chief Boo Hoo, the Lilith Grotto of the Church of Satan, Then there's..."
>
> She ticked off a few more on her fingers.
>
> "Enough!" Hitler cried. "I have heard of none of these organizations!"

One day while the young novelists were passing a bowl of hashish back and forth at the UPS loft, Forcade produced a newspaper item announcing a "Special Moon Shot Cruise."

The SS *Statendam* would be carrying such notables as Norman Mailer and science-fiction authors Arthur C. Clarke and Isaac Asimov down to Cape Kennedy to witness the last of the scheduled Apollo missions to the moon. There'd be seminars by geophysicists, astronomers, anthropologists, and biochemists. Even Wernher von Braun, the V-2 rocket designer who the United States had recruited from Nazi Germany's aerospace program and who cameoed in *Visions of Hitler*, was scheduled to appear. Cabin rentals started at $750.

"They've shut out the underground press again," Forcade pronounced, brooding. "We're going to have to do something about it."

As they continued puffing, Forcade laid out his theory that the elites were preparing to leave behind the hoi polloi, that the Apollo cruise and seminars were just the visible layer of a more insidious plot for the rich to abandon mothership Earth for interstellar colonies. "Mailer is either in on the scam or they've suckered him into it," Forcade declared. "We have got to get on board that ship, find out what these motherfuckers are up to, blow their cover, and rescue Mailer before it's too late."

On the day the *Statendam* set sail, they packed an ounce of marijuana and some clothes, donned black leather jackets, and—along with Cindy and writer Deanne Stillman, and Cindy's cousin Blair Sabol, who was covering the event for the *Village Voice*—sauntered onto the boat at Pier 40 on the Hudson River. After trying a series of doors, they managed to find an unlocked and unoccupied stateroom cabin, right next to the captain's quarters, with a starboard view, a wet bar, and keys sitting on the dresser. After a bon voyage toast—Wild Turkey, champagne, and Twinkies and Cheetos for Forcade—Cindy and Deanne returned to shore, and the stowaways were off.

It wasn't hard to blend in with the other passengers, Forcade wrote. "All we had to do was carry around cocktail glasses all the time. There was plenty of room, too, since the ship was less than half full." Even when word got out that there were two uninvited guests, it became a kind of open secret that excited and intrigued the shipmates. Forcade and Weiner caroused with Katherine Anne Porter, the eighty-two-year-old author of the novel *Ship of Fools* who was writing a piece for *Playboy*, and with a group of Canadians who told them they were filming a documentary called *Starfuck*. At one gathering they asked science-fiction writer Robert Heinlein about his old friend L. Ron Hubbard, the founder of the Church of Scientology. No dice, Heinlein said. A few moments later, though, amid bawdy bantering between the sci-fi writers and their wives, Heinlein turned to Asimov and said, "Why don't we start a church of our own—a Church of the Heterosexual? If Ron can do it, we can!"

Forcade was intrigued by the various lectures, about the benefits of extracting resources from colonized planets and plans for a space shuttle program, but still worried that a plot by the "techno-elite" was afoot. "The fact that the ship was filled with those wealthy enough to pay the fare raised the chilling possibility that the rich were planning to split the planet and leave us with their mess," he wrote. "It didn't help any when they promulgated a list of ecological rules for the next planet we occupy, but made no mention of applying those rules to this ruined planet."

Mailer's fiery speech, positing that NASA should be conducting experiments on ESP, levitation, and magic, was the exception. "We are trying to become gods," he ranted. "If that is our deepest desire, then we also have to recognize that we may also be evil!"

"I *am* evil," Forcade groaned to himself, but he was soon applauding the contrarian novelist.

At an onboard screening of *2001: A Space Odyssey*, Forcade and Weiner shared their stash, passing joints to the tweedy Hugh Downs, who'd just left the grind of the *Today* show...and Norman Mailer himself. "We gotta talk to you, man," Forcade informed Mailer when the lights went up, but the novelist skedaddled before they were able to corner him into discussion of conspiratorial goings-on.

Forcade fell into a dark mood after that—the darkest Weiner had ever seen.

"I confronted him finally—what's up with you, man? Tom confessed what few people knew at the time, the sort of confession that fellow travelers tend to share aboard sea cruises: he was a clinically diagnosed manic-depressive. He said a doctor had recently prescribed medication to control his wild ups and downs....Now here we were in the middle of the ocean and Tom was on a downswing. Worse, he'd forgotten to take his pills along. His prescription pills, that is. He had a whole pocketful of other pills: Quaaludes, Valium, Vicodin, Codeine, Dexedrine, Dexamyl, some orange barrel LSD, a whole gamut of uppers and downers, and he was popping them like jellybeans."

On the night of the Apollo launch, they again got stoned with Mailer, Downs, and Porter. As the rocket rose from flames in the distance, and the ocean liner shook from distant vibrations, the passengers oohed and ahhhed.

"Incomparably beautiful," gushed Robert Heinlein.

"When I saw them take off, I wanted with all my soul to be going with them," said Porter.

Blair Sabol found Forcade downstairs afterward, in a green vinyl booth of a restaurant. "I dunno," he told her. "I found the whole thing a stone drag. I felt like I had seen it on television and better. I mean it was better than the Rolling Stones but...so what?"

The following day, Forcade went missing, until Weiner found him leaning over the stern railing. "If I jumped overboard now," he asked, "how long do you think I'd last in the water?" After Weiner locked him in their room, Forcade passed out on quaaludes.

Further exacerbating the situation was a *New York Times* piece that was filed while they were still on board, and which named the two stowaways.

> The two young men, who said they thought they deserved a vacation after the rigors of fomenting demonstrations at the political conventions in Miami Beach, set themselves up in a comfortable cabin, which they vacated early each morning after making the berths and tidying up.
>
> They spent their days sunning themselves, accepting drinks from the many passengers who were in on their secret, and hinting broadly that they had some really spectacular deviltry up their sleeves.
>
> "We were thinking about opening the seacocks," said Mr. Forcade, "when we realized that we didn't have any seats in the lifeboats."

It was one thing for the writers and scientists to know of their fugitive status, another for the Holland America cruise line crew to learn that it was being cheated publicly out of expensive fares. Katherine Anne Porter hid the two in her cabin for a spell. Forcade was by now practically catatonic, clenching his fists and grinding his jaw. "I had to drag him around the ship and stuff him in rope lockers to keep him from being discovered," Weiner recalled.

They bolted as soon as the boat docked at St. Thomas, but not before finally cornering Mailer.

"There's a conspiracy," Forcade managed. "You have to be careful, you dig?"

"I know," Mailer responded with conviction and compassion. "I know. You be careful, too."

In January 1973 the Watergate burglars' criminal trial finally commenced. They stonewalled a district court, pleading guilty but offering little information. Their cover story—that they'd been gathering information to prevent leftist extremists from making violent attacks at the Republican convention—raised suspicions, and Senate Democrats prepared to begin their own investigation.

The head of the Justice Department's Internal Security Division alerted the FBI director that the ISD planned to show "nefarious plans by Zippie leaders" to commit violence at the Republican convention. The Justice Department had since obtained the candles and gasoline that Miami Dade police had seized from Forcade's truck in August; Acting FBI Director L. Patrick Gray III wrote to the bureau's Miami office multiple times, urging that any leads be "vigorously pursued in an effort to establish any violation of Federal firearms statutes on [Forcade's] part." The candles and gasoline that were earlier classified as "cans containing a wax-like material with a match-type item sticking out" and "inflammable liquid" were now, according to the FBI, "illegally manufactured and unregistered destructive devices."

On February 8, 1973, a grand jury in Miami delivered a sealed indictment of Forcade and Cindy, for violating the National Firearms Act.

The FBI visited Cindy's parents and had a talk with the building superintendent of the Underground Press Syndicate offices on West 10th Street. They were ready to make their move.

On February 9, White House Chief of Staff H. R. Haldeman recorded a meeting with President Nixon in his diary: "He got into Watergate strategy. He wants to get our people to put out that foreign or Communist money came in in support of the demonstrations in the campaign, tie all the '72 demonstrations to McGovern and thus the Democrats as part of the peace movement. Broaden the investigation to include the peace movement and its leaders."

The following afternoon, six FBI agents trailed Cindy Ornsteen's purple Camaro through Greenwich Village traffic and, police radios crackling, filed behind her and Tom into the basement of 204 West 10th Street.

"Thomas Forcade?"

"He's not here," said Forcade.

They consulted with their copies of the mug shots before leading Forcade and Ornsteen out to the street in handcuffs.

"If I'd known that you had a warrant for my arrest, I wouldn't have been taken alive," Forcade told the agent taking him to the car. He vowed that members of the Weather Underground, of which he said he was a member, would rescue him.

By evening, Forcade was sitting in a federal detention center downtown, and Cindy was in Riker's Island.

YIPPIES ARRESTED IN FIRE BOMB CASE, read the next day's *New York Times* headline. Bail was set at $50,000. They were facing up to twenty years each.

The high bail meant they each had to get their parents to post property bonds. Tom's mother did that from Phoenix; Cindy's parents traveled to the New York court from their Main Line home.

Three days later, the pair appeared before a federal magistrate in Miami and entered pleas of not guilty.

Cindy asked attorney Helene Schwartz, who'd witnessed the Miami tear-gassing firsthand, to represent her at the trial—but first, she said, "You have to tell me when your birthday is." Cindy still believed in the stars, even though her astrologer had told her she'd be safe if she stayed with Tom (Uranus rising), and here she was charged with a felony.

Schwartz was a Scorpio on the cusp of Libra. Cindy told her she'd have to check with her astrologer before hiring her. The astrologer gave approval, but then Cindy learned that Mercury was going to be in retrograde for the opening day of the trial.

"What does that mean?" Schwartz asked.

"It's terrible. It means we're going to lose. I might as well bring my toothbrush to the courtroom, all prepared to go to jail. You've got to ask the judge for an adjournment. The trial can't start that day."

The stars aligned: an issue with witness availability pushed the trial back, and a Mercury-in-retrograde trial was avoided.

The day after she got back from Miami, Cindy was driving with a UPS colleague when a police car's flashing lights popped up behind her. She guided her Camaro to the side of the street and handed over her driver's license. When the officer ran the number, the reply over the radio was urgent: these were armed and dangerous criminals.

Four more cars rushed to the scene and out flooded more police, .38s and shotguns drawn, ordering the two out of the car. They were frisked and handcuffed.

"But I've already been arrested in this charge," she told them at the precinct house.

"Maybe you have. Maybe this is all a mistake."

Then the FBI showed up and, because she wasn't in the custody of her parents, threatened to charge her with Unlawful Flight to Avoid Prosecution.

By the time it was straightened out, her purple Camaro had been impounded.

As the threat of a twenty-year prison sentence loomed, it became clear to Forcade that the movement itself was also fading.

A mellowed John Sinclair was managing rock bands and working for the Michigan Marijuana Initiative. "We never until very recently even had a policy of having somethin' to say that made sense to straight people," he said. "We'd just try to freak people out, especially the press—just say crazy stuff, you know, just put people on . . . it didn't make any difference." Now more pragmatic, he had endorsed McGovern and gotten involved in local city council elections.

"As the sun sets for good on America's empire, it also sets on the once vaunted American counterculture," Forcade wrote in a guest column for the *International Times*. "All our old heroes are dead in America. Antiwar minstrel Bob Dylan turns out to be a millionaire with investments in war stocks and New York office buildings." He noted that the Black Panthers' Eldridge Cleaver and Huey Newton had, respectively, left the country and returned to college. Acid advocate Timothy Leary and acid chemist Stanley Owsley were in jail, Abbie Hoffman was in hiding, and Weather was underground.

"Understandably, people in America are confused. Nixon calls for law and order. Abbie Hoffman and Jerry Rubin tried to stop the Third Annual July 4th Smoke-In, while a government commission calls for legalizing grass.

"Nothing is real. Reality is staged according to scripts. Nobody trusts anybody," Forcade concluded. "Paranoia is in fashion. Everybody seems to be a part of some conspiracy, and everybody's afraid they're being manipulated, and they're probably right."

At the United States District Court for the Southern District of Florida, the Forcade-Ornsteen trial opened with Miami patrolmen testifying that they'd stopped the Zippie truck for driving on the wrong side of the road. They opened the cab doors and saw four cans on the floor of the truck. Two of the cans, they testified, "contained heads of matches embedded in a hard substance," so they'd called the bomb squad. Jerry Rudoff—the Miami Dade officer formerly in undercover guise as Salt, the Vietnam veteran—testified, too.

"They were trying to describe various things that happened to cops as a result of Zippies attacking them," Forcade said. "They described the people on the truck as having two by fours with four-inch nails sticking out of them."

The prosecution, he complained, painted the Zippies as "some Mansonesque love/death violence cult. That wasn't what was going on at all. We were people doing revolutionary dada actions, more accurately. We were ten years ahead of our time. That's not my fault."

On the second day, the Department of Justice lawyer called bomb and chemistry experts who confirmed that the items were potassium nitrate.

But the last witness for the prosecution, the chief of the FBI's laboratory explosives unit in Washington, offered some nuance. "It's an incendiary device," he testified, "but it's not a bomb."

The defense exchanged looks of disbelief.

Tom and Cindy's lawyers immediately moved to dismiss.

"Their own witness testified that it wasn't a bomb!"

The judge, a Nixon appointee, denied their motions.

"If we reach the point that you can get indicted for possession of a candle," Schwartz cried, "all the housewives in Florida better beware!"

That line made it into the papers, but the judge still refused.

The prosecution rested its case.

On the third day, Cindy, Tom, and the Gooks' equipment manager all testified that they'd never seen the potassium nitrate device before.

On cross-examination, the prosecution tried to play up the idea of Zippies as a cult.

"Is she your girlfriend?" the prosecutor asked Forcade, indicating Cindy.

"It depends on how you define girlfriend," he replied. "Define girl-friend for me and I'll be glad to answer."

"Did you introduce her as your wife?"

"No, I have never introduced her as my wife."

"Have you ever introduced her as your girlfriend?"

"I may have. I don't recall ever doing so."

"During the time that you were down here in July and August of 1972, were you and Cindy together all the time?"

"No."

"Were you living together?"

"Objection!" shouted Schwartz.

"Objection sustained."

"Does Cindy more or less follow you around?" the prosecutor asked.

"Good heavens," Schwartz objected. "She is not a sheep!"

After that, when talking to her lawyer, Cindy always referred to her-self as "your client, the sheep."

Then the defense called a criminologist to testify that no, none of the items qualified as bombs. The defense rested its case.

The jury was sent out, and the lawyers approached the bench to dis-cuss jury instructions.

But when the court reconvened, the judge at last granted the defense's motion to dismiss, ruling that the federal firearms statute under which Forcade and Ornsteen were charged was not intended to cover the two cans and candle: "not, by definition in the federal statute, firebombs, gre-nades, or missiles of any kind."

Despite seven months of behind-the-scenes coordination by the gov-ernment, the case never even made it to the jury. The US attorney filed for appeal, in hopes of taking the case to the Fifth Circuit Court in New Orleans, but in May the solicitor general advised that it would not continue to pursue charges. Still, the New York FBI office advised investigating the shotgun that had been seized from the Coconut Grove house, the one Pat Small had hidden in the garage. The United States wasn't done with Tom Forcade yet.

The dismissal of the trial hadn't done much to quell Forcade's concerns about state surveillance or the role of political corruption within law enforcement. "It's been suggested," he said afterward, "that bringing down our indictment in a hastily strung-together Grand Jury after the Watergate people were found guilty but before they were sentenced—then rushing us to trial before they were still yet sentenced—was an attempt to justify lighter sentences for them. It could be."

> I would like to say one thing for the record. Very clearly, they're beginning with anti-hijack laws and they're talking about anti-terrorist laws worldwide, supposedly in response to the thing that happened in Tel Aviv or in Munich at the Olympics and they're beginning to push that line more and more in the media. It's being pushed by the government and by established interest. It seems to me that three superpowers want to lock things up so that there will be no more freelance violence, it'll all be done by the government.

> What I'm saying is that in the past, there were three superpowers, and you, if you were an oppressed people in, say Cuba, you could play one off against the other and obtain some freedom for yourself. But what they are talking about now is that they'll just freeze everyone who's in power in every country in the world now will remain in power, and any kind of violence to attempt to overthrow any government will be strongly opposed. And there will be no going to Algeria, there will be no sanctuary in Cambodia, there'll be no sanctuary anywhere. There will be total cooperation in terms of maintaining the status quo between China, Russia and the US. I think that's going to be the issue of the 70s and 80s—worldwide 1984. You can't have a 1984 unless it's worldwide, because once you can play them off against one another, or split to a country where there is no totalitarianism, it won't

work. It's gotta be worldwide. That seems to be the linkup they're establishing now, right down to the point where if you don't pay your electric bill in Mohawk, NY, you can't get electricity in Leningrad without paying your bill back in Mohawk.

I'm against all of this control politics. It gets in the way of everybody having a good time, which is my goal.

I really think that that's what YIP should be dealing with, the encroaching 1984. It's the thing that people are afraid of and the thing we should be fighting the hardest. It's the most evil, because once it gets established there aren't going to be any changes of any type.

Mind-freedom is like the last defense, the final barrier.

By the time the televised Senate Watergate hearings began, the lines between campaign dirty tricks and national security abuses had gotten so blurry that governmental and journalistic investigations delved into both. Shortly after Richard Kleindienst resigned as attorney general, the Associated Press reported that FBI agents and informers had infiltrated the leadership of "most groups" demonstrating in Miami and taken part in the planning of the demonstrations, and that Kleindienst had shared the intelligence in several meetings with his old friend Robert Mardian, who was working for the Nixon reelection campaign.

The *Miami Herald*, speaking with government sources, learned that the Zippies had been especially prone to government infiltration. Forcade gamely conceded that they'd set out to embarrass the Democratic Party, and that every organization in Miami had its share of spies, but he insisted that government agents "had not infiltrated the Zippies on the decision-making level." And anyway, Forcade said, the Zippies' ultimate purpose had been simply "to advance the cause of international surrealism."

Senate investigators and journalists soon learned that not only had the 1970 Hoover-vetoed plan for domestic spying and burglaries been secretly implemented but also the operation had passed its intelligence to the Nixon reelection campaign committee. They also discovered that Watergate conspirators had tried to organize a group of fake "hippies" to disrupt McGovern campaign headquarters at the Democratic National Convention.

A *Newsweek* bombshell feature entitled "What the Secret Police Did" reported that "illicit methods—including burglary and unauthorized wiretaps—were widely used to try to stop sensitive leaks, to monitor the domestic left and gather information for the prosecution of cases against radicals. The investigators have been told specifically that burglaries were committed in connection with the Seattle Seven, Chicago Weatherpeople, Detroit Thirteen and Berrigan cases." Judge Keith demanded that the FBI disclose its taps on the Weather Underground before the trial could proceed. Instead, the government chose to drop all charges. After three years, the case was dismissed.

And Guy Goodwin, the zealous prosecutor for the Department of Internal Security who'd prepared the case, got some other unwanted attention: *New York Times* muckraker Seymour Hersh reported that he had, in violation of DOJ regulations, repeatedly met directly with an undercover Weatherman informant and subsequently lied about it.

The *Times* report was the first time that the establishment press identified the Weatherman informant, Larry Grathwohl. The *Berkeley Tribe* had outed him nearly three years earlier.

But the *Berkeley Tribe* had folded in the meantime, and so had many of its UPS sister papers. In 1973, a flurry of articles began to speak of the underground press in the past tense. The factionalism of the past few years had taken their toll, as had the end of the unifying issue of the Vietnam War.

"The vitality of the alternative press was directly proportional to the health of the radical movement in general," concluded a *Washington Post* article. "The underground papers could not transcend the depoliticization of the generation that they served and now face extinction."

The establishment media that had been so hostile to the scrappy upstarts put on a serious face and lamented the passing of *The Rag*, San Francisco's *Good Times*, the *Chicago Seed*, *Quicksilver Times*, *The Rat*, the *East Village Other*, *New York Ace*, *Kaleidoscope*—all of them dropping like flies.

Forcade covered the second annual A. J. Liebling Counter-Convention in June, where a year earlier Rubin and Hoffman had surprised him with their McGovern endorsement. He marveled at how, in the year since the Watergate break-in, the media had started to resemble the former underground. The reporters "looked like cleaned-up hippies and, had a vote been taken, it probably would have gone 90 percent to impeach Nixon," he surmised. "Journalists realize they're Johnny's-come-lately, and it's resulted in a growing respect for the Levi-clad counterparts in the underground press."

"The underground papers are beginning to assimilate some journalistic principles like objectivity and good writing," he told a reporter. "And the straight papers have been picking up issues and attitudes from the underground."

Even an establishment superstar like Bob Woodward of the *Washington Post* would agree. "The underground press was largely right about governmental sabotage," he told a Berkeley audience at the height of the Watergate scandal, "but the country didn't get upset because it was the Left that was being sabotaged. The country got upset when it was the broad center, with its political institutions, that was attacked."

When representatives of forty-five independent papers gathered for their annual conference in Colorado that summer, they moved to change the name from the Underground Press Syndicate. Calling it the Alternative Press Syndicate was, in part, a reflection of the rise of newer, more professional, and locally focused weeklies like the *San Francisco Bay Guardian* and Boston's *Real Paper*, which maintained an interest in investigative reporting even in the absence of a unified movement. "It's still a leftist political medium, but it's flourishing in a new way," Forcade proclaimed. "Underground papers are becoming more oriented to serving the community rather than some abstract political goal. A lot of papers died because they became so dogmatic and predictable they boxed themselves in."

Only a few years earlier, editors patrolled the perimeter of such gatherings with loaded guns, relayed the cracked codes of police radio calls with walkie-talkies. Now they met to plot for fiscal survival, wondering if they should make public stock sale offerings or try to attract rich benefactors. The *Berkeley Barb* called the two-day conference "the final plunge in the long dive from political flamboyance to economic stability."

The weekend kicked off with entertainment from a western swing band and a weed-and-wine tasting. The politics on display were now more theoretical than desperate. They screened the Zapruder film, and Carl Oglesby, who'd been a president of SDS in the 1960s, delivered a speech about his "Yankee and Cowboy War" theory, which linked the Kennedy assassination and Watergate. Art Kunkin of the *Los Angeles Free Press* discussed Robert Kennedy assassination theories. An Attica riot survivor discussed prison reform, and a Wounded Knee fugitive made a stealthy cameo.

There was even a brief appearance by an emissary from the Divine Light Mission, which followed the fifteen-year-old "Perfect Master," Guru Maharaj Ji—and, to the consternation of movement friends, now included Rennie Davis in its ranks. When the Divine Light representative complained that spirituality was lacking in the movement, Forcade responded, "I haven't seen so much energy to fuse politics and the spiritual movement since right before the 1967 march on Washington, when we planned to levitate the Pentagon."

And then, in a prescient moment, Forcade told the assembled editors, "You're going to have to identify some sort of base that the straight press can't co-opt. Either sex, drugs, or politics."

Forcade would choose drugs. "The 'movement' was over," he later explained, "and I needed something to keep from killing myself out of boredom."

CHAPTER 11

THE FIRST TIME RONNIE VOLVOX* OF THE ALTERNATIVE PRESS SYNDI-cate realized that Forcade was involved in the marijuana trade was immediately following the 1973 Boulder conference, which they'd attended together. Volvox stopped in California for a few days, and when he returned to New York, he got a call from Mexico.

"Tom had crashed an airplane and had been in jail. I think he'd bought his way out at that point. I don't know whether he was calling to tell us he was okay, or to tell us where he was in case he *wasn't* okay. He came back in a week or so and...this was not a guy you could ask anything, so if you knew anything about Tom it was because you saw it, or he told you. He never said a word more about what happened in Mexico."

Ed Dwyer, who'd worked with Cindy Ornsteen and Michael Forman at Concert Hall in Philadelphia, was now in New York, working as an

---

* A pseudonym.

editor at magazines like *Coronet*. He got a phone call one night out of the blue from Tom, who was worried for some reason that the APS office was about to be raided. Would it be okay if he stored some things at Ed's apartment? Tom and Cindy showed up in true Bonnie-and-Clyde fashion: she was wearing hot pants; he was carrying a gym bag with a sawed-off shotgun and a revolver in a suitcase. Dwyer stuffed the items in his closet, where they'd stay untouched for months.

The year before, Forcade had met some entrepreneurs with an eye to the future: Colombian weed, grown by farmers all along the country's Caribbean coast. When Forcade began selling it in New York, he found that he could get $350 a pound, roughly double the price of Mexican. By 1973, discerning customers were looking for strains like Santa Marta Gold, Chiba, and Maui Wowie; the Mexican weed of yesteryear was for high schoolers and bums.

The concept of the "smoke-easy," a formalized update of the Harlem tea pads of the 1930s, was perfected by a friend of—and pot dealer to—Mayer Vishner, one of the jurors on the *Steal This Book* trial. Chris Kearns was a draft card–burning member of the Catholic Worker movement who'd begun dealing hashish when he found a Lebanese Red connection from two local rabbis. Then he bought a loft on a cobblestone street in SoHo, fixed it up, and installed a bar that he customized for selling marijuana. The bar—or "candy shop," as Kearns called it—became known simply as Crosby's, after the name of the street it was on.

Behind the bar were six bins in which he put a few hundred pounds of product. In those days, that might mean various strains of Mexican, Colombian, and Jamaican imports, as well as mushrooms and hash. Prices were on a blackboard. "The most difficult thing about a trip to Crosby's was finally having to make a choice, assuming you could get through the sampling process without passing out," recalled Ron Rosenbaum.

"I had other people smuggling for me mostly," Kearns said. "But I would finance loads—people would come to me, tell me about what they wanted to do, and if I liked that idea, I'd give them money, you know?"

"Mayer introduced me to Tom because Mayer just bought for himself, but Tom and I could do, you know, tons together," Kearns recalled.

Forcade quickly found a wholesale source in New York. A friend of a friend named Larry Hertz, a Sheepshead Bay–raised taxi driver, showed up at the UPS offices with two upright American Tourister suitcases filled to the brim with Colombian. He found Forcade in the back, surrounded by tanks of nitrous oxide and sucking from a yellow balloon. "Hey, what's happening?" Forcade asked him, in an Alvin-and-the-Chipmunks-register voice.

Repeated trips into an office that had been under surveillance by the FBI with hundreds of pounds of product, though, didn't appeal to Larry. "I said, 'Tom, this is crazy, we can't keep doing this. I'm getting paranoid. I shouldn't be taking all this shit here.'"

It was time for Forcade to start a smoke-easy of his own. Forcade's two-room Greenwich Avenue operation, in the shadow of the recently shuttered Women's House of Detention, lacked the charm of Crosby's; the entrance was a steel door. Visitors entered to find a white-carpeted, cork-walled, and curtained room, illuminated, Rosenbaum wrote, "by the blood red glow of an artificial fireplace complete with bogus-seeming Naugahyde logs."

The second room was behind another steel door. "The biggest safe I ever saw," one customer marveled. "It filled the whole back of that place, a converted industrial loft. Inside were suitcases stacked to the ceiling. You paid your cash and he handed you a suitcase filled with dope and you could go right to the airport and split." Forcade stayed back there, rolling joints and listening to Derek and the Dominos' "Key to the Highway" over and over again on the absurdly giant speakers he'd hauled around three years earlier on the Medicine Ball Caravan.

"He had other people bringing him stuff, and I was going there once or twice a week constantly refilling him," Larry says. "I'd bring the bulk, and he'd break it down into smaller amounts with Big Bertha, a triple-beam scale with a round plate on top, almost a foot in diameter. Anything you placed on that platform would fit. We even weighed bales on it."

Larry helped him write a black book of rules and regulations: Customers had to follow elaborate procedures requiring multiple payphone calls and parking protocols; once they arrived, they had to keep their voices down. And, of course, "Do not tell anyone of the existence of this book."

Forcade made about five thousand dollars a night.

"He did it quite differently than I did," Chris Kearns, the proprietor of Crosby's, said. "He was a hell of a lot more paranoid than I was. I had a bar where people could hang out; it was a pretty groovy scene. But he separated the people. It didn't have a good vibe. When a customer would come, he'd put them in the room and shut the door, so they wouldn't see anybody else there. He hired one of my ex-customers, and she would reel this cart around with the samples on it, and...it wasn't real fun. It wasn't anything like Crosby's." Product was usually sold by the pound.

"It was," said A. J. Weberman, "like a whorehouse without beds."

"Out of the 300 or 400 papers that were in the underground press service, there are only about 15 or 20 left," Jerry Powers of Miami's *Daily Planet* told a reporter in 1973. "We find the *Planet* now is into the whole youth market, sponsoring rock concerts, planning charter trips, the works." He enthusiastically announced plans to "develop a chain of subculture papers" that would form a publicly traded conglomerate called the New Underground Products Corporation, or NUPCO. "Did you ever hear of an underground paper going public?" Powers asked rhetorically. "I guess not, so we're not really underground anymore."

But like so many other UPS papers in 1973, the *Daily Planet* was feeling the pinch, and within a matter of months Powers decided to fold both the paper and the plans for NUPCO. He ended up in New York, where he paid a spontaneous visit to one of the *Planet*'s unlikely investors, a Fort Lauderdale businessman named Ken Burnstine.

"He'd called me about a month earlier, and I called him back and he said he was in New York at the Hotel Navarro on Central Park South, and he said, 'Come on over.' I was about two blocks away."

As Powers was walking in, he said, Forcade was walking out.

"And at that time, I started to put one and one together, because by then I had learned that Burnstine was a smuggler."

Ken Burnstine and Jerry Powers had first met in the autumn of 1969. "He called me up out of the clear blue and he said, 'You know...I got your newspaper, I love it. I'm with you on all of this political stuff. I live in Fort Lauderdale. Let's have lunch.'

"I remember my assistant Tina saying, 'Jerry, there's a Rolls-Royce outside.' It was so the opposite of what we were doing. And this, you know...suntanned Miami Beach kind of looking guy came out, and we had lunch and he just said, 'Look, I can give you $50,000 in return for twenty percent equity in the company.' I looked at him and I said, 'You know, you may never see this money again because we don't make money.'

And he said, 'Don't worry about it, we'll figure it out. I'm going to send in my brother'—totally very straight, heavyset, the opposite of Ken—'as our accountant and CPA.' He said, 'Let me give you $50,000. Put 10 or 15 aside and give him a nice salary,' and I did. That was it. It was very innocent.

"He said, 'I'm into the Movement, I believe in you guys,' but in the meantime, there was the Rolls-Royce, and the thirty-million-dollar mansion with guards, private planes, and God knows what. So how much of a hippie he really was, I don't know. . . . I didn't think there was anything more to it than a rich guy who maybe was a little sexually kinky, and wanted to be around young hippie girls. I think he wanted to, you know, I think he bought himself an education to the counterculture."

Burnstine made his name in Florida as a real estate developer. After he overextended his finances in the mid-1960s, he'd started a charter airline to the Bahamas called Florida Atlantic Airlines; a former Marine, he piloted many of the flights himself. By 1969, he was planning a comeback in real estate with a $35 million apartment complex, and his former secretary and mistress had become his second wife. Burnstine wore silk shirts, bell bottoms, big rings, and gold medallions. He lived in a shag-carpeted mansion with a bar that seated twelve, an indoor reflecting pool and fountain, and a swinging bookcase that opened to reveal a pistol range with moving targets.

There were also two Great Danes, a chimpanzee, a number of lions, and a sign at the gate that warned TRESPASSERS WILL BE EATEN.

Burnstine invited Powers and his wife to visit him in Fort Lauderdale. "When we got there," said Powers, "he took us over by the lions and tigers and . . . for the first time, all of a sudden, something changed, and he said, 'Fuck with me and they will eat you.' And that was scary enough, and then we got into his house, and his wife gave me and my wife some hash brownies. And we got a little freaked out and paranoid, so we left."

Martin Blitstein was a Florida attorney who represented both Burnstine and Powers. "Powers had these sex ads in the back of the paper," said Blitstein, "and Burnstine wanted all the pussy he could fucking get. He invested in the paper so he could get access to what was in there.

"Burnstine was not actually a drug player in the beginning," Blitstein said. But then Burnstine happened to meet yet another of the firm's colorful clients: the owner of a topless shoeshine business who'd gotten into smuggling.

"Ken needed money at the time, and it was the only way he could see to make that much so quickly. His basic business became renting airplanes to dope smugglers. I used to go and rescue them. They crashed one plane in the Bahamas. Busted one in Chillicothe, Ohio. That's all I did, run around the world defending guys he was leasing planes to." Burnstine offered to put arrested men on salary for the duration of any prison sentence they might face.

The first time Burnstine's name was publicly tied to drugs was in late 1972, when one of his marijuana-laden Lockheed Lodestars—and one of its two pilots—burned up in a crash in Jamaica. Burnstine claimed the plane had been stolen. By the time Jerry Powers saw Forcade coming out of Burnstine's Central Park South apartment a year later, more planes had crashed, more pilots had died, and more marijuana had been seized.

A single document connecting Ken Burnstine to Tom Forcade survives. It's on the letterhead of one of Burnstine's real estate companies, and it's from nearly four years before Powers saw the two of them together.

Dear Tom:

Enjoyed talking to you on my last visit to New York, Sorry for the delay in this letter, but I was hit with, of all things, pneumonia, two days after I got back, and have been flat on my back for the past ten days.

As we discussed via telephone, I am enclosing a complete set of the financial analysis of The Daily Planet. I will greatly appreciate it if you will study this yourself and give me the benefit of your comments concerning the analysis of the Planet, and also, if you would obtain similar financial data from the various newspapers you have suggested we try to acquire, and set it up for me in a similar comparative form, so that we can see how these other papers compare with the Planet, and visa-versa....

I look forward to hearing from you at your earliest convenience. I am still as much interested as ever in putting together the NUPCO organization as ever, and I am particularly interested in seeing you be a part of this organization. Please let me hear from you as soon as possible. Best personal regards.

Sincerely,
Ken

"So that meant," asked Powers upon being told of the letter years later, "that when Ken Burnstine called me out of the blue and came into my life, he and Tom had already known each other?

"Burnstine could have had no business rationale for investing with me, because in those days, if we got lucky, we might make $5,000. There was no money in it. And he was building condos in Florida. I saw the way he lived. The profit from the *Daily Planet* maybe could have paid for his security guard for about a week. He said, 'We're going to make this big, we're going to make this national,' and it wasn't there, there was no potential for it.

"Looking back at it, I believe Burnstine was trying to recruit me, to get me into that pot game. I ran all the concerts; he knew I had the biggest network going. I was so naive. I didn't pick up on his hints at all. But Tom did, and Tom also had access....

"Up until the time I saw them together," continued Powers, "Ken had never mentioned Tom's name to me, and it was a fluke that I even went to see him, because I just happened to be in New York. We went to lunch, and that was about the only time the three of us were together.

"At that point, Burnstine told me a few things. 'You know how I invested the money in Miami, we were thinking we could make 10 or 20 grand?' He goes, 'If you want to see real money, talk to Tom.' Which I never did. But I knew exactly what was going on at that point. Tom was definitely smuggling with Ken Burnstine. The role he played, I have no idea."

The Zippies, meanwhile, had taken up calling themselves Yippies, since nobody was using that name anymore. They poured their time into the *Yipster Times* newspaper, an outgrowth of the newsletters they'd published in Miami. Forcade was still involved, but he had distanced himself a bit. An item in the Alternative Press Syndicate's *Press Revue* even expressed surprise that the *Yipster Times*'s circulation had quickly grown from one thousand to fifteen thousand, "considering its zany humor, foamy-mouthed politics, and slap-dash layout."

That July Fourth, the Zippies held a demonstration on the Mall in Washington, DC, to impeach Nixon and legalize marijuana. The sound system was late, though, and then the bullhorn wasn't working, and even the *Yipster Times* admitted that the protesters were "wandering around in circles on the Mall for fifteen minutes while the organizers tried to remember what the march permit said." They had perhaps given out too many free joints.

"A lot of people were too burned out on pot to make the march," Aron Kay observed of the disappointing crowd.

"C'mon, people," Beal shouted between sets by rock bands. "Let's get up and dance! Show some action! You're like you're all out on quaaludes."

"These people are our own constituents, they're mostly from the YIP chapters," Forcade told the *Washington Post*. "All the other people in America don't know what they're missing."

Still, the FBI was there to record it for posterity:

During the afternoon of July 4, 1973, the Yippies just lounged around the grass on the Mall, smoking marijuana and listening to "several rock" bands. They were in no mood to rally at the U.S. Capitol Building and were worn out by the heat.... An estimated 600 persons participated in the march, with participants dropping out during the course of the march. After the marchers arrived on the steps of the Capitol, the Yippies jumped into a fountain and some Yippies tore apart the anti-Nixon props. Beal was "freaked-out" and could not get the Yippies to cooperate.

And:

It was recently learned that [Dana Beal] will probably be asked to have less leadership in YIP. [Beal], A.J. Weberman and TOM FORCADE have had some disagreement, but now appear to be coming together in their ideas.

"The park was emptying out after the rally," remembered *Yipster Times* staffer David Spaner, "and Tom came up in his Cadillac with Cindy, rolled down the window, stuck out his head, and screamed at me, 'Get over here! Where the fuck is Dana?' I went over to him and said, 'Don't fucking talk to me that way!'

"The next time I saw him in New York," said Spaner, "he offered me a job at UPS."

That summer, at a Detroit Common Council meeting, a Zippie named Pat Halley pied the Guru of Divine Light Mission. "I always wanted to throw a pie in God's face," Halley quipped. Afterward, two men told Halley they had information about corruption within the group. They asked if they could come to his apartment. After he let them in, they administered blows to his head and fractured his skull.

Just three months earlier, Aron Kay had attempted to pie Divine Light follower Rennie Davis at New York's Anderson Theatre, but when security guards intervened and jostled him, the cherry pie ended up on the ground. (Subsequent targets of Aron Kay would include William F. Buckley, Daniel Patrick Moynihan, E. Howard Hunt, Phyllis Schlafly, Abe Beame, G. Gordon Liddy, William Colby.) Now the New York YIP, including Forcade, retaliated for the attack on Halley at the Divine Sales store in the East Village. A brawl spilled out into the street before police broke it up.

"It's all-out war," the *Yipster Times* declared.

On the tenth anniversary of John F. Kennedy's assassination, Forcade and Weberman held a demonstration at the National Archives. To publicize their action, they made a stop at Georgetown University in Washington, DC, where the Committee to Investigate Assassinations was holding a conference that several members of Congress and their staffs were scheduled to attend. Forcade and Weberman arrived armed with posters and leaflets that asked, "Who Stole Kennedy's Brain?" A cartoon depicted Richard Nixon holding and stroking JFK's gray matter.

"When I arrived there shortly before the conference began, I saw the horrible posters on trees and poles and the sides of buildings all around the area," the committee's Richard E. Sprague wrote to a colleague. "I must admit my immediate reaction was to want to vomit, and my next reaction was a desire to run around the campus tearing down all of the posters.

"Several congressmen and their staff people were planning to attend the CTIA conference. It was not the kind of material any of us wanted to see associated with the conference. Nor did we want to have the CTIA conference in any way connected in the minds of the senators and representatives with the demonstration in front of the Archives."

Sprague kept his wits and headed to the auditorium, but just as he settled into his seat, he heard a disturbance emanating from the lobby, where a woman named Sally was registering guests.

"I looked out and saw two men in straw-like derby hats colored black with a gold or yellow trim, creating a scene with Sally. I later found out they were Weberman and Forcade. I had never seen either of them before.

"Weberman and Forcade came storming into the foyer, demanding they be allowed to enter the auditorium while the conference was in progress and distribute the 'brain missing' leaflets. Sally told them no and before she could do anything else, Forcade grabbed one of the CTIA registration tables and literally threw it on top of Sally, scattering books, forms and literature in all directions, grabbing handfuls of them while wildly running around the foyer. Sally's finger was broken in the action, and she was badly shaken up. I don't know exactly what Weberman was doing during Forcade's performance, but he surely was making no effective effort to stop it."

Campus police arrived to throw out the disrupting duo. But the next day, Weberman returned to harass a conference speaker about working for "a government organization"—Amtrak.

It was clear that, even with Hoffman and Rubin out of the picture, accusations of double agentry would continue to fly. Following the demonstration at the National Archives, a writer for the DC underground paper *Daily Rag* questioned the reputation of a conspiracy researcher who had joined the action, asserting that his "affiliation with the Zippies was an exercise in 'who-was-using-who.'" These were confusing times—the *Daily Rag* writer was, himself, a former intelligence agent who'd cofounded an organization that billed itself as a "watchdog on the government spy apparatus."

For Weberman, the trip would be the beginning of an obsession with the Kennedy assassination and the multiple mysteries that surrounded it. He'd start working on a book called *Coup d'Etat in America*, and the pages of the *Yipster Times* would increasingly find space for coverage of spycraft and assassination plots.

Allen Ginsberg, still angry about what had happened a year earlier in Miami, was also seeing conspiracies. In an interview with the *Georgia Straight*, he railed against the Zippies, saying that the handouts attacking Hoffman and Rubin "were, as far as I'm concerned—if they weren't paid for by the CIA or the Watergate people, might just as well have served the same purpose."

"Everybody was accepting the UPS reporting inspired by Tom Forcade," Ginsberg said. "But Forcade also, in addition to attacking Abbie and Jerry in jail, levelled his hand at David Dellinger, who was on a

30-day fast, and said, 'We ruined Abbie and Jerry and we'll ruin you if you don't watch out,' which I have a record of—a tape. . . . And that's the failure of the whole underground—its own bad faith.

"It got so bad," Ginsberg continued, "that we went to Jack Anderson to see if we could find out if Forcade was paid by the Republicans or the CIA or the police or something. But I guess not, I think he's just naturally nutty."

The *Straight* received a long rebuttal letter from Forcade. "First, it was I who was in jail, not Abbie or Jerry," it began. "Second, I did not 'ruin' Hoffman or Rubin. Their own behavior discredited them." Forcade also denied threatening to "ruin" Dellinger, who, he complained, had refused to testify as a material witness at his firebomb trial.

> Since it was Dellinger's organization, MCC-PCPJ, which had RE-QUESTED my arrest, by their own admission, I was not surprised at Dellinger's reluctance to testify. I do think the "movement" has been singularly myopic in not investigating the close relationship, financial and otherwise, between MCC-PCPJ and the CRP-government. I would be glad to provide any information I have to any qualified researcher.
>
> In regard to Ginsberg's quotes of my supposed statements on tape, HE IS A LIAR. I HEREBY PUBLICLY BET GINSBERG $1,000 IN CANADIAN MONEY THAT HE DOES NOT HAVE SUCH A TAPE AND PUBLICLY CHALLENGE HIM TO PRODUCE SUCH A TAPE WITH THAT STATEMENT ON IT. THE LOSER TO PAY THE MONEY TO THE GEORGIA STRAIGHT LEGAL DEFENSE FUND.
>
> Despite the fact that I dislike and avoid public appearances of any type, I further challenge Ginsberg to repeat such statements to my face, in a debate format or otherwise, publicly or privately, anytime, anyplace.
>
> My extreme preference for personal privacy may make me seem mysterious to many. Nevertheless, this does not justify Ginsberg's McCarthyite ravings and factionist rantings. We need to come together, the over 30s alike, Ginsberg, Rubin, and Hoffman, and those under such as myself and the YIP people. Lies and gratuitous badmouthing don't help. We are all beginning to understand more and more why in his final years, Jack Kerouac loathed and despised Allen Ginsberg.

A few weeks later, the *Georgia Straight* received a second letter with a Forcade signature, claiming that the first had been "a cleverly contrived put-on, because I don't give a flying fuck what Ginsberg says and wouldn't bet him ten cents on it." This letter closed with the assessment that "Ginsberg's o.k.," but a postscript asked, "Incidentally, what the hell was Ginsberg doing taping people's conversations? Sounds like Nixon. I don't care if he doesn't have the tape. But if he does have the tape, the question is why?" The paper printed the Forcade signatures side by side and told readers to judge for themselves.

Meanwhile, Rubin's and Hoffman's paths had led them in different directions. Rubin had renounced drugs and taken to practicing yoga and something called Bioenergetics, which involved laying on a bed, yelling, and kicking very hard. "My energy was all external in the 60s," he said. "In the 70s I want to find out what's within." Rubin tried various other forms of self-help, physical and spiritual, and these karmic realignments would eventually lead him to issue public apologies:

> During the election year of 1972, I was involved in a misguided attempt to remain a national political leader of YIP (Youth International Party) during the conventions in Miami Beach. In that crazy activity I was in a group which became involved in a factional fight with another faction of YIP called the Zippies....
>
> The Zippies came to Miami, in their own words, "to make trouble—trouble for McGovern, trouble for Nixon, trouble for all politicians, left or right!" I used my relationship with the media to help project the idea that the Zippies were either "police agents" or "police provocateurs," although I did not believe this at the time, or now.
>
> Unfortunately, at the end of the summer, various people, including Tom Forcade, Dana Beal, and Pat Small, were busted. I now see that such left-McCarthyist tactics—labeling activists as "CIA agents" or "police provocateurs" because of political or personal disagreements—is destructive. I don't intend to ever get involved again in such negative, divisive political factional fights, which turns people you disagree with into "enemies."

Rubin also issued his regrets for banning Zippie women from the women's center of the Miami YIP office and for pressuring A. J.

Weberman to apologize to Bob Dylan "in our mutual hopes that Dylan would then appear at pro-movement concerts." And he forgave the Zippies for smashing his car when he got back from Miami.

Abbie Hoffman wasn't in a position for such public apologies. During a sweltering, late-August brownout night, he was arrested for selling cocaine to undercover police in the Hotel Diplomat, the same place that the Zippies had held their beach ball press conference just a year and a half earlier.

A syndicated Associated Press article ran the following week, under headlines like YIPPIES STILL ALIVE AND STRUGGLING. It depicted the Youth International Party as underfunded and unorganized bumblers, "a honeycomb of cells in different cities across the country, guided by relative unknowns." Or, as it quoted Forcade, "ex-Weatherpeople, old White Panthers and others—a potpourri."

It opened by describing sixteen people waiting on an East Village sidewalk for a meeting to start as news comes that the key to the building has been lost.

"The tiny, hot dark office is above a darker, danker two-room basement with bare mattresses, rats, roaches, stacked newspapers and a shower stall with a view—a gaping hole to the alley above. When it rains, the apartment floods."

"Without strong personalities, YIP is going to disappear," A. J. Weberman told the reporter. "They're failing to capture people's interest, the interest of intellectuals, college students, *Rolling Stone* readers....What we need is an angle. I don't believe in just standing on a street corner giving out pamphlets."

"I look at myself as a custodian," said Dana Beal, "but I'm too stoned to do a good job. We need people that the media can focus on, somebody to get funds....We're committed to neither violence nor non-violence at this stage. We're committed to self-determination."

Capitalizing on Hoffman's arrest, Forcade organized a "Legalize Cocaine" benefit at the Grand Ballroom of Hotel Diplomat, promising that all money collected would go toward "cocaine research." (The published results, he promised, would be available for legal defendants like Hoffman.) Shipped from Missouri were a couple hundred copies of a special "Legalize Cocaine" issue of the Kansas City underground *Westport*

Trucker, which included an unsigned essay on cocaine that was, according to *Trucker* editor Dennis Giangreco, written by Forcade. "Cocaine is
much like marijuana, in that it can be a stimulant, a relaxant, a psychedelic, an aphrodisiac, or anything it needs to be," Forcade waxed. "Indeed, unlike marijuana, it is possible to injure yourself with coke. But
the precautions are scarcely known, causing unneeded paranoia and un-
necessary injury.... We feel that cocaine has potentially fantastic physical
and psychic properties, far beyond a simple high.... Further, we feel that
hedonism and only hedonism can be the basis for future society, and so
we propose to bring this issue into the wide open, here and now, by advocating the legalization of cocaine."

On the occasion of the benefit party, Forcade announced that the
American Arbitration Association had ruled in his favor for the amount
of $3,409.76, for work done on *Steal This Book*. "I consider this a great
victory," he said. "Now the problem is collecting it."

Within months, Abbie Hoffman had skipped off to Mexico. He'd
spend the rest of the decade underground, under an assumed name.

Forcade was scarce after that, too. He'd made excited plans with Giangreco to publish a national version of the *Trucker*, but suddenly he was
unreachable.

"He just kind of disappeared for a few months," recalled Giangreco.
"He reappeared and was flush with cash."

In later years, there'd be countless versions of the origins of *High Times* magazine. Cindy Ornsteen and Tim Hughes would say that it was conceived
in late 1972, at the farmhouse in Florida. A dealer friend said it came to
Forcade like an epiphany during an Orange Sunshine trip at his apartment.
("What do people want even more than drugs? They want information
about drugs!") Another account—"We were sitting around getting stoned
on nitrous oxide and laughing gas one day when someone said 'Hey, why
not write about getting high?'"—got a lot of traction over the years. Dennis
Giangreco maintained that *High Times* had roots in Forcade's attempt to
bring the *Trucker* to a national audience. (Indeed, when the *Trucker* changed
to magazine format in 1973, its masthead bore the names of several future
High Times staffers, including Forcade.) "The working title for a while was
The High Life: The Magazine of High Society," recalled Giangreco.

Much of the early conceptualizing for *High Times* certainly came from Ronnie Volvox and Ed Rosenthal, who'd been working for the Alternative Press Syndicate and realized that microfilm royalties weren't covering operating costs.

Rosenthal had led a bit of a double life. After college, even as he was working as an assistant compliance officer on Wall Street, he was occasionally involved in Yippie and Zippie actions—he'd been at the 1967 Tompkins Square Park rally where Dana Beal was arrested. He also grew his own cannabis in a six-bedroom Bronx apartment—until he realized that he could use his knowledge to construct and install marijuana greenhouses for other people, including residents of upscale Central Park West and Park Avenue. So he cleared the pot out of his own place and started the Clearlight Company. "I would come and install it in your home," Rosenthal said. "Everything but the seed." Rosenthal even made a bold prediction to a reporter for the *Philadelphia Inquirer*: "As grass gets more acceptable, as more certified public accountants start smoking and want to save money, you'll get more people interested in growing their own. This is only the start of something big. I'm going to go big-time before it goes legal. Tell GE to watch out."

Rosenthal had been pulled further into Forcade's orbit when the two marketed mail-order hemp rolling papers under the aegis of "Amorphia East," selling them out of the UPS office; Tom and Cindy crashed at his Bronx apartment after Miami. As Rosenthal remembered it, the talks that evolved into *High Times* started with plans to start a marijuana news service. "Then I did some figuring on the economics of the potential advertising, and we decided to do a magazine."

What *Playboy* had done for sex, *High Times* would do for dope—the difference being, of course, that one was legal and one was not.

In late 1973, Tom and Cindy moved into a large basement apartment at 283 West 11th Street with Hughes, Rosenthal, and Volvox, where they could dedicate themselves full time to working on *High Times*. It was big enough that they were able to construct walls in the back—some with drywall, some with stacks of old underground newspapers—for living spaces and fill the front with metal desks and metal folding chairs. The linoleum floors didn't look pretty, especially under the bright overhead lighting, but it got the job done.

Forcade returned to Ed Dwyer's apartment, retrieved his shotgun and pistol, and offered him the position of editor of *High Times*.

"He left a bag of Colombian behind," Dwyer added, "to help me decide."

Once he'd signed on, it was time to produce a magazine. "There was just me and Ed Dwyer," Forcade later recalled. "We were usually so wiped out we could barely crawl up to put our hands on the keyboard of the typewriters." They added a photostat camera, an enlarger, and a Compugraphic typesetting unit.

That autumn and winter, visitors to 283 West 11th Street were greeted by an old bronze plaque that read INSTITUTE FOR ADVANCED STUDIES and, often, tanks of nitrous oxide. Inside the doors, brainstorming commenced. Many of the brainstormers, which included Dana Beal, A. J. Weberman, cartoonist Alan "Yossarian" Shenker, and Bob Singer, were alumni of the *East Village Other* and the *New York Ace*.

"We put together a list of about 100 articles that would appear in the magazine over a period of time," said Rosenthal. "And actually, over a period of years, those articles did eventually appear."

Andy Kowl, Bob Lemmo, and Bo Sacks put out a Long Island underground paper called *The Express*. Forcade called them one day to ask if they would typeset UPS newsletters, and then he impressed them by riding the Long Island Railroad out to Hicksville with an open shopping bag of pot, showing up at their offices in his black suit, hat, and cowboy boots.

They knew how to drum up publicity—Kowl rented a gorilla suit and handed out promotional *Express* pens on the campuses of Long Island colleges—and they had figured out that they could trade advertising space for albums, clothes, even a motorcycle. But that didn't pay the bills. So, like many underground newspaper employees before them, they dealt grass.

"Two guys named Mike and Corey, from a syndicate in Texas, were our main suppliers," said Kowl. "Mike and I would meet at the airport, with identical suitcases, mine with the money, and his with ten or twenty pounds of pot. We would sit in the lounge, and I would talk to him while he was waiting for the plane that would take him back to Texas, and then we'd get up and take each other's suitcase.

"At some point, I was talking to Tom, and he said, 'I hear you know Mike and Corey.' He said, 'It's kind of a pain in the neck, the way we have it arranged, so they thought you wouldn't mind if I became your supplier for them.' I said, that sounds good to me. So that put our relationship on another level. I started going to New York more often, to get as much poundage as possible, and spending time with Tom down in the basement of West 11th Street."

Within a year, all three partners of *The Express* would be working for *High Times*.

Ken Landgraf, a young Vietnam War veteran, was heading into a class at the School of Visual Arts when someone outside started loudly asking the students, "Is there anybody that can illustrate a catalog?"

Landgraf said he could, skipped the class, and was immediately ushered to see Forcade, who asked him to render pen-and-ink illustrations of bongs, design "Eat the Rich" rolling papers, and help paste up layouts.

Then Forcade narrated a story about smuggling. "He wanted a rope with one of those giant pallets of pot, going down in the swamp," said Landgraf. "I didn't even know what he was talking about because I didn't know about the drug world. Girls were coming in there, like, giggling, and I think he was selling them drugs.

"I fell asleep on the floor, finally, because he was taking uppers of some sort, amphetamines. So that's how he was staying up for days, working on the magazine."

Diana Drucella, a customer at Crosby's smoke-easy, came to work in the art department, as did Karin Limmroth, a friend of Ed Rosenthal who'd worked at *Essence* and *Penthouse*. Limmroth arrived at the office to find Forcade, surrounded by books on mushroom growing and bomb making, with a primitive prototype. "Tom has these pieces of five-by-seven red construction paper stapled together, with nothing on them, and he says, 'Can you help me?'"

For the cover, an ex-girlfriend of Ed Dwyer photographed her friend holding a supermarket mushroom to her mouth, managing a sensuous evocation of psilocybin tripping without need of illegal props. Cindy Ornsteen picked out the foil stock on which that image was printed. "I think silver and turquoise are beautiful," she said, "and I thought we needed a good cover to clean marijuana on."

Twice a year, merchants swarmed several floors of the Garment District's Hotel McAlpin to sell wares—denim and polyester, leathers and feathers, incense and necklaces, and no small amount of junk—to retail buyers. "Beautiful people who wouldn't go near business a few years ago, now getting involved in the so-called Establishment," one of the cofounders crowed. "They are going to be our new market princes."

They were also a fit for *High Times*. Rosenthal used his connections to secure *High Times* a giant space in the basement, but the finished magazine wasn't ready in time for the January event. So they sublet the area to various paraphernalia dealers. Volvox designed a brochure ("Sticks and stems removed—you'll get the straight dope"), and Rosenthal passed those out to potential advertisers and distributors among the eight hundred exhibitors eagerly aiming at the funky and groovy dollars of a post-hippie clientele.

But what should have been a moment of triumph was immediately thwarted by unexpected rifts.

"I was working on the booth, setting the place up," said Rosenthal, "and Tom comes in with Tim Hughes. Tim says a few words in Tom's ear. Tom is saying, 'You should do it this way, you should do it that way.' I said, 'Why don't you let me set it up, and then if you don't like it, then we'll change it around.' And Tim says a few more words in his ear, and Tom—it was like he's being given lines or something, I don't know what—but Tom blows up, slashes stuff off his table.

"I don't know if it was staged or what, but Tim provoked Tom into some sort of rage. He had some sort of unique ability to communicate with Tom in some way that other people weren't able to. He was like his negative avatar, his black hole avatar. And he was able to manipulate Tom. It was very unusual, because Tom would usually be the person doing the manipulating, but Tim could play Tom." ("Ed always felt like everybody was undermining him in some way," said Hughes. "Before *High Times*, Tom and I were not surrounded by a lot of people, and then there was great competition for Tom's favor and attention. A few people like Ed, they felt like I had a lot of sway with Tom. That wasn't because Tom was manipulated; it's because I was his partner.")

Afterward, Forcade accused Ed Rosenthal of going to the FBI; Rosenthal said he thought Tim had been a government infiltrator. "Tim sort of planted seeds of conspiracy in Tom's head," said Volvox. "And Tom threw all of Ed's stuff out in the street. So I quit and left, which I think Tom did not anticipate at all, maybe it sort of blew his mind. But he had taken actions that I wasn't going to go along with."*

Someone *was* in touch with federal agencies. On February 13, an anonymous caller tipped the Secret Service that Forcade was "involved in the purchase and sale of marijuana and LSD. The individual stated that Forcade travels to the southern part of the United States often and returns to New York with from 25 to 100 pounds of the previously mentioned narcotics on each occasion. He thereafter sells the drugs to other individuals in the village area of NYC. The individual further advised that Forcade has an undisclosed amount of firearms in his residence on most occasions. The individual concluded by advising that he believed Secret Service would be interested in the above information."

The Secret Service contacted the FBI, which started tracking Forcade again and tried to figure out what had happened to the shotgun that Pat Small had hidden on Mary Street in Miami.

The first issue of *High Times* included an excerpt from a Timothy Leary book called *Terra II*, an interview with an anonymous "lady dealer," and a feature about a Florida smuggling ring that had appeared in the *Daily Planet*. "It was dated by the time it got in the magazine," recalled the writer, Rod DeRemer, "and they hammered the beginning and a few other parts to make it salacious." To his surprise, DeRemer was listed as both "contributing editor" and "*High Times* Correspondent from the Northern Florida Region." "They didn't pay me anything. I think they sent me one or two copies of the magazine, but there were no checks, that's for sure."

A news section rounded up drug-related scientific findings and legal developments: "California Marijuana Initiative failure to get enough signatures to get on ballot a blow to legalization, but movement stronger than ever.... National Organization to Reform Marijuana Laws (NORML) becoming more and more effective although quite straightish.... Amorphia

---

* Rosenthal moved out to California and began a successful career writing about marijuana cultivation. Even as he'd been working on *High Times*, he and another New York City–based grower, the pseudonymous Mel Frank, had been photocopying every scientific government-research paper on pot they could get their hands on, synthesizing the results, and adding them to their own empirical findings to produce the *Indoor-Outdoor Highest Quality Marijuana Growers Guide*. Rosenthal's books would go on to sell millions of copies.

[other major legalization group] having financial problems." A breathless police blotter summarized busts around the world. (One item reported that a Gainesville pilot had crashed a Lockheed Lodestar in Pompano Beach, but there was no mention that Ken Burnstine was the man behind the scenes of that failed operation.) Tucked away at the back, after a short record review section (Ash Ra Tempel and *Mushroom Ceremony of the Mazatec Indians of Mexico*) was what many readers would find to be the most indispensable feature. The "Trans-High Market Quotation" was a current-prices survey of the kind that had appeared in underground newspapers going back to *Marijuana Review*'s "Cassidy's Corner," the Ann Arbor *Sun*'s "Dope-O-Scope," and the *East Village Other*'s "Intergalactic Union Dopogram." But those were all regional—this was a national buyer's guide, with the kind of wide-ranging information to which only narcotics agents would supposedly otherwise have access. Chris Kearns of Crosby's provided Forcade with what would be the Trans-High Market's recurring photograph, depicting Operation Intercept narcs operating phones in front of a chalkboard of going rates.

A notice assured subscribers concerned about government surveillance: "the mailing list is encoded and kept in wax sealed envelope in the safe of a lawyer whose name is known only to the publisher."

High Times didn't secure paraphernalia advertising until after the first issue was published, so the sponsorship bore the distinct mark of Cindy's astrological interests. There were display ads scattered throughout from pioneering occult publisher Llewellyn Publications, and a full-page promotion for a book about the joys of nitrous oxide.

Years later, some would claim that the magazine was a lark, that it was intended to be a one-shot deal. But from the beginning, its ongoing goals were clear: "You are guaranteed the highest efficiency for your ad, if you want to reach the High Society," promised a splashy solicitation. "Back cover, $500; inside front and inside back cover, $450." With that inside front cover not yet sold, *High Times* used the space to tease stories being planned for future issues, gems like "A Visit to the Colombian Pot Fields," "Pyramids & Ancient Highs," "Child Pot Smokers: In Their Own Words," "Training the Pot Pooch," and "Getting High in the Year 2000."

Cindy even started a unique campaign to sell subscriptions by sending sample issues to drug-defendant lawyers: *"High Times* is dedicated to getting high, and that relates to your practice—news of your cases, defenses, tactics, the new drugs, the new highs. You should have a copy in your law library. And you should have a copy in your waiting room. Your partners might want copies for their offices. You might even want a copy for home.... If you'd like to be in simple possession, it will cost you $10.00 for 12 issues. If you'd like to be in multiple possession, we'll charge you only $8.00 for every subscription."

In lieu of interest from established newsstand distributors, copies went to retailers and distributors from the Fashion and Boutique show, drug paraphernalia merchants, head shops, and underground newspaper offices.

The issue was also, notably, disseminated through networks of marijuana dealers, who would buy hundreds of copies at cover price and include them in bales to friends and customers. Forcade personally carried copies when he hit the road. "In Madison, Wisconsin, he popped up in the offices of the guerrilla tabloid *Take Over*, successor to *Kaleidoscope*, with two valises, one filled with magazines and the other with pounds of Colombian pot," remembered Michael Chance.

On May 23, 1974, *High Times* was formally rolled out at a party in a rented suite of the down-at-its-heels Gramercy Park Hotel. A pair of rented brass fountains spat out red and white wine; fifty-pound nitrous oxide tanks supplied laughing gas for guests.

Forcade handed Andy Kowl a *High Times* name tag.

"I think we're going to have a big turnout," he said. "Will you wear this badge, and if anyone asks you about the magazine, just talk to them about it?" Kowl didn't even work for the magazine—yet. A few weeks later, he'd be offered a job selling advertising, and the title of Business Manager.

Initial media coverage of *High Times* was sparse, and hardly encouraging. "Is there a market for a magazine for potheads?" sniped *New Times* magazine. "No, but nevertheless *High Times* comes to you in plain brown wrapper with false return address.... More about grass than you need to know." Distributors refused to carry it.

Those dismissals didn't matter. By the time Richard Nixon left office that August, *High Times* issue no. 1 had sold out its first print run of twenty-five thousand copies.

"It's like trying to ride a rocket," Forcade said.

Andy Kowl was in his new office when Forcade brought in a hot-off-the-presses copy of the color-filled second issue.

"This," Forcade said, holding up the magazine, "is a license to print money."

SMOKE,
1974–1978

CHAPTER 12

WITH THE SECOND ISSUE, THE *HIGH TIMES* TEMPLATE WAS SET. But-tressing the usual news updates and lifestyle primers ("How to Read a Rolling Paper") were a true crime feature ("Death in the Desert," in which two sisters, walking to school, stumbled upon the aftermath of a fatal three-way shoot-out between an Arizona smuggler and two Customs agents); excerpts from the Senate subcommittee hearings on "Hashish Smuggling and Passport Fraud" (which arose after the breakup of the Timothy Leary–affiliated Brotherhood of Eternal Love ring); and a long, candid interview with the former deputy director of the Bureau of Narcotics and Dangerous Drugs, who was now advocating for decriminalization ("Operation Intercept," he told *High Times*, "was a mistake and a fiasco."). "I Was JFK's Dealer," by the pseudonymous Lesley Morrissey, signaled another mainstay for the magazine, one that threatened to undermine the more serious claims of journalism: whole-cloth fabrications. There was also, significantly, a full-page ad for the National Organization for the Reform of Marijuana Laws, which had emerged as the leading voice for legislative action. *High Times*'s support for NORML included not just monetary contributions and cosponsored events but also free-of-charge space in every issue that garnered a steady stream of donations from the readership.

Finally, the issue included the inaugural edition of the *High Times* centerfold, which lovingly depicted, sometimes in gauzy close-ups, rare and notable drug specimens. It was a ridiculous monthly hallmark whose notoriety would transcend the magazine's actual readership. The magazine borrowed *Playboy*'s sexualized language to introduce its "budding beauty," a twenty-pound cube of Colombian cannabis that "grew up close to the soil with her shapely stems planted firmly in the ground" and whose "rich golden tan bespeaks of months spent basking in the sensuous sunshine."

The launch party for the second issue was a bigger affair. Forcade conscripted Bob Lemmo, Kowl's colleague from *The Express*, to drum up interest from national media and deep-pocketed luminaries like Stuart Mott. Staff from the *Times*, *Vogue*, *Newsweek*, and *Time* and a phalanx of Japanese businessmen were among the two hundred curious souls who made their way into the ballroom of the Gramercy Park Hotel decorated with the original painting Forcade had commissioned for the cover. WNEW's *10 O'clock News* arrived as guests were served pieces of a cake iced with a magic-mushroom design.

Cindy, wearing a Girl Scout uniform open to the waist and a tiny coke spoon around her neck, used the pseudonym "Anastasia Sirrocco" when speaking to an Associated Press reporter. "If a couple of thousand airplane pilots can have 20 glossy magazines, why can't 26 million dope smokers have one, too?" she asked rhetorically and admitted that "contacts in the drug underworld" provided the market quotations. "We don't advocate the use of drugs," she said, "but do feel that a trade magazine for the drug industry is necessary."

"Channel 5 got two guys to come out in the hall and snort cocaine, and blacked out their faces," Lemmo said. "That was the first cocaine snorting on television."

In the cloakroom, a white-coated dentist operated two blue nitrous tanks, handing out balloons emblazoned with the *High Times* logo. At first, the older journalists looked on quizzically; by the end of the night, they were holding empty balloons, and elbowing one another to get back to the front of the line.

The dentist was a neighbor of Karin Limmroth, the art director, who spent the evening serving hash brownies on a silver tray. "No one knew what was in anything, and we didn't talk about it. I kept saying, 'Please, you might want to just have this half and see how you feel in about an hour,' but they were greedy, grabbing them by the handful. People were really scared of the punch, but that, in fact, was just punch. You know, the brownies were *good*. But they were strong, and a lot of middle-aged people were expanding their minds for the first time in their lives. The next day there were calls on the RSVP line, 'How do you come down?' I think a couple people ended up in the emergency room." According to Bob Lemmo, three indulging guests subsequently brought lawsuits against the magazine.

Within four weeks, *High Times* had sold out its fifty-thousand-copy run of the second issue. For the third issue, they printed eight-five thousand copies. Meanwhile, they kept going back to press for reprints and sold subscriptions to college libraries, government agencies, and district attorneys.

The magazine quickly became an informational network not just for consumers but for paraphernalia manufacturers, distributors, and head shops, a guidebook to the lay of the land. This was the way America was going to standardize its idea of what different strains of marijuana looked like, tasted like, felt like, and cost.

"We figure we're getting in below the ground floor of a new industry," Forcade—using the pseudonym "Michael King"—told *Newsday*. "By the time dope is legal, we'll be firmly established."

And anyway, he said, the magazine "isn't about drugs. It's about getting high. We foresee a time when there'll be more sophisticated ways of getting high, like meditation, but right now it's marijuana."

Forcade wasn't the only one who wanted to keep his name off the *High Times* masthead. Karin Limmroth panicked when she saw an issue come off the presses with her name on the masthead. "Oh, but I thought that was, like, your pseudonym," someone responded. "Nobody uses their real name around here."

Diana Drucella, who succeeded Limmroth as art director, remembered that Forcade often thought he was being tailed and that "everything we paid for was in drug money—small denominations of twenties, tens, fives. Tom once trusted me with a fat *High Times* envelope containing five hundred dollars to go and pay the typesetters. So, I walked from the basement office, stopped to make a call at a Sheridan Square pay phone on my way, and I got to the typesetters, and I didn't have the envelope. I'd left it at the pay phone. I was absolutely terrified to go back to the office and tell him. He got crazy mad, but it blew over.

"Two days later, Tom got a phone call from a good friend who said, 'Tom, I have to tell you, you saved my life.' Tom said, 'What do you mean?' And he said, 'I was down to my last dime, I had nothing going on in my life, I was completely desperate, and I passed a phone booth in Sheridan Square, and I found $500 in an envelope with the *High Times* logo and phone number.' Tom came to me and said, 'How did you know how to leave that money with my very good friend?' So, we got over the misery. But I was intimidated by him. You'd almost not want to mention something that needed to get done, because you didn't know if he would kind of lose it on you."

Forcade began to express concern about informants. "There's a cop here," he would say to staffers. "We just don't know which one of you it is."

According to Dennis Giangreco, Forcade set up a shadow *High Times* staff, in case of emergency. "Peter Bramley [of *National Lampoon*] was to be the art director if there was a wipe-out of the senior staff by New York State or the feds. The idea was to turn on a dime and maintain all schedules and contracts. Duplicate business and subscription records were maintained at separate locations, and separate accounts were kept at Manufacturers Hanover. It was a very closely held affair, since Tom found that nearly everyone associated with *High Times* either had a very big mouth or, he believed, were likely to blab at the slightest threat of imprisonment. Tom bounced back and forth between no worries and the conviction that it could happen any day."

Another venture was growing too.

"Tom and I were getting weed from old friends of his in Phoenix and bringing it back to New York," said Tim Hughes. "I would go out with $50,000 in my cowboy boots and arrange for the stuff to be shipped."

Forcade rented the second floor of 714 Broadway to use as a marijuana retail location, a kind of prototype marijuana dispensary. The space was partitioned into six private rooms for customers, painted completely white, plus a reception area sparsely furnished with a couch and a coffee table. In the back was a stash room with metal shelves and a safe. They mostly sold by the pound at 714,* although the real goal was to offer a sampling of what was available to buy in bulk.

"Whenever I had anything to deal, Tom was like a bank," marveled Chris Kearns. "When we were rolling, when we were hot, we used to trade $15,000 a day—not gross, net."

Forcade and Hughes purchased fifty empty guitar cases for transporting product in and out of the building—although occasionally, when more was on hand, they'd pack it in crates, dress up in jumpsuits, and move everything in and out with hand dollies.

---

* Everyone remembered the address, because 714 was also the number on quaalude pills.

Again, there were house rules: Call first, don't bring a friend unannounced, don't call attention to yourself. Customers could call, but only using loop lines—the numbers—so that nobody knew their landline number. And they were instructed to only speak in code. ("Do you have the new Rolling Stones album?" "Yeah, we've got seven of them.") There was nothing on the walls, and no paperwork—if the premises had to be quickly abandoned, there would be no chance of tracing anything. This turned out to be a good policy.

"Tom and I went up there one afternoon," Hughes said, "and the locks had been broken on the front door. On that particular day, we'd had a little bit of weed, three or four pounds, that couldn't fit in the safe, and that was gone. Then we got a phone call from Redbeard, one of our regular customers, who asked if he could come and buy three pounds of weed—which he never bought; this was a one-pound guy at the most. It was like he was returning to the scene of the crime. 'Yeah, come on over,' we said.

"He walks in the door, and says, 'I see you got your door fixed.' Tom and I held guns on him and had him lay down on the floor. We handcuffed him and took him to a chair in the room in the back, where we'd arranged chains and bags of cement mixture for him to see. We asked where the weed was. He said he didn't know, so we left him in the room for twenty minutes."

In the face of more denials, Forcade mixed a bag of cement in a tub while they impressed upon him the seriousness of his infraction. Finally, Redbeard spilled. "Okay, okay," he said. "It's at my house."

They spirited their captive downstairs to a van; Hughes held him while Forcade drove.

"Turns out the fucking guy lived all the way out in Staten Island," Hughes said. "At a stoplight near Orchard Street, a cop car pulled up next to us, and Redbeard started flinging himself at the window. I'm punching him, and Tom starts panicking. We double back to 714 so I can stay with Redbeard while Tom goes out to Staten Island."

While Forcade unlocked the front door of the building, Redbeard made a break for it. Hughes caught him, sat on him, and began pummeling him right there in the middle of Broadway. Then another police car appeared. Hughes stood up and tried to blend in with the passersby, but the long arm of the law grabbed him.

"There's a marijuana factory up there!" Redbeard shouted. The police removed his handcuffs, and he started pointing at the second floor. "There's another guy up there!"

The police walked Redbeard and Hughes inside and put Hughes up against the door. "If your friend comes out blazing," the cop told Hughes, "you're going to be tomorrow's headlines."

Forcade, though, was gone. Hughes was taken to the police station. "They brought the chains and concrete into the room," he said, "and then tossed a pound of weed on the table, which was not ours. They charged me with kidnapping, assault, and armed robbery, just because I'd taken Redbeard's wallet out and tossed it across the room."

For a while, Diana Drucella worked two nights a week rolling joints and offering samples at 714, making more money than she did at the magazine. Now floor-mounted police locks and additional bolts protected the loft.

"One night, two cop cars pulled up in front of 714," Drucella recalled. "Tom said, 'We're getting out of here.' We left everything, ran up the staircase to the roof. I had just bought a pair of Earth Shoes—it was the first day I was wearing them—so I was feeling a little bit off balance to start with. He jumped and he reached out his hand, and I jumped to the next roof, and we got out through the Lafayette side of the building."

"I didn't last long there," Drucella said. "Every minute of being there was scary as hell."

B eing at the magazine was getting scary, too.

Karin Limmroth had left the job after a tree came crashing through the office window and landed near the layout table she worked at. Forcade had hit the tree with a delivery truck he was driving. "I was, like, stunned," she said, "and Tom strolled through the door like nothing had happened."

Even more unsettling was the tripod sentry. "It was a mess in his office, and he would lose stuff," said Giangreco. "He would say 'Well, if it's not on top of anything, then it must be underneath something.' And he would start turning over stuff. In one instance, he was certain that something that was missing had been lifted—that someone had been getting into his office. He took his shotgun, and he cocked that sucker. You could hear it.

And he was working on trying to set it up on a tripod; his door was closed but you could hear him rushing and banging around in there."

When Forcade finally emerged, he announced, "There's a gun set up in my office! Don't go in there, you'll be shot." It was pointed toward his door and right beyond at Drucella's chair. Another employee remembered her working "with wide, saucer eyes, terrified."

Forcade was keeping guns and large reserves of cash at Cindy's Bank Street apartment. After the police knocked on the superintendent's door one day, Cindy decided she'd had enough and demanded he move it elsewhere.

"I have nowhere else to put it!" he pleaded.

The next day, Cindy came into the office and found herself out of a job. She was gone before the third issue was published.

"We had a huge amount of income from distribution of the magazine because we had no wholesale middleman, and we would see the money immediately," said Dennis Giangreco.

> But there was money coming in from distributors that I had never heard of, that had no phone numbers, that did not exist. To put it bluntly, Tom was using *High Times* to do some money laundering, and that was a massive vulnerability because all somebody had to do was go into the books.
>
> I was saying, "Tom, you can't do this. You're putting everything at risk." He was trying to defend it, saying that, with the decentralized structure of the different fly-by-night organizations and companies that were distributing the publication, it would just look like one of them. I said, "Tom, do you think that the FBI and the Treasury Department don't know who is out there distributing magazines?" Finally, I was able to appeal to his paranoia: "You are going to get busted, or they're going to say we'll let you off if you cooperate." But then after about another month and a half, he started doing it again, and in a big way. My last month there, I was waiting for the search warrants to be served at the door.
>
> I gathered up the Manufacturers Hanover checkbooks and got the signature cards so that Andy's name could be on them; he wasn't even a signer on three of the accounts.

I said to the comptroller, "You know, you better get Andy to put his name on these accounts. Otherwise, the only person who's going to be a signer is Tom. Do you want Tom to be the only signer on these accounts?" But I don't know what transpired after that. She didn't stick around much longer, either.

Shortly after that, Forcade walked into Kowl's office with $20,000 in cash. "Get a safe deposit box," he directed. "In case I'm not around and the company needs it, you have a cushion here. Just tell me where it is— and give me one of the keys."

This was the charged atmosphere in which Forcade offered Kowl the title of publisher.

"I had to think about that a lot," Kowl said. "If you publish a photo of an illegal substance, is that prima facie evidence? If the name of the photographer is credited, is he liable? If you write about a plane coming in, and offloading a ton of weed, were you a journalist or a participant? That's why nobody's name was in the first issue. If anybody walked in and said, 'Who's in charge?' people were gonna point to me.

"I agreed to take the title. But we just didn't know what to expect."

The times certainly called for caution. Word had gotten around that Timothy Leary had turned snitch—specifically, that he was cooperating with that old radical hunter, Guy Goodwin—and had given up friends. Criminal charges against Leary for involvement with the hash-smuggling Brotherhood of Eternal Love were quietly dropped, and even his old friend Allen Ginsberg joined a group called PILL, or People Investigating Leary's Lies. *High Times* changed the ad copy for *The Curse of the Oval Room*—the volume that bore a High Times Books imprint and which the magazine had hawked on the back cover of its first issue and boxes of which were still stacked throughout the office—to "Timothy Leary's last book before he fell victim to the curse himself."

The most explosive news in the country at the end of 1974, though, was the revelation of decades' worth of skeletons in the CIA's closet, which included the maintaining of intelligence files on more than ten thousand American citizens.

In the fallout from the Watergate scandal, the director of the agency had commissioned a report on its so-called Family Jewels, and excerpts from this compendium of dirty laundry and illegal acts splashed across the front pages of Christmastime editions of the *New York Times*.

But the CIA's "massive, illegal domestic intelligence operation . . . against the antiwar movement and other dissident groups in the United States"—a higher-octane counterpart to the FBI's COINTELPRO project—was just the tip of the iceberg. A presidential commission and bipartisan select committees in both the House and Senate dedicated themselves to further investigations, an unprecedented excavation that would result in the media calling 1975 "The Year of Intelligence."

One of the CIA programs that came to light had been launched in 1967 and targeted, among other radical groups, underground newspapers. "Operation CHAOS" was originally intended to determine whether other countries had backed anti-war activities in the United States—but eventually domestic spying, complete with CHAOS agents sent into the field, became as much a priority for the CIA as foreign operations. One agent, for example, had been asked in 1971 "to travel to Washington D.C. to work on an interim basis; the mission was to 'get as close as possible' and perhaps become an assistant to certain prominent radical leaders who were coordinators of the imminent 'May Day' demonstrations. The agent was to infiltrate any secret groups operating behind the scenes and report on their plans."

Meanwhile, Jack Anderson's column revealed that one of the founding staffers of the DC underground *Quicksilver Times* had been a government agent. Sal Ferrera had interviewed Abbie Hoffman and Jerry Rubin, photographed the May Day demonstrations, and reported extensively on the movement—for the underground press and the Central Intelligence Agency, simultaneously. He had also, of course, kept tabs on other UPS papers.

As these reports surfaced, the year-old Drug Enforcement Administration faced its own scandals. The Senate Permanent Subcommittee on Investigations began looking into the influx of CIA agents into the DEA and evidence that top DEA officials had perused catalogs of assassination equipment. Magazines and newspapers reported that members of the Nixon administration had discussed assembling "hit squads" to target narcotics traffickers.

Forcade, in other words, was by 1975 at the intersection of multiple groups—radicals, journalists, and drug dealers—that were in the cross-hairs of the government.

Forcade's old accomplice Ken Burnstine had gotten into some heavy-duty operations. Along with one Mitchell WerBell III—a Scotch-swilling, sword-toting arms dealer and covert operative who invented a submachine-gun silencer and ran a training camp for mercenaries out of his Georgia home—Burnstine had been selling MAC-10s, manufactured without serial numbers, to Pinochet's junta government in Chile.

Unfortunately, Burnstine had picked partners unwisely. According to later testimony by a Drug Enforcement Administration agent, WerBell, who once described himself as "to the right of Attila the Hun," passed along word to the DEA that he wanted Burnstine investigated.

He wasn't the only one. At about the same time, Watergate burglar Frank Sturgis had just been sentenced on a separate charge—for an older scheme involving transporting stolen cars to Mexico—and he encouraged Jerry Buchanan, his codefendant in that enterprise, to work with the feds to entrap Burnstine.

Buchanan met with Burnstine, and undercover DEA agents discussed their plans at meetings in Guadalajara, Mexico City, Vera Cruz, and a Denny's Restaurant in Hollywood, Florida. Buchanan had the international contacts and Burnstine had the fleet of planes. Their grand plans included a weapons-for-drugs trade in Central America. The amount of product they figured to move in their first year of business approached a value of $900 million.

In late 1974, DEA investigators gathered two pounds of seeds and stems Burnstine had neglected to scrape from a Lodestar he'd landed in a Texas field. When he returned to retrieve it, they arrested him, and tacked on a charge for the ten grams of cocaine they found in his suitcase. This served to speed along the indictment that prosecutors had been already building in Florida: for conspiracy to import cocaine and marijuana.

Frank Sturgis, out of jail on bond awaiting his appeal on the Watergate break-in charges, even showed up to the courtroom to watch Buchanan testify against Burnstine.

Burnstine staged a novel defense, claiming that he was working as an informant for the Federal Bureau of Alcohol, Tobacco and Firearms; he produced letters that he'd written about it. His alleged ATF case agent, however, said that their arrangement had never progressed beyond the conversation stage.

As soon as Burnstine was convicted, Sturgis and Buchanan received reduced sentences for their own crimes, as thanks for their "support and guidance during the six-month investigation prior to grand jury indictment."

From where Burnstine was sitting, providing "support and guidance" must have looked like a good move. After he received a seven-year sentence, he appealed his case and posted $100,000 bond. Then he set about turning on *his* former partners, including a Florida state representative who was soon indicted for selling him a map of the state's anti-drug strike-force locations. Burnstine began to appear at numerous other secret grand juries, giving up names—including that of Mitchell WerBell III.

WerBell's own public profile had risen since his arms-dealing partnership with Burnstine had dissolved into rancor. In January 1975, someone passed documentation to Senator Lowell Weicker that one of WerBell's weapons companies had presented a number of James Bond–like assassination devices (exploding telephones, cigarette packs, tennis balls, et cetera) to a heretofore unknown Special Operations Group within the DEA. The head of this covert anti-narcotics group was Lucien Conein, a decades-old friend of WerBell from their days in the OSS.* Their mandate was to identify and eliminate narcotics traffickers. "When you get down to it," a DEA official later admitted, "Conein was organizing an assassination program. He was frustrated by the big-time operators who were just too insulated to get to."

So, while WerBell was under fire for supplying lethal aid to the DEA so that it could neutralize kingpins, Burnstine was helping the DEA put the screws to WerBell.

Although several of its staff members wanted to remain anonymous, *High Times* still needed publicity. It was growing without the benefit of a national wholesaler, keeping track of distribution centers on a thumbtack-spotted US map in the back of the office.

So when a writer for *New York Magazine* approached about a story, it was a golden opportunity—the publication had, like the *New York Times*, refused to run ads for *High Times*.

---

* Another of their OSS friends was Watergate burglar E. Howard Hunt.

The writer, Albert Goldman, had been hipped to *High Times* through his research partner, a lifelong criminal named Philip "Chic" Eder who'd gotten out of the California Men's Colony in San Luis Obispo, headed east, and immediately started hanging around the *High Times* offices. Goldman had seen the third issue's "Interview with a Dope Taster" and wanted to talk to the mysterious sommelier of sinsemilla for a series he was doing on the drug trade. Goldman was summoned to *High Times* to meet with Dwyer and Kowl, and negotiations for the interview began.

Finally, on the appointed evening, Dwyer ushered into Goldman's Upper East Side apartment "Mike the Marijuana Maven," who looked like "a wasted, blinking hippie scientist with a pale mushroom face and eroding hairline" and soliloquized softly but nonstop, like a caffeinated late-night DJ.

While Eder supplied joints of various origins, the Maven philosophized about tetrahydrocannabinol and isomers, about a "society of grass dealers" that operated like the New York Stock Exchange, about the relationship between crop altitude and serotonin levels.

> Up and up a line of thought would climb, like the smoke from his smoldering joint; then, inevitably, at a certain point, like the coil in the smoke stream, the drift of the thought would reverse itself and start down in the opposite direction. After each of these elaborate mental somersaults, the Maven would pause for a moment and a sly, dissociative giggle would emerge from the side of his frozen face. Then, his eyes would blink, blink, blink, like a computer receiving a fresh set of signals, and he would be off again.

Goldman was intoxicated by Mike's insights, which provided him with pages of material for his article. It was only later—after the article ran in *New York*, in fact—that Goldman learned that there was no such thing as a professional dope taster, and that Mike, the marijuana maven, was a fictional character played by Tom Forcade.

Such playacting had, in fact, a semiregular mode of operation at *High Times*. Forcade would take on a larger-than-life persona—like, say, "Dope Taster" or "Smuggling Ace"—and have Ed Dwyer and Bob Singer interview him in an improvisatory rap session. "Tom would come over to my place about eleven in the evening with Bob in tow," Dwyer said. "Then he proceeded to expound. What he said generally left us either dazed or laughing. He never gave us any timetable. He just expected that at some point his ideas would be crystallized. He allowed us to improvise and cop our own styles. 'Ventriloquize' is a good word for the way he operated." By bringing in the unwitting Goldman, they were in effect taking their charade on the road.

Meanwhile, were anyone paying attention, a more factual portrait of Forcade emerged publicly. The ongoing lawsuit he'd joined, in an effort to obtain press credentials, had continued to wend its way through the court system, and after an FBI agent's deposition made reference to confidential files on Forcade, the judge ordered them unsealed. Never given a reason for the withholding of credentials, Forcade had assumed that the 1970 pieing of the obscenity commissioner was the reason. He'd even apologized for it in an affidavit, calling it "a juvenile prank which, in hindsight, I believe was foolish."

Now, in 1975, the curtain was lifted.

The government's eye had started fixing on Forcade back in 1968, when, at an Underground Press Convention, he'd handed a leaflet to an informant. Included in the Forcade files was the 1972 report that he had threatened to assassinate Richard Nixon.

Unfortunately for the government, the only witness to that alleged assassination plan was an informer whose identity the Detroit office of the FBI refused to reveal. So the FBI and Secret Service had accessed Forcade's private bank records, telephone records, and credit records and had opened mail, all without legal process. The Secret Service had then teamed with the Madison, Wisconsin, police department's undercover Affinity Squad to monitor Forcade's activity there. On July 13, 1972— the same day that the Florida Department of Law Enforcement was impounding Forcade's Cadillac in Miami—FBI agents were frantically sifting through a Convention Hall postal box, worried that Forcade had put an explosive in a package he was sending to the UPS accountant in Detroit. They opened it and found only "numerous writings, checks and other envelopes."

This only scratched the surface of the government's ongoing surveillance. Its sources had also included "infiltrators in Yippie meetings in Madison and in Florida, a Florida printer who turned down a Yippie job, credit bureaus, bank clerks, gun salesmen, undercover policemen and clerks who had access to Forcade's tax and medical records." Even Forcade's New York City mailman, it turned out, had been a source.*

The fourth annual A. J. Liebling Counter-Convention was held in San Francisco in February 1975. The newly flush *High Times* hosted a party in room 666 of the Sheraton Palace, and Forcade even broke out his white three-piece suit—the same one he'd worn three years earlier—to preside over the now-customary two tanks of nitrous oxide.

Among those stepping over the deflated balloons that were strewn about the suite were Jerry Rubin, Garry Trudeau . . . and Gabrielle Schang, whom Forcade had not seen since the fraught Miami summer.

Following the convention, Gabrielle had gone out to California and started working at the *Berkeley Barb*—first doing layouts, and then covering Patti Hearst's kidnapping and the exploits of the Symbionese Liberation Army and the spin-off New World Liberation Army. She'd also endured a personal trauma: after hitching a ride from the Berkeley campus one night, she'd been robbed, assaulted, and shot in the back as she jumped out of a van, a .38 bullet lodged near her spine. Police believed that the attack was related to the notorious Zebra Murders that were sweeping the Bay Area.

Schang had, more recently, been in the papers for refusing to answer a federal grand jury's questions about a communique the *Barb* had received from the New World Liberation Army, which had claimed credit for the bombing of a San Francisco bank building.

Forcade was besotted. "He'd been keeping tabs on me," Schang said. "He was reading everything I was writing." Now, while Forcade

---

* John Shattuck, the ACLU lawyer handling Forcade's case, included some of these documents when he testified at a congressional hearing on wiretapping in February. Forcade's files included information about another Madison activist, whose subsequent lawsuit eventually led to the release of all Affinity Squad files. In June, yet more disclosures were made about surveillance of the underground press. An investigation of the Special Service Staff of the Internal Revenue Service found that in 1971 the FBI had sent the SSS a list of every known US underground newspaper—148 of them. The SSS "made a special examination of these newspapers and their editors."

was running a magazine, it was Schang who was inarguably closer to the pulse of revolution.

"It was very hard to get back into his good graces," Schang said. "He was paranoid, and he was bitter." But he kept in touch with her after he returned to New York. "He invited me to go to Arizona. We went to Bisbee, an old, deserted copper-mining town, we stayed at a hotel, drove to Mexico, went to Laramie. We drove around Tombstone, all these desolate places, talking and smoking joints and driving." Eventually, he confided to her that he'd never been completely open in the past because he was a dealer.

Come back to New York, Forcade urged her.

After Forcade's return, paranoia only grew. In his "Michael King" guise, he acknowledged to an interviewer that the magazine's sources and its readers were largely criminals and that he was spending a third of his time listening to "an army of overpaid attorneys."

When the grand jury for Tim Hughes's kidnapping and assault charges rolled around, he and Forcade decided to bluff that they had caught Redbeard's theft on a security camera. "We hired a couple of people to sit outside the grand jury room with a projector and a pile of tapes to look like we had a visual presentation planned," said Hughes. Redbeard walked into the room and recanted.

But, perversely, Forcade moved the magazine's headquarters into the now-conspicuous space at 714 Broadway. The morning after he and Drucella escaped to the roof, Forcade sent Bob Lemmo and three others to set up new office space in what had nearly been a crime scene.

So perhaps it shouldn't have been surprising when an employee came to Andy Kowl to share her concerns about a messenger *High Times* had hired, who was taking too long on his deliveries and pickups and asking too many questions. Kowl brought the issue to the attention of Forcade, who immediately decided to hire a private detective to tail the potential fink.

The messenger, they soon learned, was stopping midroute at windowless telephone company switching centers and meeting police, who would open the packages, review the contents, and send him on his way.

Forcade summoned one of his attorneys, who asked what kind of information the police might have.

"Not much," Forcade replied. *High Times* had instituted a policy to shoot photographs of contraband off the premises, and the staff was told not to bring drugs to the offices... well, he clarified, "only enough joints to get them through the day."

"Of course, I'm scared," Forcade admitted. "How would you feel if you knew one of your employees was out to get you? I'm not a martyr. Jail was a Sixties scene."

At times, it seemed like Forcade had moved on from the sixties scene entirely. No longer working shoulder to shoulder with everyone in a basement office or sleeping in a teepee, he'd rented out Room 214 of the Fifth Avenue Hotel, where editors brought him *High Times* pages to look over. It was also, precariously, where Forcade was operating a drug distribution business with Albert Goldman's jailbird pal Chic Eder.

When Forcade learned that Michael Horowitz and Cynthia Palmer were editing an anthology of Aldous Huxley's writings about psychedelics, he sent a driver to pick them up and lead them through a padlocked back entrance to an apartment with no number on the door. "Tom was sitting in a chair across the room from us," said Horowitz. "He had been holed up for a long time and wore a haunted look. He explained that he was hiding out from the Feds, who were after him." The paranoia was only heightened after they shared a joint, Horowitz said, but Forcade was eager to run an excerpt from the book. A deal was made, and they were escorted home. Horowitz later interviewed Albert Hofmann, the Swiss creator of LSD, for the magazine, and coauthored the *High Times Encyclopedia of Recreational Drugs*, but he never saw Forcade again. Another contributor summoned to the Fifth Avenue Hotel was Paul Kirchner, the cartoonist behind the graphically bold, surrealistic Old West comic strip "Dope Rider." Forcade had responded to Kirchner's first submission with an effusive midnight phone call that lasted ninety minutes. "He was kind of rambling, kind of high, but very enthusiastic," Kirchner remembered. "He said, 'Oh man, I love the way you just parodied all the clichés of psychedelia.'" Kirchner hadn't intended parody, but graciously accepted the compliment. After the third installment, *High Times* editor Bob Singer told Kirchner that Forcade wished to meet him in person.

When Kirchner arrived at Forcade's suite, he was surprised to find the publisher well groomed, hair shorn and mustache short, and dressed in a three-piece suit. "He looked like someone going to a trial, trying to look their best. But he also had an intense look in his eyes that reminded me of photos I'd seen of Jesse James."

One or two *High Times* editors worked in the background, filling up balloons from a nitrous tank in the corner of the main room and taking hits. But apart from admiring the Smith & Wesson patch on the shoulder of Kirchner's denim jacket, Forcade was strictly business.

He looked over Kirchner's sketches. "So how much are we paying you for these?"

"Uh, I don't know," said the cartoonist, and Forcade froze.

"You don't know?" Forcade asked indignantly. "Why would you do work when you don't know what you're getting paid? Suppose I said that you were getting $5,000—you wouldn't be doing enough work for that! Or $25—you wouldn't be getting paid enough! Anybody uncomfortable talking about money is someone you don't want to work with."

A short distance away, Bob Singer was talking quietly with the other editor.

"Hey, Bob," snapped Forcade, "could you stop talking?"

"Sure, Tom."

"'Cause, you know, I'm talking to Paul here. You *get* that, right?"

Silence.

"I mean, when I'm *talking to someone*, and someone else is talking at the same time, it bothers me, you know? 'Cause it's *distracting*, you know? It's distracting!"

Forcade turned his attention back to Kirchner's work. This episode of "Dope Rider" was set during the Mexican Revolution, and Pancho Villa was standing in front of his own Wanted poster, facing a firing squad.

"He looks like Joe Stalin," Forcade said.

"Yeah, you know, they had the same head," Kirchner said.

He'd meant it literally, but Forcade stared back and smiled at the profundity. "Yeah, their head was in the same place!"

Forcade asked Kirchner if he wanted to smoke some $200-an-ounce grass. Kirchner, not much of a toker, declined.

Forcade looked back at him thoughtfully. "That's good," he said, "because this isn't $200-an-ounce grass."

For all his success, Forcade was careful to maintain an underdog image. "One of the most persistent rumors is that *High Times* is being bankrolled by somebody big—*Playboy*, *Penthouse*, NORML, the Brotherhood, the CIA, an international cartel of rolling paper manufacturers, the tobacco industry, or a big-time dope syndicate," fretted one editorial. "But we're not backed by anyone with that kind of clout."

The magazine walked a fine line, acknowledging that its advertisers were a cottage industry of paraphernalia manufacturers hawking "a hash-pipe-in-a-bottle or a 500-yard-long roll of cigarette paper" and insisting to readers that the magazine itself was above such crassness. "If you're waiting for *High Times* rolling papers, *High Times* hash pipes, *High Times* massage oil, *High Times* clubs, etc., forget it, because there probably aren't going to be any. *High Times* is into information and entertainment, not empires."

But the magazine's profile was rising everywhere. A giant billboard— with a smiling pilot in a bomber jacket in front of a DC-3, giving a thumbs-up next to the words "Ask Your Local Dealer"—went up along Sunset Boulevard. Editor Bob Singer traveled to McLeod Ganj in India for an exclusive audience with the Dalai Lama. (*High Times*: "Have you ever taken any drugs?" Dalai Lama: "No...enlightenment should be curried by the full alert mind.") When a New York City man held ten hostages in a New York bank for eight hours, the gunman demanded $10 million in gold, an airplane, and to speak with someone from *High Times*. "There is nothing I wanted more than to have some of your people come in to join me for a nice long chat and friendly smoke-in," the robber later wrote from Rikers Island.

The offices moved yet again, this time uptown to 27th Street, near Madison Square Park, where there was room to run things like a real magazine, with copyeditors and proofreaders, drawing tables and a stat room, and offices for each editor.

The imagined readership had gotten fancier, too. Where an early issue had included a guide to the best scales one could buy, now there were illustrated spreads on "Dealers' Wheels" (recommending a Lamborghini Countach for speed and a four-door Chevy station wagon for stealth) and "How to Fly Low."

With the addition of Toni Brown as art director, *High Times* achieved a sheen of hip glamour and professionalism. Brown, a hypersocial lesbian who favored bright orange flight suits and aviator sunglasses, commissioned work from high-profile fashion photographers and brought the magazine's visual style in line with the slickest of consumer periodicals on the newsstands.

As it approached the end of 1975, *High Times*'s circulation had sky-rocketed past 250,000 per issue. The page count had more than doubled to more than a hundred pages, about a third of which were paid ads—for pipes of glass, oak, brass, plastic, teak, or rosewood; for sterling coke-stash pendants; for seashells you could smoke out of; for quaalude paper-weights; for joint chimneys attached to under-the-jacket plastic tubes that could be sucked on "at a concert, at a ballgame, on a picnic." The Mary-gin ($5) would clean your weed, and the Isomerizer ($275) promised to extract oil, turn CBD to THC, and "convert low-rotating forms of THC as found in low-quality marijuana and hashish to the more psychedelic and spiritual high-rotating forms." If you were tired of marijuana, you could order "lettuce opium," which could be "smoked alone or blended with favorite herbs."

The Christmas 1975 issue—a whopping 148 pages—also featured ads from record companies, hi-fi manufacturers, and, in a unique post-Watergate sign of the times, a manufacturer of anti-bugging devices. "Tom was totally hung up on getting non-paraphernalia ads," recalled Shelly Schorr, who came on to sell advertising. "Film ads, record ads—it didn't make a difference, he loved it." Of course, there were limits. "He knew that Chevrolet wasn't gonna buy ads."

High Times was now a glossy travelogue of high adventure and a well-spring of news about "the business" from an international network of sources. With regular updates on price fluctuations, tips for would-be entrepreneurs, and its alliance with NORML, it had simultaneously le-gitimized and commodified the drug culture.

And the drug culture was winning battles.

As the magazine scornfully covered anti-narcotics government task forces with names like Operation Dragnet (the first maritime blockade in US waters since the rum patrols of the Prohibition era), Operation Buc-caneer (targeting Jamaican traffic), and Operation Star Trek (utilizing the Air Force's NORAD system to track smuggling planes), it gleefully reported that the Drug Enforcement Administration's embattled first di-rector, John Bartels, was resigning and that the Senate was preparing to investigate the agency.

Most importantly, thanks to the growing popularity of marijuana, successful lobbying, and quickly developing scientific research—not to mention Nixon's absence, and the wave of new Democrats who'd been elected in midterms—legalization was moving quickly. Alaska, Maine, Colorado and California, and Ohio all decriminalized marijuana in the spring and summer of 1975.

Higher times, it seemed, were coming to America.

At the beginning of the bicentennial year, *High Times* expanded even further. Forcade launched an oversize spin-off tabloid, *National Weed*, a sort of *National Enquirer* for potheads, complete with scare-quote-laden headlines ("Henry Kissinger Is a Russian Agent"; "Reggae Star Jimmy Cliff Hates Jamaicans"; "Narcs Escalate Viet Nam-Type Dope War in Mexico"), plus space for A. J. Weberman's dissection of Jackie O's trash bins and a full-color comics section for underground cartoons by Kim Deitch, Spain Rodriguez, Bill Griffith, and Gilbert Shelton.

When Gabrielle Schang decided to return to New York, Forcade offered her a job reviving *Alternative Press Revue* as *Alternative Journalism Review* and, finally, *Alternative Media*.

Forcade also began plans to produce a glossy paraphernalia-industry trade magazine called *Dealer*, in which the pure-capitalist side of the drug world could spread its wings. Reports on catching thieves ("In-Store Security: 25 Ways to Protect Your Profits") and "dealing with the heat" ran alongside interviews with head-shop proprietors and rolling-paper barons and articles about the FCC's resistance to allowing paraphernalia ads on the radio.

But the smooth sailing ended suddenly on a Sunday night in January of 1976, when Forcade, cruising past the Fifth Avenue Hotel, noticed silhouettes in the windows of his room. Further scrutiny revealed that the visitors to his suite—which housed his passport, business papers, and a half-dozen variety of drugs—were a group of police and firemen.

So he called Chic Eder, the seasoned criminal, for help casing his own joint. Chic promptly reported that the locks had been changed, so the two of them removed the door from its hinges, and Forcade ran in to retrieve a satchel of money. He handed it to Chic.

The story that Forcade soon pieced together, after his lawyer spoke with police, was that a window had been left open, allowing the water pipes to freeze and burst; when the room started to flood, the hotel sent in cleaners, who found a hundred pounds of weed in a closet. The hotel immediately summoned the NYPD, and the felonious appurtenances of Room 214, from cocaine adulterants to cocaine, began to pile up. Forcade suspected that this story was a ruse, that he'd been set up by the hotel or the police, but such theories were immaterial.

The following day, he sent Chic back to recover whatever else he could from the room—cash in the refrigerator, gold in a safe, stray drugs— while he headed into the office to make arrangements.

"Tom called me in his office, we were talking about business, and I just saw a physical change happen in front of my face," remembered Andy Kowl. "I don't know how to describe it except it was like shades being pulled down behind his eyes."

"He said, 'Look, I'm leaving for a while. You're not going to be able to get a hold of me most of the time, but I'll try to check in. You're in charge, you sign the checks. Make a lot of money, go out of business—do whatever you've got to do. I'm sure you'll be fine. We'll talk down the road.' And he was gone."

Kowl called Stanley Place and Paul Tornetta, the middle-aged men Forcade had just hired as circulation director and marketing director, into his office to break the news.

They'd been wined and dined by Forcade, who'd turned on the charm, presented himself as a responsible businessman, and lured them to be a part of the *High Times* success story. They had mortgages and families—and now they realized that their new boss was skipping town.

When Chic returned Forcade's satchel, Forcade opened it up and showed him more than a hundred thousand dollars in large bills. "Take what you want," Forcade said.

"Nah, that's punk change," Chic said. "I just want in."

"In on what?"

"In on *High Times*, and in on everything," Chic said.

The pinch was on. A week later, Tim Hughes, now working as a receptionist at *High Times*, requested a raise, noting that he was about to get married and that "I am almost invaluable at the position I work at. I make reference not only to the current situation with Tom, but at any other time I am the insulation for this office. Any other person would be a security risk. I'm sure that Tom would agree."

One Monday night a month later, Chic and Tim were with Forcade in Florida, when a forty-four-foot trawler brought in two tons of Santa Marta Gold from a Colombian freighter anchored thirty miles off Florida's Gulf Coast.

The next transfer point was set up at a ranch a few hundred feet from US 41, popularly known as the Tamiami Trail. From there, Forcade, Chic, Tim, and Larry Hertz were to unload bales of marijuana from Zodiac inflatable boats and haul everything eighty-five miles southeast to Palmetto Estates, near Miami.

While the marijuana was loaded into trucks, Larry served as the lookout, sitting on a grass mound and holding his arms like he was fishing from the narrow canal that ran along the dirt road to the ranch. *If anyone gets close enough to you to see you don't have a fishing line*, Forcade told him, *it'll be too late and it won't matter anyway.*

Larry's truck was packed up first with the smaller load—a little under a ton of weed. He started to write down the directions to the safehouse.

Forcade stopped him. "What are you, out of your fucking mind?"

Larry was feeling a little stoned from the samples.

"You can't write it down," Forcade said. "If you get pulled over, they'll know where it is, and I'll be in back of you. I'll be driving into a house full of police. You don't want that to happen, do you?"

"Of course not, Tom," said Larry.

The route was pretty direct, luckily, but Larry, a city boy, had never driven a stick shift, except for the two hours of lessons Forcade had given him the day before.

"I'm gonna be in the next truck," Forcade assured him. "We just gotta load it up—I'll be maybe an hour behind you."

Shortly after Larry left the scene, however, one of the trucks became mired in the mud. While Forcade was struggling to free the truck, he saw a game warden's vehicle come to a stop on the main road. Forcade got out of the truck and walked over.

"I thought they were hunting to start with," the warden told a local newspaper the next day. "I asked the occupant where his friends were. He said they were looking for a place to camp."

Forcade walked back toward the canal. Chic and Tim squeezed into the cab and Forcade took his place behind the wheel.

"We could have stopped right there," Tim said later, with regret. "We could have subdued the warden, put him in his trunk, but Tom was insistent."

This time, the wheels pulled loose. Moments later, the Chevy camper emerged, blowing by the game warden.

The warden followed the camper east on Tamiami Trail, from a distance of about fifty feet, and turned on his flashing lights. The camper kept going, shifting from side to side from heavy weight, and the warden called for a roadblock ahead.

Inside the camper, the three heard the roadblock calls on a citizens band radio. As they approached the trap, Chic called for Forcade to take the truck off the road. He made a hard right into the swampy land.

The camper came to a halt almost immediately. Forcade grabbed a briefcase filled with money, and the three men jumped out and ran into the woods.

The converging authorities chased after the three men, but once they disappeared behind trees, the game warden admitted, "there wasn't much we could do. Besides, we had to find out why we were chasing them to start with."

That question would be answered within minutes. The wildlife officer approached the abandoned Chevy camper, adorned with Tennessee license plates and bumper stickers that read "George Wallace for President" and "Happy Birthday, America!" Opening the doors, he was surprised to find that it was a "hollow shell," with the bed and sink removed to make room for the 2,800 pounds of marijuana stacked inside wrapped in burlap and two layers of plastic. The only other items were the CB radio, binoculars, a Styrofoam cooler, a pair of chukka boots, and three books: a poetry anthology, a paperback biography of criminal financier Robert Vesco, and a *Red Sonja* comic book.

As sheriff's deputies and wardens from the Florida Game and Fresh Water Fish Commission spread out on the ground, police helicopters hovered in the sky above.

Larry got back to the safehouse and found that he had to deflate the tires to fit the truck into the garage. Then he had to bring the bales into the house through the side door, and finally move his truck down the street to make room for Forcade's truck, because the garage was only big enough for one vehicle at a time.

Unfortunately, Larry realized, there was no basement, and there were no shades on the windows, which meant the entire load had to fit into closets.

There was also no food in the house, and he was getting hungry while he waited, sitting in the empty, weed-smelling living room, with no phone, not even a watch. As the hours passed, he started to figure that Tom was either busted or dead. Did he have an accident? Who would leave this much weed in the middle of the smuggle?

Tuesday morning turned to Tuesday afternoon. Tom was about ten hours behind schedule.

Larry walked down the street until he found a phone booth. He called New York, called the magazine offices. No answer. He went back to the house and tried to sleep.

The three fugitives had split up as they waded into the swamp but reconnected hours later in the dark. They'd debated heading to the highway to hitch a ride but realized they wouldn't know whether headlights belonged to a police car until it was too late. Amid the distant sounds of helicopters and barking dogs, they brushed away a seemingly infinite number of mosquitoes and flies, so many that they were getting bitten through their clothes. Forcade buried the briefcase of money at the foot of a cypress tree, and over Chic's initial objections, they snuggled together for warmth in the late-winter cold.

When night fell on Tuesday, they split up again. "There's a pay phone at a gas station about a mile up the road," Forcade said. "If I'm not back in an hour, assume I'm caught. Good luck."

Three hours later, with no word from Forcade, Tim told Chic he was going up to the road to find out what was going on. He crouched by a bridge that was, unfortunately, right next to the Everglades City sheriff's substation. A patrol car pulled up, and an officer got out.

"What are you doing?" he asked Hughes.

Hughes, caked with mud and covered in bites, burst into tears with a story about hitching a ride with a lecherous motorist. "I jumped out," he cried. "Thank God you're here."

"You're lucky," the officer said. "We're out here looking for drug smugglers." He offered Hughes a seat in the front.

"Just a second," he said when Hughes was buckled in. He reached for his radio. "I gotta check in with the lieutenant."

When the lieutenant appeared at the window, he asked to see the treads of Hughes's Adidas sneakers. They matched with footprints in the swamp. The charade was up.

After Hughes was taken into custody, the search was called off. Forcade and Chic replenished themselves with briny water and crawled through the nearby parking lot of squad cars on their elbows, making their way to the foot of the bridge, which they traversed from beneath, hanging from the rungs like they were monkey bars. Once they were far enough away from everything, they walked back out onto the highway and made their way back to the ranch.

Meanwhile, the 2,800 pounds of marijuana headed to the county incinerator.

On Wednesday morning, Larry returned to the pay phone and called his friend Steve in Staten Island and explained the situation. Steve knew guys in a Florida-based smuggling group called the Black Tuna Gang. Larry gave Steve the number of his phone booth.

Larry then tried New York again, no answer.

But Bob, from the Black Tuna Gang, called back quickly.

"You're sitting on a lot, huh?" Bob asked.

"Yep."

"How much?"

"Oh, roughly... bring enough cash for about a thousand pounds."

"Where are you?"

Larry didn't know Bob enough to trust that he wouldn't come armed or have someone with him, so he gave an address near the phone booth. Then he walked back to the house and moved a thousand pounds out of the closets and into one room.

An hour later Larry met Bob down the street.

"Give me the keys to the car," Larry said. "Put your head down, and I'll drive us back to the house. You got the money?"

Bob showed Larry the money.

When they got to the house, Bob cut into a bale, took an approving sniff, and gave him the money. Larry stashed it in the dishwasher. Then he drove Bob back to the street, headed to the pay phone, and called New York again.

This time he reached Forcade's assistant at *High Times*.

"I don't know what's going on," she said, "but Tom called here and he's a nervous wreck. He sounded out of it or something… he's going crazy. He wanted to know if you were there."

"I'm not there now, because I'm calling you, there's no phone there."

"Well, Tom said to get back to wherever you're supposed to be."

When Larry returned to the safehouse, he noticed that the door was no longer locked. And sitting in the middle of the kitchen table was a bottle of calamine lotion that hadn't been there before. His heart racing, he made his way to the dishwasher when a figure lunged at him.

"You motherfucker, I'm gonna kill you!"

The attacker wrapped his hands around Larry's neck.

It was Forcade. "Where's my fucking weed, you motherfucker?"

"Tom, I sold it!"

Forcade loosened his grip. "I smell weed in here!"

"I didn't sell it *all*. I left a few hundred pounds that we're going to take back to New York, and we can break it down into five-, ten-pound pieces."

"How could you fucking sell it?" Forcade demanded.

"Every bale had been weighed! Each one was marked by gross weight, and I had the scale. I figured out how much it was going to be for the net after we took off the burlap bags and the plastic."

Forcade looked at him, then smiled and hugged him.

"You're the fucking best. This is like a fucking dream, Larry! Where's the money?"

Larry pointed to the dishwasher. As Forcade started counting the money, he said, "This is great, because we're in big fucking trouble."

"You're in big trouble? Tom, where's the fucking loot? Where's the rest of the weed?"

Forcade told him about the chase, the swamp, and Hughes's arrest.

"Okay," Larry said. "Well, at least we got this."

"What about the rest of the weed here?"

"I'll get my friend John. He'll come down. He has a Navajo twin engine, we can get a lot in there. And I'll fly it back to New York. You don't have to worry about anything. I got rid of all of this so far, let me get rid of the rest. Take a few pounds for yourself."

"I don't want to wait for your friend to come down. I've been through a lot of hell here. I'm bitten up, mosquito bites everywhere. We're going to take this and we're flying back by regular airlines. Get your friend to meet us by the airport."

"I don't want to fucking take all of this by commercial, Tom. What are we doing here? My friend Paul has a plane. He could fly us back."

"No, no, no, no," Forcade protested. "We can just take a flight into LaGuardia; there's another one going to Kennedy."

"Let me just fucking hold it. I don't want it out of my sight."

"No, it's cool—let's just get back. Let's do it."

Larry opened each bale and inhaled deeply, choosing the best of the beautiful, bright gold and separating it into stacks.

They went to the Jordan Marsh department store, bought up the American Tourister luggage, bought extra plastic bags, sprayed the bales with Lysol to cover the smell, and packed them into ten 27-inch Pullman suitcases. Then they hopped on separate flights back to New York.

Forcade and Larry met by the baggage carousel, but the luggage never came through. One of the handlers, they suspected, had taken it for themselves.

A few days later, Forcade returned to Florida. He took Gabrielle to see Bob Marley and the Wailers perform at the National Association of Record Merchandisers convention in Miami, where Andy Kowl and Shelly Schorr were working to sell ads to the music business. It was the first time anyone at *High Times* had seen Forcade in two months.

The following day, while Gabrielle enjoyed the hotel pool, Forcade took a side trip to the Everglades. This time, quite miraculously, he located the briefcase.

Forcade brought the suitcase back to Michael Kennedy in New York. Kennedy, recently relocated from San Francisco, had nearly unparalleled credentials as a radical lawyer, working on the defenses of the Chicago Eight, Timothy Leary, Huey Newton, and members of the Weather Underground and the Brotherhood of Eternal Love. Soon he would be defending Tim Hughes, who was facing five years to life for the 2,800 confiscated pounds, and whose arrest threatened to complicate the ongoing New York investigation that stemmed from the January raid of Forcade's Fifth Avenue Hotel room.

When Forcade opened the water-logged suitcase, the perplexed lawyer stared at the contents: mud.

"We've got a serious money-laundering problem here," Forcade said.

Kennedy realized that under the "mud and scum and grime and alligator shit" was, in fact, several hundred thousand dollars, hopelessly stuck together. They tried to figure out a way to get it redeemed by the Bureau of Engraving and Printing—Kennedy even visited a mint—but that would, of course, bring unwanted attention. They tried using a hairdryer, they tried putting some of the money in an oven. Eventually Forcade rented a loft directly across from the *High Times* office on 27th Street and set to cleaning the money. It took days of peeling bills—all tens and twenties—and setting them out on tables to dry.

The magazine had managed without its founder—in fact, while Forcade was in the swamps hiding from police, *High Times*'s Craig Copetas had gotten Jimmy Carter to go on the record in favor of marijuana decriminalization.

But after the Everglades fiasco, Forcade's behavior was even more erratic. *High Times* pages were brought across the street to the loft for his approval. "If he didn't like it, he would rip it in half," said Andy Kowl. "If it were a piece of artwork that had cost $1,500 and he didn't dig it, he would throw it on the floor."

"The first time I met him, I was sort of granted an audience and went over to the loft and hung out with him," said Glenn O'Brien, a former *Interview* and *Rolling Stone* editor who'd been recruited to *High Times* months earlier by Bob Singer and Ed Dwyer. "I was told that this is the guy who runs things, and he owns the magazine. He was already cryptic and mysterious, but then when you have someone kind of playing that role, it's even stranger."

One could be forgiven for being confused about the chain of command at the magazine. "Andy Kowl thought he ran things in Tom's absence," said *Dealer* editor Keith Deutsch. "The guys in advertising thought *they* ran things. And the top people in editorial like Bob Singer thought *they* ran things. Tom let everyone believe they ran things after he returned, and maybe they did in a way. He seemed to be in the background, reading *Trade-A-Plane* magazine and plotting economic revolutions."

Bob Lemmo recalled that Forcade would swoop in at the last minute and reject articles by proxy, to the confusion of writers who'd never heard of Forcade because his name was still kept off the masthead. "The people listed as 'Editor' would have already approved stuff, then Tom would kill it and they'd say, 'Well, it's been killed.' And they would say, 'By who?' They'd say, 'Well, by the, uh, boss. You know, the boss of the boss.'" When Shelley Levitt began working as an assistant at *High Times* in the middle of 1976, she said, "Tom was just a rumor." Once she finally laid eyes on him, she saw "a skulking, huddled figure walking through the office with his hands in his pockets. You would feel his presence before you caught sight of him."

As the magazine grew, it became even easier for Forcade to not interact with its contributors. "He was like somebody who doesn't want to be seen," said Steve Cooper, who photographed many of the centerfolds. "When Toni Brown introduced us, I'd been working for them for six months. I thought I would get *something* from him. I remember it being like a black hole. Cold, dark, melancholic—walking doom."

At other times, Forcade was very much in the foreground, but with his face red with anger, breaking out in hives, throwing heavy objects, kicking in doors, or tearing up pages after they'd been laid out and typeset. One art director remembered the "berserk" fury that erupted when an article on smuggling made its way to Forcade's desk with Colombia spelled "Columbia" throughout.

"Tom would come in like a whirlwind, and then slam the door," recalled Scott Cohen, who worked in the art department. "If you needed him, there was a note on Tom's door saying you must knock and wait for an answer before entering."

Once, enraged that the office had been carpeted, he accosted a passing assistant. "That's your raise on the floor," he snarled. He might fire off draconian memos, like one that required that every item in the production department needed to be affixed to bulletin boards. When he next entered the production area, everything not on a bulletin board was torn down. A hurled painting narrowly missed one employee. The magazine schedule lay on the floor in shreds.

An employee who voiced excitement at one of Forcade's editorial ideas risked a withering response: "Ah, we have a *Yes Man*." He often hired people in whom he saw potential, who weren't yet qualified for their positions, and encouraged them to grow into them. But he'd also make sure they maintained a certain level of fear in his presence. "If you can't do it, maybe I need to find someone who can," he'd threaten. A firing might be accompanied with the warning "You have thirty seconds to get out of here." He'd command one of his editors to yell at art director Toni Brown; when she'd come to him, upset, he'd comfort her.

"He was a master of being able to manipulate one person against another," said Shelly Schorr. "It was kind of like a check-and-balance system, where he knew that this person hated that person. Sooner or later, one of them would try to outfox the other, and he let them play on one another."

"Tom would come in and it was like a dark cloud descending," said Diana Marchand, who worked with Toni Brown. "It seemed like either Tom was going to come in and kill us all, or the police were going to come and arrest us."

Those who'd known Forcade for years saw a different side. "At work, the man was borderline evil," remembered Ed Dwyer. "On the other hand, he'd call out of the blue (again late at night), and the next morning we'd be on a flight to the Florida coast to lend moral support to a pal of his on trial for dealing. Then he'd rent a four-seater to fly low over the Everglades by moonlight to Miami, where we'd gobble quaaludes and blast away with .44-caliber Magnums in a buddy's Coconut Grove backyard."

With the cooperation of Ken Burnstine, undercover narcotics officers had spent seven months busy arranging meetings and making plans with Mitchell WerBell III. After WerBell was finally indicted—along with an ex-cop and members of the Cleveland Mob—on charges of conspiring to import marijuana into the United States, the Miami DEA boasted that Ken Burnstine's testimony would result in the "collapse of the entire structure of the drug smuggling business in south Florida." The unfolding events captured the attention of Forcade and the pages of *High Times*, which dubbed the upcoming trial a "Marijuana Watergate"—without, of course, mentioning Forcade's own longstanding connection to Burnstine. To *National Weed*, Burnstine fumed that "Sturgis is a rotten motherfucking liar. He's a two-bit, penny-ante thief who works both sides of the street. Sturgis is an A-1 shit pot."

"After the trial is over," he promised, "I'll tell you all."

But Burnstine never had the chance to tell all—not to *National Weed*, and not to the federal court. On June 16, 1976, the week before he was set to testify, Burnstine (who'd not only never spent a day in jail but also never had to surrender his arms license or pilot certification) was preparing for an air show in which he was competing. Five thousand feet over Mojave, California, he pushed his P-51 Mustang into a split S maneuver, lost control, and hit the ground at 300 miles per hour.

The explosion made forensics difficult. "Identification was made exclusively from a fingerprint taken off a left thumb that was found by investigators combing the rubble," reported Carl Hiaasen of the *Miami Herald*.

"The man had a lot of enemies," an official told Hiaasen. "The crash was in bits and pieces. You have to look at the man's record and draw your own conclusion."

Days after the crash, another *Herald* reporter revealed that, in an earlier, off-the-record conversation, Burnstine had confided that he'd been double-crossed by the government, for which he'd worked since the early 1960s. Eventually, Burnstine had promised the reporter, the "whole story" would come out. Justice Department officials refused to comment on the claims.

"I used to consider Ken one of my very best friends," Mitch WerBell told *High Times*, "but in a way, the son of a bitch turned on everybody. As they say in China, 'It couldn't have happened to a nicer guy.'"*

At about this time, the men's magazine *Argosy* published an interview with a former WerBell employee who'd also been, with Sturgis, part of an early-1960s paramilitary outfit called the International Anti-Communist Brigade. Gerry Hemming had been known to fabricate stories, and had his latest claims involved any other group of men, they might have been easily dismissed.

Hemming said that, in the lead-up to the 1972 conventions in Miami, Sturgis had offered to obtain automatic weapons for Florida law enforcement in return for law enforcement credentials that would allow Sturgis's "people" to carry automatic weapons.

ARGOSY: What were they planning?

---

* WerBell's earlier assassination-device scandal with the DEA now became his best defense at trial. He insisted that he'd been secretly working for Conein's Special Operations Group, and that *he* had been trying to trap *Burnstine*. WerBell's lawyer assured the court that his client "would never get involved in a conspiracy to import marijuana. Guns, revolutions, maybe even assassinations, but he's not being tried on that."

HEMMING: Create a shoot-out, using the Yippies and Zippies and the other "hardcore Commies" they were so worried about. The people I spoke to were gonna put some of this equipment in their hands, and some in law-enforcement hands, and use some of the local vigilantes to start the shoot-out. This would finally straighten out Washington as to where the priorities were on overcoming the "domestic Communist menace."*

ARGOSY: What stopped it from happening?

HEMMING: I think some other people created enough heat to prevent the equipment from falling into those hands. I think [James] McCord was one who did something about it. I've been told [J. Edgar] Hoover and certain Agency people were upset that certain other people were trying to create a private Gestapo in the US. So they penetrated it and took measures to stop it.

Multiple elements of Forcade's compartmentalized life suddenly seemed, at the very least, claustrophobic with coincidence, all part of one Möbius strip of intrigue.**

---

* "We were deeply concerned by extremist elements," Sturgis's fellow Watergate burglar Howard Hunt had written in his memoir *Undercover*, singling out Yippies and Zippies as "groupings of the counterculture directed by the counter-government, whose purpose seemed clearly aimed at the destruction of our traditional institutions they could not hope to eliminate through elective process."

** Mitch WerBell's legal team subpoenaed Hemming—along with Watergate figures Egil Krogh, John Ehrlichman, and former President Nixon—to testify for the defense. Although Nixon and Ehrlichman never did testify, Egil Krogh, the former head of the White House Special Investigation Unit, better known as "the Plumbers," did. (Krogh assured the court that he knew nothing about an assassination program and that he had never met any of the defendants.) Gerry Hemming, who'd given the magazine interview about right-wingers plotting to mow down Zippies with machine guns, also showed up to testify for the defense and was arrested in the courtroom corridor on his own cocaine-and-marijuana smuggling charge. None of this mattered too much to Mitch WerBell. With the death of star witness Ken Burnstine, the prosecution fell apart. WerBell and his fellow defendants were acquitted of all charges.

After four years, the *Yipster Times* had bumped up its production values, introducing slick layouts and color illustrations, but had never lost its conspiratorial bent. There was an uptick in theorizing about the deaths of John F. and Robert Kennedy—there was a regular column called "Assassin Nation"—spurred on by A. J. Weberman's research for his book *Coup d'Etat in America*. The paper was also edging into weird allegations and innuendo, with anonymous sources fueling stories about the US military causing a swine flu outbreak or weaponizing weather overseas.* Without evidence, the *Yipster Times* asserted that Jimmy Carter's campaign had intervened in a Georgia drug investigation swirling around the orbit of the Allman Brothers Band, whose label head was a major Carter fundraiser. Thus did the *Yipster Times* become the first national publication to put presidential candidate Carter on its cover, with a headline that blared JIMMY CARTER COKE SCANDAL. ("How can Abbie Hoffman's people be down on coke?" Carter's press secretary, Jody Powell, allegedly said when presented with the issue.)

The Yippies even found a new media platform for themselves: public access television. As soon as Channel J was launched in Manhattan, *The Jelly Bread Show* agitated for the legalization of marijuana every Friday night. The Yippie hosts brazenly brought their product into the studio, smoking joints on the air, which meant that the literal haze of the proceedings was visible to anyone who tuned in.

Meanwhile, they ratcheted up their stunts for the election year. A Yippie named Ben Masel spit on Democratic hopeful Henry "Scoop" Jackson at the Madison airport and earned the distinction of being the first person indicted under a law that made it a felony to assault a member of Congress. In New York, Aron Kay revived Forcade's old baked-goods-as-protest-tool, garnering press for nailing William F. Buckley with a shaving cream pie and Daniel Patrick Moynihan, who was running for the Senate, with banana cream.

Not all of the Yippie publicity of 1976 was voluntary. When the *Chicago Tribune* ran a fevered article about a supposed assassination plot, under the front-page double-decker headline TIE CUBAN SPY TO PLOT AGAINST FORD, REAGAN—it identified the "terrorist turned informer" as a member

---

* As with many conspiracy theories, there were kernels of truth: the 1976 swine flu outbreak did originate at Fort Dix, New Jersey, and the Defense Advanced Research Projects Agency (DARPA) did conduct research on weather control.

of the Youth International Party. (The *Yipster Times* had simply once published a letter from the informer, whose tips to the feds turned out to be questionable anyway.) This, the Yippies would later claim, was what led to FBI wiretaps, mail opening, and false arrests in the coming months.

This was exactly the kind of attention that Forcade was eager to avoid. "The sense I got was that Tom felt like it was time for him to move on to something else," said Yippie Steve D'Angelo. "He still had an affinity for the Yippie politics, but he didn't really feel like it was the zeitgeist anymore. And Tom viewed Dana Beal as sort of a junior varsity team leader who could sort of keep the flame burning while he stepped away. There was also a business relationship there. So Tom subsidized the Yippies by giving exceptionally good weed deals. We always had the very best cannabis in the world, cannabis that nobody else could get from anywhere. When the rest of the world was dealing bricks of Mexican, we were getting Temple balls from Nepal, vacuum sealed Thai sticks, cannabis from Burma and Belize. We were getting hand-rolled hash from the valley, all these incredible, exotic products of exceptionally high quality, and that allowed folks in the Yippie network to become fairly significant players in local cannabis markets. Months later, those exact same products would be in the centerfold of *High Times*."

The relationship between Forcade and the Yippies was seemingly inextricable. That spring, an ambitious junior high school student from Long Island was determined to get a professional freelance assignment. Smarting from a few dozen rapid rejections, R. J. Cutler called the Underground Press Syndicate phone number in *Steal This Book* and finally found an encouraging audience: Gabrielle Schang at *Alternative Media*, who told him to come into the office. Feeling emboldened, Cutler hung up the phone and tried the other numbers that were listed in the book. All of them rerouted to the *High Times* switchboard. "I remember thinking, 'Oh, all of these publications are really one.'"

The next day Cutler went to 714 Broadway, the former *High Times* office that now housed *Alternative Media* and *National Weed*, and found Schang ensconced in the back, sitting at a desk surrounded by piled-up magazines, "almost like a clearinghouse. It felt temporary, everything was in boxes. It felt like there had been, or was going to be, a lot of activity, but there wasn't any when I was there. There was just Gabrielle Schang, this beautiful woman in the middle of this underground paradise."

Brainstorming for an appropriate topic, they noted that Jerry Rubin's *Growing (Up) at Thirty-Seven*, in which the former Yippie renounced his former ways in favor of meditation, Bioenergetics, acupuncture, Rolfing, and carrot juice, had been published that week.

"You should write about Jerry," Gabrielle said. "It'll be great, the 14-year-old kid talking to the sellout."

She picked up the phone and called Jerry, who wasn't interested.

"Why don't I write about the guys he left behind?" Cutler suggested.

"Brilliant!" she said, writing him a short note of introduction. "Take this to 9 Bleecker Street," she told him, and gave him directions to the Yippie headquarters, where *Yipster Times* was published and where a rotating cast of activists lived. "They are paranoid as hell," she warned.

Upon arriving at 9 Bleecker, Cutler pounded on the door. "I could hear the music inside. It was like a vault. Finally, a slot opened, and a voice said 'Whaddaya want?' He invited me in, introduced me to Dana Beal, Aron Kay, and a few other guys."

Inside was a giant hippie pad clubhouse, reeking of weed, the walls lined with posters and the black-and-red Yippie flag. After they subjected Cutler to a summary interrogation, he was invited to attend their Yippie National Convention, where they planned their agenda for the upcoming election. After the Yippies had run Pigasus the Pig in 1968, and a rock in 1972, their candidate in 1976 would be a marsupial they named J. Edgar Kangaroo—"hopping back and forth over the issues."

As Schang had warned, they *were* a little bit paranoid. "We assume that the phones are bugged," Beal told Cutler. "But not only that. They tap the phones here, and then they tap the phones of all the people who call here, and all the people who call them."

But they were thrilled about the press coverage of their latest antics and about the latest issue of their paper. "Take the cocaine scandal involving Carter," Chance offered. "We went right up to him and asked him to comment about it. That's the kind of thing that a paper has to do if it's going to have the kind of flash and class of *Yipster Times*."

According to Mike Chance, who wanted *High Times* to follow up on the *Yipster Times* story that linked Jimmy Carter to a cocaine investigation, Forcade was afraid that negative coverage of Carter would make waves. "If we run that story," Chance quoted Forcade as saying in an editorial conference, "it's only a matter of time before they bust us on some pretense or another." The *Yipster Times* pulled no such punches. It ran an article about Carter's deputy campaign manager (and future drug czar) Peter Bourne with the headline CARTER AIDE IS MURDER SUSPECT. It even took a shot at *High Times* when it printed a picture of the magazine's news editor Craig Copetas walking alongside Jimmy Carter. "Who's fooling whom here?" asked the caption. "The magazine, which could have plugged any of 10 deserving Democrats? Or the candidate, who endorses nothing, leaving it to the states? Trying to reform the DEA is like reforming the Gestapo."

It was true that *High Times*—or rather, the Trans-High Corporation (THC), as the parent company of *High Times* was called—wasn't so pure in its radicalism. At that year's National Fashion and Boutique Show, it had handed out engraved invitations to the launch party for the first issue of *Dealer*, its paraphernalia trade magazine, held at an Upper West Side discotheque that catered to "the beautiful people, the trendsetters"—admittedly, a strange claim of exclusivity for a disco situated within a chain restaurant.

At the same time, Forcade was deeply concerned about the Trans-High Corporation not abandoning its ideals. In an unsigned editorial published in *High Times*—entitled "When Freedom Is Outlawed, Only Outlaws Will Be Free"—he provided the closest thing to a manifesto he'd penned since the UPS days.

> THC is owned by a non-profit trust fund, and the staff makes very modest salaries indeed. Should we make any excess profits, they will be given to organizations concerned with social, cultural, political, and economic change.... We have no desire to be limited to being the magazine of substances that people put in their mouths. In this issue, you will notice more general news, more diverse features, much more music coverage, and more cultural and political coverage than ever before.
>
> The Big Five national distribution monopoly has boycotted *High Times* because of THC's radical structure. Obviously, any magazine that can sell 420,000 without a national distributor represents a serious threat to the hegemonic monopolistic control of the Big Five over what the public will be allowed to read. The Big Five are now financing a brace of "dope" magazines (*High Times* is not a dope magazine) intended to break the back of THC.

Making money is not enough for us. Money and political "power" (often a goal in publishing) strike us as irrelevant. We are faced with a future that needs help. We know that as far as the future is concerned, we are playing for keeps. Our goal is to go all the way, whatever that may bring.

Forcade continued to support radical causes. When Madison Square Garden was announced as the site of the Democratic National Convention, Forcade excitedly informed Andy Kowl that he'd rented the entirety of the nearby Diplomat Hotel—earlier the site of a Zippie press conference and of Abbie Hoffman's cocaine bust—for the entire week, offering to provide space for any interested protest group. Kowl quickly stepped in to reduce *High Times*'s expenditure by about 75 percent, but even then the "Counter-Convention" was the central gathering for activist groups. They charged three-dollar admission, sold one-dollar beers, and gave out nitrous balloons for free. Delegates wandered over from the Garden. Wavy Gravy was there and founding Yippie Paul Krassner, and, to the consternation of A. J. Weberman, Jerry Rubin showed up, too.

"You ain't comin' in here, man!" Weberman barked at Rubin, shaking with anger. "You're not wanted here!"

"No more Jerry Rubins!" David Peel shouted. "No more Abbie Hoffmans! Just marijuana! Marijuana and ourselves! Do what the fuck you want! We smoke pot and we like it a lot!"

Someone ran and got Andy Kowl, who insisted A. J. let Rubin pass. Later on, the music was lowered to broadcast a phoned-in message from a special guest: Abbie Hoffman, still on the run.

The following month, the Republican National Convention was held in Kansas City; *High Times* ran a free full-page ad soliciting YIP contributions and urging people to show up for protests. Across an eight-foot-high wire fence and a traffic median, Yippies screamed insults and waved middle fingers at the candidates' hotel. They held banners reading STOP GOVERNMENT SPYING, END AMERICAN IMPERIALISM, and FUCK SOUTH AFRICAN FASCIST MURDERERS. But they admitted that the end of the Vietnam War had taken away a major rallying point. They even missed Richard Nixon, who they now said they wanted to draft as the VP running mate for their kangaroo candidate. "Without the Yippies in 1968, there would have been no Nixon," lamented Dana Beal. "Now we want him back."

"I don't know for sure what we're going to do before we're through in Kansas City," one Yippie spokesman told a journalist. "But you better keep your eyes open."

Kansas City's police chief, Joe McNamara, was dismissive. "They're the leftovers from the Chicago and Miami conventions mostly and they've got problems in their own ranks, fighting for leadership spots," he said. "The 1976 Yippie is fighting more for attention than for any cause."

"Once demonstrators had struck fear in the hearts of Republicans," wrote Watergate felon John Dean, now covering the convention for *Rolling Stone*. "The promised demonstrations for Kansas City never materialized and those that did were spectator sport. It was curious to watch three dozen shouting protesters across from the Crown Center Hotel, Ford's headquarters. Ford supporters sat on the grass and gawked as if Yippies were relics who'd climbed from Conestoga wagons."

The *Berkeley Barb*'s words were even harsher, especially coming from the last remaining founding paper of the Underground Press Syndicate. "They were pathetic," a *Barb* writer said of the Yippies. "No one doubted for a moment where the power lay."

Gabrielle Schang was also in Kansas City, and she managed to get a microphone in front of Nelson Rockefeller. She'd hoped to ask the former New York governor, who'd presided over the handling of the Attica riot, "How does it feel to be a mass murderer?" But when the moment came, the question she posed was "How does it feel to be vice president?"

"It's very exciting," he said.

"What's so exciting about it?"

"Well," said Rockefeller, "the president could die."

After the convention, Schang headed to San Francisco with two *Yipster Times* writers to interview aboveground liaisons of the New World Liberation Front–sympathizing *Urban Guerilla* for a magazine article. On the way back from the interview, their car was pulled over by two unmarked FBI cars and a motorcycle cop. They were dragged from the car, frisked at gunpoint, and fingerprinted. The FBI said it had been tipped that a member of the Symbionese Liberation Army was in the car.

While Schang was in California, an old roommate of hers, San Francisco–based cartoonist and graphic designer Becky Wilson, was in New York to show around samples of her work. Schang told Wilson she could stay at her SoHo loft, which she was renting from Forcade. (It was, in fact, a safehouse for marijuana. "I didn't realize when I had that place," Schang said, "that Tom had all these secret compartments there for stashing pot.") Forcade made it his business to escort Wilson around town, arriving at the loft every evening to take her to restaurants, where they ordered dinner and talked. But she never saw him eat the entire week; she thought it was like he survived on air. He was full of restless energy, always talking about places he'd gone the night before, after he'd dropped her back off at the loft. During the days, he set up appointments for editors to look at her portfolio, invariably with skin magazines like *Hustler* and *Screw*. Forcade told her he was interested in integrating underground comics into *High Times* and floated the idea of Wilson editing a section of the magazine with work by women. She eagerly agreed but wasn't sure he'd follow through. Who knew what to believe with this guy?

At the end of the week, Forcade brought her to a midtown hotel, where the American Numismatic Association was holding its annual convention. They took an elevator up to the top and entered an ultra-modern suite, with floor-to-ceiling windows and white leather furniture.

Forcade pulled out a briefcase, put it on a glass coffee table, and suddenly began assembling an automatic weapon. He expertly clicked the metal parts into place and added a suppressor and a scope. Then he pointed it out the window, at different objects in the room, and finally at Wilson.

She dove onto the floor.

"Sorry," Forcade said. "I didn't mean to scare you." He quickly disassembled the weapon and put it back in its case.

Wilson was still in shock when a couple of strangers, in town for the convention, arrived at the room. They'd brought a suitcase filled with gold bars. She was pretty sure that they were laundering drug money. She never asked.

After Wilson was back in San Francisco, she got a call from the *High Times* office. They were sending a contract for a seven-page insert, to be called *Vamp*, of cartoons and stories by women.

fter Schang returned to town, she and Forcade looked out her loft windows to a vacant storefront down the street and talked about how the neighborhood could use a bookstore. "We both loved magazines and newspapers," she said, "and there was nothing at the time—maybe a *Daily News* at the subway when you got to Sixth Avenue." Let's open one, Forcade said. He had Larry Hertz rent the place immediately.

Schang had a manager in mind—a bookstore owner named Jim Drougas, who she'd met at the Alternative Press Syndicate offices. "You have to meet Tom Forcade," Schang told him. "He's gonna like you."

Drougas and his girlfriend were summoned to meet Forcade at his *High Times* office. "He was this little guy sitting at this little desk about twenty feet in front of our seats, in this giant office," said Drougas. "He had these two giant speakers on either side of his desk. He would joke about it later, 'Yeah, I'm like the Wizard of Oz. I like to intimidate people like that.'"

Forcade talked about his vision of a bookstore catering to subcultures and how he envisioned stores throughout the nation. "We'll reach the masses," he said. "We're gonna bring our culture to the whole country."

They were talking for about ten minutes when a *High Times* employee knocked on the door.

"Come in," Forcade said. The staffer didn't hear, and knocked again, after which Forcade leapt to his feet, opened the door, and yelled. "You fucking bastard! I told you to come in. And if people are here, why are you bothering me?" He slammed the door and returned to the meeting. "They're idiots," he said to his guests. "They don't listen."

To each suggestion Drougas made, Forcade would respond with enthusiasm and that he'd call "a guy" to put it in action, resting his feet on the desk and dialing the phone. Finally, he said to Drougas, "I dig that you're into all the right things I want for the store, but how do you feel about your ability to *run* a store?"

His girlfriend jumped in. "He doesn't know anything about this. I'm the expert."

Forcade looked at Drougas with wide, shocked eyes, and then chuckled. "You're hired."

The store opened in a matter of months, stocking a carefully curated selection of counterculture literature, underground comics, and fanzines, some of which it even helped distribute elsewhere throughout the city. Allen

Ginsberg, Amiri Baraka, and Susan Sontag did readings. The artists Art Spiegelman and Mark Beyer created a signed and numbered illustration advertising the store. Jane Fonda even came in once, to ask if Tom Forcade was around.

"He lived there, so we'd see him passing through," said Drougas. "He'd come in, gather 25 magazines and just walk out. Then he'd say, 'What the hell is going on with your security?' I'd say, 'Look, Tom, everyone knows who you are. They're not going to stop you.' Once I said, 'Tom, how do you want to handle shoplifters?' He said, in a very serious tone, 'We should have machine guns mounted in each corner of the store, which will be remote controlled.'"

Working on the bookstore further solidified the renewed friendship between Forcade and Schang. When she was trying to work up the nerve to ask for a job from a television producer with a reputation for screaming, Forcade gave her a pep talk and stayed with her while she made the phone call. "You're going to be a natural," he told her.

"I would have never let someone else sit and listen to my conversation," Schang said. "But Tom made me feel stronger, and I didn't back down—I didn't give a damn that this guy screamed at me."

Not that she didn't retain some reservations about Forcade. "I was still a tiny bit scared of him," she said. "He was so intense."

They both saw other people. Forcade had been involved with a woman involved in the marijuana trade, and with Estela Matta, a woman in her early twenties who worked as a translator for John Wilcock. She'd been impressed by this "quiet little guy with piercing blue eyes, listening to everybody bullshit, not saying very much."

Matta became not just his lover but another lieutenant. "I would hang out in his loft, go to business meetings with him, fly around the country with him—a lot of trips to Florida, a lot of trips to the Caribbean. He liked to have me on hand because I was level-headed—I was never an embarrassment, and I didn't ask questions that I didn't need to." After the Everglades police chase, she'd let Forcade stash Chic Eder and a member of the Colombian ring at her Brooklyn apartment. At one of the NORML conventions, she'd spent three days ensconced in a hotel room rolling joints, using bed sheets to shake out seeds from pounds of weed.

Another constant companion for Forcade at this time was Jack Combs, a warm, bear-like six-foot-four Kentuckian who'd been a member of the Free Ranger Tribe back in 1970 and who'd recently moved back to New York from a years-long stretch in Puerto Rico. Combs's background as a signals man in the Coast Guard was put to quick use as he and Forcade worked on launching a *High Times* radio program from the 27th Street loft. (The sight of the two men wearing headphones and focused day and night on the boards of banks of recording equipment, one staffer recalled, led many people to wonder if Forcade had bugged the offices.)

There was something strikingly incongruent about the short, scheming Forcade and the bighearted Combs, something out of *Mutt and Jeff*, perhaps, or maybe *Of Mice and Men*.

Combs was often described as Forcade's bodyguard. One *High Times* editor remembers seeing Combs and Forcade at a party crouched in a corner, their backs to the crowd, and being told that the two men were "inspecting Forcade's gun."

But this suggests a more thuggish role than Combs, a compassionate caretaker for Forcade, actually played. "Jack was very loyal and friendly," observed Gabrielle. "And unlike Tom, who looked suspicious—he had that long and stringy hair—Jack always looked kind of wholesome and clean-cut. So I think they were a good couple, whatever they were out there doing."

CHAPTER 13

FORCADE NOW ENACTED REBELLIONS IN A DIFFERENT TAX BRACKET, A manifestation of the *Magic Christian* fantasies he'd played at during the Medicine Ball Caravan. He appeared, Guy Grand style, at the offices of the financially struggling *Punk* magazine, which was among the first to chronicle the crusty subculture that swirled around the New York club CBGB. Decked out in western wear, charging past a secretary, Forcade threw his feet up on the desk of *Punk* cofounder John Holmstrom and announced, "I'm going to make you rich and famous." His plan was to pay the printer's bill for the next issue of *Punk*, run an eight-page *Punk* supplement in *High Times*, and watch the magazines fly off the stands. To demonstrate his power, he handed crisp hundred-dollar bills to everyone in the office, then floated away.

Weeks later, he whisked Holmstrom out to Long Island in a limousine to see a show by the Dictators and provided powerful marijuana on the way. "I was so stoned that I couldn't function after a few puffs, but it seemed to energize Forcade," remembered Holmstrom. Once they arrived, the Dictators launched into a careening version of "America the Beautiful," and Forcade "ordered pitchers of beer and started banging the glass pitcher on the table so hard that I got totally paranoid it would break."

Forcade was thrilled by the burgeoning punk rock scene, of course—it was all part of the continuum of loud, anti-authoritarian music he'd been smitten with since encountering the proto-punk MC5 in their days as the official band of the White Panther Party. It was a tradition he'd tried to continue when he took David Peel cross-country as a punk provocateur in 1970, and when the Free Ranger Tribe had given the New York Dolls its first professional gig at a Dana Beal fundraiser. So it was with some pride that Forcade invited Holmstrom to hear "Kick Out the Jams" at top volume in his loft, sitting before the twelve-foot-tall Minuteman missile-silo speakers he'd hooked up to his stereo.

Holmstrom was a little bit spooked by his unpredictable new patron, who kept referring to "his enemies" and insisting that everything was "top secret." But he got to work on the next issue, a fumetto starring members of Talking Heads, Blondie, Patti Smith Group, and Richard Hell & the Voidoids. The press run of twenty-five thousand copies was five times that of the previous issue. But by the time the eight-page *Punk* supplement ran in *High Times*, Forcade had already, citing poor sales, pulled the plug on financing future issues.

Punk wasn't the only large impulsive expenditure Forcade took on that summer. Keith Stroup of NORML told the *Washington Post* that he'd been working late in his office when a "very normal looking" man with short hair, slacks, and a sport shirt strolled in with a black briefcase, eager to chat about decriminalization legislation. Stroup excused himself to retrieve some literature, and when he returned, his exiting visitor handed him a note and said, "I made a contribution. It's in your attaché case."

The note read:

> *The Confederation (an association of independent marijuana, hash-ish, and hashish oil smugglers; ton dealers; growers; transporters; and workers) donates this $10,000 to NORML to hasten the day when our contributions to the betterment of society will be legalized.*
>
> *We regret the small amount—last year we could have given 100 times this—but since then the molecular totalitarianism of the ruling class has seriously depleted our resources. Nevertheless, we will attempt to continue to keep America high.*
>
> *We invite and entreat all others in the cannabis trade and otherwise to give to NORML as much as they can afford—now!*
>
> *Karma prevails. Venceremos!*

The "Confederation," of course, was simply Forcade, as Stroup knew. Forcade had asked him to release the note to the press.

High Times and Forcade were now the top financiers of NORML, an occasion for celebration at a fundraiser in late October. The Park Avenue home of society matron Diana Bonnor Lewis, widow of a managing partner of Bear Sterns, was packed with cocktail-hoisting upper-crust socialites and attorneys. Keith Stroup, fearing a dull party, had invited Forcade.

Forcade shot in from the private elevator, escorted by nearly the entire *High Times* staff, who were straight from closing the December issue. He headed away from the party and into the dining room, where he proceeded to light a candelabra, situate himself at the head of the table, hoist his cowboy boots up on the polished wood, and begin rolling joints of Colombian.

Stroup was in the thick of the party, angling for possible donors when the hostess took him aside. "There are some strange men in the next room. I'm sure they can't have been invited. My butler says they're smoking marijuana." Stroup darted into the dining room and found Forcade.

"Tom, you crazy fucker, cool it!"

Forcade ignited a joint from the candelabra flame. "What's the problem?" he said, handing the spliff to Stroup. "It's a dope party, isn't it?" Stroup shrugged and accepted the offering.

When the distressed hostess walked into the dining room and began insisting that he and his friends leave, Forcade played dumb for a while, until finally he shouted at her: "Go fuck yourself!"

As guests started to edge away from the action, the butler dropped his tray and grabbed Forcade by the shoulder and tried to guide him to the elevator. Then Forcade took a swing at him. The butler dodged the blow.

It was at this time that Shelly Schorr and an editor emerged from a bathroom, freshly coked-up, and saw the butler returning the punch. They jumped into the scuffle, as did Ms. Lewis's fleet of waiters and bartenders.

While Jack Combs, the largest and most imposing figure present, stood still, the action swirled around him. Forcade hurled antiques, including a Ming vase, which struck a guest before shattering on the marble floor. The hostess knocked one of Schorr's teeth loose as the partygoers fled.

Mrs. Lewis resigned her NORML membership.*

I t was just a taste of the chaos soon to come. On the November afternoon when the proofs of the new issue made their way across the street, Forcade called *High Times* general manager Paul Tornetta.

"I want you to fire everyone except yourself and Stan [Place, the circulation director]," Forcade said. "Collect all the money from the people who owe us money. Sell all the furniture and typewriters. We're closing down the magazine."

"What? Tom, I'm not gonna do that. If you wanna do that, you're gonna have to do it yourself."

Paul rushed into Andy Kowl's office.

"Tom sounds totally fucked up. He wants to shut down the magazine. What are we gonna do?"

"Send everybody home," Kowl said. "Tell them to come back tomorrow. And pay no attention to anything they hear or see."

Within minutes, Forcade emerged from the elevator on the third floor, his head down as usual. The receptionist buzzed him in. He walked up to her desk, tore the telephone switchboard out, and threw it. "You can go home," he said calmly. "*High Times* is closed."

---

* The next day, *New Times* magazine, having been tipped to the fracas, reached Ms. Lewis for comment. "That young man," she said, "must have come from a deprived home."

Then he made his way through the office hallways cutting phone lines. At each door he would announce, in monotone, "You...are... terminated."

Half an hour later he was gone, returned to his sanctuary across the street. The staff gathered at a bar downstairs for an impromptu group therapy session. Some of them discussed pooling their money to buy the magazine.

The following day, Kowl appeared at Forcade's loft, urging his boss to take another sabbatical. When Forcade refused, Kowl put forth the offer of a purchase: fifty thousand a year for ten years, ten thousand down. A document was drawn up by hand, a cashier's check proffered.

Forcade, couchbound in his bathrobe, nearly catatonic, was being tended to by Jack Combs, who was trying to nurse him back to health. "No, no, it's over," Forcade managed from his semi-supine position. The magazine had become too successful, he said, had gotten away from its mission.

Over the coming days, the negotiations would go back and forth, always getting close to an agreement but always ending with Forcade backing out at the last moment.

Kowl and Tornetta even appealed to recent *High Times* subject Jimmy Buffett, in town for shows at the Bottom Line nightclub, to come by and deliver the pep talk: "Tom, our founder, is your biggest fan, and he's having a lot of problems," they told him. Amazingly, Buffett consented. But when he arrived, Forcade simply looked up at the singer and said, "What are you doing here?"

The episode reached its climax shortly afterward, on another visit.

"Look, man," Kowl said, "we started this thing together, we went through a lot, and you made me a lot of promises."

"I made you a lot of promises? I'm breaking these promises?"

"Yeah!"

"Get me my piece," Forcade said to Jack, who tossed Forcade's pistol to him.

Forcade stared at the gun, then looked up at Kowl.

"If I broke all these promises," Forcade said, putting the gun in Kowl's hands, "kill me." Tornetta snatched the gun away.

After more back-and-forth, Forcade agreed to sign over the magazine. Kowl and Tornetta handed him an envelope of cash and headed for the door.

"This paper is never going to stand up in court," Forcade called out. "I'm crazy. I'm not in my right mind!"

"So don't sell us the goddamned contract!" Kowl shouted, and the dance began again.

Forcade asked his older cousin, a staunchly anti-drug estate lawyer named John Goodson, to fly in from Phoenix to work out an arrangement. Goodson was in for a shock when he arrived at the magazine offices. "Everyone in the room was taking some type of drug," he remembered. "Tom was laying on the floor, looking up at me. It was very difficult to get people to concentrate on what we were doing. They kept interrupting the meeting to lay down powder on the table and divvy it out with a razor while I was trying to conduct a meeting." There was even, Goodson recalled, a psychiatrist on hand "to make sure there weren't emotional issues."

"His guys were carrying guns up on the seventh floor," said Kowl. "People up there were scared, coming to my office, saying, 'Something's wrong, Andy.' So at that point I called one of the private detectives we'd hired, to guard the lobby, because I didn't know what the fuck was going on."

When Forcade finally agreed to reactivate the magazine, it was with a complicated resolution entailing a family trust and a charitable trust, and the provision that loyal employees who stayed on for more than ten years would accrue shares of the Trans-High Corporation; in the year 2000, they would become beneficiaries. *High Times*, Forcade declared, would eventually be owned by its workers.

Gabrielle, meanwhile, began a relationship with *High Times* editor Glenn O'Brien, who was understandably wary of Forcade, who he secretly referred to as the "Prince of Darkness."

"As soon as I started going out with her," O'Brien later marveled, "he wanted her back. It was kind of crazy, because then I became his rival or something."

Forcade *did* seem a little eager to keep O'Brien out of town on extended assignments. He began coming by Schang's loft, leaving romantic postcards.

On Christmas Day 1976, Becky Wilson was preparing dinner with her roommates when she received a phone call from Forcade. She hadn't heard from him since the week he'd pointed an automatic weapon at her. His words were slurred, but she gathered that Gabrielle had gone to the Caribbean with Glenn. "He wasn't talking much—he wanted me to talk—but every time I started to get off the phone, he'd ask me another question. We spoke for hours. Finally, he told me he'd OD'd on some medication." She offered to call Forcade an ambulance, but he wouldn't tell her where he was or a number at which he could be called back. She asked him if he had any friends nearby who could come over to make sure he was okay.

Eventually, her roommates began petitioning her for use of the telephone. She made Forcade promise to call back in a half hour; to her relief, he did. "Even if I'd known where he was, I wouldn't have wanted to call the police to rescue him," she said. "Who knows what they'd find."

Schang returned from vacation to a visit from Forcade, who proceeded to swallow a handful of pills—"Look, I'm taking my vitamins," he taunted—and then crumpled to the ground. Unable to move him, she ran across the street to the New Morning bookstore and grabbed Jim Drougas, who came back and helped her drag Forcade down the stairs and into a cab to Bellevue Hospital.

Forcade wrote Gabrielle a letter in turquoise ink where he let it all hang out, telling her that he couldn't live without her, that he kept other relationships going only out of a fear that she would turn him down. "Being without you I feel incomplete, empty, sick, paralyzed."

There were, packed into its two pages, apologies, vows, and a marriage proposal. "I was thinking about kidnapping you," he confessed. "I am dead serious. I'm a desperate man. I think I am right for you and I love you and I think you love me and it is ridiculous to be apart. I want you, I need you. . . . Please say yes."

"I was living with Glenn at the moment I eloped with Tom," Schang admitted. "I left in the middle of the night. He said, 'Pack your suitcase, and meet me downstairs at 3 a.m.'"

They flew to Phoenix—she wouldn't marry him, she said, until she met his mother and verified that he wasn't from outer space—where she signed a prenuptial agreement prepared by Forcade's cousin, John Goodson. Then, on St. Patrick's Day, they were married at City Hall.

It was not a conventional marriage. "One day I was in his loft," Estela Matta said, "and he called me up and said, 'I want you to meet me at the airport at LaGuardia. We're going on my honeymoon.' I said, 'What are you talking about, Tom?' 'I just married Gabrielle.' I said, 'Oh, that's nice. Congratulations, and fuck you!' He said, 'Yeah, I know, we'll talk about it.' We went down to Miami and spent a couple days, he and Gabrielle and I on our honeymoon."*

Forcade and Schang also went to visit Tim Hughes at the Collier County Stockade in Immokalee, Florida. After a year of legal negotiations following the debacle in the swamp, Hughes had pleaded to a possession charge and was serving a nine-month sentence. His "cooperation with authorities" did not extend to implicating Forcade. Throughout the term of imprisonment, Forcade paid for Hughes's wife, mother, and a parade of others to fly down to Florida.

Michael Kennedy met with New York City's Special Narcotics Prosecutor about the grand jury investigation that had begun after the Fifth Avenue Hotel raid, and for which *High Times* employees were being subpoenaed. He threatened to bring suit against the DA's office "on grounds that they were trying to break the magazine." The investigation was quashed, another year-old burden removed.

Forcade had other reasons to celebrate. *High Times* was evolving, evidenced not just by rising circulation numbers and advertisements but also by the expanding scope of its coverage. "Forcade was able to bring to hundreds of thousands of kids and Middle Americans a different perspective on American society in the 70s than they could get from almost any other magazine," observed Ron Rosenbaum, who, under the simple pseudonym of "R.," became *High Times*'s in-house marijuana critic. "Since the organized and mass Left died out after the Vietnam war, it was very valuable in that sense. He didn't want to make it a relic of the Sixties, but to point out there were things going on in the Seventies—it was not *totally* a dead decade."

Forcade was quick to embrace the hippest parts of the downtown New York City arts scene in which Glenn O'Brien and Toni Brown both circulated, and the magazine began to make room for a sophisticated celebrity culture. Interviews with Susan Sontag and Gil Scott-Heron appeared; Debbie Harry of Blondie and Andy Warhol both posed for covers. (Forcade sometimes took *High Times* further from its ostensible hippie roots than his employees wanted to abide: "We the undersigned

---

* "That was not our honeymoon," Schang said.

herby declare a total violent disapproval of the proposed October cover featuring Mr. Johnny Rotten," read a missive from eighteen members of the staff. "For aesthetic, political, and pure mercenary reasons, we hope that management will please consider another alternative." The cover ran anyway.)

The mini-edition of *Punk* wasn't the only supplement section the magazine ran—*Vamp: Fantasy and Humor by Women* ran as a seven-page insert. A media section was devoted to publications that focused on various subcultures, from gay magazines to rock fanzines. Articles about the dangers of white sugar, or the benefits of biofeedback and ionized air therapy, now surrounded the steadfast marijuana centerfolds.

Those centerfolds had gotten imaginative, though. Steve Cooper photographed Toni Brown's girlfriend aloft on "three hundred pounds of primo Colombian Cheeba Cheeba," like a stoner Scrooge McDuck. The photo crew brought it in barrels up a freight elevator and into an apartment. They shoved the furniture to one side, laid out a tarp, and dumped everything on the floor before piling it up with a snow shovel. "You could smell the pot out on the street, I swear," said Corinne Tynan, a photo assistant. "Everyone was fucked up from the contact high." Forcade showed up at the end to pick up the pot. As it was being loaded onto a van, one of the barrels fell over and spilled out into the street, just outside the 10th Precinct. Forcade started furiously kicking marijuana into the gutter and commanded the driver to pull away.

The following day, Cooper got a call from the office that the loaned product had been returned underweight. "I got a scientist friend to sign a bunch of affidavits," Cooper said, "saying that six pounds of moisture evaporated from the buds during the shoot."

If anyone asked about the contraband items in the photographs, employees were told to say that all shoots were done on a ship in international waters, beyond the three-mile limit.

Sometimes, there was no product at all. Photographer John Farrell showed up at a Manhattan warehouse to create a centerfold illustrating one of Forcade's favorite maxims: "There are two kinds of dealers. Those who need forklifts and those who don't." The forklift was there, but the bales of marijuana were not. "Oh, I don't have any," Forcade told him. "You're going to have to wing it." Farrell ran over to West Broadway and scared up cardboard boxes and fifty pounds of tea. Then he spray-mounted the tea onto the boxes. "It looked pretty good," Farrell said. "When they went to do the color separations, they changed the color to gold, because Tom didn't want any green stuff. He was into gold, because that's what he was selling from Santa Marta."

For the first few years of the magazine, much of the news in *High Times* was aggregated from other sources with the help of clipping services, but increasingly Forcade was sending Craig Copetas around the globe to cover issues relating to law enforcement, smuggling, or pharmaceuticals. There were also writers from Reuters, the Associated Press, ABC News, and the *New York Times* contributing under pseudonyms.

Certainly, Forcade's connections facilitated an access to the underworld that was unique among glossy periodicals. Like the time that Forcade told Copetas that Chic Eder had a line on a drug-packed freighter due to arrive at the Brooklyn docks, and that this was an opportunity to observe the ins and outs of offloading. Upon Forcade's insistence, Copetas and a photographer tagged along, following Eder in the middle of the night through wire-cut openings in a chain-link fence.

But there were higher-level contacts, too—much higher. By the time Jimmy Carter was elected president, the magazine had been covering him for over a year, traveling with the campaign and getting to know the people around the candidate.

In the spring of 1977, Forcade surrendered his longtime personal fight for White House press credentials when he declined to join Robert Sherrill on the latest appeal in their lawsuit. Perhaps he didn't want to tempt further scrutiny. *Forcade v. Knight* became *Sherrill v. Knight*.

But by then, *High Times* itself had already gotten that access. "I got the credentials, and I got into the White House," said Copetas, who even accompanied First Lady Rosalynn Carter on a trip to Colombia. "When I told him, he cried a little bit. He was so happy that it finally happened."

High Times poured money into travel expenses, sometimes tens of thousands of dollars at a time. A particular focus was the drug war being conducted in Mexico, the source of the vast majority of the United States' marijuana and also, following the cutting off of the French-Turkish connection in 1971, 90 percent of its heroin. Domestic interdiction strategies having failed, emphasis was placed on international diplomacy; agreements were signed for extraditions and the destruction of crops. The

US State Department applied pressure and donated planes, helicopters, and electronic detection equipment that had been developed for the Vietnam War, and in Mexico began a heavy herbicide-spraying campaign on marijuana and poppy fields throughout the Sierra Madre region. Some saw this international, supply-side focus as a convenient cover for political repression; the influx of military-grade aid to Mexico occurred amid an ongoing battle between that government and the peasants of the Sierra Madre.

High Times reported on shoot-outs between rival traffickers and between campesinos and the Mexican police, and on bounties placed on the heads of drug lords. Its coverage was aided by its sources in, of all places, the Drug Enforcement Administration, with whom, one magazine staffer recalled, there was a kind of "friendly rivalry."

The reporting that gained the most traction was about those herbicides spewing from the air. Alarms about paraquat had been sounded in thinly sourced underground newspaper reports, which the magazine duly picked up and ran with. Drug dealers asked Keith Stroup about it at a NORML conference, and *High Times* ran a six-page color-photograph spread showing the destruction of fields. But the story didn't break out to the mainstream press until an internal report by a chemical expert from the USDA leaked. "Paraquat probably has caused more deaths, both purposefully and unintentionally, than any other herbicide I know of," Walter Gentner told journalists. It was still unclear what smoking paraquat-contaminated marijuana might do to a person, but oral ingestion was said to cause damage to the heart, lungs, and kidneys. By the end of the year, Mexican marijuana and heroin exports to the United States would be halved—but the paraquat story would make it to the pages of the New York *Daily News* and the *Washington Post*, causing a headache for the Carter administration. The White House bumped *High Times* from a press corps flight to Mexico, until Sam Donaldson stepped in. "ABC is not going to go on this trip," he vowed, "unless *High Times* goes too."

The success of the magazine continued to synergize with that of the growing paraphernalia industry, which in the course of a year had doubled from $120 to $250 million annually. And there was an undeniable tide change in marijuana laws: in the spring and summer of 1977, Mississippi, New York, and North Carolina became the eighth, ninth, and tenth states to pass decriminalization legislation. NORML had its sights set on ten more states, plus the District of Columbia.

In August, President Carter delivered a speech in favor of federal decriminalization, eliminating penalties for possession of up to an ounce of marijuana. "Penalties against possession of a drug should not be more damaging to an individual than the use of the drug itself," he said, "and where they are, they should be changed." In a phenomenal triumph of lobbying power, and a testament to NORML's access to Carter drug czar Peter Bourne, the language had been drafted by Keith Stroup. Legalization seemed so assured that the old rumors about the tobacco industry standing by and ready with machine-rolled joints and trademarks on strain names like Acapulco Gold reemerged.

In another promising development, Larry Flynt, the publisher of *Hustler*, approached *High Times* with an offer to become its distributor. Flynt had built up an extraordinary pipeline for his pornography—by doing away with the middleman national distributors that eked a profit in getting magazines from publisher to regional wholesalers, he was keeping more than half the cover price of each issue of *Hustler* sold. It was only natural that he should branch out into distributing other magazines as well, and the vice-embracing *High Times*, he felt, was a good match.

But on Labor Day 1977, Michael Kennedy delivered news that would end Forcade's streak of victories and send him into another tailspin.

Chic Eder had been arrested months after the Everglades adventure, with 5,300 pounds of marijuana. In the process of defending Eder on the later charge, Kennedy learned that Eder was an informant for federal agencies, including the FBI and the DEA. Notably, Eder had helped to ensnare telephone hacker John "Captain Crunch" Draper, who, before working for *High Times*, had made the hubristic mistake of tapping into FBI lines.

Eder would later insist in a deposition that he had never informed on Forcade, even though he bitterly accused the *High Times* publisher of ripping him off for fifty pounds of marijuana. Eder stated that he'd stopped doing business with Forcade after that and then hurled an insult that seemed custom-made to hurt the proud renegade. "He was not," Eder said, "an honest outlaw." Eder also accused Forcade, with whom he'd imported "many thousands of pounds" into the country by boat, of once pulling a gun on him. (This claim was later repeated by attorney

Gerald Lefcourt, who told the writer Albert Goldman that "Tom pulled a .45 and put it to Chic's head, and Chic suddenly realized that after all the conning and bullshitting he was up against someone just as hardcore as he was.") Still, Eder maintained that when the assistant district attorney in New York tried to lean on him to testify against Forcade before a grand jury, even threatening to interfere with a prior immunity deal Eder had cut with the DEA, he'd responded with a curt "Get fucked."

But Forcade was blindsided by what he considered an absolute betrayal. *High Times* promptly ran a cover story about government cooperators with a title that was, to those who knew the background, a thinly veiled swipe at Eder. It was called "Informer Chic."

Now paranoia extended to nearly everyone in the office. When a bottle of Vin Tonique Mariani cocaine wine, sent to the office by a reader, went missing, Forcade hired private detectives to find it. Then he insisted that lie detector tests be administered to the staff.*

Forcade did allow one fresh face into his inner circle. Maureen Mc-Fadden arrived at her *High Times* interview dressed collegiately in corduroy suit and sweater. Forcade, looking to hire an assistant, was sitting in his office chair, silhouetted by the light reflecting from the Chrysler Building behind him, twirling a Thai stick in one hand and sucking from a bottle of vanilla extract.

"Do you know what this magazine is all about?" he asked.

"Absolutely! I've been reading it since it started."

"So you don't mind that it's all about drugs?"

"No, actually! I do them as often as I can."

She started the next Monday. Sorting his mail, she rolled a joint and left it on top of the pile. He buzzed her to come into his office.

"Who put this here?" he demanded.

"I wanted to say thank you for the job," she said.

Forcade looked at her. "No one has ever done that before."

After President Carter's speech, language was included in the US Senate's sweeping 360-page proposal for federal criminal code reform (S. 1437) that called for the decriminalization of under ten grams

---

* The *Washington Post* printed an announcement shortly thereafter that *High Times* would pay a $20,000 reward for the cocaine wine.

of marijuana. This apparent victory became another wedge between NORML and the Yippies—who'd always been a little wary of one another, even though Keith Stroup had finally agreed to speak at their annual Smoke-In that year.* To the further-left Yippies, the crime bill's "under ten grams" qualifier was an affront, and its other, non-marijuana-related elements were encroachments on civil liberties.

NORML and the Yippies were also in conflict over the subject of paraquat, the herbicide that Mexico, thanks to $35 million in US funding, was spraying on poppy and marijuana fields. Whereas NORML saw paraquat news as a motivating issue that was gaining steam, the Yippies claimed that the threat of contaminated crops was overblown, a threat ginned up to scare marijuana smokers and cripple the livelihoods of dealers.

Paraquat spraying also was a source of tension between NORML and the White House's Peter Bourne. After pressure from Senator Charles Percy, Bourne directed the National Institute on Drug Abuse (NIDA) to conduct a study of paraquat but said that he saw no "demonstrable health hazard of any consequence" and that "people who disagree with that do so on a largely emotional basis without any scientific substantiation."

So Bourne and Stroup were already feuding when Bourne made a surprise appearance at the packed Washington, DC, townhouse Stroup had rented for the Saturday-night party of the December 1977 NORML conference.

Yippies, smugglers, and members of the media establishment all watched as the White House drug czar was quickly whisked upstairs, away from the six hundred common people, to an exclusive party-within-the-party, a bedroom where about a dozen guests—including Hunter S. Thompson, Forcade, and Copetas—were passing around joints.

Soon after, a mound of cocaine was laid out on a mirror and passed around with a razor blade. When that was finished, a *High Times* publicist produced a vial, and Copetas tapped some into a tiny spoon and handed it to Bourne.

---

* The Yippies were not the first to voice suspicion of NORML. All the way back in 1971, John Wilcock, in his syndicated "Other Scenes" column, had warned, "Be wary of the money-raising NORML, which sounds like an FBI front," because it had placed an ad in the "allegedly CIA-backed *Ramparts*" that declared, "We do not advocate the use of marijuana."

"My God, man," Hunter Thompson said to Copetas, "we'll all be indicted now."

Bourne left the party soon afterward.

That weekend's conference was lousy with Yippies, whose registration fees had been paid by Forcade. Aron Kay asked Stroup for suggestions on who might be a good pie victim, and Stroup actually had an answer. He suggested Joe Nellis, chief counsel of the House Select Committee on Narcotics Abuse and Control, who'd be on a Sunday panel. The chair of that committee had recently recommended the closing down of all stores that sold rolling papers, pipes, or other marijuana paraphernalia. Stroup not only handed Kay six dollars to buy a pie; he gave him directions to a local bakery.

Stroup soon had second thoughts and called off the pie hit. Kay and a few other Yippies started digging into the dessert. But then, during the panel discussion, Nellis responded to a question—from Dana Beal—by insisting that international drug treaties took precedence over the Bill of Rights. This was a bridge too far for Kay, who moved quickly to lob half of the pie at the panel. It missed its target and dropped onto the floor, but a NORML staffer's move to deflect it knocked a water pitcher onto Nellis.

Stroup quickly denounced the Yippies as "impotent and irrelevant" and "terribly disruptive," but the pieing touched off a feud that now went beyond him and Bourne. Some meringue had splattered a White House aide named Bob Angarola who was sitting next to Nellis. Weeks later, someone leaked to Angarola an internal NORML memo in which Stroup admitted his part in the pieing. Angarola sent a pointed letter to Stroup on official White House stationery, cc'ing people at both NORML and the White House. Stroup, furious and feeling threatened, pushed back with implied threats about Peter Bourne's exposure risk. "My constituents know I do drugs," he told a State Department official. "Do Peter's know that he does? You tell Dr. Bourne he'd better repudiate that letter!" Then he called up one of Jack Anderson's reporters and told him—off the record, for now—that Bourne had snorted cocaine at the NORML party.

Not everyone was so shy about cocaine use—days after the Nellis pieing, Geraldo Rivera came to the *High Times* office to interview Andy Kowl, and Forcade gave him a friendly bit of media-training advice. "You're only going to get a few minutes, so stretch it out. Why don't you lay down some coke while you're talking to him and snort it, and then we'll get more time?" On December 14, 1977, ABC News viewers saw Kowl become the first person to snort cocaine on national television.

CHAPTER 14

IN AUGUST 1975, A DC-4 CARGO PLANE LOADED WITH NEARLY TWO TONS of Colombian marijuana and hashish made a virtuosic landing on a short, makeshift runway on the top of Treat Mountain, in Polk County, Georgia. "It looked like a bumblebee on a postage stamp," one pilot said admiringly. Fourteen men were arrested, but the authorities couldn't figure out how to remove the aircraft. The strange sight made for an instant tourist attraction, and a Georgia state legislator named Jim West had a vision of making a movie about the whole thing. At auction, he paid $20,000 for the plane—and purchased the mountain itself, for an additional $278,000. Then he began casting locally, hired a crew, and in the summer of 1977, *Polk County Pot Plane* hit theaters. It was a hokey, low-budget redneck caper.

Forcade took notice. With the right repackaging, he thought, it might be blockbuster material—a *Smokey and the Bear* for dopeheads. He offered half a million dollars, with a fifty-thousand-dollar down payment, and informed Andy Kowl that he was taking half of that money from the magazine.

On the January 1978 morning that Forcade prepared to head to Georgia to deliver the cash payment for *Polk County Pot Plane*, he received a phone call from Lech Kowalski, a young filmmaker who was scrambling for backing to make a documentary about the Sex Pistols' first US tour. He'd heard that the publisher of *High Times* might help him. As it turned out, the Sex Pistols were starting the tour two nights later, in Atlanta. He needed $10,000 to get started.

Forcade put Kowalski on hold for ten minutes and returned to the line. "Pack your bags and bring all your equipment. Come down here around three o'clock, and we'll go down to Atlanta."

At the office, Kowalski was in for a long wait. People were passing out joints, so he accepted. A spacey paranoia began to overtake him, exacerbated when, at long last, Forcade invited him in and looked him up and down. "Give me a list of five people that you know in the business," Forcade said. "Wait out there, and we'll see what happens."

An hour later, when an impatient Kowalski returned, Forcade told him he didn't want to back his film after all. Kowalski was overwhelmed with panic. "This is really fucked up, to do this," he spat out. "I waited all day, and it's too late to call my other connections."

"Why don't you get out of here," Forcade said, and disappeared. But the next time he came out, Kowalski, still parked in the reception area, convinced Forcade to loan him enough money for a plane ticket—the banks were now closed—so he could make it to Atlanta when the Sex Pistols arrived.

Forcade instructed Maureen McFadden to reserve a helicopter. Then he disappeared back into his office. As the workplace began emptying out for the day, a well-dressed middle-aged man entered the reception area and quietly stepped into Forcade's office, where the lights were off. Another hour later, they emerged together. "Come on, let's go," Forcade muttered to Kowalski, and they got in the elevator. Forcade struggled with the key and violently kicked the doors. The three men went downstairs in silence and stepped into a black Cadillac, Forcade behind the wheel, the middle-aged man next to him, and Kowalski in the back.

As they weaved in and out of traffic, running red lights and hurtling seventy-five miles an hour down the FDR Drive toward the helicopter terminal, the still-very-high Kowalski deduced that the unfazed man in front, quietly urging Forcade to relax, was his psychiatrist. After the men ran into the waiting helicopter, Forcade produced an envelope packed with hundred-dollar bills and handed it to Kowalski without explanation. As the chopper was landing at the airport, and Kowalski prepared to jump out, Forcade warned him about avoiding the rotors. "He grabbed me affectionately and told me not to walk towards the back," Kowalski remembered. "I felt he was mainly sending me a message: Things are going to get wild. Be on your toes, because if not, it can get dangerous."

Forcade flew first-class; Kowalski sat in coach. Upon arrival in Atlanta, Forcade instructed the filmmaker to rent a room in the Peachtree Plaza Hotel—"the highest room you can get. I'll be in touch."

The next morning, Forcade called Kowalski to come upstairs—the publisher had already rented a suite of five rooms on the top floor, where plentiful amounts of dope were out. "Tom was very paranoid. He's going, 'Who's this, what's this, what's going on here?' He doesn't trust any of the people who are coming in with the food and drinks we're ordering."

Initial overtures to Warner Brothers were a failure. "Forcade wanted to do a pirate documentary, a rebel documentary," said Ted Cohen, who was the director of artist relations for Warner Brothers at the time. "Forcade thought the Sex Pistols were the first sign of the Armageddon and the complete disillusionment with the American government, and this was going to be the beginning of chaos. And it wasn't a mercenary kind of thing—he really thought he was filming a documentary on the collapse of Western civilization." This did not, unsurprisingly, align with Warner Brothers' own plans.

But Forcade was feeling inspired. McFadden had contacts at Warner Brothers who got her the Sex Pistols' itinerary. He called the Squire Inn and got their road manager, Noel Monk, on the phone, and informed him of his intentions to make a movie about the tour.

"You have to speak to Warner Brothers about that."

"No, Mr. Monk, I've tried that once. I didn't like it. I don't think you understand. We're going to make it worth your while."

Monk made up an excuse to put him off, but Forcade kept calling back, increasingly agitated. He decided that the best way to procure the cooperation of the group was to deliver a rented 1934 Duesenberg and chauffeur to them. Then he called up Johnny Rotten. "Look out the window and you'll see a car," he said, and then hung up the phone. He told the chauffeur to circle around the hotel and keep checking in with him for further instructions ("Drive in," "Okay, now drive away," et cetera). Meanwhile, he'd had McFadden ship down stacks and stacks of copies of the *High Times* issue with Rotten on the cover and sent those via the chauffeur, who he then grilled for details by telephone: "What was the reaction?" "What color is the room?" The plan did not endear him to Rotten, who later wrote that he suspected *High Times* was a front for the Central Intelligence Agency.

The following night, Kowalski and his small, locally assembled crew managed to shoot some footage from the front of the Great Southeast Music Hall, before the Sex Pistols' roadies physically picked them up and deposited them in the back. When Kowalski's crew moved back up front, they were accosted again—but this time, Forcade's chauffeur pulled out a gun. Then he put Kowalski up on his shoulders. Ten rolls of film were shot that night; the chauffeur immediately couriered them back to New York.

The next show, to which they took a private plane, was in Memphis. Forcade flew down John Holmstrom and Roberta Bayley of *Punk*, hoping that they might be able to infiltrate the Sex Pistols' inner circle. He also summoned two Puerto Rican martial artists from New York, to act as bodyguards. Forcade had a thousand *High Times* T-shirts printed to hand out to Sex Pistols fans, and color xeroxes of the Johnny Rotten *High Times* cover.

The evening of the concert, Sid Vicious was nowhere to be found. According to Noel Monk, Forcade called the road manager from a Holiday Inn and said, "I believe you're missing someone, aren't you.... If you come to my room by yourself, we can talk—about my documentary, that is, and then perhaps the two of us will have an opportunity to talk about where Sidney is." Monk showed up with reinforcements, and Forcade professed not to know where the bassist was—but if they'd talk about the documentary, he'd find out. At that point, Monk looked out the window and glimpsed Vicious by the swimming pool swinging his studded leather belt at armed hotel security. In other tellings of the event—by Lech Kowalski, and by Michael Duck, who was traveling with Forcade— Sid Vicious showed up asking Forcade to score heroin. Forcade wondered how he might place him into rehab and even considered smuggling him to Jamaica, where Forcade had contacts. "The idea was not to kidnap Sid in order to hold him for ransom," Kowalski insisted. "The idea was to kidnap Sid for his own health. But it was just an idea." Duck says that the road crew handlers arrived at Forcade's suite with FBI agents in tow. Regardless, Vicious was subdued and delivered to the Taliesyn Ballroom for the performance.

After the show, Kowalski was sitting in the limousine with Forcade when their still photographer came up and broke the number one rule: he photographed the publisher. Forcade flipped out. "I want this guy off the shoot!" he yelled. "If I ever see him again, I'll kill him." Kowalski, convinced that Forcade was a lethal danger, now flew in his own bodyguard—a production manager who was also a leather-wearing, motorcycle-riding knife collector.

The next morning, Forcade picked Holmstrom up in the limo and explained his plans: while Kowalski made the movie, Holmstrom would write everything he could about the tour.

"He wanted to be their manager, basically," said Holmstrom. "He felt they were on the same political wavelength; he really liked what they were doing."

Warner Brothers, Forcade confided, was holding Sid Vicious against his will, so they were going to have to get the band their bicycle chain belts to use for their own protection. And Holmstrom was not to say a word to anyone that he was working with Forcade.

"Not only did Warner Brothers not trust Forcade, but the band was also trying to figure out what he wanted," said McFadden. "It was like espionage. Tom called me and said, 'I want you to go my apartment, and get a brick of pot, and someone else is going to bring it down here. This is how we're going to get in the door with the band.'"

Forcade's ability to locate the band's hotel rooms at every stop—thanks to the intercepted itinerary—only stoked the paranoia of the band and label as the tour continued to zigzag through the South, from San Antonio to Dallas to Baton Rouge. The route had been plotted for maximum confrontation value—the scary punks invading rural America—but now Forcade added another front to the war. And his entourage kept growing. A cameraman was hired away from a San Antonio television station, in hopes of obtaining press access. By then, Forcade had more people on the tour than the record label did.

"Every venue we would go to, they would show up somehow," said Ted Cohen of Warner Brothers, "and we would have them thrown out. And they'd be back 15 minutes later because Forcade would pay a guy from the venue: 'Here's $200, look the other way.'"

But Forcade's camp had its own fissures. Kowalski remembered Forcade haranguing the crew as they rode around in a truck. "He was in the front of the truck with the driver, facing all of us sitting in the back with the equipment, yelling out orders. Really shouting. 'You go here, you do this.' If someone interrupted, he would turn his back until the guy finished speaking, then turn around and talk about something totally different."

In Dallas, Forcade urged Kowalski to rent a helicopter and hover over the Sex Pistols' bus during a snowstorm in Dallas. "Give me the fucking camera and I'll do it myself," Forcade said, and Kowalski gave him a Bolex and rolls of film. But then he couldn't convince the helicopter pilot to fly through the blizzard.

Money was running out. The crew, lacking the necessary funds for things like film stock, were making purchases with Forcade's credit card numbers and selling the goods for cash in Tulsa. Forcade phoned *High Times*, demanding that seven blank checks immediately be delivered via airplane.

Kowl refused. "Tom, we got those plane tickets just like you asked, and we took care of the equipment rental, but I can't send you blank checks. I have to pay the printer, I have payroll to make."

"But it's my company!"

"I understand that, Tom."

"Well, you can quit."

"I'm not going to quit, and I'm not going to send you blank checks."

Furious, Forcade reached Paul Tornetta, another signer on the account, who was home sick with the flu. "I want you to fire Kowl!" he screamed. "And I want you to take seven blank checks and send them to Tulsa—"

"Listen, Tom, I don't know what you're saying. I can't talk to you." Tornetta hung up the phone.

Despite all the challenges, the footage piled up. "He knew how to create a fantasy world for us as we worked," said Kowalski. "He created an outlaw atmosphere. Tom created a psychological state in which all of the crew—including myself—felt invincible. We felt like the world was revolving around us; he did it in many little ways such as getting us chauffeurs and bodyguards."

The Sex Pistols, for their part, were barely communicating with one another, and tensions between Johnny Rotten and the band's manager, Malcolm McLaren, were rising. After the last performance, in San Francisco, the band was finished.

Back in New York, there were rumors that *High Times* was having trouble with cash flow—so much so that its Wisconsin-based printer flew into New York after hearing that the magazine had abandoned its March issue. Kowl and Tornetta told him not to worry, that everything was business as usual.

But two days later, the recently returned Forcade distributed a memo that called for a staff meeting at the Diplomat Hotel that afternoon. Shareholders, the memo announced, would determine a course of action to be taken with the magazine. (Forcade was the only shareholder.) "Tom comes in that morning," said Andy Kowl, "with a carton of Mao's Little Red Book, and red star pins. He had somebody hand one of each out to everybody in the company, and then he had a bus come and take them to the Diplomat."

At the Diplomat, Forcade, wearing a Chinese Red Army hat, presided over the meeting from behind a desk that was dialectically decorated with how-to-run-a-corporation books and volumes about Marxism. Then he asked everyone not employed by Trans-High to leave the room. When everyone stayed put, he began pointing out individuals.

"Who are you?" he demanded.

"I'm Michael Kennedy, Tom."

"What are you doing here?"

"I'm your attorney," Kennedy replied.

"Who is the woman with you?"

"This is my wife. She's my counsel."

Eventually, one person was kicked out, an outside accountant. Forcade called for the "Sergeant at Arms," Jack Combs, to remove the man. Then Forcade walked over to the door of the ballroom, locked it behind the accountant, and kicked the door.

Forcade announced the firings of Kowl and Tornetta, whose refusal to send blank checks was unforgivable. "The workers," he said, "have been vindicated. Power to the people!"

When the meeting was adjourned, Forcade invited everyone to return to the Diplomat later that night for a "Victory Party."

Forcade hadn't given up on the Sex Pistols, even though the band was finished. He tracked down Johnny Rotten, who was staying in New York with a photographer named Joe Stevens. "This is Thomas K. Forcade," he announced imperiously when he got Stevens on the phone. "I can come around with a shoebox full of greenbacks. All he has to do is sign a release for whatever we want to use in the movie. Fifteen thousand dollars, I'll bring it over." Stevens relayed the message to Rotten, whose response was instant: "No fucking way."

Shortly after that, Forcade heard rumors that Rotten had headed to Jamaica and was there with Richard Branson of Virgin Records. Forcade set out to find him. He chartered a plane to Jamaica for himself, Jack Combs, Craig Copetas, and John Holmstrom. (They were unable to locate the singer.)

There were so many possible ways to spend money. Forcade discussed starting a fourth television network and even had Maureen McFadden scope out an entire floor of the North Tower of the World Trade Center. He talked about buying a Concorde, or a Sikorsky amphibian, and opening his own bank. Then, to show he was in on the joke, or at least self-aware, a day later he'd follow these grand pronouncements with a self-effacing line, like, "Gabrielle, give me my lithium."

Unfortunately for *High Times*, Forcade wasn't the only one going through a frenzied phase. Shortly after the announcement that the magazine would be distributed nationally by Flynt Publications, Larry Flynt had begun exhibiting stranger-than-usual behavior as well. While flying on his private jet, he saw the apparition of a bearded man in a robe and sandals and dropped to his knees in prayer. He soon announced that he was a born-again Christian. (He would later write that his conversion was most likely "the outcome of a manic-depressive episode.") Flynt made moves to turn his company into a nonprofit and make large charitable donations but complained that family members were undermining his efforts. Flynt's brother attempted to have him committed for a sanity hearing. Then Flynt began a buying spree: he purchased three newspapers, including the oldest of the undergrounds, the *Los Angeles Free Press*. He took out full-page ads in the *New York Times*, *Washington Post*, and other metropolitan papers offering a million-dollar reward for information leading to the solving of JFK's assassination. Soon he hit a cash flow problem and cut personnel and delayed plans to introduce two new magazines.

Flynt railed to his employees about loyalty. "They were plotting against me," he told a reporter in March 1978. "A lot of people thought I was crazy. I didn't mind them thinking I'm crazy, but I did mind the plotting. If I was screwing twenty women a day and smoking coke, they'd think I was okay."

The day after he gave that interview, Flynt was ambushed by a rifleman outside a Georgia courthouse and paralyzed from the waist down.

Theories abounded as to who the shooter might be. The periodical business, with its longtime ties to organized crime, wasn't exactly open to outsiders—Flynt was the first new national magazine distributor to come along in decades. Mark Lane, the lawyer and writer Flynt had hired to investigate the assassinations of John F. Kennedy and Martin Luther King Jr., now turned his staff's attention to Flynt's own shooting. He contended that "government agencies" were involved.

"I knew who did it even before I was shot," Flynt claimed. "The CIA did it, the same people who assassinated President Kennedy, his brother Bobby, Martin Luther King Jr., Malcolm X."

And the same people who'd come for Flynt—whether it was wholesalers, puritans, or the CIA—just might be after Tom Forcade. Not long after the shooting, Forcade declined an interview for a *Los Angeles Times* profile of *High Times* and told the reporter that his name was not in the masthead of the magazine because of a "desire not to be hassled by nuts, with or without guns." Once, walking down the street with Larry Hertz on LaGuardia Place, Forcade turned to Hertz and said, "Don't walk that close to me. If somebody takes a shot, I wouldn't want you to get hit."

To Albert Goldman, Forcade was more direct. "I feel like, in the end, I'm gonna get bumped," he said. "It's gonna be the straight media that bumps me, and my lengthy list of so-called friends will be eager participants, in due time. My efforts will be reinterpreted by history as unacceptable to the System."

When Chic Eder's surreptitious work as an informant came to light, Albert Goldman had already picked a younger, sexier muse around whom to build his drug-world articles. Smuggler Tommy Sullivan was only twenty-one when Goldman met him in a Colombian hotel restaurant on New Year's Day 1976. Two years later, Sullivan met photographer Peter Beard at Studio 54, and almost immediately, the Tampa-raised kid who'd survived three plane crashes and hauled millions of dollars' worth of marijuana was embraced by the New York jet-set world, hopping between exclusive parties with wads of hundred-dollar bills stuffed in his front jean pockets and leaving a trail of unfinished room-service champagne and caviar in his wake. He became an unlikely fixture on the haute celebrity circuit, appearing as a boldfaced name in *Interview* magazine and in newspaper tabloids as the companion of Margaret Trudeau, the wife of the Canadian prime minister. He bankrolled a movie called *Cocaine Cowboys*, in which he cast himself as a rock musician and dealer of heavy weight and for which he would rent Andy Warhol's Montauk summer home.

Sullivan also made plans with Tom Forcade. They decided to purchase a plane's worth of Santa Marta Gold from Raul Davila-Jimeno, the Colombian supplier also known as Black Tuna.

Forcade had never removed himself from the drug trade, although he managed to compartmentalize his life enough that few of his friends knew the details of what he was up to, including his wife. "We'd stay at this hotel called the Mutiny in Coconut Grove," said Schang. "I was one of those ladies who'd stay at the pool all day swimming, even though I was just 25. At night he'd come back; I didn't ask him what he did all day. I knew it was illegal, I knew he was smuggling. I didn't want to know. He didn't want me to know either. Tom took an inordinate amount of care to keep me out of it."

Larry Hertz recalled one of those trips. "There were a few of us bringing the shipment in, and we were all in the same hotel to make things easier. Gabrielle was in Tom's room, and I came in, and he went, 'Get out of here. I don't want her to see who you are.' He didn't trust anybody. I mean, he couldn't. His life was at stake at all times."

Forcade and Jack Combs had been talking about buying an airplane for themselves—"laying plans and sharing dreams," as Gabrielle put it. Forcade subscribed to *Janes Aviation* and scoured the ads in *Trade-A-Plane* and took Gabrielle to browse at Sky Books International, which specialized in volumes about aircraft. He also paid for Combs to take flying lessons in Columbus, Georgia, so that Combs could be near his fourteen-year-old daughter. "When he started flying, I made some joking comment about flying drug planes," she remembered, "and he said, 'No, I'm not gonna get caught.' I was like, 'Okay, my daddy flies drugs.'"

"I wanted to go," said Hertz, "to learn how to fly. Forcade goes, 'No, I'll use my friend Jack, he's a very bright guy.' He really loved Jack. Tom said, 'I need *you* to sell the weed. I want you on the ground. I'm gonna send Jack to flight school. I want him to be the co-pilot on this thing.'"

Meanwhile, Hertz went to Florida to purchase a plane for the trip to Colombia, a 1946 Beechcraft D18 that Forcade had found in a classified ad.

"The seller could tell after a few minutes that I didn't know anything about planes," said Hertz. "And he knew that the person actually doing the smuggle, the main man, doesn't buy it—he wants to buffer himself, doesn't want them to know who he is. He said, 'I'll give you some addresses, in case you need any parts or anything in South America, some guys that can help you.' I go, 'Who said anything about South America?' And he just laughed."

At the end of April, Jack Combs and Joe Rockwell, an old friend of Tommy Sullivan's, flew the Beechcraft out to Barranquilla; Hertz met them at the Hotel Del Prado, where payment was delivered to Raul Davila. The loaded Beechcraft was to come up through Florida and toward Atlanta. At that point, Forcade, in a second plane, would rendezvous with the Beechcraft to guide it over the drop spot, where the cargo would be dropped by parachute. On the ground, Hertz's recovery crew, driving trucks and armed with stun guns, would collect the bales.

Sullivan was stationed in a Peachtree Plaza penthouse, the same spot Forcade had stayed months earlier at the beginning of the Sex Pistols tour. At midnight, he received an ETA from the plane and contacted Forcade. Their best friends would soon be zipping in from another continent with a fortune's worth of grass.

Forcade met the Beechcraft in the air, made visual contact, and turned around to lead the way, flying low to stay under radar detection.

"Get lower!" he commanded, cruising above a stand of pine trees in a rural area near Interstate 75. Then he heard an explosion and saw the fireball.

Forcade had guided them too low. He circled around in desperation, hoping to see something to give him hope, but there was only flaming wreckage. At last he landed. Forcade placed anonymous phone calls to the Marion County Sheriff's Department and the Federal Aviation Administration, trying to give them approximate coordinates, but it was four days before the charred remains of the Beechcraft were found. The fuselage was in ashes; only the tail of the plane was intact. It took the police days to determine whether the bones found in the ash were human.

"I'd never seen Tom cry until he came home and told me Jack was gone," said Gabrielle. "He was so distraught, he was sobbing. He loved Jack."

Forcade couldn't even bear to tell Larry Hertz what happened over the phone. He just told him that he didn't need to wait around with his ground crew, that he needed to come back to New York. When Hertz arrived at Forcade's apartment, Tom was soaking in a bath, curled up in a fetal position. He described the crash, and then he produced a tiny, pearl-handled gun—so small it could almost disappear in someone's hand.

"What are you doing with that?" Hertz asked. "Is it loaded?"

"Of course it's loaded. What am I gonna keep a gun for if it's not loaded?"

"What do you need this for, Tom?"

"It's my toy," Forcade said.

"We had all of Jack's things in our loft when he died," Schang recalled, "but it took him a long time to call Jack's parents, to have to face them."

Albert Goldman—whose friendships with both Sullivan and Forcade meant that he was one of the few people privy to the details of the smuggling operation—observed Forcade's frenetic response in the aftermath of the tragedy. "Though there was no hope of survivors, he wouldn't relinquish his belief that Jack had escaped and was lying up somewhere in the hospital, too sick to make contact. Tom hired private investigators and attorneys to work on the case." Forcade eventually began to construct alternative narratives about what had actually caused the crash, wondering if someone—the DEA, perhaps—had possibly planted an altimeter-triggered bomb.

"I guess he felt like they were closing in. His paranoia went up several notches," said Maureen McFadden. "Tom was really never the same after Jack's death." Forcade had her dispose of all his flight-related books.

Jack Combs's father, a retired army colonel, was convinced that his son was working undercover for the government, and he had gone to his congressman to find out what had happened. Before long, Cyrus Vance, the US secretary of state, was cabling back and forth with the US embassy in Bogotá.

No one, however, had told Jack's daughter that her father was missing.

"When I left a message on his answering service, he would always call that night or next day. I must have called three or four times. When he didn't call back, that's when I called Tom."

"Oh my God, you don't know?"

Her grandparents had tried to shield her from the news, and it was left to Forcade to explain what had happened.

A few weeks after the crash, Joe Rockwell's body was identified using his dental records. Forcade sent McFadden to his dentist's office to retrieve his X-rays. If something happened to *him*, he told her, he didn't want anyone to be able to identify him.

It would be four months before Combs's death was confirmed, when his daughter identified the remains of his belt buckle and watch. Everything else had burned beyond recognition.

"We heard from the police that someone had been at the crash site," she said. "There were van tracks. The mystery's always been, what did they put in or what did they take out? They were saying it was drug related. My grandfather wanted to find out who, when, how, but the Sheriff said, 'You need to leave it alone. These people don't play.'"

A part of him even questioned if Michael Kennedy was telling the truth about Chic Eder. "If someone told me right now the lawyer was CIA," he said to Albert Goldman, "that it was the other way around, I wouldn't be surprised either!" Then he let out a laugh. "I don't have your total cynicism," Goldman said, and Forcade's laughter faded.

Shortly after the crash, Forcade called Gary Stimeling, *High Times*'s science editor, into his office and told him that he had a friend who'd been confined to a mental hospital after a suicide attempt. Did Stimeling know of any good antidepressant drugs?

"He was very obviously emotional," Stimeling recalled. "His whole body was vibrating, and sometimes when he spoke, I could see the veins in his neck and head stand out. I told him that Stelazine and Thorazine, the drugs usually given at that time for depression, were terrible—I knew this from experience—and said I thought the best things were marijuana or maybe some peyote or magic mushrooms. It just did not occur to me at the time that he was probably talking about himself."

The paraquat story continued to grow and sow division. When the NIDA tests were complete, the government had to admit that 21 percent of the marijuana samples were contaminated and that "paraquat contamination may pose a serious risk to marijuana smokers." At the White

House, Peter Bourne seemed unmoved. "If the risk exists," he said, "the guy still has the option not to smoke the grass to begin with."

NORML held a press conference to announce that it was suing four government agencies. In the back of the room, Yippies and *High Times* employees passed joints and heckled.

Stroup called Forcade that afternoon. "You crazy fucker!" he yelled. "You're just like every other businessman. All you care about is your profits, and you don't care if people die!"

High Times immediately issued a press release accusing NORML of "promoting paranoia among potheads with dangerous and irresponsible claims" and offering Keith Stroup "a $1,000 reward if he can score just one ounce of paraquat-contaminated weed on the streets anywhere in the United States."

But not everyone at the magazine was so dubious. Copetas and Stimeling had also been at the NORML press conference, fuming at the Yippies' heckling, at what they saw as a reckless disregard for science. Those in the newsroom felt an ever-widening gulf between what they perceived as their journalistic duties and the agitprop tendencies that had existed from the beginning, a holdover from the underground press.

"I'd witnessed the spraying of fields in Mexico," said Copetas. "I'd taken samples and had them tested. Gary and I also had samples of paraquat pot sold on the street, which we'd shown Tom."

Stimeling had found the number for a poison hotline run by one of the paraquat manufacturers and called up, posing as a doctor. A patient in his hospital, he explained, who had been smoking marijuana was now indicating symptoms of lung disease. The company had one of its physicians call Stimeling back armed with information about all the cases that had been pouring in. When the scientific jargon finally got too complicated for Stimeling to continue his bluff, he hung up. Then he and Copetas spent the rest of the day writing a report that went out the next day to the two hundred radio stations across the country that were running *High Times* news segments.

High Times scheduled its *own* press conference to explain the science behind the defoliant. Mike Chance, who was in the unusual position of dual employment at *Yipster Times* and *High Times*, subscribed to the theory that paraquat poisoning was a hoax, and he pleaded with Forcade to cancel the press conference, but Forcade wouldn't hear of it. "Since it's going to be such a big story," Forcade reasoned, "we'd better be the ones spreading the bad news."

Copetas and Stimeling appeared with charts, showing that the tanks used for paraquat were also sometimes used for the herbicides 2-4-D and 2, 4, 5-T, and diesel fuel, and sometimes not drained between uses. There was potential, this meant, for a paraquat–Agent Orange concoction to be sprayed over the fields.

With a jar of paraquat in one hand and a fuel-insecticide brew in the other, prodded on by a *High Times* advertising manager, Stimeling held his breath and poured sludgy brown liquid from the left to right, "just to show how easy it would be to make this super-deadly herbicide. I didn't spill a drop and immediately got the lids back on tight."

The journalists assembled for the press conference panicked and scattered.

"It was around that time," Copetas said, "that Tom told us to stop reporting."

Future trips to Mexico and South America were put on hold, and when Ed Bradley of CBS approached Copetas about doing a segment on the *High Times*'s paraquat reporting, Forcade got suspicious. "It was kind of an insecure place at times," said Gary Stimeling. "One day, Tom calls Craig into his office. Craig's girlfriend had just broken up with him, so he was pretty sad already. And Tom calls him in and accuses him of being a CIA agent and fires him. Craig came out just hysterical, crying 'What the hell is going on?'"

The time that Copetas spent with his sources at law enforcement agencies had also begun to make Forcade anxious. After Copetas's firing, Stimeling was even more cautious about mentioning his own DEA contacts to other *High Times* employees.

Forcade rehired Copetas shortly afterward, but the magazine was walking a fine line in its coverage. It ran color photographs, supplied by NIDA, of paraquat-contaminated pot and published an address to which pot could be sent in for testing. But *High Times* continued to insist that no one had suffered from smoking it. "There hasn't been a single certifiable case of paraquat-dope poisoning anywhere in this country," Dean Latimer assured readers in one column, and then, in the next breath, warned: "Don't believe the government…they've been knowingly poisoning American citizens for three years, and now that the news is out, they're scared stiff of catching hell for it."

The White House received more calls and telegrams about it than any other topic, including the then-heated debate about the United States relinquishing control of the Panama Canal. An opening sketch on *Saturday Night Live* featured John Belushi and Gilda Radner playing Mexican marijuana harvesters getting the pesticide dumped on them. Their weed makes its way to Bill Murray in New York. "Are you sure this stuff is okay?" Murray asks his source, the house band's bassist. "Oh yes, man—I swear it's Colombian," he says, as Murray coughs, barely managing a hoarse "Live from New York, it's *Saturday Night!*"

Interviewed in the magazine, *SNL*'s Laraine Newman weighed in on the State Department's warning about paraquat spraying: "It may just be something to intimidate people from buying it. If it's true, it's diabolical! You get cirrhosis of the liver with alcohol, but marijuana doesn't harm you, so the government tried to devise a way to make it harm you."

Network television making jokes about different strains of marijuana without demonizing the user would have been unthinkable just a few years earlier, but cannabis had permeated America's consciousness. It had, indeed, become normalized. *High Times* had guided its readers through the world of marijuana, in economic, political, and botanical detail; it had popularized home cultivation and provided field guides to international products. The paraphernalia industry, which had exploded as a result of the magazine's reach, was now retailing $300 million annually.

By 1978, eleven states had decriminalized marijuana. Four states— New Mexico, Florida, Louisiana, and Illinois—had even *legalized* marijuana for therapeutic purposes, after studies showed its effectiveness in providing relief for glaucoma and chemotherapy patients. Peter Bourne set his sights on adding medical marijuana to federal programs for cancer treatment.

A backlash was inevitable. "Paradoxically," Forcade wrote in a *High Times* editorial, unsigned as always, "these victories may have come too easily to us. For today, at the crossroads of history, America is waging war on us.... We face defeat by the current government attack on pot—the most violent assault it has ever made on marijuana and the people who smoke it."

To Forcade's mind, the paraquat threat was psychological warfare, the government "making Americans afraid to smoke pot." Political attacks on the legality of marijuana paraphernalia, however, comprised a tangible economic and constitutional threat. The targeting of paraphernalia had been a key agenda of middle-class parents' groups that had been popping up in recent months, groups that made little distinction between "soft" and "hard" drugs and that were horrified to see pipes in record stores and a magazine about weed at 7-Elevens.

Bob DuPont, the director of NIDA, commissioned the leader of one of those parents' groups to write the agency's drug-prevention handbook. Then he resigned—amid charges that NIDA was improperly awarding contracts and grants—and set out on a tour about the dangers of marijuana. "I get a very sick feeling in the pit of my stomach," he told the *Washington Post*, "whenever I hear talk about marijuana being safe."

Suddenly, anti-paraphernalia bills were passing through legislatures—in New York, in Chicago suburbs, and in Carter's home state of Georgia.

Since politicians could not legislate the size of spoons or outlaw razor blades, rolling papers, or scales, Forcade argued, "what they are going to attempt to outlaw is their cultural context—the packaging, the advertisements, the instructions, the headshops and, of course, the magazine—*High Times*." Sure enough, some of the new paraphernalia legislation called for bans of "drug-related literature."

Then, at this crucial moment, a bombshell dropped. On July 19, 1978, the *Washington Post* reported that drug czar Peter Bourne had written a quaalude prescription for an aide, using a fake name for the patient. A legman for Jack Anderson's column, who'd been at the NORML party and who'd gotten Stroup to confirm Bourne's cocaine snorting off the record, was now desperate to run *that* story.

"I won't tell you not to use it," Stroup said.

The next morning, Jack Anderson went on *Good Morning America* with the scoop that Carter's drug advisor used cocaine.

Within hours, Peter Bourne resigned. In a kind of exit interview with the *New York Times*, Bourne poured gasoline on the political flames, claiming that there was a "high incidence" of marijuana and cocaine use among the White House staff. ("We told you so," crowed the *Yipster Times*, seizing the moment to remind readers that it had tried to connect the Carter administration to cocaine use.)

"Peter Bourne," said Keith Stroup, "was indeed a victim of paraquat—and there'll be more victims if Carter doesn't change his policy. This was a power play, a recognition that in the long run, you can't go against the constituency you claim." But Stroup had miscalculated the power play.

At a press conference that evening, on national television, Craig Copetas asked the president if he would support a bill in the Senate that would outlaw "money, men, or D.E.A. material to Mexico" for spraying.

"I'm not familiar with the bill," Carter said. "My understanding is that American money is not used to purchase the paraquat. I think Mexico buys the material from other countries and they use their own personnel to spray it with."

Copetas, gobsmacked, pointed out that $13 million a year was going to Mexico.*

But Carter was more interested in driving home the new direction of the administration. "My preference," the president said, "is that marijuana not be grown nor smoked."

Bourne's departure would mark a sea change in official policy. The drug czar had been more than just another special assistant with Carter's ear—the president had once called him "about the closest friend I have in the world." This privileged position meant that Bourne had held at bay the more hawkish desires of the Drug Enforcement Administration. As soon as Bourne was out of the picture, his replacement, a Nixon holdover named Lee Dogoloff, welcomed input from DEA administrator Peter Bensinger, who falsely claimed that marijuana represented a more serious cancer threat than cigarettes and called for marijuana-smuggling sentences to be tripled, saying that cocaine and heroin traffickers were now switching their attention to pot. Dogoloff also solicited advice from the parents-against-pot groups, who carted duffel bags of bongs and *High Times* issues into his office to make their case.

Decriminalization activists, on the other hand, were now personae non gratae in the White House. There would be no more mentions of decriminalization from the Carter administration.

A few weeks after Peter Bourne's resignation, Stroup organized a blowout week of partying in Miami. Forcade and Copetas both flew down for the celebration, timed to coincide with a series of Jimmy Buffett

---

* "He lied through his teeth," Copetas later said of the president, "which led to a whole other series of leaks and stories about how much we were funding paraquat."

concerts that were to be recorded for a NORML-benefiting live album, and were surprised by the orgiastic tenor of the party.

Jimmy Buffett skipped Stroup's closing-night party. His management later told Stroup that because of expenses, NORML wouldn't be getting any money from them.

It wasn't just NORML going through changes—the entire drug culture was shifting, especially in Miami, which was starting to feel like Chicago in the 1920s. On a visit to the bar at the Mutiny in Coconut Grove, Copetas noticed, for the first time, patrons brazenly carrying guns. Cocaine was no longer something thrown in with a marijuana load as an afterthought, a bonus export to pay for the cost of fuel. It was the whole game.

At the week's end, Forcade asked Stroup if he wanted to fly to Colombia with him. Stroup reminded the publisher that he'd been busted for cocaine in Canada only months earlier. "Don't worry," Forcade assured him. "In Colombia the cops are on our side."

Near the end of August, at Madison Square Garden's Felt Forum, the actor Rip Torn codirected a production called *Haven Can't Wait*, staged to benefit the effort to have charges against Abbie Hoffman dropped. Paul Krassner, William Burroughs, Allen Ginsberg, Jon Voight, Ossie Davis, and others performed in sketches, while most of Hoffman's fellow Chicago Eight—David Dellinger, Rennie Davis, Jerry Rubin, Bobby Seale, and John Froines—offered reminiscences. (Tom Hayden was busy running for governor of California.) Twenty-seven winners of an Abbie Hoffman look-alike contest were granted admission in order to confuse the police when they came to the Garden looking for the fugitive, who'd now been underground for five years.

Four days later, Dana Beal—one of the organizers of *Haven Can't Wait*—was in Chicago marching to Grant Park with the new wave of Yippies to celebrate the tenth anniversary of the 1968 convention that had set off the Conspiracy Trial and made Abbie Hoffman and Jerry Rubin household names.

"Let's get a nice group picture. We need a few more people," Beal directed with a bullhorn. "We're on national television." But the press was quick to uncharitably contrast 1968—12,000 police, 6,000 National Guard troops, and Mayor Daley asking police to shoot to kill anyone with a Molotov cocktail and shoot to maim anyone looting a store—with the

150 current-day Yippies, who were smarting from camping-permit deni-als, lamenting lack of funds ("there used to be some radical chic money in Chicago," Beal sighed), and hawking a new *Yipster Times* interview with Abbie Hoffman. Why were they chanting "Stop the war"? one reporter asked incredulously. The answer he got—"the war against the working class, against women, against Blacks, against young people, against gyp-sies and native Americans"—only seemed to further agitate the reporter.

"Why don't they just shut up?" a local bystander told another reporter. "People don't care about cops and dope anymore."

In September, days after Forcade's thirty-third birthday, *High Times* threw a party at a spare loft he owned on West Broadway. "We played with it to make it look like that's where he lived," Maureen McFadden said, "so that people would think they were at Tom's apartment." Tele-visions were set up all around the rooftop, tuned in to the premiere of ABC's ersatz *Star Wars* series, *Battlestar Galactica*, a broadcast briefly in-terrupted with the breaking news of the Camp David Accords signing. Forcade was in a good mood, the best mood anyone had seen him in in a while. He handed one of his editors a gram of cocaine and mingled with the guests. He walked over to *High Times* art director Toni Brown, who was talking to Andy Warhol. That week, she'd persuaded the artist to pose for a cover with Truman Capote.

"Get some photos of us!" Brown shouted over to Mick Rock, the pho-tographer of stars like David Bowie, Lou Reed, and Iggy Pop, who was lined up to shoot the Warhol and Capote cover later that week. Forcade beckoned managing editor Shelley Levitt over. "Get Shelley into the pho-tograph," he told Mick. "We can always crop her out afterward!"

Suddenly, Aron Kay appeared and pied Andy Warhol in the face as Rock snapped away.

Brown was furious. "I don't know what to do," Forcade said to Levitt while Warhol was getting cleaned off. His carefully compartmentalized worlds were colliding. "Andy Warhol's our guest. But I look at Aron Kay, and...I've created him! I can't censor him!"

No one else shared Forcade's belief in *Polk County Pot Plane*. "There was no level of artistry," said Maureen McFadden, "although it was the first film to have a 40-foot semi driving through a house."

Ed Dwyer left a screening halfway through and ran into Forcade in the hallway outside. "Tom, if you keep putting your money into this," Dwyer said, "I'd better get home and print up some cash." Larry Hertz couldn't understand why Forcade didn't just put their own adventures on-screen. "I saw it and I said, 'How could you buy this piece of trash? We could've made our own movie.'"

Forcade was resolute. After the success of Cheech and Chong's *Up in Smoke* (tagline: "*Don't* go straight to this movie") and *National Lampoon's Animal House*—a movie about marijuana and a movie branded by a magazine, each filmed for under $3 million and grossing more than $100 million—a magazine-branded marijuana movie should be a slam dunk.

In October, Forcade flew out to Los Angeles with copies of *Polk County Pot Plane* and Tommy Sullivan's vanity project *Cocaine Cowboys*.

High Times contributor Victor Bockris, whom Forcade had hired to act as a kind of roving West Coast correspondent, picked him up at the airport.

"We need to get about an ounce of cocaine," Forcade informed him. "Can you get it right away?"

When they got to Forcade's penthouse suite at the Chateau Marmont, Bockris made some calls. "These girls came over with top quality cocaine," he recalled. "One of them tried to seduce him, which annoyed him very much. He gave them cash and disappeared."

"My wife is my best friend," Forcade told Bockris the next day, as they were driving up the coast. "She's the only person I trust." The marriage, Forcade said, also provided him with a form of protection. "Otherwise, these girls would always be hitting on me for money and drugs."

They were headed to a house that Tommy Sullivan and his band—the stars of *Cocaine Cowboys*—had rented. But the once-luxurious home had been abandoned. It was a spooky scene—doors left open, food on the floor, a dirty swimming pool, and a neglected dog. It felt like something terrible had happened, Bockris thought. Forcade fed the dog and then started searching for papers that he said he needed to get rid of. He spent hours looking.

Forcade started playing strange power games in Hollywood. When Bockris came to pick him up for a dinner meeting at an agent's house, Forcade stalled for three hours, taking hits of nitrous oxide every fifteen minutes, sprawled on his bed in suit and cowboy hat. Inevitably, phone calls started coming, questioning where the guests were. "They already left; they're on the way," Forcade would insist.

They showed up at midnight, Forcade breezing past the sputtering agent, beelining for the couch, where he sat and stared at the wall. Then he asked for a scotch.

Miraculously, this charmed the host.

"He hit it perfectly; he had them wrapped around his finger," said Bockris. "I apologized to him. I said, 'You're a genius. I didn't understand.'"

At a meeting with producer Gene Taft, an associate of the legendary Robert Evans, Forcade took out a gold canister filled with cocaine and conspicuously set it down on the table as the meeting began. He hired the industry-connected Taft to act as a middleman and set up more meetings, including one with Robert Evans. Then he picked up the canister, put it in his pocket, and left.

The next morning, Maureen McFadden picked up Forcade and Bockris in a gray limousine and drove them to the Bel Air home of Evans, who greeted them in white pajama bottoms and a long white bathrobe. Ushered past the swimming pool and into the screening room abutting the tennis court, they sat around a black coffee table. Evans spent forty-five minutes breaking down the problems of the film, while a butler brought them cigars and candy.

"Tom was so depressed afterward," said McFadden. "He'd dropped about a hundred thousand dollars into *Polk County Pot Plane*, and Evans told him he should have just released it as it was. It was just a midnight movie; he couldn't make it better."

Now he'd hit a wall—people were happy to meet the man behind *High Times*, but they didn't want to touch the films. Gene Taft confided to Bockris that the only reason the producers were taking meetings was because they thought Forcade could get them Merck pharmaceutical cocaine. Forcade kept playing Betamax copies of *Polk County Pot Plane* and *Cocaine Cowboys* for visitors in his hotel suite, hoping someone would like them. It was hopeless.

Bockris hosted a party for William Burroughs at his suite at the Tropicana Hotel. Christopher Isherwood, Kenneth Tynan, Timothy Leary, and John Paul Getty Jr. were there. Forcade lay on the bed with his cowboy hat over his face for the duration of the party.

"He wasn't there at all," Burroughs later said.

A few days later, just before Forcade left Los Angeles, Bockris brought Burroughs to Forcade's Bel Air suite for a steak dinner. They bonded over their shared interest in guns and made plans to go shooting the next time Burroughs was in New York.

"I think when you die," Forcade said at one point, "you're just dead."

"Oh, Tom, do you really believe that?" asked Burroughs. "I don't believe it at all."

"Well," Forcade said, "I want to believe it."

A few weeks later, back in New York, Forcade woke up Gabrielle at 4:00 a.m. one morning and asked her to interview him on the spot. Roused from bed, she gamely played along with his suggestions for questioning, yielding a flurry of quotable lines:

> "I never met a drug I didn't like, but I never violate any local, state, or federal laws. I believe in clean living, and I stay away from sugar."
> "It's an all-American magazine with a section on world news. We support America 100%, especially South America."
> "Q: What are the magazines' politics? Radical, alternative...?"
> "A: Astral."

He spoke kindly of Abbie Hoffman and Jerry Rubin, plugged his favorite magazines ("I read a couple hundred a week"), from *New Woman* to *Road and Track*, and said that the *High Times* atmosphere was "a lot healthier now" than in the old days. "Things are more in perspective. We have the high without the hassle."

But the conversation was also, at times, shot through with darkness and paranoia. "The entire media has been bought up and has become a subsidiary of big business," he said, and it was now about as independent as the Soviet Union's TASS or *Pravda*. He was motivated by "a deep fear of killing myself out of boredom." Asked if he worried about being imprisoned, he said that he'd been under such close surveillance that he'd effectively "spent the last ten years in jail."

"They have tapped the phones where I live, including my bedroom," he said. "They've read my mail, they've used superintendents where I live and work. To this day they've got informers planted against me. They've planted women informers to try to fuck me, they've planted informers in positions as *High Times* office boys, office managers, and accountants. They don't stop there, either. The government has used informers against me as dope dealers, dope smugglers, pseudo-radical activists, gun dealers, explosives dealers, and even lawyers."

It wasn't as if Forcade's suspicious nature was new. "I don't think he would ever relax if there was more than one other person in the room," said Copetas. "He was fearful that people were coming after him, taking precautions for his life, which he really didn't need to take." But his anxieties now seemed to be growing. A member of NORML's board of directors recalled Forcade worrying that the growing popularity of soccer in the United States might lead to stadiums being used as prison camps, as they had been in Pinochet's Chile.

"It was really hard for me to get through to him," said Shelley Levitt. "Even though Tom and I had become really good friends, and we had in fact talked about his previous suicide attempts, there were times when he would become really reticent and withdrawn, and it was really difficult to penetrate the shell."

And his wit was increasingly macabre. "If all else fails," he joked to Larry Hertz, "there's always suicide."

Forcade's feelings about "the movement" had gotten pretty morbid, too. He wrote an editorial for *Yipster Times* that touted a new organization called the Revolutionary Independent Party, an entity whose fictitiousness became clear as he started riffing on the group's acronym. "RIP America? RIP the world? RIP for under thirties? RIP for over-thirties *and* under thirties."

At work, Forcade was nearly catatonic, lying on the couch in his office, begging off from meetings that he said he was too tired for. He carried out another spontaneous round of *High Times* terminations at the end of October. "He went upstairs," said Bob Lemmo, "and it was like everyone he saw, he fired."

Victor Bockris returned from Los Angeles and called Forcade, eager to pick up the new friendship where it had left off. "He was like a different person," Bockris said. "He said, 'Listen, man, I'll get together with you soon. I'm just dealing with some problems.'"

A week later, Forcade called back.

"Hey, man, could you come over?"

"I'm writing right now, Tom," said Bockris.

"No...ahh...I don't want to put you through changes, man...but..." Bockris was startled by Forcade's faltering voice.

"I'll be there in twenty minutes," he said, and headed through the November snow over to LaGuardia Place.

Gabrielle opened the door. Forcade was lying on the couch.

"How's it going, man?" Bockris asked. Forcade turned over and passed out.

"He's quaaluded out," Gabrielle said. She tried to wake him up, turned him over and gave him a shake, to no avail. "He's really out of it this time," she said.

Bockris was speedy from the Desoxyn he'd taken to race toward his writing deadline. *Call Tommy Sullivan,* he kept thinking. *We'll get a helicopter! Forcade's so fucked up chemically, maybe Sullivan could...give him coke or something.* But Bockris couldn't reach Sullivan anyway.

The next night, Forcade called Maureen McFadden, three times. Everyone wanted him for his money, he complained. In Hollywood, he said, people only wanted to buy coke from him. He called Shelley Levitt to get a writer's phone number and stayed on for forty-five minutes. He said he had a lot on his mind and that he might not be around much in the coming weeks.

"Do whatever you have to do to get the magazine out," he said. "You're in charge. The magazine is so good—there's so much goodness there, you can't make it bad. It's just a question of what *degree* of goodness you're going to achieve. *High Times* is the only thing standing between us and Western barbarism."

She'd never heard him so depressed. After they hung up, she thought about going over to his loft, but it was after 1:00 a.m.

The next day was Thursday, November 16. NIXON APPROVED BREAK-INS, EX-FBI AIDE TELLS COURT, announced front-page headlines in the *Washington Post*, for a story about how the bureau had secretly implemented parts of the illegal 1970 Huston Plan after all.

Forcade called Levitt from home and told her he wasn't going into the office.

"Listen," he said, "it's really important that you understand exactly what I said to you last night. And if you have any questions, ask me now."

"Tom, maybe you're not going to be around for the March issue, but that's lined up already, you've seen everything. And by April, maybe you'll be feeling better."

"You're really great. And you can run the magazine as well as I can."

"Tom, that's not true. I can't."

"Yes, you can," he said, and then raised his voice: "Yes, you can!"

She asked him about an upcoming article. "It's up to you," he said. "Do what you want."

Craig Copetas called Forcade from the airport. Forcade had asked him to represent *High Times* at a NORML fundraiser at the Playboy Mansion and also to visit Larry Flynt to talk about distribution issues. But Copetas didn't feel right leaving Forcade behind.

"I really think you should come," Copetas said. "Everyone out there wants to see you. Why don't you change your mind? I'll cancel my ticket, and we'll take a later flight."

Forcade began babbling. "No... no, no, you go and take care of the magazine. Whatever you do, take care of the magazine. And make sure you get good lawyers, so people don't try to steal it. Don't trust the lawyers we have now."

"Okay, Tom," Copetas said. "I'll call you when I get there and maybe you'll change your mind."

Not long afterward, McFadden called. She heard Forcade's phone pick up, but nobody said hello. Sometimes he was weird like that, just waiting for her to start talking. So she went ahead and told him she was at a film vault picking up a print of *The Smugglers*. But he still didn't say anything, and then the receiver fumbled back into place. The son of a bitch hung up on her, she thought, and went back to work.

Jim Drougas, manager of the New Morning Bookstore, stopped by Tom and Gabrielle's loft on his way back from the bank. She'd invited him to join them for lunch.

Shortly after 12:30 p.m., Forcade asked Gabrielle for a Valium. "Wait twenty minutes," she said, "and see if you can sleep without it."

"You'll hear from me at one," he said.

At 1:00 p.m., Jim and Gabrielle were talking, food in the oven, when they heard a strange popping noise. They looked at each other, and she went in to check on her husband.

Drougas heard Gabrielle cry out. He ran in and saw a .45 next to Forcade, who was lying on Gabrielle's side of the bed in a paisley shirt and blue jeans, his body convulsing. He was unconscious.

Frantically, they called for an ambulance.

Members of the homicide squad and forensic unit appeared at the door instantly. "If your husband lives," a detective told Schang, "you won't hear from me anymore. But if he dies, you will."

"They wanted to take her to be interviewed at the precinct," said Drougas. "I said, 'Look, I'm not comfortable with you taking her and putting her through this right now. If you're gonna take her, you're going to have to go through me and her lawyer first. She didn't do anything, I was there. I'm a witness.' And he backed off."

Forcade was taken in an ambulance to St. Vincent's Hospital, about fifteen blocks away.

Hunter Thompson picked Copetas up at the airport in Los Angeles. "You hear what happened?" he asked. "Tom blew his brains out while you were flying."

"We were just in complete and total shock," recalled Copetas. "I think it was the only time Hunter ever drove slow."

Shelley Levitt got a call at the office from WPIX radio.

"Do you know Gary Kenneth Goodson?"

"There's no one at the magazine by that name," she said, and started to hang up.

"Who's the publisher of *High Times*?" the caller asked.

This was not information she was going to give out. "Let me put you through to our PR department."

"Before you hang up, let me just tell you what this is about. The police just found someone who shot himself who is believed to be the publisher of *High Times*."

"Well, Gary Kenneth Goodson is not the publisher of *High Times*. Where was he found?"

"506 LaGuardia," the reporter said, and then Levitt knew it was Tom.

"What's his condition?"

"He's not expected to live," the reporter said.

Levitt put down the phone.

Everyone left the office and went over to the hospital to say goodbye to Tom.

Forcade's living will had stated that he did not want to be kept on life support. The respirator was disconnected on Saturday. At 7:24 p.m. the former Gary Goodson was pronounced dead.

The next day a wake was held uptown. Forcade, hair combed neatly and wearing a mushroom-patterned necktie, lay in a gray casket in a blue-carpeted chapel with a chandelier and curtains. The bullet hole in the right temple had been so tiny that the damage was nearly invisible. "He looked so together there, he was so ready to go," Tommy Sullivan told Victor Bockris. "I was thinking, 'Let's get it on, Tom!' You know how he would lie and sleep. He had his hands folded like he always did, and he was just ready to jump up and say, 'All right! Let's get it on! Let's do it!'"

At the Diplomat Hotel, which now primarily functioned as a disco, a press conference enumerated Forcade's achievements, from the Underground Press Syndicate to *High Times*, his activism and philanthropic projects. Press kits with photos of the mysterious Forcade were handed out "so that you know what the guy looked like." The still-in-shock speakers, there to testify about his impact—Craig Copetas, Ed Dwyer, Dana Beal, Toni Brown, Jim Drougas, Ron Rosenbaum, and Keith Stroup—wore nametags, slumped amid a background of neon fixtures and mirror balls. Even Jerry Rubin was in the audience.

Michael Kennedy introduced himself as Forcade's "lawyer for a number of legal and illegal things over the years" before ceding the floor to Gabrielle Schang.

"He was a guy who was a genius, and I can't begin to simplify what was going on in his brain," she said.

He was maybe a manic depressive, okay? He was either really, really high during which time he produced movies, came out with three or four magazines, wrote books, anthologies, and did incredible things. And then during those lows, you know, I mean, this time he chose to off himself. What can I say, you know? It's not like he was a drug casualty at all. He was not an addictive personality. . . . He provided a cultural context for the people who may have been disillusioned and not known what to do when the war ended and all the revolutionary activity stopped.

"When people went their separate ways, Tom carried forth with the vision and culture of the Sixties," Jerry Rubin told a journalist. "He was a brilliant journalist and editor who captured the ideas of a generation and expressed it. Anyone who spent any time talking to him knew they were in the presence of genius."

But Forcade's death was crowded out of the news. That same weekend, in the South American country of Guyana, minister Jim Jones directed the members of his Peoples Temple congregation, who had followed him from the Bay Area, to drink cyanide-laced Flavor Aid. More than nine hundred people, including more than two hundred children, died in what Jones claimed to be "an act of revolutionary suicide" but which was in fact a massacre—many had been forcibly administered cyanide. In addition, a visiting congressman from Northern California, a defecting member, and three journalists were assassinated by gunshot. It was, at the time, the greatest loss of American life in a single incident.

And it was, in a strange way, one more nail in the coffin of 1960s idealism. Although Jones was an abusive megalomaniac, the Peoples Temple had supported the Black Panther Party, worked against capital punishment, donated funds for slain police officers and bail for activists, and established medical clinics, drug rehabilitation programs, and childcare centers. History would only remember that it had become a death cult.*

Nine days later, the prominent gay rights advocate Harvey Milk was murdered by a former colleague from the San Francisco Board of Supervisors. Also killed was San Francisco mayor George Moscone, who three years earlier, as the Democratic leader of the California Senate, had written the bill that decriminalized marijuana in that state.

A few weeks later, a wake was held at Windows of the World restaurant at One World Trade Center, where guests would be literally as high as possible. Some of his cremated ashes were to be given to Gabrielle, and some to his mother.

"Everyone there was just completely in a stoned haze," said Copetas. "I don't know why, but I was given the wooden urn with his ashes. We

---

* Theories that the People's Temple was a psychological operation of the CIA have persisted. The slain congressman, Leo Ryan, had been a leading critic of agency overreach, and had introduced legislation that restricted its covert actions.

were starting to leave, and we're in the lobby of the restaurant, and people decide that they want to scatter some of Tom's ashes from the roof. I said, 'You can't get up there,' but they didn't want to hear about that. So someone got out a dime and put the urn in their hands while this other person tried to unscrew the bottom. And of course, some of the ashes—in fact, quite a bit—fell on the floor. Within moments, a busboy emerged with a vacuum cleaner, and you can imagine the chaos that ensued. Some of them were actually vacuumed up. It was tragic. It was a comedy of tragedy, a calamity."

Forty years later, an article in the *New York Times* reported that some of Forcade's ashes were rolled into joints and smoked "atop the World Trade Center." The source of that story was not named.

The legend of Thomas King Forcade continued to grow.

EPILOGUE

"Tom was the kind of guy who'd shoot himself in the head just to show his friends how pointless it was to shoot yourself in the head," wrote Zippie Steve Conliff in a letter shortly after Forcade's death. Then he qualified the statement: "If he shot himself. Who can be sure nowadays?"

"When I went to his funeral, I just wanted to touch him, to see if it was really Tom in that box," said Glenn O'Brien. "I really didn't believe he was dead. He was so smart and cool and such a scam artist....If you could ever imagine somebody faking his own death, it would have been Tom Forcade."

Perhaps unsurprisingly, rumors swirled. People whispered about a government-sanctioned hit or a cover-up job. A story about someone breaking into Forcade's loft and tearing up the floorboards even made it into the *Village Voice*. Maureen McFadden said she heard that the bullet didn't match the gun in Forcade's hand. Another contributor claimed that "mysterious black cars" followed Forcade in his last weeks. "I'll never believe, till the day I die, that Tom committed suicide," one of the earliest *High Times* staffers declared, decades later.

It was as if all the suspicions that had been once directed at Forcade were now looking for new places to attach themselves.

Although the CIA's CHAOS program began on August 15, 1967, it was probably a coincidence that Forcade first contacted the Underground

Press Syndicate in New York on that very day—the CHAOS operations weren't enacted immediately. And although the "CIA's inquiry into foreign ties of American dissidents intensified at the end of October 1967," as the Church Report stated, presumably "precipitated by the October 21 demonstrations and arrests at the Pentagon," it was probably also a coincidence that this was the time and place at which Forcade first met prominent activists. There were, after all, a hundred thousand of them there that weekend.

It was, perhaps, curious that the science-fiction novel that he had treated like a bible was called *Agent of Chaos*. At the book's conclusion, the director of the Brotherhood of Assassins is on the brink of defeat at the hands of the Hegemony when he thinks he sees a way out in what he terms the "Ultimate Chaotic Act": suicide. But Forcade's bipolar condition and the trauma of losing his best friend seem more likely to have brought about tragedy than any kind of wish for fulfillment of a literary prophecy.

Still, somehow, even after he left the world, Forcade continued to confound everyone. "Tom said I was the only person he could trust," Shay Addams confided to fellow Zippie Rex Weiner. "That's what he told *me*," Weiner replied.

"There are a lot of things that I don't think anybody will ever know," said Forcade's sister Judy Goodson. "He might say one thing to one person, another to somebody else, and something else to a third person. Which story do you want to take as the accurate one?"

Andy Kowl remembered that he had the key to the safe deposit box into which, upon Forcade's instruction, he'd placed tens of thousands of dollars during the early *High Times* days. Kowl went back to the bank and found the box empty.

Gabrielle Schang discovered that Forcade had kept safe deposit boxes at a Chase Manhattan branch under the name "John Thomas Mason." One was filled with $175,000 of the moldy, singed money that had been recovered from the Florida swamp. There were bars of gold, too, or so it seemed at first. They turned out to be painted lead.

Two weeks after Forcade's death, the William Burroughs–honoring festival for which Forcade had provided the last-minute funding was held in Manhattan. The Nova Convention bridged generations of the New

York arts scene, from John Cage to Patti Smith. Jean-Michel Basquiat and Keith Haring, as yet unknown, were in attendance and invigorated by the readings and performances. "We didn't realize that this huge event would be an adieu to the American avant-garde," said one of the convention organizers, decades later. "No other event after that gathered so many of the artists, poets, musicians of the underground scene."

Abbie Hoffman, still underground, donned a disguise and attended the Nova Convention's closing-night party and recorded his thoughts in the third person in "The Fugitive," an essay for the *Village Voice*:

> His associate/antagonist, Tom Forcade had just blown his head off. The Fugitive and Tom had made their peace two years ago. He felt relieved their conflict had been settled in time. "How," he thought, "could you ever pay back a dead man?" He was saddened by Tom's death. Down in Guyana poor souls by the hundreds were trying to keep up with the Jones and, in San Francisco, post-Vietnam white insanity had cut down the Mayor and a courageous freedom fighter—Harvey Milk. Horrible Horror. The Fugitive shivered.

> Hoffman surreptitiously caught up with old friends. He spoke to Allen Ginsberg and Timothy Leary. Hoffman had been quoted condemning Leary; he told Leary not to believe "all you read in the magazines." They embraced.

> On the way out, he saw Gabrielle.

> "He must pay his respects," Hoffman wrote of himself, "to the bereaved widow of *High Times*. 'Sadness will pass, Gaby, soon you should get onto the next movie.' She's strong, he thinks, a student of the streets. 'Yes, the next movie,' she concurs. He is very pleased Tom gave half the magazine money to marijuana's future legalization. An honorable will. 'We are all getting more mature.'" Hoffman headed to the subway.

> Inside, Aron Kay found Timothy Leary and got him in the face with a cheesecake—cheese, for being a rat.

> That same night, in Washington, DC, Keith Stroup delivered a farewell address to NORML. He was leaving the post of national director after the Bourne fallout. Stroup had heard rumors that a pieing was planned for him, too, but that never came to pass. He began his speech by honoring the recently departed George Moscone and Tom Forcade

for their contributions to the movement. Then he spoke about NORML's decision to shift its demands from decriminalization to full legalization of marijuana.

"We want the right to as much marijuana as we can put in our homes, as well as the right to legally grow our own," he said. "The people who sell marijuana are also our friends, not violent criminals. It's about time we started backing them right along with the smoker."

Afterward, he was plied with Dom Pérignon, methamphetamine, cocaine, quaaludes, and of course premium marijuana. Finally, in a Hyatt Regency suite, he passed out.

"Watch the light from San Francisco; it will light up the world," Vietnam veteran Dennis Peron wrote from his five-by-seven-foot Northern California jail cell near the end of 1978, in a letter published in *High Times*. Peron's Big Top "marijuana supermarket" was a larger and more public establishment than Forcade's own smoke-easies had ever been, serving thousands of customers; he'd been busted ten times in the previous three years. But just before accepting a deal for a six-month sentence, Peron had coauthored a ballot initiative called Proposition W, which called for San Francisco policy to prohibit arrests for sale or cultivation.

The nonbinding initiative passed, but the celebration was short-lived. Former San Francisco city supervisor Dan White—who had once angrily expressed shock that his colleague Harvey Milk had supported Peron's probation—murdered Milk and Mayor George Moscone. Proposition W was never recognized in the city. Peron's bold prediction to *High Times* was correct, but it would take a while.

In the meantime, the drug war raged on. It had already started to grow more militaristic in the middle of 1978, when the White House, concerned by the increased involvement of organized crime in the drug trade, agreed to coordinate not just the DEA, Customs, Coast Guard, and FBI but also the Navy, Air Force, and State Department. Soon the US attorney general announced the first big fish of the joint FBI–DEA operations: the Black Tuna Gang. One of the leaders of the $300 million drug ring had learned about the marijuana market from reading *High Times*'s Trans-High Market Quotations, which determined the wholesale price for its product.

The trade had changed. As drugs became the largest retail business in the state of Florida and Colombian cartels vied against one another as well as CIA-trained Cuban exiles, drug-related homicides increased dramatically, and with the infamous July 1979 machine-gun shoot-out at the Dadeland Mall in Miami, the era of the cocaine cowboy had arrived.

But now the marijuana plant was available from other, closer sources. "If people in America want to get high, they're going to have to grow their own," Forcade had predicted in 1976. "As those who have gotten into high horticulture know, the best dope in the world is grown in windowboxes and closets." The late-seventies paraquat scare resulted in an increase in the number of US citizens growing their own marijuana, just as Operation Intercept's throttling of the Mexican border traffic had a decade earlier. By now, though, the methods of both cultivation and distribution were more sophisticated. Marijuana flourished in Hawaii, where *pakalolo* crops were estimated to outpace the sugarcane industry; in the Emerald Triangle of Northern California, where growers specialized in seedless sinsemilla; even in the moonshine counties of Tennessee. By the end of the seventies, a third of the grass smoked in California was grown in state.

The federal government did what it could to yoke marijuana to harder drugs as the drug war intensified during the Reagan years. The Anti-Drug Abuse Act of 1986 imposed draconian mandatory sentences; Democrats and Republicans engaged in a game of tough-on-crime one-upmanship.

But cannabis's medicinal value would, over the years, be the key to legalization, and San Francisco would indeed be the beacon. Galvanized by the AIDS crisis, Peron and other activist-dealers supplied Bay Area patients with appetite-stimulating, nausea-suppressing marijuana; slowly, the tenor of news coverage began to change as the benefits of marijuana became not just undeniable but also unavoidable. In 1996, California's Proposition 215 made the possession and cultivation of marijuana for personal use legal with a doctor's recommendation. By 2012, seventeen more states had followed. And that year, the first states—Colorado and Washington—expanded their legalization to recreational use. Today, in nearly half of the United States, Forcade's 1975 description of an ideal dispensary has come to pass:

"Each dealer would have his small store, like a tobacco shop. The finest varieties of marijuana would be available from hermetically sealed bins, to be scooped out fresh, weighed precisely and sold over the counter like fine pipe tobaccos or good liquor."

The path of *High Times* itself was perhaps even rockier than that of legalization. "When Forcade shot himself," said writer Dean Latimer, "he put a bullet through everything."

Forcade had left behind an intricate maze of paperwork: a will, a family trust, and something called the Trans-High Charitable Trust, which administered the Trans-High Corporation. The charitable trust named as its beneficiaries NORML and the Alternative Press Syndicate—with common stock to be turned over in the year 2000 to loyal *High Times* employees who'd served for ten years or more. His widow, Gabrielle Schang, challenged the validity of the charitable trust immediately.

The next few years would be a bonanza of billable hours for legions of attorneys and a nightmare for everyone else involved in *High Times*, filled with accusations of substance abuse and self-dealing, threats, lawsuits, and confidential settlements.

In early 1979, two of the trustees—*High Times* circulation director Stanley Place and design director Toni Brown—were named president and vice president of the Trans-High Corporation. They quickly moved seven Trans-High companies out of the charitable trust and consolidated them under the creatively named THC Joint Holding Corporation. Schang charged that they were looking for a "pot of gold" and angling to be the only long-term employees by the year 2000. In July, Schang, along with Michael Kennedy and Forcade's mother and sister, entered the office with two bodyguards, removed Place, and left a note of termination on the desk of Brown, who was on vacation.

"When I walked into *High Times*," Schang said, "there were 70 people, and a good half of them were just bombed, stoned on something. There were people in the bathroom holding other people's heads while they puked. The people who were stoners, just down and out all the time, not working at all, Tom just let hang on. I let them go." The Thursday drug bazaars, in which dealers came through the office to make sales on payday, came to an end.

She told a reporter that, although Forcade made a "fairly impressive display of sharing power," he never trusted his employees. "I think it was hard for him to be a radical leftist and a successful capitalist, too," she told another. "I don't have that guilt."

There was blowback. Bricks crashed through the *High Times* office window, and late-night anonymous callers hissed and grunted at Schang. Accusatory graffiti seemed to stalk her, from the office to the New Morning bookstore and finally to her apartment building. She and her mother received graphic death threats.

There were shifting alliances within the magazine as everyone vied for power. "One faction or the other would try to curry favor with the staff," said one employee. "I remember someone dumping a bag of coke on my desk, meaning that I should stick with their side."

Schang changed the *High Times* tagline from "the magazine of getting high" to "the magazine of feeling good." She planned articles on alternative energy, scuba diving, and natural healing, as well as critical looks at PCP and prescription drugs. Back-page ads for *Airplane!* and *The Blues Brothers* replaced ads for home-freebasing kits. ("It's clean, simple, fast and effective.") But it was a challenging shift, since more than 90 percent of ad revenue came from paraphernalia companies. The trustees fired Schang.

Rampant cocaine centerfolds and ads for caffeine-and-ephedrine pills moved *High Times* into ever more controversial territory. A late-eighties course correction in content was too little to escape the crosshairs of the United States' escalating drug war. By the turn of the decade, the DEA was targeting paraphernalia and gardening-equipment sellers directly from the pages of *High Times*: Operation Green Merchant raided retail stores in forty-six states and demanded the names of customers who'd purchased fluorescent lamps or plant food.

The magazine never again reached the heights of its late-1970s peak, but it maintained reasonable stability until 2016, when Michael Kennedy's death kicked off another wave of internal lawsuits. Amid battles at the management level, *High Times* signed partnerships with clothing designers and promoted "pop-up" events. Models posed in pricey outerwear that incorporated the old marijuana-and-red-star Yippie flag, along with copy that eagerly commodified dissent. ("Original media badass Thomas King Forcade, the founder of *High Times*, inspired much of the line, which will drop a new collection each season.") The company announced that it was even setting its sights on branded furniture and casinos.

A private-equity firm called Oreva Capital acquired the Trans-High Corporation in 2017. Its CEO donated to right-wing politicians and positioned *High Times* as a lifestyle brand and "platform for cannabis entrepreneurs." But after the number of lawsuits brought against the company reached double digits, and following resignations and layoffs, an announced public stock offering was delayed indefinitely. In 2020, Trans-High suspended publication of *High Times* for five months.

Colleen Manley, the daughter of Forcade's cousin John Goodson, maintains an interest in the company and hopes to see *High Times* rise "like the Phoenix bird from Thomas King Forcade's ashes."

"Can we be the voice for journalism that everybody's afraid to publish?" she asks. "If Tom were alive today, he would be pushing boundaries."

Contrarianism was hard-wired into Forcade's personality. It's what made him so brilliant, to a point, when he worked to subvert the system from within.

But part of Forcade's story might serve as a cautionary tale. His political involvement began in the late 1960s, just as the anti-war movement was beginning to splinter. Government meddling was a key part of that division, as were conflicting priorities among activists. It was a particularly difficult time to sustain alliances; when one cultivated an air of mystery and even distrust, the challenge was even greater. Some of the provocations of the Zippie movement, while entertaining from a distance, could be seen as a foreshadowing of the dangerously adversarial factionalism that now plagues America.

Half a century later, the echoes of Forcade's condemnations—of runaway corporatism, governmental oppression, and media distortion—are heard across the spectrum from the Far Left to the Far Right, often in glib rhetoric that flattens everything into a generalized rage. Stripped of sarcasm and partisan associations, though, such sentiments might give common cause to all citizens.

"The same people that own the Fortune 500 also own the networks and the daily newspapers," Forcade complained to Albert Goldman in a particularly revved-up conversation a few months before his death. "They don't want to acknowledge the alternative economy, and the alternative culture that it represents. To acknowledge the size and scope of it would be to give it credibility. To give it credibility would force an inevitable confrontation; a confrontation would mean that they lose because they don't have any cards in their hands—they're bluffing.

"What good is the free press if you don't use it? None of this incredible stuff you hear in Washington about the CIA: people can't even say that they've heard it, or that the rumor's going around! None of this stuff will ever see print in any straight media place because it can't be proven. Well of course it can't be proven as long as you don't start leaning on them and start putting it in print."

Marijuana, Forcade said, "is just a small aspect of everything that's being kept down, like this 'managed news'—not managed by some overlords at the top, but just by a general attitude of *fear*—the fear that's in the media."

Beyond the legalization of marijuana, Forcade can claim another irrefutable triumph. From his Underground Press Syndicate advocacy to his battles for Senate and White House press passes and his self-distribution of *High Times*, he was a committed First Amendment activist.

Forcade's legacy was highlighted in November 2018: after the Secret Service seized the security credentials of CNN reporter Jim Acosta, the network sued. In its argument that President Donald Trump had no authority to arbitrarily deny access to "White House press facilities," CNN's counsel cited *Sherrill v. Knight*, formerly known as *Forcade v. Knight*. That case, which had dragged on through three presidential administrations and involved multiple government agencies, had been a battle waged by oppositional journalists.

With high stakes, the journalistic establishment resurrected the case in a new century. Forty years to the day after Forcade shot himself, a judge ordered the White House to restore a reporter's credentials.

ACKNOWLEDGMENTS

I'D LIKE TO THANK JUDY GOODSON BAKER, COLLEEN GOODSON MANLEY, John Holmstrom, Andy Kowl, Maureen McFadden, Gabrielle Schang, Leni Sinclair, Alice Torbush, and Rex Weiner for their encouragement and generosity.

Terese Coe, Jere Herzenberg, and Jane Krupp permitted me the use of archival material that brought the past to life. Thanks also to Chris Bois at the Senate Press Gallery; Kate Donovan at the Tamiment Library & Wagner Archives, New York University; Patrick Lawlor at Columbia University; Rossy Mendez, NYC Department of Records & Information Services; Abigale Mumby and Caitlin Moriarty at the Bentley Historical Library; Michael Rush and Timothy Young at the Beinecke Rare Book and Manuscript Library at Yale University; Jeremy Smith at the University of Massachusetts, Amherst; and Rose Spijkerman at the International Institute of Social History, Amsterdam.

For advice and support, thanks to Spencer Ackerman, Jason Altman, Jamie Atlas, Reuben Atlas, Jay Babcock, Rachel Bien, Doug Brod, Dale Brumfield, Sabina Burdzovic, Isaac Butler, Caleb Crain, Joshua Clark Davis, Brian Doherty, Jon Dolan, Laura Dolan, Emily Dufton, Kristin Earhart, Mark Eckel, Sean Fennessey, Victoria Ferrigno, Gillian Flynn, Caryn Ganz, Matt Giles, Daniel Greenberg, Andy Greenwald, Joe Gross,

Joe Hagan, James Hannaham, Sharon Harkey, Ross Harris, Laurie Charnigo Heathcock, John Hilgart, Gina Hirsch, Jason Horowitz, Matthew Houston, Andrew Hultkrans, Dave Itzkoff, Ted Jalbert, Jesse Jarnow, Steve Kandell, Jason Katzman, Aaron Kimbrell, Carrie Klein, Chuck Klosterman, David Jacob Kramer, June Kress, Phil Lapsley, Jason Leopold, Jonathan Lethem, Stu Levitan, Lisa Lucas, Melissa Maerz, Mackenze McAleer, Bernard McCormick, John McMillian, Amanda Miller, Greg Milner, Annie Nocenti, Tom O'Neill, Christopher Othen, Alex Pappademas, Kiel Phegley, Ally Polak, Brian Raftery, Jennifer Raftery, Michael Ravnitzky, Laura Regensdorf, Phoebe Reilly, Brad Ricca, Abraham Josephine Riesman, Lawrence Roberts, Jennifer Romolini, Chris Ryan, Lucy Sante, Jon Savage, Ingrid Schorr, Mark Schwartzbard, Will Sheff, Rob Sheffield, Chris Simunek, Benjamin T. Smith, Gabe Soria, Christopher Sorrentino, Matthew Specktor, Stephanie Ruocco Spry, Stephanie Steiker, Julie Taraska, Peter Terzian, Sam Thielman, Pat Thomas, Michael Tisdale, Danielle Troy, Jessica Troy, Dominic Umile, Sandya Viswanathan, Ken Wachsberger, Deborah Wassertzug, Bill Weinberg, Michael Weinreb, Peter Werbe, Tyler Wilcox, Bryan Wizemann, Sabina Wizemann, Erin Wrightsman, and Jason Yung.

I'm deeply indebted to my editor, Brant Rumble, who supported this project from the beginning, sometimes against odds, and over a number of years. At Hachette, I'd like to also thank Michael Barrs, Kara Brammer, Michael Giarratano, Amanda Kain, Seán Moreau, Monica Oluwek, Mollie Weisenfeld, and Jeff Williams. I was lucky to work with copy editor Christina Palaia, and I appreciate the fine work of indexer Robie Grant and proofreaders Erica Lawrence and Susie Pitzen.

Thank you to my agent, David Patterson, at the Stuart Krichevsky Literary Agency, for tireless guidance. Thanks also to Chandler Wickers.

Thank you to Bill Sienkiewicz for the extraordinary cover illustration. Maximum appreciation to Jeff Trexler.

Love and gratitude to the extended Howe, Knowles, Sheridan, and Mulvihill families; to Laura Burkart, Donal Sheridan, Jim Sheridan, John Sheridan, and Diane Willaum; to Erin Howe, Marc Schuricht, Isla Schuricht, Valerie Howe, and Gary Howe; to Miss Geraldine and Emily Sheridan for brilliance, patience, encouragement, wisdom, partnership, and making everywhere feel like home.

SOURCES

Much of this book is based on the personal recollections of nearly two hundred people; I'm deeply grateful to all of them for sharing their memories and insights:

Shay Addams
Michael Aldrich
Michelle Aldrich
Jill Anderson
Michael Antonoff
Jarratt Applewhite
Stu Arrow
Leslie Bacon
Judy Goodson Baker
Joe Barton
Roberta Bayley
John Beadle
Dana Beal
Daniel Ben-Horin
Chip Berlet
Lowell Bergman
Harold Black

Martin Blitstein
Larry Block
Victoria Bochat
Victor Bockris
Leslie Brody
Bart Bull
John Cahal
Scott Camil
Michael Chance
Laurence Cherniak
Bill Choyke
Lola Cohen
Ted Cohen
Kristine Combs
Steve Cooper
A. Craig Copetas
Lynda Crawford

Lynn Cummings
R. J. Cutler
Monson Davis
Steve DeAngelo
Paul DeRienzo
Keith Deutsch
Mark Diamond
John Draper
Jim Drougas
Diana Drucella
Michael Duck
Richard Dupont
Ed Dwyer
Robert England
John Farrell
David Fenton
Bob Fiallo

Darlene Fife

Michael Forman

Randy Forman

Jim Fouratt

Bruce Frank

Charlie Frick

Bill Gast

Dennis Giangreco

Michael Gilbreath

John Goodson

Sigil Goodson

Lisa Gottlieb

Fred Graham

John Grissim

Joseph Gross

Judy Gumbo

William Hermann

Larry Hertz

Arthur Hine

Geary Hobson

John Holmstom

James Horwitz

Tim Hughes

Craig Karpel

Aron Kay

Chris Kearns

Steve Kenin

Michael Kennedy

William Kirkley

Susan Knight

Jane Hopper Koehl

Lech Kowalski

Andy Kowl

Corinne Kowl

Michael Kuziv

Frank Lauria

Laurence Leamer

Bob Lemmo

Shelley Levitt

Ron Lichty

Karin Limmroth

Uli Lommel

Roger Lowenstein

Scott MacNeill

Diana Mancher

Estela Matta

John Mattes

Bill McCune

Maureen McFadden

Ken McKechnie

Bob Merlis

Jeffrey Michelson

Tom Miller

George Misso

Kim Moody

Rick Namey

Jerrold Neugarten

Jeffrey Nightbyrd

Dave Noland

Glenn O'Brien

David Obst

Daniel Page

Victor Pawlak

Abe Peck

Chris Peebles

David Peel

Jerry Powers

Daria Price

Jim Retherford

Terre Richards

Bill Ritter

Andy Romanoff

Barry Romo

Frank Rose

Mike Roselle

Ed Rosenthal

Sue Rouda

Diane Rouda Abell

Nancy Rouda Fogel

Jerry Rudoff

Carol Ryder

Blair Sabol

Gabrielle Schang

Shelly Schorr

Ann Hirschman

    Schremp

Allen Sheinman

Dennis Shlaen

Craig Silver

John Sinclair

Leni Sinclair

Larry Sloman

Pat Small

David Spaner

Deanne Stillman

Gary Stimeling

Keith Stroup

Melany

    Thum-McAleer

Alice Torbush

Paul Tornetta

Ron Turner

Gary van Scyoc

Wavy Gravy

A. J. Weberman

Rex Weiner

Jackie Weisberg

Becky Wilson

Don Wirtshafter

Susan Wyler

Allen Young

In addition to interviews conducted by the author, this book draws from numerous archival collections, books, government hearings, reports, and periodicals. Specific quotations from these are cited on a page-by-page basis in the Notes section.

Archival Collections

Terese Coe Papers, privately held.*

Albert Goldman Papers, 1953–1994, University Archives, Rare Book & Manuscript Library, Columbia University Libraries.

John Holmstrom Papers and Punk Magazine Records, General Collection, Beinecke Rare Book and Manuscript Library, Yale University.

John and Leni Sinclair Papers, Bentley Historical Library, University of Michigan, Ann Arbor.

Rex Weiner Collection of Underground Press Material, 1955–1981, Beinecke Rare Book and Manuscript Library, Yale University.

John Wilcock Papers, University Archives, Rare Book & Manuscript Library, Columbia University Libraries.

Books

Acton, Jay, Alan LeMond, and Parker Hodges. *Mug Shots: Who's Who in the New Earth.* Meridian, 1972.

Albert, Judith Clavir, and Stewart Edward Albert. *The Sixties Papers: Documents of a Rebellious Decade.* Praeger, 1984.

Albert, Stewart Edward. *Who the Hell Is Stew Albert? A Memoir.* Red Hen, 2003.

Alpert, Jane. *Growing Up Underground.* William Morrow, 1981.

Anderson, Jack, with George Clifford. *The Anderson Papers.* Random House, 1973.

Anderson, Patrick. *High in America.* Viking, 1981.

Armstrong, David. *A Trumpet to Arms: Alternative Media in America.* J. P. Tarcher, 1981.

Badman, Keith. *The Beatles Diary, Volume 2: After the Break-Up, 1970–2001.* Omnibus, 2001.

Bakke, Kit. *Protest on Trial: The Seattle 7 Conspiracy.* Washington State University Press, 2018.

Bamford, James. *The Puzzle Palace.* Penguin, 1983.

Bates, Tom. *Rads: The 1970 Bombing of the Army Math Research Center at the University of Wisconsin and Its Aftermath.* HarperCollins, 1992.

Baum, Dan. *Smoke and Mirrors.* Back Bay Books, 1996.

Bernstein, Carl, and Bob Woodward. *All the President's Men.* Simon & Schuster, 1974.

Bingham, Clara. *Witness to the Revolution: Radicals, Resisters, Vets, Hippies, and the Year America Lost Its Mind and Found Its Soul.* Random House, 2016.

Bird, Kai. *The Outlier: The Unfinished Presidency of Jimmy Carter.* Crown, 2021.

---

* Coe's interviews were conducted in person on various dates from 1978 through 1981 in Manhattan, New York City. Tape recorder was clearly visible at all times.

Bonnie, Richard J., and Charles H. Whitebread II. *The Marijuana Conviction: A History of Marijuana Prohibition in the United States.* Lindesmith Center, 1999.

Brauntstein, Peter, and Michael William Doyle, eds. *Imagine Nation: The American Counterculture of the 1960s and '70s.* Routledge, 2002.

Brecher, Edward M. *Licit & Illicit Drugs: The Consumers Union Report on Narcotics, Stimulants, Depressants, Inhalants, Hallucinogens, and Marijuana—Including Caffeine, Nicotine, and Alcohol.* Consumers Union, 1972.

Britto, Lina. *Marijuana Boom: The Rise and Fall of Colombia's First Drug Paradise.* University of California Press, 2020.

Brumfield, Dale M. *Independent Press in D.C. and Virginia: An Underground History.* History Press, 2015.

Burke, Kyle. *Revolutionaries for the Right: Anticommunist Internationalism and Paramilitary Warfare in the Cold War.* University of North Carolina Press, 2018.

Burrough, Bryan. *Days of Rage: America's Radical Underground, the FBI, and the Forgotten Age of Revolutionary Violence.* Penguin, 2015.

Canfield, Mark, and A. J. Weberman. *Coup d'Etat in America.* Third Press, 1975.

Carey, James T. *The College Drug Scene.* Prentice Hall, 1968.

Carroll, Peter N. *It Seemed Like Nothing Happened: America in the 1970s.* Rutgers University Press, 2000.

Carson, Clayborne. *In Struggle: SNCC and the Black Awakening of the 1960s.* Harvard University Press, 1995.

Carson, David A. *Grit, Noise, and Revolution: The Birth of Detroit Rock 'n' Roll.* University of Michigan Press, 2005.

Chard, Daniel S. *Nixon's War at Home: The FBI, Leftist Guerillas, and the Origins of Counterterrorism.* University of North Carolina Press, 2021.

Churchill, Ward, and Jim Vander Wall. *The COINTELPRO Papers: Documents from the FBI's Secret Wars Against Domestic Dissent.* South End Press, 1990.

Citizens Research and Investigation Committee and Louis E. Tackwood. *The Glass House Tapes.* Avon, 1973.

Clark, Evert, and Nicholas Horrock. *Contrabandista!* Praeger, 1973.

Colby, William Egan, and Peter Forbath. *Honorable Men: My Life in the CIA.* Simon & Schuster, 1978.

Collins, William S. *The Emerging Metropolis: Phoenix, 1944–1973.* Arizona State Parks Board, 2005.

Constantine, Alex. *The Essential Mae Brussell: Investigations of Fascism in America.* Feral House, 2014.

Conway, Flo, and Jim Siegelman. *Snapping: America's Epidemic of Sudden Personality Change,* 2nd ed. Delta Books, 1979.

Cowan, Paul, Nick Egleson, and Nat Hentoff. *State Secrets: Police Surveillance in America.* Holt, Rinehart and Winston, 1974.

Coyne, John R. *The Impudent Snobs: Agnew vs. the Intellectual Establishment.* Arlington House, 1972.

Crowley, Walt. *Rites of Passage: A Memoir of the Sixties in Seattle.* University of Washington Press, 1995.

Davis, Joshua Clark. *From Head Shops to Whole Foods: The Rise and Fall of Activist Entrepreneurs*. Columbia University Press, 2017.

Dean, John. *Blind Ambition: The White House Years*. Simon & Schuster, 1976.

DeBenedetti, Charles, and Charles Chatfield. *An American Ordeal: The Antiwar Movement of the Vietnam Era*. Syracuse University Press, 1990.

Dellinger, Dave. *More Power Than We Know: The People's Movement Toward Democracy*. Anchor, 1975.

Dellinger, David. *From Yale to Jail: The Life Story of a Moral Dissenter*. Pantheon, 1993.

Dickinson, William B., Jr. *Watergate: Chronology of a Crisis*. Congressional Quarterly, 1973.

Dickstein, Morris. *Gates of Eden: American Culture in the Sixties*. Basic Books, 1977.

Doggett, Peter. *There's a Riot Going On*. Canongate, 2007.

Dokoupil, Tony. *The Last Pirate: A Father, His Son, and the Golden Age of Marijuana*. Doubleday, 2014.

Donner, Frank J. *The Age of Surveillance: The Aims and Methods of America's Political Intelligence System*. Knopf, 1980.

———. *Protectors of Privilege: Red Squads and Police Repression in Urban America*. University of California Press, 1990.

Downie, Leonard, Jr. *The New Muckrakers*. New Republic Book Company, 1976.

Dufton, Emily. *Grass Roots*. Basic Books, 2017.

Eckstein, Arthur M. *Bad Moon Rising: How the Weather Underground Beat the FBI and Lost the Revolution*. Yale University Press, 2016.

Emerson, Gloria. *Winners & Losers: Battles, Retreats, Gains, Losses, and Ruins from the Vietnam War*. Random House, 1976.

Emery, Fred. *Watergate*. Touchstone, 1994.

Epstein, Edward Jay. *Agency of Fear: Opiates and Political Power in America*, rev. ed. Verso, 1990.

Fairfield, Richard. *Communes USA*. Penguin, 1972.

Farber, David. *Chicago '68*. Chicago University Press, 1988.

Feldstein, Mark. *Poisoning the Press: Richard Nixon, Jack Anderson, and the Rise of Washington's Scandal Culture*. Farrar, Straus and Giroux, 2010.

Felton, David, ed. *Mindfuckers: A Source Book on the Rise of Acid Fascism in America*. Straight Arrow Books, 1972.

Flynt, Larry, with Kenneth Ross. *An Unseemly Man*. Dove Books, 1996.

Fonzi, Gaeton. *The Last Investigation*. Basic Books, 1993.

Forcade, Thomas King. *Caravan of Love and Money*. Signet, 1972.

———, ed. *Underground Press Anthology*. Ace, 1972.

Frank, Thomas. *The Conquest of Cool: Business Culture, Counterculture, and the Rise of Hip Consumerism*. University of Chicago Press, 1997.

Fuss, Charles M. *Sea of Grass: The Maritime Drug War, 1970–1990*. Naval Institute Press, 1996.

Gitlin, Todd. *The Sixties: Years of Hope, Days of Rage*. Bantam, 1987.

Glessing, Robert J. *The Underground Press in America*. Indiana University Press, 1970.

Goines, David Lance. *The Free Speech Movement: Coming of Age in the 1960s*. Ten Speed Press, 1993.

Goldman, Albert. *Grass Roots*. Harper & Row, 1979.

Goldstein, Robert Justin. *Political Repression in Modern America: 1870 to 1976*. University of Illinois Press, 2001.

Goodman, Mitchell, ed. *The Movement Toward a New America: The Beginnings of a Long Revolution (A Collage), A What?* Knopf, 1970.

Grathwohl, Larry. *Bringing Down America: An FBI Informer with the Weathermen*. Arlington House, 1976.

Gray, Francine du Plessix. *Adam & Eve and the City*. Simon & Schuster, 1987.

Gray, L. Patrick. *In Nixon's Web: A Year in the Crosshairs of Watergate*. Times Books, 2008.

Green, Timothy. *Encyclopedia of Espionage: The Smuggling Business*. Danbury Press, 1977.

Greenfield, Robert. *Timothy Leary: A Biography*. Harcourt, 2006.

Grissim, John. *We Have Come for Your Daughters: What Went Down on the Medicine Ball Caravan*. William Morrow, 1972.

Gugliotta, Guy, and Jeff Leen. *Kings of Cocaine*. Simon & Schuster, 1989.

Gumbo, Judy. *Yippie Girl: Exploits in Protest and Defeating the FBI*. Three Rooms Press, 2022.

Haden-Guest, Anthony. *The Last Party*. William Morrow & Co., 1997.

Hagan, Joe. *Sticky Fingers: The Life and Times of Jann Wenner and Rolling Stone Magazine*. Knopf, 2017.

Haldeman, H. R. *The Haldeman Diaries: Inside the Nixon White House*. G. P. Putnam's Sons, 1994.

Halstead, Fred. *Out Now! A Participant's Account of the American Movement Against the Vietnam War*. Monad Press, 1978.

Hager, Steven, ed. *High Times Greatest Hits*. St. Martin's Press, 1994.

Hinckle, Warren, and William Turner. *The Fish Is Red: The Story of the Secret War Against Castro*. Harper & Row, 1981.

Hoffman, Abbie. *Revolution for the Hell of It*. Dial, 1968.

———. *Soon to Be a Major Motion Picture*. Perigee, 1980.

———. *Steal This Book*. Pirate Editions, 1971.

———. *Woodstock Nation*. Random House, 1969.

Hoffman, Abbie, Jerry Rubin, and Ed Sanders. *Vote!* Warner Paperback Library, 1972.

Hoffman, Jack, with Daniel Simon. *Run Run Run: The Lives of Abbie Hoffman*. Putnam, 1994.

Holmstrom, John, and Bridget Hurd, eds. *Punk: The Best of Punk Magazine*. It Books, 2012.

Hougan, Jim. *Spooks: The Haunting of America—the Private Use of Secret Agents*. William Morrow, 1978.

Howard, Mel, and the Reverend Thomas King Forcade. *The Underground Reader*. Plume/New American Library, 1972.

Hunt, Andrew E. *David Dellinger: The Life and Times of a Nonviolent Revolutionary*. New York University Press, 2006.

Hutchison, Robert. *Vesco*. Praeger, 1974.

Jacobs, Harold, ed. *Weatherman*. Ramparts Press, 1970.

Jarnow, Jesse. *Heads: A Biography of Psychedelic America*. Da Capo, 2016.

Jenkins, Philip. *Decade of Nightmares: The End of the Sixties and the Making of Eighties America*. Oxford University Press, 2006.

Jezer, Marty. *Abbie Hoffman: American Rebel*. Rutgers University Press, 1992.

Johnson, Loch K. *A Season of Inquiry Revisited: The Church Committee Confronts America's Spy Agencies*. University Press of Kansas, 2015.

Johnson, Nick. *Grass Roots: A History of Cannabis in the American West*. Oregon State University Press, 2017.

Jonnes, Jill. *Hep-Cats, Narcs, and Pipe Dreams: A History of America's Romance with Illegal Drugs*. Scribner, 1996.

Kamstra, Jerry. *Weed: Adventures of a Dope Smuggler*. Harper & Row, 1974.

Katzman, Allen, ed. *Our Time: An Anthology of Interviews from the East Village Other*. Dial Books, 1972.

King, Dennis. *Lyndon LaRouche and the New American Fascism*. Doubleday, 1989.

Kinoy, Arthur. *Rights on Trial*. Harvard University Press, 1983.

Kleindienst, Richard. *Justice: The Memoirs of an Attorney General*. Jameson, 1985.

Kleps, Art. *Millbrook*. Bench Press, 1975.

Kopkind, Andrew, and James Ridgeway, eds. *Decade of Crisis: America in the '60s*. World Publishing, 1972.

Kornbluth, Jesse, ed. *Notes from the New Underground: An Anthology*. Viking, 1968.

Kostelanetz, Richard, ed. *Seeing Through Shuck*. Ballantine, 1972.

Krassner, Paul. *Patty Hearst & the Twinkie Murders: A Tale of Two Trials*. PM Press, 2014.

Krieger, Susan. *Hip Capitalism*. Sage Publications, 1979.

Krüger, Henrik, and Jerry Meldon. *The Great Heroin Coup: Drugs, Intelligence & International Fascism*, updated ed. Trine Day, 2015.

Kuhn, David Paul. *Hardhat Riot: Nixon, New York City, and the Dawn of the White Working-Class Revolution*. Oxford University Press, 2020.

Kutler, Stanley. *The Wars of Watergate*. W. W. Norton, 1992.

Lapsley, Phil. *Exploding the Phone*. Grove Press, 2013.

Lattin, Don. *The Harvard Psychedelic Club: How Timothy Leary, Ram Dass, Huston Smith, and Andrew Weil Killed the Fifties and Ushered in a New Age for America*. HarperOne, 2011.

Leamer, Laurence. *The Paper Revolutionaries: The Rise of the Underground Press*. Simon & Schuster, 1972.

Leary, Timothy. *Confessions of a Hope Fiend*. Bantam, 1973.

———. *Flashbacks: A Personal and Cultural History of an Era: An Autobiography*. J. P. Tarcher, 1990.

Lee, Martin A. *Smoke Signals: A Social History of Marijuana*. Scribner, 2012.

Lee, Martin A., and Bruce Shlain. *Acid Dreams: The Complete Social History of LSD*. Grove Press, 1985.

Lehman, Christopher P. *Power, Politics, and the Decline of the Civil Rights Movement: A Fragile Coalition, 1967–1973*. Praeger, 2014.

Lerner, Kevin M. *Provoking the Press: [MORE] Magazine and the Crisis of Confidence in American Journalism*. University of Missouri, 2019.

Lewis, Roger. *Outlaws of America*. Penguin, 1972.

Liddy, G. Gordon. *Will.* St. Martin's Press, 1980.

Loren, Cary, and Lorraine Wild, eds. *Motor City Underground: Leni Sinclair Photographs 1963–1978.* Museum of Contemporary Art, Detroit, 2021.

Luckingham, Bradford. *Phoenix: The History of a Southwestern Metropolis.* University of Arizona Press, 1989.

Lukas, J. Anthony. *Don't Shoot—We Are Your Children!* Random House, 1971.

———. *Nightmare: The Underside of the Nixon Years.* Viking, 1976.

Mackenzie, Angus, with David Weir. *Secrets: The CIA's War at Home.* University of California Press, 1997.

Mailer, Norman. *St. George and the Godfather.* New American Library, 1972.

Makower, Joel. *Woodstock: The Oral History.* Doubleday, 1989.

Marchetti, Victor, and John D. Marks. *The CIA and the Cult of Intelligence.* Dell, 1974.

Marks, John. *The Search for the Manchurian Candidate.* Times Books, 1979.

Massing, Michael. *The Fix.* Simon & Schuster, 1998.

McAuliffe, Kevin. *The Great American Newspaper: The Rise and Fall of the Village Voice.* Scribner, 1978.

McCoy, Alfred W. *The Politics of Heroin in Southeast Asia.* Harper Colophon, 1973.

McKenna, Kristina, and David Hollander, eds. *Notes from a Revolution: Com/Co, the Diggers & the Haight.* Foggy Notion, 2012.

McLendon, Winzola. *Martha: The Life of Martha Mitchell.* Random House, 1979.

McMillian, John. *Smoking Typewriters: The Sixties Underground Press and the Rise of Alternative Media in America.* Oxford University Press, 2011.

McNeil, Legs, and Gillian McCain. *Please Kill Me: The Uncensored Oral History of Punk.* Grove Press, 1996.

McNeill, Don. *Moving Through Here.* Knopf, 1970.

McWilliams, John C. *The Protectors: Harry J. Anslinger and the Federal Bureau of Narcotics, 1930–1962.* University of Delaware Press, 1990.

Medsger, Betty. *The Burglary: The Discovery of J. Edgar Hoover's Secret FBI.* Vintage, 2014.

Melville, Keith. *Communes in the Counter Culture.* Morrow, 1972.

Messick, Hank. *Of Grass and Snow.* Prentice Hall, 1979.

Miles, Barry. *Hippie.* Sterling, 2004.

Moldea, Dan. *The Hoffa Wars: Teamsters, Rebels, Politicians and the Mob.* Paddington Press, 1978.

Monk, Noel E., and Jimmy Guterman. *12 Days on the Road: The Sex Pistols and America.* Morrow, 1990.

Moretta, John Anthony. *The Hippies: A 1960s History.* McFarland, 2017.

Morgan, Bill, ed. *The Selected Letters of Allen Ginsberg and Gary Snyder, 1956–1991.* Counterpoint, 2009.

Morgan, Neil. *Westward Tilt: The American West Today.* Random House, 1963.

Muller, Robert H., Theodore Jurgen Spahn, Janet M. Spahn, and Janet Peterson Spahn. *From Radical Left to Extreme Right.* Campus Publishers, 1970.

Mungo, Raymond. *Famous Long Ago: My Life and Hard Times with Liberation News Service.* Beacon Press, 1970.

Musto, David. *The American Disease: Origins of Narcotic Control*, 3rd ed. Oxford University Press, 1999.

Musto, David F., and Pamela Korsmeyer. *The Quest for Drug Control: Politics and Federal Policy in a Period of Increasing Substance Abuse, 1963–1981*. Yale University Press, 2002.

Nelson, Jack, and Ronald J. Ostrow. *The FBI and the Berrigans*. Coward, McCann & Geoghegan, 1972.

New Yippie Book Collective. *Blacklisted News: Secret Histories from Chicago to 1984*. Bleecker, 1983.

New York Times staff. *The End of a Presidency*. Bantam, 1974.

———, ed. *The Watergate Hearings: Break-In and Cover-Up*. Bantam, 1973.

Nicosia, Gerald. *Home to War: A History of the Vietnam Veterans' Movement*. Carroll & Graf, 2004.

Nocenti, Annie, and Ruth Baldwin, eds. *The High Times Reader*. Nation Books, 2004.

Obst, David. *Too Good to Be Forgotten: Changing America in the '60s and '70s*. John Wiley & Sons, 1998.

Olmsted, Kathryn S. *Challenging the Secret Government: The Post-Watergate Investigations of the CIA and FBI*. University of North Carolina Press, 2000.

———. *Real Enemies: Conspiracy Theories and American Democracy, World War I to 9/11*. Oxford University Press, 2009.

O'Sullivan, Shane. *Dirty Tricks: Nixon, Watergate, and the CIA*. Hot Books, 2018.

Pardun, Robert. *Prairie Radical: A Journey Through the Sixties*. Shire Press, 2001.

Payne, Cril. *Deep Cover: An FBI Agent Infiltrates the Radical Underground*. Newsweek Books, 1979.

Peck, Abe. *Uncovering the Sixties: The Life and Times of the Underground Press*. Pantheon, 1985.

Perlstein, Rick. *Before the Storm: Barry Goldwater and the Unmaking of the American Consensus*. Hill and Wang, 2001.

———. *Nixonland: The Rise of a President and the Fracturing of America*. Scribner, 2008.

Perry, Charles. *The Haight-Ashbury: A History*. Random House, 1984.

Plamondon, Pun. *Lost from the Ottawa: The Story of the Journey Back*. Trafford, 2004.

Powers, Thomas. *The Man Who Kept the Secrets: Richard Helms and the CIA*. Knopf, 1979.

Prados, John. *The Family Jewels: The CIA, Secrecy, and Presidential Power*. University of Texas Press, 2013.

Press Freedoms Under Pressure: Report of the Twentieth Century Fund Task Force on the Government and the Press. Twentieth Century Fund, 1972.

Pulliam, Russell. *Publisher: Gene Pulliam, Last of the Newspaper Titans*. Jameson, 1984.

Rafalko, Frank J. *MH/CHAOS: The CIA's Campaign Against the Radical New Left and the Black Panthers*. Naval Institute Press, 2011.

Raskin, Jonah. *For the Hell of It: The Life and Times of Abbie Hoffman*. University of California Press, 1996.

Richardson, Peter. *A Bomb in Every Issue: How the Short Unruly Life of Ramparts Magazine Changed America*. New Press, 2009.

Rips, Geoffrey. *Unamerican Activities: The Campaign Against the Underground Press.* City Lights, 1981.

Robbins, Christopher. *Air America: The Story of the CIA's Secret Airlines.* G. P. Putnam's Sons, 1979.

Roberts, Lawrence. *Mayday 1971.* Houghton Mifflin Harcourt, 2020.

Rolling Stone staff, ed. *The Age of Paranoia.* Pocket Books, 1972.

Romm, Ethel Grodzins. *The Open Conspiracy: What America's Angry Generation Is Saying.* Stackpole Books, 1970.

Roselle, Mike, with Josh Mahan. *Tree Spiker.* St. Martin's Press, 2009.

Ross, Andrew. *Bird on Fire: Lessons from the World's Least Sustainable City.* Oxford University Press, 2011.

Rubenstein, Richard E. *Comrade Valentine.* Harcourt Brace, 1994.

Rubin, Jerry. *Do It! Scenarios of the Revolution.* Simon & Schuster, 1970.

———. *Growing (Up) at Thirty-Seven.* M. Evans and Company, 1976.

———. *We Are Everywhere.* Harper & Row, 1971.

Rudd, Mark. *Underground: My Life with SDS and the Weathermen.* HarperCollins, 2009.

Sale, Kirkpatrick. *SDS.* Random House, 1973.

Sanders, Ed. *The Family.* Dutton, 1972.

———. *Fug You: An Informal History of the Peace Eye Bookstore, the Fuck You Press, the Fugs, and Counterculture in the Lower East Side.* Da Capo, 2011.

Santelli, Robert. *Aquarius Rising: The Rock Festival Years.* Dell, 1980.

Saunders, Nancy Miller. *Combat by Trial.* iUniverse, 2008.

Savage, Jon. *England's Dreaming: Anarchy, Sex Pistols, Punk Rock and Beyond.* St. Martin's Griffin, 1992.

Sayre, Nora. *Sixties Going on Seventies*, rev. ed. Rutgers University Press, 1996.

Schnell, Jonathan. *The Time of Illusion.* Vintage, 1976.

Schorr, Daniel. *Clearing the Air.* Berkley Medallion, 1978.

Schou, Nicholas. *Orange Sunshine: The Brotherhood of Eternal Love and Its Quest to Spread Peace, Love, and Acid to the World.* Thomas Dunne Books, 2010.

Schrag, Peter. *Test of Loyalty: Daniel Ellsberg and the Rituals of Secret Government.* Touchstone, 1974.

Schwartz, Helene E. *Lawyering.* Farrar, Straus and Giroux, 1976.

Scott, Peter Dale, and Jonathan Marshall. *Cocaine Politics: Drugs, Armies, and the CIA in Central America.* University of California Press, 1991.

Shannon, Elaine. *Desperados: Latin Drug Lords, U.S. Lawmen, and the War America Can't Win.* Viking, 1988.

Sheff, David, with G. Barry Golson, ed. *The Playboy Interviews with John Lennon and Yoko Ono.* Playboy Press, 1981.

Shermer, Elizabeth Tandy. *Sunbelt Capitalism: Phoenix and the Transformation of American Politics.* University of Pennsylvania Press, 2013.

Shore, Elliott, Patricia J. Case, and Laura Daly, eds. *Alternative Papers: Selections from the Alternative Press, 1979–1980.* Temple University Press, 1982.

Sinclair, John. *Guitar Army.* Douglas Book Corporation, 1972.

Sloman, Larry. *Reefer Madness.* Bobbs-Merrill, 1979.

————. *Steal This Dream: Abbie Hoffman and the Countercultural Revolution in America*. Doubleday, 1998.

Slonecker, Blake. *A New Dawn for the New Left: Liberation News Service, Montague Farm, and the Long Sixties*. Palgrave Macmillan, 2012.

Small, Melvin, and William D. Hoover, eds. *Give Peace a Chance: Exploring the Vietnam Antiwar Movement*. Syracuse University Press, 1992.

Smith, Benjamin T. *The Dope: The Real History of the Mexican Drug Trade*. W. W. Norton, 2021.

Solomon, David, ed. *The Marijuana Papers*. Mentor, 1968.

Solomon, Norman. *In the Belly of the Dinosaurs* [booklet]. Out of the Ashes Press, 1972.

Southern, Terry. *The Magic Christian*. Berkley Medallion, 1961.

Spinrad, Norman. *Agent of Chaos*. Belmont, 1967.

Spitz, Robert Stephen. *Barefoot in Babylon*. Viking, 1979.

Steadman, Ralph. *The Joke's Over*. Harcourt, 2006.

Stevens, Jay. *Storming Heaven: LSD and the American Dream*. Grove Press, 1987.

Stewart, Sean, ed. *On the Ground: An Illustrated Anecdotal History of the Sixties Underground Press in the U.S.* PM Press, 2011.

Stroup, Keith. *It's NORML to Smoke Pot*. High Times Books, 2013.

Talbot, David. *The Devil's Chessboard: Allen Dulles, the CIA, and the Rise of America's Secret Government*. Harper, 2015.

Tendler, Stewart, and David May. *The Brotherhood of Eternal Love*. Panther, 1984.

Teodori, Massimo, ed. *The New Left: A Documentary History*. Bobbs-Merrill, 1969.

Thomas, Evan. *The Very Best Men: The Early Years of the CIA*. Simon & Schuster, 1995.

Thomas, Pat. *Did It! From Yippie to Yuppie: Jerry Rubin, an American Revolutionary*. Fantagraphics, 2017.

Thompson, Hunter S. *Fear and Loathing on the Campaign Trail '72*. Popular Library, 1973.

————. *The Great Shark Hunt*. Summit, 1979.

Torgoff, Martin. *Can't Find My Way Home: America in the Great Stoned Age, 1945–2000*. Simon & Schuster, 2003.

Trimble, Marshall. *Arizona Outlaws and Lawmen: Gunslingers, Bandits, Heroes and Peacekeepers*. History Press, 2015.

Tully, Andrew. *The Secret War Against Dope*. Coward, McCann & Geoghegan, 1973.

Ungar, Sanford J. *FBI: An Uncensored Look Behind the Walls*. Little, Brown, 1976.

Unger, Irwin. *The Movement: A History of the American New Left 1959–1972*. Dodd, Mead & Company, 1974.

Valentine, Douglas. *The Strength of the Pack: The Personalities, Politics and Espionage Intrigues That Shaped the DEA*. Trine Day, 2009.

————. *The Strength of the Wolf: The Secret History of America's War on Drugs*. Verso, 2004.

VanderMeer, Philip. *Desert Visions and the Making of Phoenix, 1860–2009*. University of New Mexico Press, 2010.

Varon, Jeremy. *Bringing the War Home*. University of California Press, 2004.

von Hoffman, Nicholas. *We Are the People Our Parents Warned Us Against*. Quadrangle, 1968.

Wachsberger, Ken, ed. *Voices from the Underground: Insider Histories of the Vietnam Era Underground Press: Part 1*. Michigan State University Press, 2011.

Wagner, Dave. *The Politics of Murder: Organized Crime in Barry Goldwater's Arizona*. Gracenote, 2016.

Walker, Jesse. *The United States of Paranoia: A Conspiracy Theory*. HarperCollins, 2013.

Weiner, Rex, and Deanne Stillman. *Woodstock Census: The Nationwide Survey of the Sixties Generation*. Viking, 1979.

Weiner, Tim. *Enemies: A History of the FBI*. Random House, 2012.

———. *Legacy of Ashes: The History of the CIA*. Doubleday, 2007.

Weissman, Steve, ed. *Big Brother and the Holding Company: The World Behind Watergate*. Ramparts Press, 1974.

Wells, Tom. *The War Within: America's Battle over Vietnam*. University of California Press, 1994.

Wheen, Francis. *Strange Days Indeed—the 1970s: The Golden Age of Paranoia*. Public Affairs, 2010.

Whitmer, Peter O., with Bruce VanWyngarden. *Aquarius Revisited: Seven Who Created the Sixties Counterculture That Changed America*. Citadel Underground, 1991.

Wiener, Jon. *Come Together: John Lennon in His Time*. Random House, 1984.

———. *Gimme Some Truth: The John Lennon FBI Files*. University of California Press, 2000.

Wiley, Peter, and Robert Gottlieb. *Empires in the Sun: The Rise of the New American West*. Putnam, 1982.

Wise, David. *The American Police State: The Government Against the People*. Random House, 1976.

Wolf, Leonard, and Deborah Wolf, eds. *Voices from the Love Generation*. Little, Brown, 1968.

Wolfe, Tom. *The Electric Kool-Aid Acid Test*. Bantam, 1969.

Wynkoop, Mary Ann. *Dissent in the Heartland: The Sixties at Indiana University*, rev. ed. Indiana University Press, 2017.

Zarbin, Earl. *All the Time a Newspaper: The First 100 Years of the Arizona Republic*. Arizona Republic, 1990.

Zaroulis, Nancy, and Gerald Sullivan. *Who Spoke Up? American Protest Against the War in Vietnam*. Doubleday, 1984.

United States Government Hearings

US House of Representatives, Committee on Armed Services, Special Subcommittee on Intelligence, Inquiry into the Alleged Involvement of the Central Intelligence Agency in the Watergate and Ellsberg Matters, Ninety-Fourth Congress, First Session, 1973–1974.

US House of Representatives, Committee on Internal Security, *Domestic Intelligence Operations for Internal Security Purposes*, Part 1, Ninety-Third Congress, Second Session, 1974.

US House of Representatives, Committee on Internal Security, *Investigation of Students for a Democratic Society, Part 7-A (Return of Prisoners of War, and Data Concerning Camera News, Inc., "Newsreel")*, Ninety-First Congress, First Session, 1969.

US House of Representatives, Committee on the Judiciary, Subcommittee on Courts, Civil Liberties, and Administration of Justice, *The Matter of Wiretapping, Electronic Eavesdropping, and Other Surveillance*, Part 1, Ninety-Fourth Congress, First Session, 1975.

US House of Representatives, Select Committee on Intelligence, *US Intelligence Agencies and Activities: Domestic Intelligence Programs*, Ninety-Fourth Congress, First Session, 1975.

US Senate, Committee on Governmental Affairs, Permanent Subcommittee on Investigations, *Organized Crime and Use of Violence*, Ninety-Sixth Congress, Second Session, 1980.

US Senate, Committee on Government Operations, Permanent Subcommittee on Investigations, *Federal Drug Enforcement*, Ninety-Fourth Congress, First Session, 1975.

US Senate, Committee on the Judiciary, Subcommittee on Constitutional Rights, *Federal Data Banks, Computers, and the Bill of Rights*, Ninety-Second Congress, First Session, 1971.

US Senate, Committee on the Judiciary, Subcommittee to Investigate the Administration of the Internal Security Act and Other Internal Security Laws, *Extent of Subversion in the "New Left,"* Ninety-First Congress, Second Session, 1970.

US Senate, Committee on the Judiciary, Subcommittee to Investigate the Administration of the Internal Security Act and Other Internal Security Laws, *Hashish Smuggling and Passport Fraud: "The Brotherhood of Eternal Love,"* Ninety-Third Congress, First Session, 1973.

US Senate, Select Committee on Presidential Campaign Activities, *Presidential Campaign Activities of 1972*, Senate Resolution 60, *Watergate and Related Activities: The Hughes-Rebozo Investigation, and Related Matters*, Ninety-Third Congress, First Session, 1973.

US Senate, Select Committee to Study Governmental Operations with Respect to Intelligence Activities, *Intelligence Activities*, Senate Resolution 21, *Unauthorized Storage of Toxic Agents* (Vol. 1); *Huston Plan* (Vol. 2); *Internal Revenue Service* (Vol. 3); *Mail Opening* (Vol. 4); *The National Security Agency and Fourth Amendment Rights* (Vol. 5); *Federal Bureau of Investigation* (Vol. 6); *Covert Action* (Vol. 7), Ninety-Fourth Congress, First Session, 1975.

United States Government Reports

Commission on CIA Activities Within the United States, *Report to the President by the Commission on CIA Activities Within the United States*, 1975.

US House of Representatives, Committee on Foreign Affairs, *The World Heroin Problem: Report of a Special Study Mission, Composed of Morgan F. Murphy, Illinois, Chairman, and Robert H. Steele, Connecticut*, Ninety-Second Congress, First Session, 1971.

US Senate, Committee on the Judiciary, Staff of the Subcommittee on Constitutional Rights, *Army Surveillance of Civilians: A Documentary Analysis*, Ninety-Second Congress, Second Session, 1972.

US Senate, Select Committee to Study Governmental Operations with Respect to Intelligence Activities, *Final Reports*: *Foreign and Military Intelligence* (Book I); *Intelligence Activities and the Rights of Americans* (Book II); *Supplementary Detailed Staff Reports on Intelligence Activities and the Rights of Americans* (Book III); *Supplementary Detailed Staff Reports on Foreign and Military Intelligence* (Book IV); *The Investigation of the Assassination of President John F. Kennedy: Performance of the Intelligence Agencies* (Book V); *Supplementary Reports on Intelligence Activities* (Book VI), Ninety-Fourth Congress, Second Session, 1976.

NOTES

Chapter 1

2   **"I am starting a campaign"**: "1-Man Marijuana 'Crusade,'" *San Francisco Examiner*, August 17, 1964.

2   **"When the citizens"**: Allen Ginsberg, "The Great Marijuana Hoax," *Atlantic Monthly*, November 1966.

2   **a number of "smoke-ins"**: See "Dope-O-Scope," *Ann Arbor Sun*, April 1967; "Be-In Turns Nasty, Police Arrest 20," *Philadelphia Daily News*, May 15, 1967; Allen Katzman and William Bowart, "Sgt. Pepper's Lonely Hearts Political Club and Band," *East Village Other*, July 1–July 15, 1967; Stephen A. O. Golden, "Police Look On as Hippies Stage a Park Smoke-In," *New York Times*, Monday, July 31, 1967.

2   **"Let's go and get high"**: Untitled article, *Ann Arbor Sun*, January 20, 1969.

3   **agents of the US Postal Service:** Philip D. Carter, "Buffalo Has 'Symposium' on Drugs," *Boston Globe*, March 3, 1969.

3   **their manager:** Don Lenhausen, "MC5 Rock Boss Guilty in Assault," *Detroit Free Press*, April 18, 1969.

3   **Nearly fifty members:** Bill Halpin, "Police Arrest 4 in Area 'Pot Raid,'" *Scranton Tribune*, December 9, 1968.

3   **Leslie Fiedler:** "Dr. Fiedler, Advisor to LEMAR, Is Arrested on Narcotics Charges," *The Spectrum* (SUNY Buffalo), May 2, 1967.

3   **police raided:** Nicholas von Hoffman, "The Grass Is Growing Like Weeds in Buffalo," *Washington Post*, May 7, 1967.

3   **"If you try to see":** Mike Power, "Drug Group—Tune In, Tune Out—Meets," *Rochester Democrat and Chronicle*, February 28, 1969.

3   **"We were all put up":** Ken Kelley to Albert Goldman, December 21, 1983, Box 20, Tape 20, Albert Goldman Papers, 1953–1994, University Archives, Rare Book & Manuscript Library, Columbia University Libraries.

4   **"Although local evidence"**: Paul Schatt, "Underground Press Plans Establishment of Free Zone," *Arizona Republic*, May 24, 1969.

4   **"You shouldn't talk"**: Associated Press, "Newspaperman Socks Poet for Insults," *Arizona Republic*, May 1, 1969.

4   **"You are dirty people"**: "'Dirty People' Evicted" [clipping from unknown underground paper], May or June 1969, in possession of author.

5   **"Did you notice the charred marks"**: Gene Luptak, "House Near State Capitol Links Underground Press," *Arizona Republic*, June 1, 1969.

6   ALARMED EXPERT: "Alarmed Expert Ranks Phoenix Among Widest Open Drug Towns," *Arizona Republic*, June 1, 1969.

6   **narcotics arrests:** James Cook, "The Drug Drivers," *Arizona Republic*, May 11, 1969.

6   **Charles Tignor:** "Drugs in State Tied to Red Conspiracy," *Arizona Republic*, May 3, 1969.

6   **"It's hard to believe"**: Jack West, "Become Involved in Fight on Crime, Parents Urged," *Arizona Republic*, March 7, 1969.

7   **On June 17:** "LSD Charges Are Dropped," *Arizona Republic*, November 14, 1969.

7   **According to Forcade's account:** Gary Goodson, "U.P.S. and Downs of Law and Order," *Rebirth* 1, no. 2 (1970).

7   **Perhaps looking:** Rev. Thomas King Forcade, "Think About Drugs," *Rebirth*, July 28, 1969 (reprinted from the *North Mountain News*). The article "Experts Warn Drug Gamble Is Game Without Winners" was produced by the Office of Information, XVIII Airborne Corps at Fort Bragg and was reprinted widely in various Department of Defense publications in 1969.

7   **In an editorial:** Jerry Hicks, "Behind the Headlines," *North Mountain News*, June 25, 1969.

8   **In a letter to UPS cofounder:** Letter from Tom Forcade to John Wilcock, undated but from late 1967 or early 1968.

8   **He sent dummy pages:** Letter from UPS coordinator Bob Rudnick to Thomas King Forcade, September 19, 1967 (copy in author's possession).

9   **The *Orpheus* crew:** Liberation News Service, no. 158, April 26, 1969.

9   **The *Orpheus* announcement:** Rev. Thomas Forcade, "Let's Stop the Game!" *Rebirth* 1, no. 2 (mid-1969?).

10   **Burks made no mention:** John Burks, "The Underground Press: A Special Report," *Rolling Stone*, October 4, 1969.

11   **"We're going to New York"**: Goodson, "U.P.S. and Downs of Law and Order." The *Orpheus* bus departed for Ann Arbor on July 6.

11   **Along the way:** Thomas King Forcade (writing as Peter Rabbit), "UPS Oddyssey" [*sic*], *Rebirth*, August 1969. The route was re-created by the author, using various gas station receipts that Forcade saved.

11   **At 4:00 a.m.:** Forcade (writing as Peter Rabbit), "UPS Oddyssey."

11   **A floodlight:** "Tipoff," *Detroit Free Press*, July 20, 1969.

12   **"This conference marks"**: Don DeMaio, "The Underground Press: A Special Report" (sidebar), *Rolling Stone*, October 4, 1969.

12   **"The White Panther Party"**: *Hearings Before the Senate Subcommittee to Investigate the Administration of the Internal Security Act and Other Internal Security Laws of the Committee on the Judiciary, Extent of Subversion in the "New Left,"* Ninety-First Congress, Second Session (September 25, 1970) (testimony of Det. Sgt. Clifford A. Murray, Michigan State Police, Intelligence Section), Part 8, p. 1222.

13   **east, over a bridge:** Art Johnston, "Subterranean Homesick Blues," *Fifth Estate*, July 24, 1969.

14   **"He couldn't find eggs":** Tom Tiede, "Who Killed These Girls?" Newspaper Enterprise Association (NEA) (syndicated), June 30, 1969.

14   **A psychiatrist:** Tiede, "Who Killed These Girls?"

14   **The latest police theory:** DeMaio, "The Underground Press."

14   **"The decent people":** "Dangerous Music," *Ann Arbor Argus*, July 10–25, 1969.

14   **On a patch:** Johnston, "Subterranean Homesick Blues."

15   **"We're going to set up":** DeMaio, "The Underground Press."

15   **They wore jeans:** See page of 283 of *Motor City Underground: Leni Sinclair Photographs 1963–1978*, ed. Cary Loren and Lorraine Wild (Museum of Contemporary Art, Detroit, 2021).

15   **A few visitors:** DeMaio, "The Underground Press."

15   **Art Johnston, a former Michigander:** Chris Singer, "Radical Press Agrees to Disagree on Unity," *Detroit Free Press*, July 21, 1969.

15   **Bill Schanen, the decidedly:** John Pekkanen, "The Obstinacy of Bill Schanen," *Time*, September 26, 1969.

16   **although much of Michigan:** "No Dope?" *Fifth Estate*, July 10, 1969.

16   **Forcade said he was:** DeMaio, "The Underground Press."

16   **The editor of Vancouver's:** Rev. Thomas King Forcade, "Dan McLeod and Marvin Garson: Pearls of Wisdom," *Wendre House* (newsletter), September 1969.

16   **"The trick in manipulating":** Thomas King Forcade, "Abbie Hoffman on Media," *Georgia Straight*, August 21, 1969.

17   **The singer, Terry Tate:** *Hearings Before the Senate Subcommittee to Investigate the Administration of the Internal Security Act and Other Internal Security Laws of the Committee on the Judiciary: Extent of Subversion in the "New Left,"* Ninety-First Congress, Second Session (September 25, 1970) (testimony of Det. Sgt. Clifford A. Murray, Michigan State Police, Intelligence Section).

17   **"like a panther in a bear trap":** Johnston, "Subterranean Homesick Blues."

17   **Undercover police:** "Self-Determination!" *Ann Arbor Sun*, June 9–23, 1972.

17   **banned further park concerts:** John Sinclair, "Rock and Roll Is Here to Stay," *Ann Arbor Sun*, May 7–13, 1971.

17   **"These Trans-Love people":** DeMaio, "The Underground Press."

17   **The president of the university:** Johnston, "Subterranean Homesick Blues."

17   **"invasion of weirdos":** David Dynes, "Right in the Keast-Er," *Fifth Estate*, July 24, 1969.

18   **"sit down and smoke":** Susan Jenkins, "Fiery Girl Editor Issues South End 'Bill of Rights,'" *Detroit Free Press*, July 15, 1969.

18   **A few months earlier:** Wilcock, "Other Scenes," *The Rat*; "Underground Press Conference + r.p.m.," *The Rat*, July 24, 1969.

18   **those contracts provided:** "Columbia to Stay Above Ground," *Rolling Stone*, July 26, 1969.

18   **the other television:** Letter from UPS, Liberation News Service, May 17, 1969.

18   **"junior Hearst":** Singer, "Radical Press Agrees to Disagree on Unity."

18   **contacted other Concert Hall clients:** Undated June 1969 letter from Michael Forman to John Wilcock on Concert Hall letterhead, John Wilcock Papers, Box 1, correspondence folder, Rare Book & Manuscript Library, Columbia University Libraries.

18   **One Wenner letter:** Singer, "Radical Press Agrees to Disagree on Unity."

18   **"ripping off":** Walt Crowley, *Rites of Passage: A Memoir of the Sixties in Seattle* (University of Washington Press, 1995).

18   **"Money is irrelevant":** Thomas King Forcade, "The Great Media Conference," Wendre Media, 1969. Written for syndication; copy in possession of author.

18   **"You have to make"**: Singer, "Radical Press Agrees to Disagree on Unity."

18   **The editors decided:** Ken Kelley, "United Press International," *Ann Arbor Argus*, July 29, 1969.

19   **"I realized something"**: Abbie Hoffman, *Soon to Be a Major Motion Picture*, 180.

19   **replacing its five-man coordinating committee:** UPS newsletter, March 7, 1969.

20   **"what are we, anyway"**: Burks, "The Underground Press."

20   **Big Man urged:** "Our Brothers of the Press," *Great Speckled Bird*, July 21, 1969.

20   **"mother country radicals"**: Joe Blum, "Huey Newton Talks to the Movement," *Movement*, August 1968.

21   **"pussy power"**: Mark Rudd, *Underground: My Life with SDS and the Weathermen* (HarperCollins, 2009).

21   **the women in Ann Arbor:** Walt Crowley, *Rites of Passage: A Memoir of the Sixties in Seattle* (University of Washington Press, 1995).

21   **"We're not capitalists"**: Singer, "Radical Press Agrees to Disagree on Unity."

21   **"That male supremacy"**: "Women and the Underground Press," Liberation News Service, no. 179, July 19, 1969.

22   **"Get some cat"**: Jo Hooper, "Pen Pal Meet," *Good Times*, August 7, 1969.

22   **One of the *Chicago Seed* people:** "Media Conference Raided by Shotgun-Toting Pigs," Liberation News Service, July 19, 1969.

22   **"He's not here"**: Pun Plamondon, *Lost from the Ottawa: The Story of the Journey Back* (Trafford, 2004), 134.

22   **"We have to develop"**: Singer, "Radical Press Agrees to Disagree on Unity."

22   **"We better sing"**: Kelley, "United Press International."

23   **The deputy held:** Bruce J. Smith, "Summer 1969 Meeting White Panthers, Black Panthers and Police," in *Transformation from Republican to Radical Activist in the 1960s*, Bruce J. Smith Blog (blog), https://brucejsmithblog.wordpress.com /chapter-17/.

23   **Helmeted deputies:** Kelley, "United Press International."

23   **Police moved toward the farmhouse:** "Media Conference Raided by Shotgun-Toting Pigs," Liberation News Service, July 19, 1969.

23   **"One wrong move"**: Kelley, "United Press International."

23   **Plamondon rushed:** Plamondon, *Lost from the Ottawa*.

24   **"It's a beautiful warm night"**: Abbie Hoffman, *Woodstock Nation* (Random House, 1969).

24   **"Don't know what the fuck"**: Hoffman, *Woodstock Nation*, 56.

24   **California psychic to Ann Arbor:** "Hurkos to Arrive Here Sunday," *Ann Arbor News*, July 12, 1969; "Hurkos' Visit Assured, Report Local Sponsors," *Ann Arbor News*, July 16, 1969; "Hurkos Begins Slaying Probe," *Ann Arbor News*, July 22, 1969.

25   **Police tore:** John Oppedahl, "Sinclair Given Sentence of 9½–10 Years for Pot," *Detroit Free Press*, July 29, 1969.

25   **Cindy's parents reached:** "Mail Call, Vietnam: A Labor of Love," *Lower Bucks Leader*, November 2016.

25   **"You idiot!"**: Cindy Ornsteen interview, 1980, Terese Coe Papers. Various transcriptions and other memorabilia from Terese Coe (courtesy of Trans-High Corporation).

26   **"My lady left me tonight"**: Rev. Thomas Forcade, "To Think About at Woodstock," *Other Scenes*, October 1, 1969.

26   **"It looks like"**: Cindy Ornsteen interview, 1980, Terese Coe Papers.

Chapter 2

26   **"Everyone was ready":** Abbie Hoffman, *Woodstock Nation* (Random House, 1969), 126.

26   **Eventually, they shook down:** Ted Franklin, "Woodstock: Youth Culture in the Wilderness," Liberation News Service, no. 187, August 21, 1969.

27   **"The potential of the situation":** Rev. Thomas Forcade, "To Think About at Woodstock," *Other Scenes*, October 1, 1969.

27   **Amid the ocean:** "Woodstock Festival Pledges Space for Movement," Liberation News Service, no. 183, August 2, 1969.

27   **"They were able":** Joel Makower, *Woodstock: The Oral History* (Doubleday, 1989).

27   **Hoffman took the stage:** Abbie Hoffman, "Abbie Answers Ellen Sander," *Los Angeles Free Press*, September 26, 1969.

28   **Forcade's quarters:** Brian Donovan, "Revolution USA," *Newsday*, April 21, 1970.

30   **At thirty-one:** Craig Wilson, "'Intercept' Action Disrupts Everyone," *Stanford Daily*, September 30, 1969.

30   **"Because of the lack":** Felix Belair Jr., "Operation Intercept: Success on Land, Futility in the Air," *New York Times*, October 2, 1969.

30   **What Operation Intercept:** Edward M. Brecher, *Licit & Illicit Drugs* (Consumers Union, 1972).

30   **"In the years":** Timothy Leary, "Deal for Real," *East Village Other*, September 24, 1969.

30   **A few weeks later:** Pun Plamondon, *Lost from the Ottawa: The Story of the Journey Back* (Trafford, 2004).

31   **Valler had become:** Bob Hippler and Bill Benoit, "David Valler Says, 'The Average Revolutionary Creates More Problems Than He Solves,'" *Big Fat*, June 1970.

31   **Sinclair heard about:** "CIA Conspiracy Short-Circuited," *Creem*, March 1971.

31   **The radio report:** Plamondon, *Lost from the Ottawa*, 145.

31   **Secret Service agents:** "CIA Conspiracy Short-Circuited," *Creem*, March 1971.

31   **"Our case in Phoenix":** "Write On! (Repression Comes Down, but U.P.S. Papers Write On!)," *East Village Other*, November 19, 1969.

32   **David Hilliard:** "Underground Press Spokesman Late," *San Diego Union*, November 14, 1969.

32   **who'd jumped into:** Neal Matthews, "Notes from Underground: An Incendiary History of San Diego's Counterculture Press," *San Diego Reader*, November 25, 1992.

33   CONVENTION OF PROSTITUTES: "Police Take Bait," *San Diego Free Door*, November 20, 1969.

33   **About 10:30 a.m.:** The account of Forcade's arrest has been synthesized from the following sources: "The Slogan for SDX"; "SDX: Learning How to Right the News," *San Diego Free Press*, November 28, 1969; "Underground Press Spokesman Late," *San Diego Union*, November 14, 1969; Dale Herschler, "Hey, Hey, Peter Kaye, How Many People Did You Screw Today?" *San Diego Free Door*, November 20, 1969; "Police Take Bait," *San Diego Free Door*, November 20, 1969.

33   **Forcade grabbed a water glass:** Gene Bryan, "Underground Press Holds Stormy Session," *The Quill*, December 1969.

33   **"There's repression everywhere":** Bryan, "Underground Press Holds Stormy Session."

34   **Art Kunkin:** Noel Greenwood, "Free Press Sued for Publishing Names of 80 Narcotics Agents," *Los Angeles Times*, August 9, 1969.

34   **He challenged:** [Luther Huston], "Sigma Delta Chi Welcomes Women to Full Membership," *Editor & Publisher*, November 22, 1969.

34   **"You people were":** "SDX: Learning How to Right the News," *San Diego Free Press*, November 28, 1969.

34   **The *Free Press* had been investigating:** "1969–1972: Chronology of Terror," *San Diego Door*, August 17, 1972.

34   **source for a *Penthouse* feature:** Joe Trento and Dave Roman, "The Spies Who Came in from the Newsroom," *Penthouse*, August 1977.

34   **During a question-and-answer:** [Luther Huston], "Underground Editors Fling Charges at Press," *Editor & Publisher*, November 22, 1969.

35   **The next morning Forcade:** Herschler, "Hey, Hey, Peter Kaye."

35   **"The only problem was":** "UPS Man Hit with Flag Rap," Liberation News Service, December 24, 1969.

35   **The day of the SDX conference:** "New News Agency Credited with Scoop on Pinkville," *St. Louis Post-Dispatch*, November 30, 1969.

36   **On November 14:** Ben Cole, "'Pinksville' Investigation Prompted by Phoenician," *Arizona Republic*, November 14, 1969.

36   **popsicle factory:** Dick Kleiner, "Blew Whistle on My Lai, Hopes Silent Majority Hears," Newspaper Enterprise Association (NEA) (syndicated), *Beatrice Daily Sun*, December 14, 1969.

36   **One announced:** "LSD Charges Are Dropped," *Arizona Republic*, November 14, 1969.

36   **"a trail of explosive terror":** "5 Charged for Part in Bombings," *Arizona Republic*, November 14, 1969.

36   **"revolutionary culture":** "Yip Myth Becomes Reality," *Los Angeles Free Press*, December 26, 1969.

36   **"I doubt they remember":** Forcade, "To Think About at Woodstock."

37   **Yippie Nancy Kurshan:** Stew Albert, "Viva Y.I.P.!!" *Berkeley Tribe*, January 2–9, 1970.

37   **"I've been to this meeting":** Albert, "Viva Y.I.P.!!"

37   **"Forcade finally got":** Ken Kelley to Albert Goldman, December 21, 1983, Box 20, Tape 20, Albert Goldman Papers, 1953–1994, University Archives, Rare Book & Manuscript Library, Columbia University Libraries.

37   **"If you need anything":** Tom Forcade to John Sinclair, December 4, 1969, Box 3, Folder 7, John and Leni Sinclair Papers, Bentley Historical Library, University of Michigan.

37   **"a political governing":** John Sinclair letter to Skip Taube, published as part of "Letters from Prison," *Chicago Seed* 4, no. 9 (November 1969).

37   **"They might as well":** John Sinclair to Leni Sinclair, December 18, 1969, Box 3, Folder 8, John and Leni Sinclair Papers.

38   **"It can't really be":** John Sinclair to Leni Sinclair, December 11, 1969, Box 3, Folder 8, John and Leni Sinclair Papers.

38   **"This isn't just":** John Sinclair to Leni Sinclair, December 23, 1969, Box 3, Folder 9, John and Leni Sinclair Papers.

38   **A demonstration they led:** Richard C. McCord, "Nixon Draws Protests," *Newsday*, December 10, 1969; "Viet Protesters Go on Spree in N.Y., Break Shop Windows," *Chicago Tribune*, December 10, 1969.

38   **"Dig it!":** "Weatherman SDS Meets in Michigan," Liberation News Service, January 3, 1970.

38   **"I think maybe":** Leni Sinclair to John Sinclair, December 31, 1969, Box 3, Folder 9, John and Leni Sinclair Papers.

39   **"No one can deny"**: "Intellectual Freedom ALA Midwinter," *Library Journal*, March 15, 1970.

39   **"Let's go!"**: "The Activism Gap," *Library Journal*, March 15, 1970.

40   **"organizers and energy centers"**: Sal Torey, "Interview with Abbie Hoffman," *Quicksilver Times*, January 30, 1970 (interview conducted January 17).

40   **"that the work concerning"**: Genie Plamondon, "Youth International Party," Ann Arbor, Mich., February 17, 1970; *Hearings Before the Senate Subcommittee to Investigate the Administration of the Internal Security Act and Other Internal Security Laws of the Committee on the Judiciary: Extent of Subversion in the "New Left,"* Ninety-First Congress, Second Session (September 25, 1970) (testimony of Robert J. Thoms [and Others]), Parts 8–9, Exhibit 8. Genie Plamondon signed off as minister of communications, White Panther Tribe/Youth International Party.

40   **"Attempts by New Left leaders"**: *Hearings Before the Senate Select Committee to Study Governmental Operations with Respect to Intelligence Activities of the United States Senate: Huston Plan* (vol. 2), Ninety-Fourth Congress, First Session (September 23, 24, and 25, 1975), exhibit 37.

40   **Over the next twenty-four:** Homer Bigart, "Many Buildings Evacuated Here in Bomb Scares," *New York Times*, March 13, 1970. When Nixon gave a speech about the Watergate investigation in 1973, he claimed that there had been *four* hundred threats in one day.

40   **That evening, the prominent:** James M. Naughton, "U.S. to Tighten Surveillance of Radicals," *New York Times*, April 12, 1970.

41   **"A curious thing"**: "Brief History of UPS," *Clear Head* (UPS newsletter), 1970.

42   **Forcade pulled:** Stella Mastrangelo and Bob Markus, "Winter's End," *Big Fat*, May 1970.

42   **"All the people involved"**: Parker Donham, "Dreams of 2d Woodstock Become Nightmares," *Boston Globe*, March 22, 1970.

42   **"eight groups of three"**: "Winter's End Shuck," *Quicksilver Times*, March 24, 1970.

42   **Promoters agreed:** Craig Karpel, "Das Hip Kapital: A Critique of the Youth Economy," *Esquire*, December 1970.

43   **"You the law?"**: Much of the contemporaneous dialogue in this section comes from an account Forcade wrote himself: Thomas King Forcade, "Winter's End: Free the Rock & Roll Six," *Free Ranger Intertribal News Service*, April 13, 1970.

46   **"That these dirty"**: "Promoters Arrested; Rock Beat Goes On," *Miami Herald*, March 30, 1970.

46   **Some of the seed money:** Jerry Cohen, "Mobsters Turn Monied Eye on Rock Festivals," *Los Angeles Times*, May 17, 1970.

46   **"The people who had loaned"**: Forcade, "Winter's End."

47   **A replacement ad salesman:** Robert England, "The Late, Great, Underground Press" (unpublished manuscript), October 1972, provided by England. In about March 1970, UPS's Nancy Rouda sent out a letter reaffirming exclusive contracts and saying she'd be handling through the UPS Ad Rep Co. In late June, Jeffrey Michaelson of UPS Ad Rep Co. informed Media A that UPS was issuing an injunction against it. On July 23, it filed a $200,000 lawsuit.

47   **"Sure wish you all"**: Robert Head to UPS et al., May 3, 1970, courtesy of Robert Head.

47   **"superdaily"**: Thomas King Forcade, "Free Media," *NOLA Express*, May 1, 1970.

47   **"cultural guerilla"**: Brian Donovan, "Revolution USA—the Radical Impulse: What's Behind It," *Newsday*, April 21, 1970.

47   **"Things like money"**: Donovan, "Revolution USA."

48   **"Grass breaks down"**: Brian Donovan, "Drugs and the Revolution," *Newsday*, April 23, 1970.

48   MAY DAY IS J-DAY: *The Fifth Estate*, April 16, 1970.

48   **"*Revolution for My Friends*":** Terese Coe Papers.

Chapter 3

51   **"We need better":** James M. Naughton, "U.S. to Tighten Surveillance of Radicals," *New York Times*, April 12, 1970. The aide was probably Tom Huston.

51   **In upstate:** Ron Rosenbaum, "Run Tommy Run!" *Esquire*, July 1971.

51   **"an Establishment trick":** Rosenbaum, "Run Tommy Run!"

51   **taunted students:** Howard Smith and Sally Helgesen, "Scenes," *Village Voice*, September 16, 1971; Paul Jacobs, "Informers: The Enemy Within," *Ramparts*, August 1973.

51   **Eventually, he was able:** "New York: Tommy the Traveler," *Time*, June 22, 1970.

51   **"In a few instances":** Betty Medsger and Ken W. Clawson, "FBI Secretly Prods Colleges on New Left," *Washington Post*, April 6, 1971.

51   **FBI-supervised informants:** Bob Hartley, Doug Porter, Larry Remer, and Bill Ritter, "San Diego's Watergate: Secret Police Exposed," *San Diego Door*, January 17, 1974. See also Kit Bakke, *Protest on Trial* (Washington State University Press, 2018); Frank J. Donner, *The Age of Surveillance* (Knopf, 1980); Paul Cowan, Nick Egleson, and Nat Hentoff, *State Secrets: Police Surveillance in America* (Holt, Rinehart and Winston, 1974).

51   **"I did burn":** Art Kunkin, "Your Local Bomber Might Be an FBI Agent," *Los Angeles Free Press*, October 15–21, 1971.

52   **Thus insinuated:** Michael Drosnin, "Nixon's Radical Chaser Bags a Whopper," *New Times*, October 18, 1974; Francine du Plessix Gray, *Adam & Eve and the City* (Simon & Schuster, 1987).

52   **"Burn, burn":** Martin Weil, "D.C. Police Stage Mock Campus Riot," *Washington Post*, April 20, 1970.

52   **These officers:** Christopher H. Pyle, "CONUS Intelligence: The Army Watches Civilian Politics," *Washington Monthly*, January 1970; *Hearings Before the Senate Committee on the Judiciary, Subcommittee on Constitutional Rights: Federal Data Banks, Computers, and the Bill of Rights*, Ninety-Second Congress, First Session (1971); "Looking for Trouble," *Newsweek*, May 4, 1970.

52   **"whether—because of":** Tom Huston deposition of May 23, 1975, as cited in Senate Select Committee to Study Governmental Operations with Respect to Intelligence Activities, *Book III: Supplementary Detailed Staff Reports on Intelligence Activities and the Rights of Americans*, S. Rep. No. 94-755, at 934 (1976).

52   **unprecedented domestic-intelligence strategy:** James Bamford, *The Puzzle Palace* (Penguin, 1983), 256.

53   **"Smoke at least two":** "White Panther Outburst Prompts Clearing of State Senate Gallery," *Times Herald* (Port Huron, MI), May 1, 1970.

53   **new YIP flag:** William Federici, "Panther Rally Is Short on Panthers," New York *Daily News*, May 2, 1970. The flag was previously unveiled and hung on the White House fence during Hoffman's April 25 attempt to crash Tricia Nixon's tea party.

53   **The *Village Voice* described:** Ron Rosenbaum, "Either/Or at Yale: Mayday & the Panthers," *Village Voice*, May 7, 1970. Ironically, the previous week's issue of *Black Panther* ("Will Racism or International Proletarian Solidarity Conquer?" April 25, 1970) accused the Jews of the American Left of Zionism. Huey Newton gave a qualified apology for the article at a press conference in August.

54   **Abbie started:** Allan Katzman, "Poor Paranoid's Almanac," *East Village Other*, May 19, 1970.

54   **was now being hunted:** Howard Kohn and William Schmidt, "Underground Is Protecting Young Radical from FBI," *Detroit Free Press*, June 28, 1970.

54   **"berating of people":** "Quicksilver's Back," *Quicksilver Times*, May 8, 1970. One dissenting female contributor was "thrown to the floor, slammed against the wall by six men, then interrogated on a couch and hit in the face each time she made a hesitant or 'incorrect' answer to a political question."

54   **Federal agents:** Ivan C. Brandon and B. D. Colen, "Raid Fails to Find Fugitive Radical," *Washington Post*, Friday, May 8, 1970.

54   **"The construction workers":** Michael Carliner, "Abbie Hoffman for the Hell of It," *Harry*, May 15, 1970 (despite the cover date, the interview was conducted on May 16).

54   **"endlessly repeated marches":** David Dellinger, "Carrying It On: A Third Alternative," *Village Voice*, June 5, 1970.

55   **"People should have":** Carliner, "Abbie Hoffman for the Hell of It." Sue Rouda's sister Diana remembers a slightly different version of the story. "Tom had purchased this 1934 car with a '65 Chevy engine in it—you hit the gas, it goes 0–60 in about a half second. We were driving upstate on the New York Thruway, Tom was driving like a bat out of hell, and we got stopped by the cops. For some reason, we ended up going to the police station. Tom was chatting away with the cops. I wasn't privy to a lot of the conversation. But what we also had in the car was a pan of hash brownies. Tom had his best face on: 'Would you like some brownies?' The cops were like, 'Sure!' They were munching brownies as we drove off."

56   **"The Underground Press Syndicate has repeatedly":** UPS press statement, May 13, 1970.

56   **During a momentary:** Muriel Dobbin, "Obscenity Hearing Has Slapstick Ending," *Baltimore Sun*, May 14, 1970.

57   **Only when Otto Larsen:** Nancy L. Ross, "Slapstick and *#%&*!" *Washington Post*, May 14, 1970.

57   **"I think I have the material":** Jules Witcover, "Witness Tosses Pie in Face of Authority," *Los Angeles Times*, May 14, 1970.

57   OBSCENITY COMMISSION GETS CREAMED: *Arizona Republic*, May 14, 1970.

57   THE PIE THROWER—RATED X: New York *Daily News*, May 14, 1970.

57   SMUT PROBER GETS PIE IN FACE: *Boston Globe*, May 14, 1970.

57   **"there are some people":** Letter from John Sinclair to Tom Forcade, June 7, 1970.

58   **In mid-June:** John Grissim, *We Have Come for Your Daughters: What Went Down on the Medicine Ball Caravan* (William Morrow, 1972), 113.

58   **"The Capitalist Rip-Off":** Nina Sabaroff, "Notes from the First Gathering: An Alternate Media Message," Liberation News Service, July 15, 1970.

59   **"scowl broken":** "UPS' Forcade: 'I Don't Want Peace. I Want Life,'" *Detroit News*, c. June 1970 (clipping in possession of author).

59   **"*I* took your $500":** Forcade, *Caravan of Love and Money*.

59   **"I climbed out of the car":** Forcade, *Caravan of Love and Money*.

60   **"We were all looking":** Forcade, *Caravan of Love and Money*.

Chapter 4

60   **The RYP/Off members:** Daria Price and Joyce Plecha, "Breakfast at Sardi's," *The Rat*, April 17, 1970. The RYP/Off members at the press conference were Jim Retherford,

Daria Price, and Joyce Plecha. On December 4, Plecha would be arrested—along with Sharon Krebs, who'd been at the YIP–White Panther merger meeting at the UPS loft, and four others—on charges of attempting to firebomb an Upper East Side bank. One member of their cell, it turned out, was working for the NYPD's Bureau of Special Services and Investigations. They later pled guilty to second-degree conspiracy.

61   **"If you find these"**: John Zeh, "Woodstock Nation '70: Invasion or Rip-Off?" *Village Voice*, May 21, 1970.

61   **When Warner Brothers:** Ron Rosenbaum, "The 'Exploited' Culture Demands Its Dues," *Village Voice*, July 16, 1970.

61   **At the film's:** Dennis Levitt, "Woodschuck Boycott," *Los Angeles Free Press*, May 22, 1970.

62   **On the afternoon:** John Da Swede, "Mu$icBuckNews," *East Village Other*, June 23, 1970.

63   **promoter named Teddy Powell:** Richard Robinson, "Problem for Black Promoters," Pop Scene Service, *Fond Du Lac Commonwealth Reporter*, August 7, 1968.

63   **"I'd like to see Teddy":** Rosenbaum, "The 'Exploited' Culture Demands Its Dues."

63   **"You people":** Dialogue from *Free* (Bert Tenzer Productions, 1973).

64   **"Members of the collective":** Rosenbaum, "The 'Exploited' Culture Demands Its Dues."

64   **"At one point":** Thomas King Forcade, *Caravan of Love and Money* (Signet, 1972).

64   **"There's a pig":** Craig Karpel, "Das Hip Kapital: A Critique of the Youth Economy," *Esquire*, December 1970.

64   **"I was put off":** John McMillian, *Smoking Typewriters: The Sixties Underground Press and the Rise of Alternative Media in America* (New York: Oxford University Press, 2011), 119–120.

65   **"Listen. Capitalists will":** Karpel, "Das Hip Kapital."

65   **Forcade told Rosenbaum:** Rosenbaum, "The 'Exploited' Culture Demands Its Dues."

65   **"Tom Forcade, who founded":** Rosenbaum, "The 'Exploited' Culture Demands Its Dues."

66   **"Brave New World Productions has":** "Rock Festival to Give Bread Back to the Movement," Liberation News Service, July 18, 1970, 3. (In stories published on July 15, the Associated Press attributed the quotation to Felipe Luciano.)

66   **"Yippies' plans hinge":** FBI Intelligence Letters (FBI INLET), Letter to the President, June 5, 1970, FBI file HQ-65-73268. Accessed via the Ernie Lazar FOIA Collection on the Internet Archive (https://archive.org/details/fbi-intelligence-letters-hq-65-73268).

66   **"YIP-WP allegedly":** Detroit SA to Detroit office, June 12, 1970, Youth International Party FBI file 100-NY-162260, serial 644. Accessed at https://www.governmentattic.org/4docs/FBI-YIPPIES_1967-1977.pdf.

66   **There had been disagreement:** "July 4th: Smoke-In!" *Quicksilver Times*, June 23–July 3, 1970.

66   **"I fell in love":** Jerry Rubin, *We Are Everywhere* (Harper & Row, 1971), 238.

67   **"utilize the YIP":** FBI memo from New York field office, June 4, 1970, FBI file 100-NY-162260, serial 630.

67   **"a higher level of revolutionary":** "Surprise Attack," *Sun/Dance*, July 1970.

67   **After receiving:** US Commission on CIA Activities Within the United States, "Chap. 10: Intelligence Community Coordination," in *Report to the President by the Commission on CIA Activities Within the United States* (Rockefeller Commission Report) (Government Printing Office, 1975), 123.

67   **"Hoffman has announced":** FBI Intelligence Letters (FBI INLET), Letter to the President, June 5, 1970, FBI file HQ-65-73268. Accessed via the Ernie Lazar FOIA Collection on the Internet Archive (https://archive.org/details /fbi-intelligence-letters-hq-65-73268).

68   **"We're gonna declare":** "Abbie," *Quicksilver Times* 2, no. 12 (May 19–29, 1970).

68   **"Amerika is":** "Youth International Party Manifesto," 1970. Viewable at https:// rozsixties.unl.edu/items/show/15, where it is misdated.

68   **"This writer personally":** "July 4th: Smoke-In!" *Quicksilver Times*, June 23–July 3, 1970.

69   **"There might be some":** "Rennie Davis Scores Honor America Day," *New York Times*, June 25, 1970.

69   HONOR AMERICA DAY BLOODBATH THREATENED BY CHICAGO 7 GROUP: Associated Press, *Maryville Daily Forum*, June 25, 1970.

69   **"moving through the water":** Mike Kazin, "Honor America Day: Grass, Gas, and Billy Graham," Liberation News Service, July 15, 1970.

69   **"Smoke dope, get high":** Jeff Shero, "Honor Amerika Smoke-In," *Sun/Dance*, October 1970.

69   **"Fuck Miss America":** Pete van Wobbly, "D.C.: July 4 Smoke-In," *The Rag*, July 13, 1970.

69   **"Before this is":** "Peak Capital Crowd Foreseen on July 4 Honor America Day," *New York Times*, June 30, 1970.

69   **"The national media mentioned":** Kazin, "Honor America Day."

69   **"We talked to":** George W. S. Trow (unsigned), "Three Festivals," *New Yorker*, August 1, 1970.

70   **So many tickets:** Coca Crystal, "Randall's Blues," *East Village Other*, July 28, 1970.

70   **A street gang:** Alfred G. Aronowitz, "Randall's Island: Festival or Fiasco?" *Jazz and Pop*, October 1970.

70   **Forcade took the stage:** John Grissim, *We Have Come for Your Daughters: What Went Down on the Medicine Ball Caravan* (William Morrow, 1972), 113.

70   **"heaved out":** Elaine Gross, "A Football Game by E.A. Poe," *Rolling Stone*, September 3, 1970.

70   **dissatisfied audience:** Richard Stim, "In Review," *Newsday*, July 20, 1970.

71   **"The psychedelic sounds":** Ramon Rivera, "Randall's Island Rip-Off," *Palante* 2, no. 8 (July 31, 1970).

71   **"The white radicals":** Carman Moore, "A Study in Mistrust," *Village Voice*, July 23, 1970.

71   **The following week:** "Ryp and Rock: Statement by the Ryp Collective," *The Rat*, August 9–23, 1970.

71   **The Young Lords told:** "Lords Reveal Mafia Plot to Murder Chairman Felipe Luciano," Liberation News Service, July 25, 1970.

71   **"had some interesting things":** John daSwede, "New York Pop: The Anatomy of a Festival (and a Story) That Wasn't," *East Village Other*, July 28, 1970.

72   **That same day:** The account of the White Panther arrest comes from Pun Plamondon, *Lost from the Ottawa: The Story of the Journey Back* (Trafford, 2004).

72   **"This kangaroo trial":** *Hearings Before the Senate Subcommittee to Investigate the Administration of the Internal Security Act and Other Internal Security Laws of the Committee on the Judiciary: Extent of Subversion in the "New Left,"* Ninety-First Congress, Second Session (September 25, 1970) (testimony of Clifford A. Murray), Part 8, p. 1215.

73   **"The so-called":** John Sinclair letter to Tom Forcade, July 29, 1970.

74   **"I think we can make it":** John Sinclair letter to Tom Forcade, July 29, 1970, Thomas Forcade Collection.

74   **Michael Forman, now living:** Grissim, *We Have Come for Your Daughters*, 114.

75   **Concert Hall's dissolution:** Robert England, "The Late, Great Underground Press" (unpublished manuscript), October 1972.

76   **Kelley proposed:** Terry Taube, *Sun/Dance*, no. 2 (October 1, 1970).

76   **"We gotta have dope!":** Steve Harris, "Hassles & Apathy in Underground Press Meet," UPS News Service, September 14, 1970.

77   **"Inside the Caddy":** Forcade, *Caravan of Love and Money*, 47.

77   **"It was a syndrome":** Forcade, *Caravan of Love and Money*, 58.

78   **"Watch this":** Grissim, *We Have Come for Your Daughters*, 41.

78   **"Forman, a showman":** Forcade, *Caravan of Love and Money*, 53.

78   **As the pill:** Forcade, *Caravan of Love and Money*, 74.

78   **"This could be":** The Donahue encounter is recounted in Forcade, *Caravan of Love and Money*, 75–79.

80   **"Tom Forcade has hardly":** Grissim, *We Have Come for Your Daughters*, 120.

80   **Rosenbaum was twenty-three:** Jay Acton, Alan LeMond, and Parker Hodges, *Mug Shots: Who's Who in the New Earth* (Meridian, 1972); Kevin McAuliffe, *The Great American Newspaper: The Rise and Fall of the Village Voice* (Scribner, 1978).

81   **"muted post horn":** Ron Rosenbaum, "The Secret Life of Tommy Rotten," *Punk*, 1981.

81   **"Forcade is one":** Ron Rosenbaum, "Hog Farm's Wayward Bus (1)—Pilgrims & Profiteers on a Cross-Country Crusade," *Village Voice*, September 10, 1970.

83   **"a death trip":** Ron Rosenbaum, "Wayward Buses (2)—Pilgrims & Profiteers: Holy for Hollywood," *Village Voice*, September 17, 1970.

83   **"Hello, we're from":** Rosenbaum, "Wayward Buses (2)."

83   **"A hip capitalist":** Most of the dialogue from this encounter comes from Rosenbaum, "Wayward Buses (2)." Additional descriptions of the scene were drawn from Forcade, *Caravan of Love and Money*; Grissim, *We Have Come for Your Daughters*; and the film *Medicine Ball Caravan*, directed by François Reichenbach (1971).

84   **"No, I'm sure":** Forcade, *Caravan of Love and Money*.

85   **"the United States Information Agency":** "Free Rock Concerts," *Washington Post*, August 24, 1970.

85   **"I told several":** Forcade, *Caravan of Love and Money*, 114.

85   **"Since literally millions":** "Caravan of Contradictions," *Quicksilver Times*, September 1–10, 1970.

85   **"Coming off the trip":** Forcade, *Caravan of Love and Money*.

85   **"The Vietnamese were":** Forcade, *Caravan of Love and Money*, 127.

86   **"a dress rehearsal":** Ralph Steadman, *The Joke's Over* (Harcourt, 2006).

86   **"being too outrageous":** Forcade, *Caravan of Love and Money*, 127.

Chapter 5

87   **"If these demands":** "The Bombers Tell Why & What Next," *Madison Kaleidoscope*, August 25, 1970.

87   **authorities thought:** "Text of the F.B.I. Affidavit Charging Four in University of Wisconsin Bombing," *New York Times*, September 3, 1970.

87   **The day after the bombing:** Tom Bates, *Rads* (HarperCollins, 1992), 31.

87   **When Angela Davis:** "The FBI's Toughest Foe: 'The Kids,'" *Newsweek*, October 26, 1970.

87   **Bombs were exploding:** Daniel S. Chard, *Nixon's War at Home: The FBI, Leftist Guerillas, and the Origins of Counterterrorism* (University of North Carolina Press, 2021), 129–132.

87   **Two women who'd:** "Ex-Brandeis Coeds Added to FBI List," *Boston Globe*, October 18, 1970.

87   **The FBI stepped:** Chard, *Nixon's War at Home*, 135–137.

88   **"Face it":** "The FBI's Toughest Foe: 'The Kids,'" *Newsweek*, October 26, 1970.

88   **"the possibility exists":** New York FBI field office investigative report, September 29, 1970, FBI file 100-NY-162260, serial 742. Accessed at https://www.government attic.org/4docs/FBI-YIPPIES_1967-1977.pdf.

88   **"It is tough":** Dick Gaik, "Speechless," *San Francisco Good Times*, October 2, 1970.

88   ABBIE OINK HOFFMAN: Jack Hoffman, with Daniel Simon, *Run Run Run: The Lives of Abbie Hoffman* (Putnam, 1994).

88   **"several anarchistic groups":** This claim was made in an October 6 letter from Attorney General John Mitchell to the Office of Management and Budget, and again in an October 12 speech that J. Edgar Hoover's assistant, William C. Sullivan, made at a conference of journalists. See also "The FBI's Toughest Foe: 'The Kids,'" *Newsweek*, October 26, 1970.

89   **"Gerald Ford might":** "Political Kidnapping Plot Tied to White Panthers," *New York Times*, March 17, 1971.

89   **"may be contributing":** John R. Coyne, *The Impudent Snobs: Agnew vs. the Intellectual Establishment* (Arlington House, 1972).

89   **"decided that the underground":** "Paranoia Food: Repression," *Clear Head!* (UPS newsletter), undated, circa November 1970.

89   **The FBI visited:** "Paranoia Food: Repression," *Clear Head!* (UPS newsletter), undated, circa November 1970.

89   **"more interviews with those":** September 16, 1970, FBI memo, quoted in Betty Medsger and Ken W. Clawson, "Stolen Documents Describe FBI Surveillance Activities," *Washington Post*, March 24, 1971.

89   **The Phoenix lawyer:** William Chapman, "Kleindienst Gave Goldwater Law-and-Order Line," *Washington Post*, February 2, 1969.

89   **He quickly earned:** Chapman, "Kleindienst Gave Goldwater Law-and-Order Line."

89   **"boisterous":** Rowland Evans and Robert Novak, "Laird Ignores Pressure," *Journal-News* (Nyack, NY), January 4, 1969.

90   **"people who demonstrate":** Elizabeth Drew, "Washington," *Atlantic Monthly*, May 1969. After the comments were published, Kleindienst insisted that he'd been misquoted, although he couldn't remember exactly what he'd said. (See Oswald Johnston, "Detention Camp Quote Stirs Furor," *Baltimore Sun*, April 26, 1969.)

90   **"One of you":** Saundra Saperstein and George Lardner Jr., "Rehnquist: Nixon's Long Shot for a 'Law and Order' Court," *Washington Post*, July 7, 1986.

90   **"an absolutely":** "The Law: Tough New Man at Justice," *Time*, February 1, 1971.

90   **"I knew a loser":** "The Law: Tough New Man at Justice," *Time*, February 1, 1971. Just after uttering those words, Mardian insisted that the reporter record that he was joking.

91   **"use immunity":** "Non-Unanimous Jury Ruling Backward Step for County," *Los Angeles Free Press* (LNS), June 9, 1972.

91   **witness was not allowed:** Arnold H. Lubasch, "Immunity Case Disturbs Many," *New York Times*, September 5, 1971.

91   **If a witness:** Donald Janson, "Witnesses Freed After 14 Months," *New York Times*, March 2, 1973.

91 **Even if a grand jury:** Tim Findley, "Farewell to the Fifth Amendment," *Rolling Stone*, December 7, 1972; Paul Cowan, "The New Grand Jury: A Kind of Immunity That Leads to Jail," *New York Times*, April 29, 1973.

91 **By November:** "9 Radicals Are on the Most-Wanted List," *New York Times*, November 28, 1970.

91 **The ISD's staff:** Walter R. Gordon, "Justice Unit Takes on Radicals," *Baltimore Sun*, February 1, 1971.

91 **Mardian found himself:** Ronald J. Ostrow, "Justice Dept. Moves to Counter Terrorists," *Los Angeles Times*, October 31, 1970.

91 **"suggested the possibility":** "If Men Were Angels," William Sullivan speech of October 12, 1970, Williamsburg, VA, printed in the *Congressional Record* of November 30, 1970.

91 **Mitchell filed an affidavit:** *United States v. Sinclair*, 321 F. Supp. 1074 (E.D. Mich. 1971).

92 **"From the rickety":** Charles R. Baker, "The Underground Press," *Homefront*, November 1970.

92 **"In general":** Baker, "The Underground Press."

93 **"Forcade's idea":** Gerald Lefcourt to Albert Goldman, September 13, 1982, Box 61, Tape 8, Albert Goldman Papers, 1953–1994, University Archives, Rare Book & Manuscript Library, Columbia University Libraries.

93 **"I urged Hoffman":** Tom Forcade, "When You Live Outside the Law." When Grove Press finally published the book, it was priced at two dollars.

93 **"It seems to me":** Jay Acton, Alan LeMond, and Parker Hodges, *Mug Shots: Who's Who in the New Earth* (Meridian, 1972).

93 **But after some haggling:** Craig Karpel, "Steal This Court," *WIN*, November 1, 1971.

94 **"too fucking academic":** Michael Antonoff, "The Thomas King Forcade Story," *Tucson's Mountain Newsreal*, December 1978.

94 **"I don't work":** Antonoff, "The Thomas King Forcade Story."

94 **"As soon as Lefcourt":** Forcade, "When You Live Outside the Law."

94 **"There is a strong":** Tom Forcade, "Dogs Run Free Why Not We," *Free Ranger Intertribal News Service*, January 20, 1971.

94 **accepted $10,000:** Letter from Nancy Hardin of New American Library to Tom Forcade, February 12, 1971.

95 **At the end of 1970:** Lesley Oelsner, "Journalist-Law Panel Advises Broad Protection for Newsmen," *New York Times*, November 17, 1971.

95 **Even the establishment:** *Press Freedoms Under Pressure: Report of the Twentieth Century Fund Task Force on the Government and the Press* (Twentieth Century Fund, 1972).

95 **"the ways in which":** Undated letter from Tom Forcade (courtesy of Judy Goodson Baker).

95 **Over the next several months:** The FBI reported Forcade was living at 1400 20th Street, NW, as of June 7. (Report from New York FBI field office, February 4, 1972, FBI file 100-HQ-469538, serial 6; copy in author's possession.)

95 **At the end of 1970, FBI director:** Frank J. Donner and Eugene Cerruti, "The Grand Jury Network," *The Nation*, January 3, 1972.

95 **He claimed:** Nancy Zaroulis and Gerald Sullivan, *Who Spoke Up? American Protest Against the War in Vietnam* (Doubleday, 1984), 341. On September 22, 1970: forty-five-minute WH briefing (Nixon, AG Mitchell, Hoover) of Republican congressional leaders, pitching for more funds for FBI hiring and authority to investigate campus violence. Hoover warns of East Coast Conspiracy to Save Lives plots. Afterward,

Gerald Ford met with Nixon, Mitchell, and Hoover and discussed the alleged White Panther kidnapping plot, according to Jeff A. Hale, "The White Panthers' 'Total Assault on the Culture,'" in *Imagine Nation: The American Counterculture of the 1960s and '70s*, ed. Peter Braunstein and Michael William Doyle (Routledge, 2001), 149.

96 **"There's goddamn no telling":** Jack Nelson and Ronald J. Ostrow, *The FBI and the Berrigans* (Coward, McCann & Geoghegan, 1972).

96 **One of the witnesses:** Michael Drosnin, "Nixon's Radical Chaser Bags a Whopper," *New Times*, October 18, 1974.

96 **"The evidence on":** "US Tapped RC Lines for Evidence, Nun Says," *Globe and Mail*, January 27, 1971.

96 **"An idea which seems":** Jeff Hale, "Wiretapping and National Security: Nixon, the Mitchell Doctrine, and the White Panthers" (PhD diss., Louisiana State University, 1995); *United States v. Sinclair*, 321 F. Supp. 1074 (E.D. Mich. 1971).

96 **After extensive meetings:** Ken W. Clawson, "U.S. to Appeal Ruling Against Wiretapping," *Washington Post*, January 28, 1971.

96 **As Jeff Hale explained:** Hale, "Wiretapping and National Security," 429–430.

96 **"from approximately fifty":** Senate Subcommittee on Constitutional Rights of the Committee on the Judiciary, *Army Surveillance of Civilians: A Documentary Analysis*, S. Doc. 79-911 (1972).

97 **"a lot of questions":** Seymour M. Hersh, "Ex-Army Agent Says He Briefed C.I.A. in 1967 on Radicals in U.S.," *New York Times*, January 11, 1975.

97 **"the overwhelming percentage":** *Hearings Before the Senate Subcommittee on Constitutional Rights of the Committee on the Judiciary: Federal Data Banks, Computers, and the Bill of Rights*, Ninety-Second Congress, First Session (February 24, 1971) (statement of Ralph Stein), 247.

97 **"political computer":** *Hearings Before the Senate Subcommittee on Constitutional Rights of the Committee on the Judiciary: Federal Data Banks, Computers, and the Bill of Rights*, Ninety-Second Congress, First Session (February 24, 1971) (statement of Christopher Pyle), 180.

97 **It later emerged:** Memo from New York SAC to FBI Director, Re: MEDBURG, FBI file 52-HQ-94527, serial 1699 (copy in author's possession).

97 **Hoover ordered surveillance:** Betty Medsger and Ken W. Clawson, "Thieves Got Over 1,000 FBI Papers," *Washington Post*, March 25, 1971.

97 **plans to develop:** Betty Medsger and Ken W. Clawson, "FBI Secretly Prods Colleges on New Left," *Washington Post*, April 6, 1971.

97 **"to get the point across":** FBI memo, September 16, 1970, quoted in Betty Medsger and Ken W. Clawson, "Stolen Documents Describe FBI Surveillance Activities," *Washington Post*, March 24, 1971.

98 **"the tactics of":** "The Administration: Bugging J. Edgar Hoover," *Time*, April 19, 1971.

98 **"We're certainly heading":** Associated Press, "Celler Warns of 'Police State' Tactics," *Miami Herald*, April 26, 1971.

98 **"We need intelligence":** Associated Press, "Mitchell Says Real Security Threat Is Here at Home," *Corpus Christi Caller-Times*, April 24, 1971.

98 **"This is not a police state":** "President Leaning to Lockheed Loan," *Atlanta Journal-Constitution*, May 2, 1971.

98 **Kleindienst cooked up:** Lawrence Roberts, *Mayday 1971* (Houghton Mifflin Harcourt, 2020).

98 **Bureau of Narcotics:** Charles H. Lutz, "Operation Bent Penny," *Vietnam*, October 2011.

98 **"Their plan is now":** H. R. Haldeman, *The Haldeman Diaries: Inside the Nixon White House* (G. P. Putnam's Sons, 1994), 284.

98 **When local precincts:** Roberts, *Mayday 1971*, chap. 18.

98 **Kleindienst and Mardian:** Nina Totenberg, "Justice Aide Alarms and Charms the Capital," *National Observer*, May 17, 1971. See also the photograph on the front page of the New York *Daily News* of May 5, 1971.

98 **Mardian snapped photos:** Ben A. Franklin, "2,680 More Demonstrators Arrested in Washington," *New York Times*, May 5, 1971.

99 **On the morning:** Leslie Bacon's accounts of her arrest come from Paul Krassner, "Conversation with Leslie Bacon," *The Realist*, May–June 1971; and David Wise, *The American Police State* (Random House, 1976).

100 **The Free Ranger Tribe got its name:** Robert D. McFadden, "Radical, Yes, but Violent? Reports Differ," *New York Times*, April 30, 1971.

100 **"Tell the grand jury":** Frank J. Donner and Eugene Cerruti, "The Grand Jury Network," *The Nation*, January 3, 1972.

100 **"Goodwin just has":** "Goodwin Is Scared to Death of Rainbows," Liberation News Service, July 14, 1971.

100 **In the next few:** John Conyers Jr., "Grand Juries: The American Inquisition," *Ramparts*, August–September 1975.

100 **grand juries would be used:** "The FBI's Toughest Foe: 'The Kids,'" *Newsweek*, October 26, 1970.

100 **Goodwin often offered:** Wallace Turner, "Girl Arrives in Seattle for Bombing Inquiry," *New York Times*, April 30, 1971. See also Michael Drosnin, "Nixon's Radical Chaser Bags a Whopper," *New Times*, October 18, 1974.

100 **under the aegis:** Jim Irwin, "Grand Juries: A New Inquisition?" *Michigan Daily*, June 10, 1971.

101 **Many of the subpoenas:** "Coming Attractions: King Kong!!!" *Berkeley Tribe*, June 11, 1971.

101 **maintained an index:** William Greider, "10,000 'Potential Subversives,'" *Washington Post*, June 13, 1971.

101 **"I said to them":** "Washington Report," WBAI, July 27, 1971, Pacifica Radio Archives.

102 **In a press release:** Thomas K. Forcade, "A Day of Hypocrisy for Journalism," 1971, Senate Press Gallery archives (in author's possession).

Chapter 6

103 **block party outside:** Patricia O'Haire, "Dylan Misses Big-30 Bash," New York *Daily News*, May 24, 1971; "Happy Birthday Anyway, Bob," *Rolling Stone*, June 24, 1971.

103 **"Happy Birthday, Bobby junkie":** "Letters: On with the Wind," *Village Voice*, undated clipping circa January 1972, p. 98.

103 **"Abbie called and said":** A. J. Weberman, Facebook post, September 11, 2015 (no longer available online).

103 **congressional report and newspaper articles:** Anderson's syndicated column ran on May 4, 1971. The Murphy–Steele Report was issued on May 27. *The World Heroin Problem: Report of Special Study Mission: Composed of Morgan F. Murphy and Robert H. Steele, Pursuant to H. Res. 109, Authorizing the Committee on Foreign Affairs to Conduct Thorough Studies and Investigations of All Matters Coming Within the Jurisdiction of the Committee* (Washington, DC: US Government Printing Office, May 27, 1971).

103 **"I come here strictly":** Forcade's announcement of a "massive marijuana smoke-in" mentioned in *Forcade v. Knight*, Civ. A. No. 73-1258, 416 F.Supp. 1025 (1976).

104 **Yippies gathered outside:** "Son of News Briefs," *The Rag* 5, no. 33 (July 1971).

104 **"the old-time Yippies":** Tom Forcade to John Sinclair, undated, circa mid-June 1971, John and Leni Sinclair Papers, Bentley Historical Library, University of Michigan.

104 **"Jerry and Abbie definitely":** UPS press release, undated.

104 **That summer:** John Kifner, "Hippies Shower $1 Bills on Stock Exchange Floor," *New York Times*, August 25, 1967.

105 **"I had remembered":** Abbie Hoffman, "Creating a Perfect Mess," *Other Scenes*, October 1, 1968.

105 **"He was a very intense":** Michael Kirkhorn, "Hoax or Hero? Yippie Case Puzzling," *Milwaukee Journal*, August 2, 1971.

105 **"very high energy":** Kirkhorn, "Hoax or Hero?"

105 **The following year:** Pete Mingle, "Paul Yippie Captured!" Milwaukee *Kaleidoscope*, no. 99 (July 22–August 4, 1971).

105 **He was credited:** Mike Aldrich, "Free Dana Beal," *Marijuana Review*, July–September 1971.

105 **Police, dodging firecrackers:** Steve Conliff, "Smoke-In," *Columbus Free Press*, July 26–August 30, 1971.

105 **Nearby on the Mall:** "Smoke-In at the Smithsonian; Yippies Want Legal Dope," Liberation News Service, no. 356 (July 7, 1971).

106 **But between songs:** "Special Flash: 2nd Annual Smoke-In Tokes Down," UPS Press Release, July 1971.

106 **"Four cops":** "Smoke-In at the Smithsonian; Yippies Want Legal Dope," Liberation News Service, no. 356 (July 7, 1971).

106 **Around seven:** Steve Conliff, "Smoke-In," *Columbus Free Press*, July 26–August 30, 1971.

106 **"CIA heroin":** Conliff, "Smoke-In."

106 **threw hypodermic:** "Mall Is Crowded; 50 Arrests Made," *Washington Post*, July 5, 1971.

106 **Ten days later:** "Dana Beal: Prison Letter," *East Village Other*, September 22, 1971.

106 **There were warrants:** "UPS Yip Busted," *Madison Kaleidoscope*, July 21, 1971.

106 **"I am convinced":** "Dana Beal: Prison Letter," *East Village Other*, September 22, 1971.

106 **"I should have taken":** Jim Hougan, "Thumb, Pot Trip Yippie," *Capital Times*, July 22, 1971.

107 **The story appeared:** "A Major Yippie Theorist Seized on Drug Charges," *New York Times*, July 26, 1971.

107 **"very few members":** William S. Becker, "Jailed Yippie Discusses Movement," Associated Press, August 18, 1971.

107 **"It has the ingredients":** Michael Kirkhorn, "Hoax or Hero? Yippie Case Puzzling," *Milwaukee Journal*, August 2, 1971.

108 **"It's all going to be cool":** Tom Forcade to Dana Beal, undated, on Senate Press Gallery letterhead, July 1971 (in possession of the author).

108 **"I am not cooling":** Tom Forcade to Dana Beal (addressing him as alias of "Jim"), undated, circa July or August 1971, Thomas King Forcade Collection.

109 **To stage a mock:** Patricia O'Haire, "Is Paul Dead? Again?" New York *Daily News*, August 27, 1971.

109 MCCARTNEY GROUPIES: Untitled photo caption, *London Daily Mirror*, August 31, 1971.

109 **"Abbie Hoffman has first":** A. J. Weberman, "Bad Vibes," *New York Ace*, March 14, 1972.

109 **"It's a family matter":** Lynn Sherr, "'Counterculture Court' Keeps Book in Family," *Miami Herald*, September 12, 1971.

110 **article on garbology:** A. J. Weberman, "The Art of Garbage Analysis," *Esquire*, November 1971. Weberman was paid $800.

110 **Hoffman refused:** Craig Karpel, "Steal This Court," *WIN*, November 1, 1971.

110 **"it would just turn":** Sherr, "'Counterculture Court' Keeps Book in Family."

110 **"What we're trying":** Michael T. Kaufman, "Abbie Hoffman Accused Before 'Court' of Peers," *New York Times*, September 2, 1971.

110 **"The guy who was":** "The Trial" (audiocassette), Box 117, Item 39002137168176, John Holmstrom Papers and Punk Magazine Records, General Collection, Beinecke Rare Book and Manuscript Library, Yale University.

111 **"We found each":** Clyde Haberman, "Did Abbie Steal His Book? Well, His Vibrations Weren't the Best," *New York Post*, September 23, 1971.

111 **they ruled that Forcade:** "To Live Outside the Law You Must Be Honest," Liberation News Service, no. 383, October 15, 1971.

112 **"my second most famous trial":** Abbie Hoffman, "Fire in the Lake: The Image of Revolution," *East Village Other*, December 23, 1971.

112 **He was tired of:** Abbie Hoffman, "I Quit," *WIN*, September 1, 1971.

112 **"I stay away from":** Hoffman, "I Quit." See also "The Red Squad," *Newsweek*, May 31, 1971.

112 **"by a 3 to 2 vote":** Luther A. Huston, "Underground Press Writer Wins Congress Privileges," *Editor & Publisher*, September 18, 1971. The application was "quietly approved" on September 2 and revealed by the *Washington Star* nearly a week later. See also Standing Committee Minutes of September 2, 1971, Senate Press Gallery archives (in possession of author).

112 **first self-described:** James Doyle, "Radical Press Gets Foothold at Capitol," *Washington Star*, September 8, 1971.

112 **"I'm just gonna play":** "The Trial" (audiocassette), Box 117, Item 39002137168176, John Holmstrom Papers and Punk Magazine Records.

113 **In Madison, two thousand:** *UPS News & Service* 2, no. 17 (October 20, 1971).

113 **"I have yet to hear":** Tom Forcade to Dana Beal (addressing him as "Jim"), undated, circa July or August 1971 (courtesy of Judy Goodson Baker).

113 **"We smoke pot":** "Letter from the Dope Organizers," *Madison Kaleidoscope*, October 6, 1971.

113 **"Our men were in the middle of them":** June Dieckmann, "Like This, Man, City Police Form 'Affinity Squad' for Protesters," *Wisconsin State Journal*, September 28, 1971. Inspector Thomas also wrote an article about his experiences: Herman J. Thomas, "One Department's Confrontation Strategy," *FBI Law Enforcement Bulletin*, January 1973.

114 **The US Secret Service had contacted:** FBI memo from Milwaukee office to director, August 23, 1971, Dana Beal FBI file 100-467404, serials 11 and 12x, https://archive.org/details/DanaBeal/page/n11/mode/2up.

114 **About a week later:** Informant report form FD-306 to SAC-Milwaukee, October 7, 1971, file 100-162260, serial 1027. See also New York FBI office report on Youth International Party, December 17, 1971, file 100-162260, serial 1033.

114 **procured the Madison:** "Police Ask Parents to Keep Children from Yippie Event," *Wisconsin State Journal*, September 24, 1971.

114 **Graham got:** Fred P. Graham, "White House Bars a Radical Reporter," *New York Times*, November 14, 1971.

114 **Upon reading it:** Mimi Schneider (secretary to Gene DuBose, American Civil Liberties Union) to Tom Forcade, November 17, 1971.

114 **Forcade announced:** Thomas Collins, "Judge and the Press Are Miles Apart," *Newsday*, November 19, 1971.

114 **"I don't know what's":** Associated Press, "Task Force Urges Press Source Shield," *Albuquerque Journal*, November 18, 1971.

115 **"two guns, like any":** Paul W. Valentine, "White House Denies Press Pass to Radical," *Washington Post*, November 16, 1971.

115 **"the Senator from":** Thomas King Forcade, "Inside D.C.," Underground Press Syndicate, December 1971.

115 **"A reporter told me":** Thomas King Forcade, "Inside D.C.," Underground Press Syndicate, January 1972.

115 **"I spent one Friday":** Forcade, "Inside D.C.," Underground Press Syndicate, January 1972.

115 **"I hope they're not":** Peter Doggett, *There's a Riot Goin' On* (Canongate, 2007), 446, citing Peter McCabe and Robert D. Schonfeld, *Apple to the Core* (Pocket Books, 1972).

116 **"I thought that when Dylan":** Jon Wiener, *Come Together: John Lennon in His Time* (Random House, 1984).

116 **Yoko Ono ensured:** A. J. Weberman, "Enemies of the People: The Truth About the Y.I.P.—Zippies," *International Times*, August 26, 1973.

116 **"Dear People":** "The Last Word," *Village Voice*, December 9, 1971.

116 **He stepped to:** Jeff Hale, "Wiretapping and National Security: Nixon, the Mitchell Doctrine, and the White Panthers" (PhD diss., Louisiana State University, 1995).

117 **Three days later, the Michigan:** Hale, "Wiretapping and National Security."

117 **"We've been planning":** Stu Werbin, "John & Jerry & David & John & Leni & Yoko," *Rolling Stone*, February 17, 1972.

118 **"the only real revolutionary":** "New Morning—Changing Weather," as recounted in Jeremy Varon, *Bringing the War Home* (University of California Press, 2004), 182–183.

118 **"Women took over":** *Hearings Before the Committee on Internal Security, House of Representatives, National Peace Action Coalition (NPAC) and Peoples Coalition for Peace & Justice (PCPJ), Part 4,* Ninety-Second Congress, First Session (US Government Printing Office, 1972), 3584 (testimony of Francis M. Watson Jr., July 21, 1971).

118 **threatened to turn:** A. J. Weberman to Albert Goldman, April 23, 1983, Box 23, Tape 5, Albert Goldman Papers, 1953–1994, University Archives, Rare Book & Manuscript Library, Columbia University Libraries.

118 **"Our staff is small":** *UPS News Service* 2, no. 26 (December 24, 1971).

118 **"a convention for":** "Convention!" *UPS Weekly News Dissemination & Intertribal Bulletins* 2, no. 18 (undated).

119 **"discriminative elitism":** FBI memo from Milwaukee Bureau to director, January 10, 1972, FBI file 100-NY-162260, serial 1042, https://www.governmentattic.org/4docs/FBI-YIPPIES_1967-1977.pdf.

119 **New and dynamic leadership:** FBI file 100-162260, serial 1054.

119 **Weberman even said:** A. J. Weberman, "Bad Vibes," *New York Ace*, January 11, 1972.

119 **"neither of these zany":** *FBI Current Intelligence Analysis* 2, no. 1 (January 17, 1972).

119 **"The Republicans don't":** *UPS News Service* 3, no. 2 (January 21, 1972).

119 **And, Forcade said:** FBI memo from Milwaukee bureau to director, January 9, 1972, FBI file 100-162260, serial 1041.

120   **"Hippies are gone":** Dave Wagner, "Yippies Huddle Here, Hatch Plans for National Convention 'Circuses,'" *Capital Times*, January 10, 1972.

120   **"Zippie Party Freek Circus":** "Zippie! Yippie Ti Yi Yo Yi Yay!" *Take Over*, January 1972.

120   **"Don't Take Youth":** *FBI Current Intelligence Analysis* 2, no. 1 (January 17, 1972).

120   **"Confusion reigns":** Thomas Forcade, "Two More Views of the Miami Convention," *The Realist*, no. 97A (August 1973).

121   **"He was like Captain Gentle":** Associated Press, "AWOL Private Indicted in Bombing Case," *Pottstown (PA) Mercury*, January 19, 1972.

121   **Days earlier:** FBI Airtel from SAC Detroit to director, Att: Domestic Intelligence Division, February 2, 1972, FBI file 100-HQ-469538, serial 8 (copy in author's possession). FBI records show that the informant and Forcade discussed business and the *Fifth Estate*. On April 1, 2011, John and Leni Sinclair told an interviewer for the Ann Arbor District Library that the *Fifth Estate* accountant was an FBI informant ("So when he'd figure out your taxes, he'd file them with the FBI first, the motherfucker.") (https://aadl.org/node/254101). In an undated (probably 1971) letter from Forcade to that same accountant, Forcade complains that he'd never received his income tax forms from the accountant and that "the income tax people are really bugging me" (letter in author's possession).

121   **"He was trying to":** FBI report from New York field office to bureau and Secret Service, February 2, 1972, FBI file 100-HQ-469538, serial 6.

121   **"the Capitol building is":** Thomas King Forcade, "Inside DC," *Sweet Fire*, January 1–31, 1972.

121   **"Our cities are":** *Address on the State of the Union Delivered Before a Joint Session of the Congress*, January 20, 1972.

121   **During the speech:** "Eye," *Women's Wear Daily*, January 21, 1972.

122   **"They had at least":** Thomas Forcade, "The State of the Onion," *UPS News Service* 3, no. 2 (January 21, 1972).

122   **"I was sitting above":** Forcade, "The State of the Onion."

122   **Three days after:** FBI memo on Thomas King Forcade, May 1, 1972, FBI file 100-HQ-469538, serial 19.

122   **"Under no circumstances":** Jerry Warren memo, January 31, 1972, Gerald Lee Warren Papers, Hoover Institution Library and Archives, Palo Alto.

122   **"Unfortunately, not too much":** A. J. Weberman, "Bad Vibes," *New York Ace*, February 15, 1972. See also "Riffs: Rock On & Rocks Off," *Village Voice*, February 17, 1972.

122   **"deeply political moves":** Robert B. Stulberg, "10,000 Non-delegates Expected Here During Democratic Convention," *Miami News*, February 2, 1972.

123   **Silver Cloud Rolls-Royce:** Memo from SAC Tampa to director, May 1, 1972, FBI file 100-HQ-469538, serial 18.

123   **In Washington, DC:** FBI report from New York field office to bureau and Secret Service, February 2, 1972, FBI file 100-HQ-469538, serial 6.

123   **FBI agents then visited:** FBI Airtel from SAC New York to director, March 1, 1972, FBI file 100-HQ-469538, serial 10.

123   **Around that time:** Mike Dorgan, "U.S. Aided Police Spying Here," *Capital Times*, February 6, 1975.

123   **"Let the Rock Speak!":** Report from Chicago FBI office on Youth International Party (YIP), February 24, 1972, FBI file 80-HQ-1353, serial 86 (copy in author's possession).

123   **"On gaining any interest":** Report from Chicago FBI office on Youth International Party (YIP), February 24, 1972, FBI file 80-HQ-1353, serial 86. After the promised

March 31 David Peel benefit never happened, the Chicago Zippies threw in the towel.

124   **Observing from chairs:** Hugh "Buck" Davis, "A People's History of the CIA Bombing Conspiracy (the Keith Case); Or, How the White Panthers Saved the Movement" (speech), Detroit and Michigan National Lawyers Guild Annual Dinner, 2010.

124   **"one of the most dangerous":** Arthur Kinoy, *Rights on Trial* (Harvard University Press, 1983).

125   **Attorney General Richard Kleindienst wrote:** Richard G. Kleindienst, *Justice: The Memoirs of Attorney General Richard Kleindienst* (Jameson Books, 1985).

125   **In the meantime, Robert:** Ronald J. Ostrow, "Justice Dept. Aide to Help Nixon Drive," *Los Angeles Times*, February 29, 1972.

125   **"Hold it!":** The altercations with Klein and Spector were assembled from the following sources: Frank Rose, "Bangladesh & Allen Klein: 'We Came for the $3 Million,'" *Village Voice*, March 9, 1972; Ben Fong-Torres, "Did Allen Klein Take Bangla Desh Money?" *Rolling Stone*, March 30, 1972; and A. J. Weberman, "Weberman Beats Up Phil Spector," *New York Ace*, March 14, 1972. A version of the "Dine with Klein" announcement appeared in the *New York Ace*, February 29, 1972, after the "Bad Vibes" column.

126   **MUSIC EXECS FREE FOOD PROGRAM:** 1972 flyer, provided by A. J. Weberman.

127   **Through Ron Rosenbaum's:** Handwritten note provided by A. J. Weberman.

128   **invited Weberman:** Peter Doggett, *There's a Riot Going On* (Canongate, 2007), 486.

129   **Arriving in Manhattan:** Coca Crystal, "The Stony Brook Conference: National Radical Attempt Fails," *New York Ace*, March 15, 1972; FBI memo from Milwaukee, April 26, 1972, FBI file 100-162260, serial 1107, which was also reproduced in Jon Wiener, *Gimme Some Truth: The John Lennon FBI Files* (University of California Press, 2000).

129   **"He lives in":** FBI memo from Milwaukee, April 26, 1972, FBI file 100-162260, serial 1107.

131   **On Monday, the US Immigration:** Keith Badman, *The Beatles Diary, Volume 2: After the Break-Up, 1970–2001* (Omnibus, 2001), 68.

131   **"Jerry couldn't keep":** David Sheff, with G. Barry Golson, ed., *The Playboy Interviews with John Lennon and Yoko Ono* (Playboy Press, 1981).

131   **The Red Squad:** Gloria Emerson, *Winners & Losers: Battles, Retreats, Gains, Losses, and Ruins from the Vietnam War* (Random House, 1976), 206.

132   **"I took the opportunity":** Gabrielle Schang (uncredited), "Pat Smells a Rat," UPS News Service, March 17, 1972. Additional details were drawn from "Rats for Pat," *New York Ace*, March 28, 1972.

132   **"I felt like I had been":** Gabrielle Schang to Albert Goldman, January 1979, Box 61, Tape 9, Albert Goldman Papers.

133   **"10,000 naked Yippies":** Robert Stulberg, "Rubin Hooked a Few Here with Flashy News Bait," *Miami News*, February 19, 1972.

133   **Forcade advised Rubin:** FBI memo from Milwaukee office, FBI file 80-MM-1353, serial 328 (copy in author's possession).

133   **"Yippies, on to Miami!":** Ernest Leogrande, "After Y Comes Z," Night Owl Reporter, New York *Daily News*, April 6, 1972.

133   **"Forcade doesn't like":** John Belknap and Nick Schaffner, "Underground's Latest Garbage, Part Two," *Cold Duck*, April 17, 1972.

133   **"Jerry had this":** Tom Forcade to Dana Beal, circa April 1972.

134   **The local undergrounds:** "1969–1972: Chronology of Terror," *San Diego Door*, August 17, 1972.

134   **"I wish there was a way":** Lowell Bergman and Maxwell Robach, "Nixon's 'Lucky City': C. Arnholt Smith and the San Diego Connection," *Ramparts*, October 1973.

134   **But in early 1972:** Doug Porter, "IT & T & GOP—Bedpartners?" *San Diego Door*, February 10–24, 1972. The *Washington Star* had earlier mentioned the $400,000 in the context of the antitrust suit, quoting M. Larry Lawrence as saying Harold Geneen "is very close to the president and was having an anti-trust problem" (Robert Walters, "Money and Politics—Convention Pledge for GOP Questioned," *Washington Star*, November 29, 1971).

134   **Weeks later, syndicated reporter:** Jack Anderson, with George Clifford, *The Anderson Papers* (Random House, 1973), 61. Nixon had told then–Deputy AG Kleindienst to drop the IT&T case; Kleindienst, nominated on February 15, was finally sworn in as attorney general on June 12, 1972.

134   **"taken steps to neutralize":** Denny Walsh and Tom Flaherty, "Tampering with Justice in San Diego," *Life*, March 24, 1972.

135   **SDCC members' tires:** "1969–1972: Chronology of Terror," *San Diego Door*, August 17, 1972.

135   **Heightening paranoia:** Citizens Research and Investigation Committee and Louis E. Tackwood, *The Glass House Tapes* (Avon, 1973). See also: Michael Blake, "Tackwood," *Berkeley Barb*, October 22–28, 1971; Richard E. Sprague, "The June 1972 Raid on Democratic Party Headquarters (the Watergate Incident), Part 2," *Computers and Automation*, October 1972; Peter Biskind, "The FBI's Secret Soldiers," *New Times*, January 9, 1976. There is also the following information from Richard Popkin, seemingly unique to his account: "[Tackwood] told of preparations to seal off and then bomb 100,000 demonstrators attending a rock concert on Fiesta Island in Mission Bay, San Diego. All sorts of mayhem was supposed to occur. Bombs were to be smuggled into Convention Center in hollow furniture, which was already being built in Los Angeles. At least one major Republican official would perish in the melee. The Democratic Party would be tied into the events, discredited, possibly outlawed.... [Tackwood] now adds that the plan also called for blowing up the podium as President Nixon was making his acceptance speech!" (Richard Popkin, "The Strange Tale of the Secret Army Organization (USA)," *Ramparts*, October 1973).

135   **"FUCKED AGAIN":** "Underground Press Zaps Journaloids," *UPS News* 3, no. 9 (May 16, 1972).

136   **"Z comes after Y":** Sally Quinn, "Journalism's New Nation," *Washington Post*, April 26, 1972.

137   **"If the Democrats are":** UPI, "Top Yippies Get Behind McGovern," *San Bernardino County Sun*, April 24, 1972.

137   **"shouts of applause":** Quinn, "Journalism's New Nation."

137   **"Apparently the people":** "Jackson Calls McGovern Spokesman for Extremism," UPI, April 26, 1972.

137   **"Hoffman, Jerry Rubin, Angela Davis":** Memo from Richard Nixon to John Mitchell, June 6, 1972, quoted in Winzola McLendon, *Martha: The Life of Martha Mitchell* (Random House, 1979).

137   **"The Yippies' Karl Marx":** Michael Kernan, "The Yippies' Karl Marx," *Washington Post*, February 13, 1972.

137   **out of jail:** Bruce Swain, "Jailing of Dana Beal Again Won't Deter the Yippies' Plans," *Capital Times*, April 12, 1972. Beal was sentenced and returned to jail on May 19.

137   **UNCLE KARL SEZ:** "Smoke-Out April 29, 1972," *Take Over*, May 1972.

137   **"Karleton Armstrong has":** Swain, "Jailing of Dana Beal."

138 **"We want a guaranteed":** Frank Rose, "Smoke-In Rocks Albany," UPS News Service, May 16, 1972.

138 **Beal was also excited:** FBI file 80-MM-1353, serials 290 and 328.

138 **"We're Yippies & we're Zippies":** "Rap with Jerry Rubin," *Take Over*, May 10, 1972.

138 **"Some New York Yip/Zips":** "Rap with Jerry Rubin," *Take Over*, May 10, 1972.

138 **On May 5, 1972:** Vincent S. Ancona, "When the Elephants Marched Out of San Diego," *Journal of San Diego History*, Fall 1992.

139 **"It's bullshit":** "High!" flyer, undated.

139 **On campus:** "Rallies, Trashing, and Shootings," *Wisconsin State Journal*, May 15, 1972.

139 **The tensions climaxed:** "Letter from the Dope Organizers," *Madison Kaleidoscope*, October 6, 1971.

139 **"creating an incredible":** Sam Martino, "Undercover Police Move Among Madison Radicals," *Minneapolis Tribune*, May 28, 1972.

139 **"Perhaps the highlight":** Herman J. Thomas, "One Department's Confrontation Strategy," *FBI Law Enforcement Bulletin*, January 1973.

140 **"They think we're going":** *The Dick Cavett Show*, episode dated May 11, 1972, John and Yoko return to the Cavett stage and perform live, written by Jean Doumanian.

140 **"Make sandcastles":** "A Delegation to the Convention," *New York Post*, May 15, 1972.

140 **"We are going to stress":** Video excerpt of Zippie press conference (in author's possession).

140 **"The Yippies called me":** Forcade to Beal, undated, c. April 1972.

Chapter 7

142 **"the American public":** Memo from Captain [redacted] to Chief Pomerance, June 1, 1972, FBI file 80-MM-1353, serial 581 (copy in author's possession); the meeting took place on May 19, 1972.

142 **"satisfying":** Robert Stulberg, "Zippies List Plans for Peaceful Protests," *Miami News*, May 19, 1972.

142 **"launch an attack":** Memo from Miami FBI field office, June 2, 1972, FBI file 80-MM-1353, serial 577.

143 **Forcade took the news:** FBI informant report sent to SAC Detroit, June 5, 1972, FBI file 100-NY-162260, serial 1181. Accessed at https://www.governmentattic.org/4docs/FBI-YIPPIES_1967-1977.pdf.

143 **According to an FBI:** Miami field office report, June 21, 1972, FBI file 100-HQ-469538, serial 23 (copy in author's possession).

143 **A pair of Miami:** Nancy Miller Saunders, *Combat by Trial* (iUniverse, 2008), 282.

143 **Then the attendees:** Saunders, *Combat by Trial*, 290–291. See also Edward Zuckerman, "Of Causeways and LSD: Rumors over Miami," *Village Voice*, July 6, 1972.

143 **The vets transitioned:** Timothy Robinson, "Antiwar Veterans Accused of Training Political Killers," *Washington Post*, August 7, 1973; Robert D. Shaw Jr., "'Political Assassination Teams' Set Up by Vet, FBI Informer-Witness Testifies," *Miami Herald*, August 7, 1972.

143 **unnamed Zippie:** George Metefsky, "More CREEP-Gainesville Links," *Yipster Times*, August 1973.

143 **On Sunday:** Saunders, *Combat by Trial*, 294; David Smith and Myra Forsberg, "Third Gov't Witness Gives Testimony," *Independent Florida Alligator*, August 16, 1973.

143 **"bag some Republicans":** David Harris, "Hogtown Justice: The VVAW and the '72 Republican Convention," *Rolling Stone*, February 14, 1974.

144 **Lemmer told a passenger:** Harris, "Hogtown Justice"; Nancy A. Miller, "Watergate South," *Computers and People*, December 1974.

144 **Camil thought:** Saunders, *Combat by Trial*, 296.

144 **The next day, Camil:** Rob Elder, "Spy Job Offer at Convention Revealed," *Miami Herald*, May 23, 1973; Rob Elder, "Police Informer Offered Guns to VVAW," *Miami Herald*, May 26, 1973; Saunders, *Combat by Trial*, 297; Gerald Nicosia, *Home to War: A History of the Vietnam Veterans' Movement* (Carroll & Graf, 2004), 261.

144 **"If you need help":** Harris, "Hogtown Justice."

144 **wearing a wire:** Doug Clifton, "Bugging of Vets Failed, Officer Says," *Miami Herald*, June 22, 1973.

144 **"If they want violence":** Warren Rogers, "Countdown," Chicago Tribune New York News Syndicate, May 22, 1972.

144 **"vigilante squad":** Raul Ramirez and Paul W. Valentine, "Phony Hippies Enlisted Fernandez," *Washington Post*, May 26, 1973. Although the *Miami Herald*'s Rob Elder broke the story of Pablo Fernandez's involvement with the Watergate burglars, Fernandez claimed that Elder had distorted his words; he told the FBI that the Ramirez/Valentine *Washington Post* story was more accurate.

145 **The reports filled out by Fernandez:** Carl Bernstein and Bob Woodward, "Spy Funds Linked to GOP Aides," *Washington Post*, September 17, 1972; Harris, "Hogtown Justice." In the White House Plumbers hierarchy, Eugenio Martinez worked for Bernard Barker, and they both operated under the command of James McCord.

145 **"The biggest problems":** "Moving on Miami," *UPS News Service* 3, no. 10 (June 1, 1972).

145 **"Let me squelch":** Frank Rose and Anastasia Sirrocco, "Rocky Raccoon: Interview with the Chief," UPS News Service, July 1, 1972.

145 **"Come out and fight!":** FBI file 100-NY-162260, serial 1185. Accessed at https://www.governmentattic.org/4docs/FBI-YIPPIES_1967-1977.pdf.

145 **They found Forcade:** FBI file 100-NY-162260, serial 1169. These events were also covered in "Potential Disruptions at the Democratic National Convention," an Intelligence Evaluation Committee report prepared for the Acting Director of the FBI on June 9, 1972.

146 **"If the case had been won":** Arthur Kinoy, *Rights on Trial* (Harvard University Press, 1983), 36.

146 **"I knew from my earlier":** L. Patrick Gray, *In Nixon's Web: A Year in the Crosshairs of Watergate* (Times Books, 2008), 62.

146 **"You could probably":** "The Law: New Curb on Bugging," *Time*, July 3, 1972.

147 **The fallout:** Because the Keith case did not address wiretapping of foreign targets, President Jimmy Carter signed the Foreign Intelligence Surveillance Act into law on October 25, 1978. The Keith case still holds for domestic wiretapping. For in-depth looks at the legacy of the Keith decision, see Trevor W. Morrison, "The Story of United States v. United States District Court (Keith): Surveillance Power," *Columbia Public Law & Legal Theory Working Papers*, No. 08155, 2008; and Jeff A. Hale, "Wiretapping and National Security: Nixon, the Mitchell Doctrine, and the White Panthers. Volume I" (PhD diss., Louisiana State University, 1995).

147 **In the coming months:** Hugh "Buck" Davis, "A People's History of the CIA Bombing Conspiracy (the Keith Case); Or, How the White Panthers Saved the Movement" (speech), Detroit and Michigan National Lawyers Guild Annual Dinner, 2010.

147 **"Depending on the rains":** Untitled Zippie press release included in FBI memo from Miami Field Office, FBI file 100-NY-162260, serial 1276.

147 **"In 1938 Chamberlain":** Edward Zuckerman, "The Siege of Miami Beach," *Village Voice*, June 22, 1972.

147 **"Tom Forcade is coming":** Fred Barger, "Miami Beach Turns Down Campsite Bid," *Miami Herald*, June 24, 1972.

147 **"You're going to throw":** Edna Buchanan, "Zippie Gets 90-Day Term in Beach Pie-Throwing Case," *Miami Herald*, July 7, 1972.

147 **Rosen, a six-foot-two:** Nicholas C. Chriss, "Pie Thrown at Official in Convention Dispute," *Los Angeles Times*, June 24, 1972.

148 **Small was thrilled:** Buzz Kliman, "Covering the Convention Disguised as a Famous Person," *Daily Planet*, August 10, 1972.

148 **"We think this attack":** AP, "Miami Council Rejects Camp for Convention Protesters," *Austin Statesman*, June 24, 1972.

148 **"Throwing a pie":** Kliman, "Covering the Convention Disguised."

148 **"construct a symbolic":** "¡LBJ Si! ¡Ché No!" Zippie press release included in FBI memo from Miami Field Office, FBI file 100-NY-162260, serial 1276.

148 **Before the convention had even:** Confidential informant report included in FBI memo from Miami Field Office, FBI file 100-NY-162260, serial 1276.

148 **At the end of one:** Confidential informant report included in FBI memo from Miami Field Office, FBI file 100-NY-162260, serial 1276; "A Split Surfaces at Tent Village," *Miami News*, July 7, 1972.

148 **"whipped to a frenzy":** Thomas King Forcade, "Childhood's End," *Daily Planet*, July 10, 1972.

150 **"Shh, they're on the line":** Helene E. Schwartz, *Lawyering* (Farrar, Straus and Giroux, 1976).

150 **On July 7:** Frank Luyando, Special Intelligence Services Comm. no. 854, July 7, 1972, Box 13, Folder 5, New York Police Department Intelligence Records, 1931–1988, Municipal Archives, City of New York.

150 **It didn't thwart:** Confidential informant report included in FBI memo from Miami Field Office, FBI file 100-NY-162260, serial 1276.

150 **They eventually gave:** Martin Walker, "Came the Revolution," *The Guardian* (UK), July 12, 1972.

150 **Forcade and Ornsteen, scouting:** Jo Werne, "Have You Seen LBJ?" *Miami Herald*, July 8, 1972; June Kronholz, "2 Zippies Freed; Pie Tosser Faces Marijuana Term," *Miami Herald*, October 25, 1972.

150 **"lack of humor":** Edna Buchanan, "Zippie Gets 90-Day Term in Beach Pie-Throwing Case," *Miami Herald*, July 7, 1972.

150 **The City of Miami Beach:** Lee Winfrey, "Hopes Mount for Peaceful Convention," *Philadelphia Inquirer*, July 9, 1972.

150 **In the basement:** Rob Elder, "Convention Spy Data Called 'Garbage,'" *Miami Herald*, June 10, 1973.

151 **"It was the earliest":** Keith Stroup, "A Founder Looks at 50: Tom Forcade, Michael J. Kennedy and High Times Magazine," NORML.org, May 29, 2020.

151 **"When I saw that huge crowd":** Bud (Michael Chance) Bogart, "The Forcade Be with You: Trans-High Market Analysis," *High Times*, June 1984.

151 **The Zippies engineered:** Michael Chance, "Report from Miami," *Take Over*, July 14, 1972.

151 **curious senior citizens:** Ken Gepfert, "Zippies Skinny Dip at Flamingo Park Pool," Associated Press, July 8, 1972.

151 **They'd figured out:** Rob Elder, "Police Admit Infiltrating Veterans Group," *Miami Herald*, July 9, 1972.

152 **The Milwaukee FBI:** Teletype from Milwaukee field office to acting director, July 5, 1972, Dana Beal FBI file 100-HQ-467404, serial number illegible (copy in author's possession).

152 **Mike Roselle hitchhiked:** Mike Roselle, with Josh Mahan, *Tree Spiker* (St. Martin's Press, 2009).

152 GET HIGH!: Rex Weiner, "Trepidation & Disgust in Miami," *Georgia Straight*, July 27–August 3, 1972.

152 **its odometer:** Tony Fuller, "Chopped Liver, Dope Mingle in Miami Park," *Chicago Daily News*, July 10, 1972.

153 **Forcade carried:** Weiner, "Trepidation & Disgust in Miami."

153 **A. J. Weberman was already:** Confidential informant report included in FBI memo from Miami Field Office, FBI file 100-NY-162260, serial 1276.

153 **"We never viewed":** Rob Elder, "Protesters Vary: Hip to Zip to Gay," *Miami Herald*, July 9, 1972.

153 **"They're under contract":** Anthony Burton, "Zippies Zap Yippie Biggies, Call 'Em Gyppies," New York *Daily News*, July 7, 1972.

153 **"There are times":** "A Split Surfaces at Tent Village," *Miami News*, July 7, 1972.

154 **"a receptionist":** Burton, "Zippies Zap Yippie Biggies."

154 **"Dostoyevskian snit-hassles":** Allen Ginsberg to Gary Snyder, July 22, 1972, as published in Bill Morgan, ed., *The Selected Letters of Allen Ginsberg and Gary Snyder, 1956–1991* (Counterpoint, 2009).

154 **Forcade led Weiner:** Weiner, "Trepidation & Disgust in Miami."

154 **"The smoke-in is actually":** Confidential informant report included in FBI memo from Miami Field Office, FBI file 100-NY-162260, serial 1276.

155 **"Trying to bust us":** Pete Gallagher, "Protest City Even Survives Public Pot-In," *Florida Today*, July 10, 1972. (The article mistakenly attributed the comments to Forcade.)

155 **The thirty-foot:** Roselle and Mahan, *Tree Spiker*.

155 **"The anti-heroin march":** *Beach Blanket Struggle*, no. 5 (July 11, 1972).

155 **"Several old people":** Nora Sayre, *Sixties Going on Seventies*, rev. ed. (Rutgers University Press, 1996), 279. The author also consulted Sayre's research files on the 1972 Convention, which reside in the Nora Sayre Papers, Box 24, Folders 4–6, Manuscripts and Archives Division, New York Public Library.

156 **"The entire march":** *Beach Blanket Struggle*, no. 5 (July 11, 1972).

156 **That afternoon, Forcade:** Chip Berlet, "Warmup for the Nixon Game," *Straight Creek Journal*, August 3, 1972.

156 **"Give George back":** Michael Chance, "Report from Miami," *Take Over*, July 14, 1972.

157 **"We're way beyond":** Ken Gepfert, "Cool Reception for McGovern by Young Radicals," Associated Press, *Santa Cruz Sentinel*, July 12, 1972.

157 **"We didn't come here":** Ben Taylor, "Day in Flamingo Park," *Palm Beach Post*, July 16, 1972.

157 **At last, around 8:00 p.m.:** William Tucker, "McGovern Confronts Demonstrators," *Miami News*, July 14, 1972.

158 **"I do not believe":** The exchange between McGovern and Beal was transcribed by the author from video of the CBS News broadcast, viewed at https://youtu.be/Cp-FJWKBIOg. For other accounts of the Doral Hotel appearance, see Mike Baxter,

"'I'm Not Shifting Position on Any Fundamental Stands,'" *Miami Herald*, July 14, 1972, and Berlet, "Warmup for the Nixon Game."

159   **"Well, Walter":** Judy Bachrach, "TV Finally Acknowledges a Convention Protest," *Baltimore Sun*, July 13, 1972.

159   **The Zippies moved LBJ:** Eric Himmel, "The Democratic National Convention: American Political Ideal?" *Middlebury Campus*, September 28, 1972.

159   **"Eat shit":** Berlet, "Warmup for the Nixon Game."

159   **George McGovern officially:** David Nyhan and Martin F. Nolan, "McGovern Wins Nomination in Runaway on First Ballot," *Boston Globe*, July 13, 1972.

159   **Forcade's Cadillac:** FBI teletype from Miami field office to acting director, July 13, 1972, FBI file 100-NY-162260, serial 1272.

159   **"We have consistently":** "A Pledge to Non-Violence & Harmony," Zippie press release, included in FBI memo from Miami Field Office, FBI file 100-NY-162260, serial 1276.

160   **A week later, the Dade County:** "Is Vets Group Backed by Illicit Drug Sales?" *Tampa Tribune*, July 20, 1972. This article also disclosed that Alton Foss, the coordinator of the 250-member Dade County chapter of VVAW, was arrested on the afternoon of July 18 for selling three tabs of LSD to undercover agents.

160   **"They called Pat Small a cop!":** Raw footage from TVTV video *Four More Years*, Tape 64a, 17-minute mark, uploaded to the Internet Archive by the Berkeley Art Museum and Pacific Film Archive Film Library & Study Center, University of California.

161   **"The acid was":** "Inside the Hall," *UPS News*, July 16, 1972.

161   **"Everywhere that the":** FBI memo from Miami field office to bureau, September 28, 1972, FBI file 100-467404, serial 25.

161   **"This was a dress rehearsal":** Terry Ryan, "Leftists More Militant Toward GOP," *Washington Star*, July 16, 1972. This quote was highlighted in the July 1972 issue of the FBI newsletter *The Extremist Speaks*.

161   **"It is almost as if":** Don Oakley, "Yippies Helping Nixon?" Newspaper Enterprise Association (NEA) (syndicated), July 24, 1972.

161   **"We won't be threatening":** Anthony Burton, "Dellinger and Davis Draw a Bead on the GOP," New York *Daily News*, July 14, 1972.

162   **"Tom Forcade, depending":** Buzz Kilman, "Movement Politics Stall in Month of the Pig," *Daily Planet*, n.d. These events describe August 13–14.

162   **"Red Star One":** Michael S. Burns, "The Veterans of Flamingo Park," *Louisville Courier & Times*, August 27, 1972.

162   **"What we don't need here":** Kilman, "Movement Politics Stall." These events describe August 13–14.

162   **"Nobody was calling":** William A. Clark, "Thursday, in the Park," *Palm Beach Post*, August 18, 1972.

162   **"Tom Forcade dealt":** "Wanted: Tom Forcade" flyer from 1972, printed in *Yipster Times*, no. 5 (March 1973).

162   **"Whenever you get":** Warren Sloat, "Even the Protesters Have Their Problems," *Home News* (New Brunswick, NJ), August 23, 1972.

162   **The section of the park:** Clark, "Thursday, in the Park."

163   **"We went over":** Interview with John D. "Gunny" Musgrave, 1541AU1593, June 12, 1978, Nancy Miller Saunders Collection, Vietnam Center and Sam Johnson Vietnam Archive, Texas Tech University.

163   **"It's not that they're":** Michael S. Burns, "The Veterans of Flamingo Park," *Courier-Journal & Times* (Louisville), August 27, 1972.

163 **On August 18:** Carl Bernstein and Bob Woodward, "GOP Aide Says Funds Used to Study Radicals," *Washington Post*, August 18, 1972.

163 **Liddy was specifically:** *Hearings Before the Select Committee on Presidential Campaign Activities of the United States Senate: Watergate and Related Activities*, Ninety-Third Congress, First Session (November 1, 1973) (testimony of Clark MacGregor), Phase II: Campaign Practices, Washington, DC.

164 **"I had a queasy":** Lucian K. Truscott IV, "The Coronation of Richard Nixon," *Saturday Review*, September 16, 1972.

164 **"When the war":** Terry Ryan, "Antiwar Action at Convention Probably Last Big Protest," Associated Press, *Racine Journal-Times Sunday Bulletin*, August 20, 1972.

164 **"I doubt if":** Larry Sloman, *Steal This Dream: Abbie Hoffman and the Countercultural Revolution in America* (Doubleday, 1998), 263.

164 **The *Gazette* informed:** *Flamingo Park Gazette*, August 22, 1972.

165 **"Piss on it!":** Chip Berlet and Henry Doering, "The Other Miami Story," *Straight Creek Journal*, August 31, 1972.

165 **It was still eighty-five:** Lee Winfrey, "Viet Veterans Against the War Make War Against Nazi Speakers at Miami Campsite," *Philadelphia Inquirer*, August 21, 1972.

166 **"Let's tear them":** John Burks, "Anti-War Vets Rout the Nazis," *San Francisco Examiner*, August 21, 1972.

166 **The VVAW tried:** Tom Fitzpatrick, "A 'Lynch Mob' in Miami Park Routs 19 Nazi Fanatics," *Chicago Sun-Times*, August 21, 1972.

166 **"The MCC told me":** "Miami Beach Demos from the Inside Out," *Liberation News Service*, no. 463 (September 6, 1972).

166 **Then the Zippie:** *Flamingo Park Gazette*, August 21, 1972.

166 **They kicked off:** "Anarchy Rock," *Yipster Times*, no. 4 (December 1972–January 1973).

167 **For the finale:** Steven Wishnia, "You Animals Don't Have Any Constitutional Rights," *The Indypendent*, May 6–June 15, 2003; Steve Jackson and Morty Rich, "Views from Both Sides of the Barricades," *Rice Thresher* (Houston, TX), August 31, 1972.

167 **They also threw:** Norman Solomon, *In the Belly of the Dinosaurs* (Out of the Ashes Press, 1972).

167 **"Because one weirdo":** "Zippie: The Living End," *Yipster Times*, no. 1 (1972).

167 **In fact, newspapers:** Anthony Burton, "Delegates Jostled, Insulted by Demonstrators," New York *Daily News*, August 23, 1972.

167 **Inside the main entrance:** Report by Lem Tucker, "ABC Evening News—1972 Republican Convention," YouTube video, 13:51, August 23, 1972, efan2011, https://youtu.be/H_O2ZybAF3E.

168 **"This truck is under arrest":** FBI interview report from Tampa field office, March 8, 1973, FBI file 100-TP-2958, serial number unknown (copy in author's possession).

168 **In the passenger seat:** Schwartz, *Lawyering*, 239–270.

168 **The streets were soon:** Tim Findley, "Outside the Convention: Cops and Confusion," *Rolling Stone*, September 28, 1972.

169 **Motorists tried to:** Mike Baxter, "More Than 800 Are Arrested After Spreading Street Chaos," *Miami Herald*, August 24, 1972.

169 **One group of Zippies:** Schwartz, *Lawyering*; and Chip Berlet and Henry Doering, "The Other Miami Story," *Straight Creek Journal*, August 31, 1972.

169 **"Look, you can't barbecue":** Steve Conliff, interview by Terese Coe, October 25, 1979, Terese Coe Papers.

169 **shouting, "Eat the rich!":** Mike Baxter, "More Than 800 Are Arrested After Spreading Street Chaos," *Miami Herald*, August 24, 1972.

169   **"We always knew"**: Mark Gallagher, "F.U.C.ed again!" *Yipster Times* 1, no. 1 (September 1972).

169   **He was charged**: Ric Reynolds, "Miami, Miami," *San Diego Door*, September 10–21, 1972.

169   **Inside the hall, the air-conditioning**: Baxter, "More Than 800 Are Arrested."

172   **Dellinger, who'd just**: Andrew E. Hunt, *David Dellinger: The Life and Times of a Nonviolent Revolutionary* (New York University Press, 2006).

172   **"aggravated assault"**: "Zippies Rescene," *Berkeley Barb*, November 3–9, 1972.

172   **two of only five**: June Kronholz, "365 Jailed Protesters Follow Freed Leaders," *Miami Herald*, August 26, 1972.

172   **She was a former beauty queen**: Carolyn Jay Wright, "Ellen Morphonios: From Beauty Queen to Criminal Judge," *Miami Herald*, July 4, 1971.

173   **On the advice**: June Kronholz, "2 Zippies Freed; Pie Tosser Faces Marijuana Term," *Miami Herald*, October 25, 1972.

173   **"If this is the guy"**: Rosa Wild, "Jailhouse Rock," *Yipster Times*, no. 4 (December 1972–January 1973).

173   **"Nixon paid me"**: Bob Kochersberger, "Felony Charged After City Man's Siege at GOP HQ," and Tom Muller, "Protest Messages Replace Nixon Posters," *Binghamton Press and Sun Bulletin*, November 1, 1972.

173   **"at a high level"**: Mike Royko, "Zippie Leader a Spy from White House?" *Atlanta Constitution*, October 19, 1972.

173   **"When the coordinating"**: Allen Katzman, "Poor Paranoid's Almanac," *Straight Creek Journal*, November 7, 1972.

174   **"the only service"**: Allen Katzman, "Poor Paranoid's Almanac," *Straight Creek Journal*, December 19, 1972.

174   **"During the Convention, the government"**: David Dellinger, *From Yale to Jail: The Life Story of a Moral Dissenter* (Pantheon, 1993).

174   **"radical, long-haired kids"**: Carl Bernstein and Bob Woodward, "Lawyer Says He Wouldn't Help GOP Stage Demonstration," *Washington Post*, November 1, 1972.

175   **"was known to have"**: Jack Anderson, "Washington Merry-Go-Round" (United Features Syndicate column), November 5, 1972.

175   **"inundated with hate mail"**: Jack Anderson, "Washington Merry-Go-Round" (syndicated column), November 9, 1972.

Chapter 8

178   **John Latham Goodson**: "Makes His Friends Pay His Way," *Omaha Daily Bee*, October 2, 1897.

178   **"The crooked transactions"**: "John L. Goodson's Financial Schemes," *Graham Post*, story reprinted in the *Savannah Reporter*, October 15, 1897.

178   **But John Goodson**: "Criminals in Jail," *Maryville (MO) Tribune*, January 26, 1899.

178   **Grace's brother**: "Suicide, Another Dead," *St. Joseph (MO) News-Press*, April 20, 1917.

178   **"It is thought here"**: "Wood Forcade a Suicide," *Beloit (KS) Gazette*, April 25, 1917.

178   **Months later**: "James A. Forcade of Graham Commits Suicide," *Maryville (MO) Daily Forum*, December 29, 1930.

179   **"Dreaming that the Germans"**: "Sailor Dreams He Is Fighting Germans, and Shoots Self," *Los Angeles Herald*, August 6, 1918.

180   **"There could be"**: "Funeral Here for John L. Goodson," *Arizona Republic*, August 18, 1918.

180   **"He was the roughest"**: Stephen Shadegg, *Barry Goldwater: Freedom Is His Flight Plan* (Fleet Publishing, 1962). Mel Goodson was born in September 1904; Barry Goldwater, in January 1909.

181   **"I shot Robertson"**: "The Page Trial," *Tombstone (AZ) Epitaph*, December 24, 1899.

181   **"There was considerable talk"**: "Murder at Pearce," *El Paso Herald*, October 25, 1899.

182   **"Page is constantly"**: "Page on Trial," *Tombstone (AZ) Epitaph*, July 1, 1900.

182   **The witnesses:** Dorothy G. Palmer, "Ethel Macia: First Lady of Tombstone," *Arizona Highways*, April 1958; Harry E. Christman, *Fifty Years on the Owl Hoot Trail: Jim Herron, the First Sheriff of No Man's Land, Oklahoma Territory* (Sage Books, 1969).

182   **Only days after:** "Old Account Settled," *Arizona Daily Star*, July 8, 1900; "Warren Earp Killed," *Arizona Republican*, July 10, 1900; "Warren Earp Killed in Willcox," *Arizona Range News*, July 11, 1900.

182   **"One pathetic side"**: "Page Convicted of Murder in the Second Degree," *Tombstone (AZ) Epitaph*, December 23, 1900.

183   **Two days after Christmas:** "Tried to Get Away from the Officers at Yuma," *Arizona Republic*, December 31, 1900.

183   **Burts was pardoned:** "Matt Burts Pardoned," *Arizona Republic*, April 18, 1901.

183   **"The result of this case"**: "Letter from Tombstone," *Cochise (AZ) Review*, December 22, 1900.

183   **In 1911:** Doris Sturgis, "Pioneer Flight Replay Set," *Arizona Republic*, June 16, 1961.

185   **In the early morning:** "Plant Manager Dies in Crash at Marietta," *Times Recorder* (Marietta, OH), April 29, 1957.

186   **"Unfortunately, I do not remember"**: "My Happiest Christmas," December 5, 1958.

186   **"Here I am taking"**: Untitled essay.

187   **"If you are going to drive"**: Letter to Gary Goodson from Allen L. Hodgson (State of Utah Department of Public Safety), May 17, 1966.

188   **In the eight years:** "140,206 Is Official Phoenix Population," *Tucson Daily Citizen*, June 30, 1955; Jack Crowe, "Growth of Phoenix Makes Lord Duppa True Prophet," *Arizona Republic*, January 27, 1963; John Barbour, "Cities Blossom in the Lonely Desert," *Hartford (CT) Courant*, December 15, 1968.

188   **The federal funding:** Andrew Ross, *Bird on Fire: Lessons from the World's Least Sustainable City* (Oxford University Press, 2011).

188   **The desert was irrigated:** Neil Morgan, *Westward Tilt: The American West Today* (Random House, 1963).

Chapter 9

192   **"a union of love"**: "The Gathering of the Tribes," *San Francisco Oracle*, January 1967.

192   **a love-in would:** C. L. Cummins, "State of June Be-In(s)," *Los Angeles Free Press*, May 19, 1967.

192   **"We fucked up"**: "How the Hippies Turned Off Hopis," *Berkeley Barb*, May 26, 1967.

192   **so vexed the residents:** "Hippies Confront Mayor at City Hall," *Arizona Republic*, October 4, 1967.

192   **"with Mexico so close"**: Don Bolles, "Modern David Faces Goliath of Narcotics," *Arizona Republic*, July 2, 1967.

192 **call for volunteer:** "Narcotics Unit Asks More Men," *Arizona Republic*, October 11, 1967 (newspaper clipping).

193 **"summarily fired":** Barry Kalb, "News for the Underground," *Washington Star*, March 24, 1968.

193 **"news of people":** Raymond Mungo, "The Movement and Its Media," *Radicals in the Professions*, January 1968.

194 **But something unexpected:** For extraordinary detail on the Pentagon action, see Larry Sloman, Michael Simmons, and Jay Babcock, "Out Demons Out," *Arthur*, no. 13 (November 2004).

194 **"Evil spirits will pour":** Naomi Fiegelson, "Mobilizing for Peace, or—Up, Up, and Away," *Village Voice*, August 31, 1967.

194 **Brown was disinvited:** Ray Mungo, "SNCC, Rap Brown Join March to 'Shut Down the Pentagon,'" *Michigan Daily*, August 31, 1967; David Greenberg, "The March on the Pentagon: An Oral History," *New York Times*, October 20, 2017.

194 **"You think that only":** Marshall Bloom in *Liberation News Service* prototype packet, via Abe Peck, *Uncovering the Sixties* (Pantheon, 1985).

195 **But when members:** Raymond Mungo, *Famous Long Ago: My Life and Hard Times with Liberation News Service* (Beacon Press, 1970).

195 **"Trotskyite fascists":** Michael Grossman, "Underground Press Joins Theater of the Absurd," *Washington Free Press*, November 23, 1967.

195 **accused Shirley Clarke:** Mungo, *Famous Long Ago*.

195 **"psychedelic recipes":** "The Periscope: Uniting the Underground," *Newsweek*, November 13, 1967.

195 **drunk on apricot brandy:** Abe Peck, *Uncovering the Sixties* (Pantheon, 1985).

195 **"Our glorious scheme":** Mungo, *Famous Long Ago*.

196 **"I loved the Washington UPS":** John Wilcock to Tom Forcade, undated.

196 **"Since your organization":** Tom Forcade to Marshall Bloom, November 1, 1967, Box 8, Folder 21, Marshall Bloom Papers, Amherst College Archives and Special Collections.

196 **"The ecology is very":** Tom Forcade to Walter Bowart, undated [1967].

196 **It would take:** Thorne Dreyer, "Law and Order Meets the Underground Press," *Liberation News Service*, no. 122 (November 27, 1968); "New Magazine Sues Printers," *Los Angeles Free Press*, April 12, 1968; lawsuit against Casa Grande.

196 **"Orpheus is a national magazine":** Undated solicitation letter from *Orpheus*.

197 **"The whole operation":** John Wilcock to UPS members, March 7, 1968, Box 1, correspondence folder, John Wilcock Papers, Rare Book & Manuscript Library, Columbia University Libraries.

197 **"Katzman got very angry":** John Wilcock to UPS members, April 1968, Box 1, correspondence folder, John Wilcock Papers.

197 **"western headquarters":** Wilcock letter draft, March 22, 1968, drafted again April 10, Box 1, correspondence folder, John Wilcock Papers.

197 **"I would prefer":** Tom Forcade letter to UPS editors, undated.

197 **"print the publication":** "Other Related Projects," press release, *Orpheus*, February 1968.

199 **"We smoke dope":** Tom Forcade to Linda Akin, undated.

199 THIS MAGAZINE HAS BEEN: *Orpheus* 1, no. 4 (1968).

200 **Hundreds of new investigations:** Robert Wall, "Five Years as a Special Agent," *State Secrets*, ed. Paul Cowan, Nick Egleson, and Nat Hentoff (Holt, Rinehart and Winston, 1974), 247.

200 **"We demand the politics":** YIP announcement reprinted in David Farber, *Chicago '68* (Chicago University Press, 1988).

200   **Rubin attended:** James R. Polk, "House Chicago Probers Are Taunted by Yippies," Associated Press, *Atlanta Constitution*, October 2, 1968.

200   **"we are LSD-driven":** "White Panther Statement," November 1, 1968.

201   **"sound of god":** Lennox Raphael, "Mini Brutes," *East Village Other*, December 14, 1968.

201   **The conference:** Thorne Dreyer and Victoria Smith, "The Movement and the New Media," Liberation News Service, March 1, 1969; Blake Slonecker, *A New Dawn for the New Left: Liberation News Service, Montague Farm, and the Long Sixties* (Palgrave Macmillan, 2012).

201   **"We in Newsreel see":** *Hearings Before the United States House Committee on Internal Security: Investigation of Students for a Democratic Society, Part 7-A, Return of Prisoners of War, and Data Concerning Camera News, Inc., "Newsreel," 1969–1970,* Ninety-First Congress, First Session (December 9–11, 16, 1969).

201   **UPS was compiling:** Dreyer, "Law and Order Meets the Underground Press"; John Sinclair, "Rock & Roll Dope," *Fifth Estate*, December 12–25, 1968.

202   **"Events have always":** *Liberation News Service*, no. 135 (January 30, 1969).

203   **"Even I am beginning":** Tom Forcade to Linda Akin (courtesy of Judy Goodson Baker).

203   **"we were stopped":** "Radical Media Bulletin Board," *Liberation News Service*, no. 149 (March 20, 1969).

203   **"Detective ___":** The original file containing this information could not be located but is referred to in an FBI report from February 2, 1972, FBI file 100-HQ-469538, serial 6 (copy in author's possession); see also FBI teletype from New York to bureau, April 12, 1974, FBI file 100-HQ-469538, serial 178 (copy in author's possession).

204   **"GOODSON, Airman Gary":** The psychiatric report of August 18, 1969, was obtained by the FBI from Goodson's military personnel file in St. Louis, Missouri, on March 5, 1974. The New York FBI field office included it in a report sent to the director by Airtel on May 30, 1974, FBI file 100-HQ-469538, serial 189.

206   **A few weeks later:** "Human Arm, Hand Lead to Discovery of Body," *Arizona Republic*, September 19, 1969; "Officers Still Seeking Dead Man's Identity," *Casa Grande (AZ) Dispatch*, September 22, 1969.

206   **"They sent two detectives":** Laurabelle Goodson to Terese Coe, 1980, Terese Coe Papers.

Chapter 10

208   **To scrape together:** FBI interview report from Tampa field office, February 28, 1974, FBI file 100-HQ-469538, serial 171 (copy in author's possession).

208   **"The more animosity":** Cindy Ornsteen interview, 1980, Terese Coe Papers.

209   **"Adolf Hitler was a super-villain":** Thomas Forcade and Rex Weiner, "Visions of Hitler" prospectus, Rex Weiner Collection of Underground Press Material, 1955–1981, Beinecke Rare Book and Manuscript Library, Yale University.

210   **"They've shut out":** Rex Weiner, "Stowaways on the Voyage Beyond Apollo," *High Times*, November–December 2004.

210   **"Mailer is either":** Rex Weiner, "A Stowaway to the Thanatosphere: My Voyage Beyond Apollo with Norman Mailer," *Paris Review*, December 31, 2012.

210   **"All we had to do":** Thomas Forcade, "Rich New World," *Berkeley Barb*, December 29, 1972–January 4, 1973.

211   **"Why don't we start":** Rex Weiner and Tom Forcade, "The Insidious Moon Cruise: A Stowaways' Tale," *Westport Trucker* (Kansas City, MO), February 1, 1973.

211   **"The fact that the ship":** Forcade, "Rich New World."

211 **"I confronted him finally"**: Weiner, "A Stowaway to the Thanatosphere."

212 **"I dunno"**: Blair Sabol, "Naked Launch," *Village Voice*, December 21, 1972.

212 **"The two young men"**: Tom Buckley, "Caribbean Cruise Attempts to Seek Meaning of Apollo," *New York Times*, December 12, 1972.

213 **"nefarious plans by Zippie leaders"**: Helene E. Schwartz, *Lawyering* (Farrar, Straus and Giroux, 1976), 245.

213 **"vigorously pursued"**: Airtel from acting director to SAC Miami, date obscured as redaction but stamped as mailed on September 29, 1972, FBI file 100-HQ-469538, serial 28.

213 **"He got into Watergate"**: H. R. Haldeman, *The Haldeman Diaries: Inside the Nixon White House* (G. P. Putnam's Sons, 1994).

214 **"If I'd known"**: New York FBI office report, February 16, 1973, FBI file 100-HQ-469538, serial 94x.

214 YIPPIES ARRESTED IN FIRE BOMB CASE: *New York Times*, February 11, 1973.

214 **"You have to tell me"**: Schwartz, *Lawyering*, 245.

215 **"We never until very recently"**: William Mitchell, "John Sinclair, Mellowed," *Detroit Free Press*, July 9, 1972.

215 **"As the sun sets"**: Tom Forcade, "All the Old Heroes Are Dead," *International Times*, April 20, 1973.

216 **"contained heads of matches"**: Ron Sachs, "Seized Substance Burned," *Miami Herald*, March 29, 1973.

216 **"They were trying to describe"**: "All the Dope: Forcade-Ornsteen," *Yipster Times*, March 1973.

216 **"some Mansonesque"**: "All the Dope: Forcade-Ornsteen," *Yipster Times*, March 1973.

217 **"If we reach the point"**: Sachs, "Seized Substance Burned."

217 **"Is she your girlfriend?"**: Schwartz, *Lawyering*, 285.

217 **"not, by definition"**: "Judge Acquits Zippies of Having Firebombs," *Miami Herald*, March 30, 1973.

218 **"It's been suggested"**: "All the Dope: Forcade-Ornsteen," *Yipster Times*, March 1973.

219 FBI agents and informers had infiltrated: Donald M. Rothberg, "FBI Linked to Convention Protests," Associated Press, *Morning Call* (Allentown, PA), May 10, 1973.

219 **"had not infiltrated the Zippies"**: Rob Elder, "Agents Infiltrated Convention Protests," *Miami Herald*, May 11, 1973.

219 Senate investigators: Jim Squires, "Justice Dept. Spy Activities Probed," *Chicago Tribune*, May 30, 1973.

219 conspirators had tried: Raul Ramirez and Paul W. Valentine, "Phony Hippies Enlisted by Fernandez," *Washington Post*, May 26, 1973.

219 **"illicit methods"**: "What the Secret Police Did," *Newsweek*, June 11, 1973.

220 Judge Keith demanded: Agis Salpukas, "U.S. Forgoes Trial of Weathermen," *New York Times*, October 16, 1973.

220 Seymour Hersh reported: Seymour M. Hersh, "FBI Informer Is Linked to Bombings and Protests by Weathermen Groups," *New York Times*, May 20, 1973.

220 The *Berkeley Tribe* had: Larry Grathwohl was identified in "Unsettled Accounts," *Berkeley Tribe*, August 21–28, 1970.

220 **"The vitality of the alternative"**: Ross K. Baker, "ZAP! No More Underground Press," *Washington Post*, April 8, 1973.

220 **"looked like cleaned-up hippies"**: Ron Lichty and Tom Forcade, "Muckraking Madness," *Westport Trucker* (Kansas City, MO), June 22, 1973.

221   **"The underground papers are beginning"**: Clark DeLeon, "Underground Press Alive and Well in Over 300 Cities," *Philadelphia Inquirer*, May 14, 1973.

221   **"The underground press was largely right"**: David Armstrong, "Opened Watergate," *Berkeley Barb*, February 1–7, 1974.

221   **"It's still a leftist political"**: Suzanne Weiss, "Alternative Press Opting to Redefine Its Purpose," *Rocky Mountain News*, June 11, 1973.

221   **"the final plunge"**: Tom Miller, "Editors Lift Up Corner of Rug at Denver Confab," *Berkeley Barb*, June 22–28, 1973.

221   **The weekend kicked off**: Rex Weiner, "Boulder: Alternative Press Conference," *Underground Press Revue*, July–August 1973.

222   **"I haven't seen"**: Stephen Foehr, "What's Happening to the Underground Press?" *Straight Creek Journal*, June 19–26, 1973.

222   **"You're going to have to"**: "Oyster River, CO," underground press meeting minutes provided by Chip Berlet to Abe Peck for *Uncovering the Sixties* (Pantheon, 1985); Paul Krassner later ran a longer version of the quote without attribution, which included parts of Forcade's essay "Obscene Scene," published in *Countdown* in 1970, grafted onto it.

222   **"The 'movement' was over"**: Gabrielle Schang, "Tom Forcade on Radical Politics, Rock Festivals, Outlaw Publishing, and Laughing Gas," *Alternative Media* 11, no. 1 (1979).

Chapter 11

223   **He got a phone call**: Rex Weiner, "High Times Takes Off," *High Times*, November 2014.

223   **When Forcade began selling**: Bud Bogart (pseudonym for Michael Chance), "The Forcade Be with You: Trans-High Market Analysis," *High Times*, June 1984. "He had been making occasional journeys back to Arizona, picking up the plentiful Mexican pot that was smuggled across the border by four-wheel-drive vehicles and light planes," Chance wrote. This could not be corroborated.

223   **"The most difficult thing"**: "R.," "The Five-Year Review," *High Times*, September 1979.

224   **"by the blood red glow"**: "R.," "The Dope Anthem," *High Times*, August 1982.

224   **"The biggest safe"**: Michael Chance, "Thomas King Forcade, Potfather," *Take Over*, November 9, 1979.

224   **rolling joints and listening**: "R.," "The Dope Anthem."

224   **"Do not tell anyone"**: Chance, "Thomas King Forcade, Potfather."

225   **"It was," said A. J. Weberman**: Steven Hager, "Tom Creates an Elaborate Smokeasy Called 'Bobby's,'" July 9, 2009, YouTube video, 2:37, https://youtu.be/zvELaTsFC0s.

225   **"Out of the 300"**: "The Underground Monthly Daily Planet Surfaces," UPI, *Fort Lauderdale News*, April 18, 1973.

225   **"develop a chain"**: Sheila Payton, "Daily Planet May Market Its Stock," *Miami Herald*, April 16, 1973.

225   **"Did you ever hear"**: "The Underground Monthly Daily Planet Surfaces," UPI, *Fort Lauderdale News*, April 18, 1973.

226   **Burnstine made his name**: Gaeton Fonzi, "Ken Burnstine Is Still Dead," *Gold Coast*, February 1982.

227   **men on salary**: Hank Messick, *Of Grass and Snow* (Prentice Hall, 1979).

228   **"considering its zany"**: "News," *Underground Press Revue*, July–August 1973.

228 **"wandering around":** Leon Yipsky and George Metefsky, "Yips Storm Capitol," *Yipster Times*, no. 7 (August–September 1973).

229 **"A lot of people":** Paul Valentine, "The Decline of the Demonstration," *Washington Post*, July 14, 1973.

229 **"These people":** Valentine, "The Decline of the Demonstration."

229 **"During the afternoon":** Memo from Cincinnati FBI office, October 31, 1973, FBI File 100-HQ-467404, Serial 39 (copy in author's possession).

229 **"It was recently learned":** Memo from New York FBI office included in Director Clarence Kelly's memo to Secret Service, January 23, 1974, File 100-HQ-467404, Serial 41.

229 **"I always wanted to throw":** "15-Year-Old Guru Slapped in Face by Shaving Cream Pie," UPI, *Los Angeles Times*, August 8, 1973.

230 **Just three months earlier:** Mark Brothers, "Free Rennie Davis!" *Yipster Times*, June 1973.

230 **Subsequent targets:** "Culture Hero: Aron Kay," *High Times*, April 1979.

230 **"It's all-out war":** *Yipster Times* clipping, date unknown.

230 **On the tenth:** A. J. Weberman, "Where Is Kennedy's Brain?" New York News Service, October 29, 1973 (4136–4138).

230 **"When I arrived there":** Richard E. Sprague to Joseph O. Okpaku Sr. (courtesy of A. J. Weberman).

231 **"were, as far as I'm concerned":** "Allen Ginsberg…Rennie Davis and the Underground Press," *Georgia Straight*, June 21–28, 1973.

233 **"a cleverly contrived":** Thomas Forcade, "Ginsberg Is a Liar," *Berkeley Barb*, August 3–9, 1973.

233 **"My energy was":** Trudy Rubin, "The 'New' Jerry Rubin," *Christian Science Monitor*, February 16, 1973.

233 **"During the election":** "Letters," *Village Voice*, October 17, 1974.

234 **And he forgave:** Jerry Rubin, *Growing (Up) at Thirty-Seven* (M. Evans and Company, 1976).

234 **"a honeycomb of cells":** Ann Hencken, "Yippies Still Alive and Struggling," Associated Press, *Tampa Times*, September 5, 1973.

235 **"Cocaine is much like":** "Legalize Cocaine!" *Westport Trucker* (Kansas City, MO), October 22, 1973.

235 **"I consider this a great victory":** "Abbie Out, Will Join Conspiracy in Chicago," NYNS, *Berkeley Barb*, October 19–25, 1973. Benefit was held October 12.

235 **Cindy Ornsteen and Tim Hughes would say:** John Holmstrom, "Interview: Cindy Ornsteen," *High Times*, September 1989.

235 **"We were sitting around":** Jack Mathews, "A Magazine to Read During High Times," *Rochester Democrat & Chronicle*, May 10, 1976. Andy Kowl, who provided Mathews with this quote, joined the magazine after the first issue had been assembled.

236 **"I would come and install":** Larry Sloman and George Barkin, "Ed Rosenthal," *High Times*, May 1984.

236 **"As grass gets":** Clark DeLeon, "Home-Grown Pot Spreads," *Philadelphia Inquirer*, May 22, 1973.

236 **"Amorphia East":** "Scenes," *Village Voice*, August 31, 1972.

237 **"He left a bag of Colombian":** Ed Dwyer, "My Life and High Times," *High Times*, November–December 2004.

237 **"There was just me and Ed":** Gabrielle Schang-Forcade, "May the Forcade Be with You," *Overthrow*, April 1979.

237 **Kowl rented a gorilla suit:** "Paper Aims at Young Readers," *Newsday*, September 28, 1972.

238 **"I think silver and turquoise":** John Holmstrom, "Interview: Cindy Ornsteen," *High Times*, September 1989.

238 **Twice a year:** Ron Rosenbaum, "Clothestrophobia: A Fond Farewell to Crap," *Village Voice*, January 27, 1975.

239 **"Beautiful people who":** Lillian Ross, "Talk of the Town: Boutique Mystique," *New Yorker*, February 6, 1971. See also Lillian Ross, "Talk of the Town: Aspects of Revolution," *New Yorker*, February 2, 1976.

239 **Rosenthal said he thought:** Peter Gorman, "The Cannabis Innovators: Heroes and Legends in the Pot Trade," *Heads*, 2003.

240 **"involved in the purchase":** FBI memo, New York field office, February 15, 1974, FBI file 100-HQ-469538, serial 163.

241 **"You are guaranteed":** Ad solicitation from initial printing of the first issue of *High Times*, Spring 1974.

241 **"*High Times* is dedicated":** Solicitation letter from Cindy Ornsteen (as Anastasia Sirroco), October 20, 1974.

242 **"In Madison":** Bogart (Michael Chance), "The Forcade Be with You."

242 **On May 23:** Rex Weiner, "High Times Takes Off," *High Times*, November 2014.

242 **"Is there a market":** John Leo, "Media: Keeping Up on Dope," *New Times*, June 14, 1974.

242 **Distributors refused:** "'High Times' a Hit," *Berkeley Barb*, January 10–16, 1975.

242 **sold out its first:** "A New Dope Magazine Appears," *Straight Creek Journal*, May 28, 1974.

243 **"It's like trying to ride a rocket":** Chance, "Thomas King Forcade, Potfather."

Chapter 12

247 **"If a couple of thousand":** Jurate Kazickas, "High Times," Associated Press, *Abilene (TX) Reporter News*, October 19, 1974.

247 **Within four weeks:** "'High Times' a Hit," *Berkeley Barb*, January 10–16, 1975.

248 **"We figure we're getting":** Thomas Collins, "Dope Sheet: 'Just Another Industry News Magazine,'" *Newsday*, January 2, 1975.

249 **"There's a cop here":** Michael Chance, "Thomas King Forcade, Potfather," *Take Over*, November 9, 1979.

249 **"Whenever I had anything to deal":** Chris Kearns to Terese Coe, Terese Coe Papers.

254 **"massive, illegal":** Seymour Hersh, "Huge C.I.A. Operation Reported in U.S. Against Antiwar Forces, Other Dissidents in Nixon Years," *New York Times*, December 22, 1974.

254 **A presidential commission:** These are colloquially known as the Rockefeller Commission and the Pike and Church Subcommittees, respectively.

254 **"Operation CHAOS":** David N. Alpern, Anthony Marro, and Evert Clark, "Who's Watching Whom," *Newsweek*, June 23, 1975; Timothy S. Robinson, "At CIA, Domestic and Foreign Spying Had Equal Priority," *Washington Post*, September 9, 1979; "Operation Chaos Spying More Widespread Than Believed," *Decatur Daily Review* (story from the *Washington Star*), September 10, 1979.

254 **"to travel to Washington":** Commission on CIA Activities Within the United States, "Chapter 11: Special Operations Group—'Operation CHAOS,'" in *Report to the President by the Commission on CIA Activities Within the United States* (Rockefeller Report) (Washington, DC: GPO, 1975).

254 **Jack Anderson's column:** Jack Anderson, "Kissinger Eyes Soviet Mideast Role," Washington Merry-Go-Round, *Washington Post*, March 21, 1975.

254 **Sal Ferrera had interviewed:** Angus Mackenzie, "Sabotaging the Dissident Press," *Columbia Journalism Review*, March–April, 1981, and Angus Mackenzie, "Darker Cloaks, Longer Daggers," *The Progressive*, June, 1982. Astonishingly, Ferrera appears to have been at least partially responsible for compiling "Know Thy Neighbor," an article in the August 26, 1969, issue of the *Quicksilver Times* that exposed the names of over two hundred people who worked for the CIA. After that issue's publication, Joseph Albright, a reporter for *Newsday*, called the *Quicksilver Times* for comment and reached Ferrera. Albright wrote that Ferrera "adopted the normal CIA protocol and refused to confirm or deny" that the names were discovered by writing down license plate numbers in a CIA office parking lot. Intriguingly, an editor at the other DC underground, the *Washington Free Press*, was the son of a veteran CIA agent who was himself involved in monitoring underground publications.

254 **Drug Enforcement Administration faced:** Lawrence Meyer, "DEA Was Offered Explosive Devices," *Washington Post*, January 23, 1975; Robert Waters, "Firm Showed Drug Unit Illegal Deadly Weapons," *Hartford Courant*, January 23, 1975; Nicholas M. Horrock, "U.S. Aide Was Briefed on Assassination Techniques," *New York Times*, January 23, 1975. On June 18, a Justice Department task force report included information that Philip Smith and William Durkin of DEA participated in discussions regarding a proposal to assassinate Panamanian military leader Omar Torrijos (Michael DeFeo et al., "Report of June 18, 1975, to the Attorney General, Subject: Additional Integrity Matters." The DeFeo report was leaked by the Church of Scientology).

254 **"hit squads":** Edward Jay Epstein, "The Incredible War Against the Poppies," *Esquire*, December 1974; Jack Anderson and Les Whitten, "Washington Merry-Go-Round," United Features Syndicate, March 22, 1975.

255 **selling MAC-10s:** Gaeton Fonzi, "Ken Burnstine Is Still Dead," *Gold Coast*, February 1982.

255 **"to the right of Attila the Hun":** William R. Amlong, "Powder Keg at Powder Springs," *Miami Herald*, July 1, 1973.

255 **$900 million:** Fonzi, "Ken Burnstine Is Still Dead."

255 **conspiracy to import:** David Esler, "Competition Scene," *Air Progress*, April 1975.

256 **"support and guidance":** A. Craig Copetas, "Trespassers Will Be Eaten," *National Weed*, May 1976. For an interesting background to Sturgis's own adventures in drug enforcement, see Seymour M. Hersh's story "4 Watergate Defendants Reported Still Being Paid," *New York Times*, January 14, 1973. Hersh reported on a book that journalist Andrew St. John was preparing to write with Sturgis. The book's outline depicted Sturgis as working for E. Howard Hunt—then consultant to the White House on narcotics traffic—"in an undercover investigation of alleged illicit drug traffic in Mexico, Panama and Paraguay."

256 **In January 1975:** Robert Waters, "Firm Showed Drug Unit Illegal Deadly Weapons," *Hartford Courant*, January 23, 1975.

256 **"When you get down to it":** George Crile III, "The Colonel's Secret Drug War," *Washington Post*, June 13, 1976.

257 **"a wasted, blinking hippie":** Albert Goldman, "Thomas King Forcade: Living and Dying the Great Adventure," *Conjunctions*, Fall 1991.

257 **"Tom would come over":** Goldman, "Thomas King Forcade: Living and Dying."

258 **"infiltrators in Yippie meetings":** Richard Bradee, "Data Shows US Snooping on Press," *Milwaukee Sentinel*, February 15, 1975.

259   **"made a special examination":** US Congress Joint Committee on Internal Revenue Taxation, *Investigation of the Special Service Staff of the Internal Revenue Service*, JSC-9-75 (June 5, 1975).

260   **"It was very hard":** Gabrielle Schang to Albert Goldman, January 1979, Box 61, Tape 9, Albert Goldman Papers, 1953–1994, University Archives, Rare Book & Manuscript Library, Columbia University Libraries.

260   **"an army of overpaid":** Michael Antonoff, "The Thomas King Forcade Story," *Tucson's Mountain Newsreal*, December 1978.

261   **"only enough joints":** Antonoff, "The Thomas King Forcade Story."

261   **"Of course, I'm scared":** Antonoff, "The Thomas King Forcade Story."

262   **"One of the most persistent":** "Flashes," *High Times*, Spring 1975.

263   **"a hash-pipe-in-a-bottle":** "Closers," *High Times*, October 1975.

263   **When a New York City:** Howie Kurtz, "Hostages Disarm Bandit," *The Record* (Hackensack, NJ), October 7, 1975.

263   **"There is nothing":** "Letters," *High Times*, June 1976.

264   **past 250,000 per issue:** "Lines," *High Times*, August–September 1975.

264   **about a third of which:** "Closers," *High Times*, October 1975.

264   **"Tom was totally hung up":** Shelly Schorr to Terese Coe, Thomas Forcade Collection.

265   **Further scrutiny:** Notes on "Fifth Avenue Hotel Incident," Box A26, Albert Goldman Papers.

266   **"I am almost invaluable":** Tim Hughes to Andy Kowl, February 4, 1976.

267   **"I thought they were hunting":** Joe Kollin, "Air, Ground Forces Hunt Pot Suspects," *Naples Daily News*, March 16, 1976.

268   **"there wasn't much":** Kollin, "Air, Ground Forces Hunt Pot Suspects."

273   **"mud and scum":** John Holmstrom, "The Ultimate Hippie: The Life and High Times of Thomas King Forcade," *High Times*, October 1989.

273   **They tried to figure:** John Holmstrom interview with Michael Kennedy, undated audiocassette, Box 117, Item 39002137168358, John Holmstrom Collection, Beinecke Rare Book and Manuscript Library, Yale University.

273   **Craig Copetas had gotten:** "Carter Gives Views on Pot," *News and Observer*, March 19, 1976.

273   **"If he didn't like it":** Andy Kowl to Albert Goldman, Box A26, Folder 8, Albert Goldman Papers.

274   **"The people listed":** Bob Lemmo to Terese Coe, Thomas Forcade Collection.

275   **"You have thirty seconds":** Bob Lemmo to Terese Coe, Thomas Forcade Collection.

275   **"He was a master":** Shelly Schorr to Terese Coe, Thomas Forcade Collection.

275   **"At work, the man":** Ed Dwyer, "My Life and High Times," *High Times*, November–December 2004.

275   **"collapse of the entire":** James Horwitz, "The Rise and Fall of Florida's Marijuana Luftwaffe," *High Times*, October 1976.

275   **"Sturgis is a rotten motherfucking liar":** Copetas, "Trespassers Will Be Eaten."

276   **"The man had a lot":** Carl Hiaasen, "Report Blames Pilot Error for Burnstine Plane Crash," *Miami Herald*, August 13, 1976.

276   **Burnstine had confided:** Jay Maeder, "Air Crash Kills Broward Drug Figure," *Miami Herald*, June 18, 1976.

276   **"I used to consider":** "Smuggler Burnstine Dead," *High Times*, September 1976. Before Burnstine's crash, WerBell implied to one journalist that he'd tried to get Burnstine to assist the DEA Special Operations team in proving that Fidel Castro was smuggling heroin into the United States via Mob boss Santos Trafficante. Naturally, WerBell said he couldn't elaborate. "I'm gonna leave all the rest blank," he said,

"because if I ever come to trial, I'm gonna need all this" (Fonzi, "Ken Burnstine Is Still Dead").

276 **"would never get involved":** Gayle Pollard, "5 Acquitted in Drug Conspiracy Case," *Miami Herald*, September 4, 1976.

277 **"Create a shoot-out":** Dick Russell, "An EX-CIA Man's Stunning Revelations on 'The Company,' JFK's Murder, and the Plot to Kill Richard Nixon," *Argosy*, April 1976.

277 **"We were deeply concerned":** E. Howard Hunt, *Undercover: Memoirs of an American Secret Agent* (Berkley Publishing, 1974), 155.

277 **arrested in the courtroom:** Tom Duncan, "The Great Pot Plot," *Soldier of Fortune*, Winter 1976.

278 **As with many conspiracy theories:** Michael Chance, "Army Researchers Revived Pig Flu," *Yipster Times*, April 1976; Craig Silverman, "Will Weather Warfare Cause World Famine?" *Yipster Times*, May 1976.

278 **"How can Abbie":** Michael Chance, "Warned of Coke Watergate," *Yipster Times*, August 1978.

278 **The Yippie hosts:** "Big Apple Agog over YIP TV," *Yipster Times*, May 1976.

278 **A Yippie named:** "Spitting Image of Yippies," New York *Daily News*, August 18, 1976.

278 **"terrorist turned informer":** Ron Koziol, "Tie Cuban Spy to Plot Against Ford, Reagan," *Chicago Tribune*, March 19, 1976.

279 **The *Yipster Times* had:** George Koppe, "2 Protesters' Groups Discount Death Plot," *Kansas City Times*, March 20, 1976.

280 **"They are paranoid":** R. J. Cutler, "Behind the Scenes at the Yipster Times," *Alternative Media Review*, May–June 1976.

280 **"If we run that story":** Michael Chance, "Thomas King Forcade, Potfather," *Take Over*, November 9, 1979.

281 CARTER AIDE IS MURDER SUSPECT: *Yipster Times*, June 1976.

281 **"Who's fooling whom":** "Carter Endorses Decrim," *Yipster Times*, May 1976.

281 **engraved invitations:** Abe Peck, "Rolling Paper Revue," *Rolling Stone*, January 27, 1977.

281 **"the beautiful people, the trendsetters":** The launch party for *Dealer* was held May 24, 1976, at Vamp's Discotheque, which was described in "Dancers Are Touching to the Bump…Walk…Hustle," UPI, *Kingston (NY) Daily Freeman*, January 4, 1976.

281 **"When Freedom Is Outlawed":** "Lines," *High Times*, November 1976.

282 **"No more Jerry Rubins!":** Leon Yipsky, "Yippies Crash Carter's Garden Party," *Yipster Times*, August 1978.

282 **"Without the Yippies":** Anthony Barbieri Jr., "Yippies Urge Nixon Draft; 'Angel' Warns GOP; Nude Runs with 'Nothing to Hide,'" *Baltimore Sun*, August 19, 1976.

283 **"I don't know for sure":** "Protesters Vie for Spotlight During Convention Sideshow," Associated Press, *Austin American Statesman*, August 17, 1976.

283 **"They're the leftovers":** Thomas Poster, "Vet of Big Apple's Hottest Days, KC's Chief Cop Keeps City Cool," New York *Daily News*, August 18, 1976.

283 **"Once demonstrators had":** John Dean, "Rituals of the Herd," *Rolling Stone*, October 7, 1976.

283 **"They were pathetic":** "Kansas City Clamor: Yippie," *Berkeley Barb*, August 20–26, 1976.

283 **"How does it feel":** Paul Krassner, *Berkeley Barb*, September 3–9, 1976.

283 **After the convention:** Gabrielle Schang and Ron Rosenbaum, "Now the Urban Guerillas Have a Real Problem: They're Trying to Make It in the Magazine Business," *MORE*, November 1976.

285   **"Come in":** Claire Prince to Terese Coe, Thomas Forcade Collection.

287   **The sight of the two:** Chance, "Thomas King Forcade, Potfather."

Chapter 13

288   **The press run of twenty-five thousand:** R. B. Gorlin, "Magazine Graffiti a La Punk," *Alternative Media*, January–February 1977.

288   **"very normal looking":** Milton Coleman, "$10,000 Gift Donated to Legalize Pot," *Washington Post*, August 16, 1976.

289   **Forcade had asked him:** Keith Stroup, "Tom Forcade & the Politics of Pot," *High Times*, November 2004.

289   **celebration at a fundraiser:** This description of the October 21 event draws from the following sources: Andy Kowl to Albert Goldman, Box A26, Folder 8, Albert Goldman Papers, Rare Book & Manuscript Library, Columbia University Libraries; Shelly Schorr to Terese Coe, Terese Coe Papers; Patrick Anderson, *High in America* (Viking, 1981), 172–173; "The Insider: Pot Shots," *New Times*, November 12, 1976.

290   **"That young man":** "The Insider: Seventies," *New Times*, November 12, 1976.

290   **"I want you to fire"** *and subsequent conversation:* Albert Goldman, "Thomas King Forcade: Living and Dying the Great Adventure," *Conjunctions*, Fall 1991; Andy Kowl to Albert Goldman, Box A26, Folder 8, Albert Goldman Papers.

290   **"You can go home":** Michael Chance, "Thomas King Forcade, Potfather," *Take Over*, November 9, 1979.

291   **"Look, man":** Andy Kowl to Albert Goldman, Box A26, Folder 8, Albert Goldman Papers.

292   **"to make sure there weren't":** John Goodson to John Holmstrom (undated audiocassette), Box 117, Item 39002137168192, John Holmstrom Papers and Punk Magazine Records, General Collection, Beinecke Rare Book and Manuscript Library, Yale University.

293   **"Look, I'm taking my vitamins":** Claire Prince to Terese Coe, November 10, 1979, Terese Coe Papers; A. J. Weberman, "Tom Forcade: Death of a Radical Romantic," *Village Voice*, November 27, 1978.

293   **"Being without you":** Excerpts of the March 11, 1977, letter from Forcade to Schang appear in John McMillian, *Smoking Typewriters: The Sixties Underground Press and the Rise of Alternative Media in America* (Oxford University Press, 2011), 244.

294   **"cooperation with authorities":** Joe Kollin, "Man Jailed in Pot Case," *Naples Daily News*, March 1, 1977.

294   **"on grounds that they were":** Michael Kennedy to Albert Goldman, January 17, 1979, Box 61, Tape 1, Albert Goldman Papers. Kennedy turned off the tape recorder to discuss Hughes's thirty-page deposition.

294   **"Forcade was able":** Ron Rosenbaum to Bruce Brown, Terese Coe Papers.

296   **in 1971, 90 percent:** Mary Jo McConahay, "Mexico's War on Poppies—and Peasants," *New Times*, September 3, 1976.

297   **herbicide-spraying campaign:** Carol Cook, "Breaking 'The Mexican Connection,'" UPI, *The State* (Columbia, SC), March 21, 1976.

297   **"Paraquat probably has caused":** Martha Angle and Robert Walters, "High-Priced Eradication," NEA, *Selma (AL) Times*, May 20, 1977.

297   **oral ingestion:** John Jacobs, "Mexican Marijuana May Be Tainted with Herbicide," *Washington Post*, December 3, 1977.

297　**"ABC is not going to go":** Craig Copetas to John Holmstrom (undated audiocassette), Box 117, Item 39002137167947, John Holmstrom Papers and Punk Magazine Records.

297　**$120 to $250 million:** Emily Dufton, *Grass Roots* (Basic Books, 2017), 73. The number was up to $350 million a year by 1978, according to Joanne Omang, "Drug Paraphernalia Sales Are Booming," *Washington Post*, December 17, 1978.

298　**NORML had its sights:** "NORML Targets 12 for 77," *High Times*, February 1977.

298　**"Penalties against possession":** Jimmy Carter, "Drug Abuse Message to the Congress," American Presidency Project, August 2, 1977, https://www.presidency.ucsb.edu/documents/drug-abuse-message-the-congress.

298　**the old rumors:** Abe Peck, "The Rolling Paper Revue," *Rolling Stone*, January 27, 1977.

298　**keeping more than half:** Wes Hills, "Hustler's Chief Reaping Riches," *Dayton (OH) Daily News*, June 13, 1976.

298　**Eder had helped to ensnare:** Phil Lapsley, *Exploding the Phone* (Grove Press, 2013), 251–259.

298　**"He was not":** Eder deposition in *Eder v. Weberman*, February 16, 1979, provided by A. J. Weberman.

299　**"Tom pulled a .45":** Gerald Lefcourt to Albert Goldman, September 13, 1982, Box 61, Tape 8, Albert Goldman Papers.

299　**"Get fucked":** Eder deposition in *Eder v. Weberman*, February 16, 1979, provided by A. J. Weberman.

299　**"Informer Chic":** *High Times*, January 1978.

299　**The *Washington Post* printed:** Ron Brodmann, "Personalities," *Washington Post*, November 3, 1977.

299　**360-page proposal:** Richard J. Bonnie, "Decriminalizing the Marijuana User: A Drafter's Guide," *Journal of Law Reform* (University of Michigan) 11, no. 3 (1977).

300　**"demonstrable health hazard":** R. Jeffrey Smith, "Spraying of Herbicides on Mexican Marijuana Backfires on U.S." *Science* 199, no. 4331 (February 24, 1978): 861–864.

300　**Yippies, smugglers:** The Saturday-night NORML party has been chronicled in, among other places, Michael Chance, "Warned of Coke Watergate," *Yipster Times*, August 1978; Patrick Anderson, *High in America* (Viking, 1981); Emily Dufton, *Grass Roots* (Basic Books, 2017); Dan Brewster and Al Brewer, "NORML Head Keith Stroup Beats Administration Threat Effort," *New Times*, August 7, 1978.

300　**a mound of cocaine:** Ronald Shaffer, "Carter Aide Bourne Resigns over False Prescription: The Cocaine Incident," *Washington Post*, July 21, 1978.

301　**"My God, man":** Patrick Anderson, *High in America* (Viking, 1981), 21.

301　**The chair of that committee:** Warren Brown, "'Pot' Material Ban Urged," *Washington Post*, March 17, 1977.

301　**Stroup soon had:** Details about the NORML convention are synthesized from interviews and the following sources: Larry "Ratso," Sloman, *Reefer Madness* (Bobbs-Merrill, 1979); Michael Chance, "Warned of Coke Watergate," *Yipster Times*, August 1978; Patrick Anderson, *High in America* (Viking, 1981); Stuart Levitan, "Yippies, Keith Stroup Clash over NORML Politics," *High Times*, May 1978; Brewster and Brewer, "NORML Head Keith Stroup Beats Administration Threat Effort"; Al Aronowitz, "Back Pages: Vote Yourself Out of Jail," *Circus*, February 16, 1978.

301　**"impotent and irrelevant":** Levitan, "Yippies, Keith Stroup Clash over NORML Politics."

301　**Some meringue:** Brewster and Brewer, "NORML Head Keith Stroup Beats Administration Threat Effort."

301 **Weeks later, someone:** Anderson, *High in America*, 231.

301 **"My constituents":** "Bourne vs. Stroup Part II: One's KO'd, the Other's Reeling," *New Times*, August 21, 1978; Anderson, *High in America*, 233.

301 **Then he called:** Anderson, *High in America*, 233.

Chapter 14

302 **"It looked like a bumblebee":** "Pilot Tells of Tight Take-Off," *Florida Today*, June 3, 1976.

302 **At auction:** Ken Willis and Rex Granum, "Rep. West Lassoes Polk Pot Plane," *Atlanta Constitution*, November 18, 1975; "Pot Plane Soars onto Screen," *Atlanta Constitution*, March 4, 1977.

302 **He offered half a million:** Andy Kowl to Albert Goldman, Box A26, Folder 8, Albert Goldman Papers, Rare Book & Manuscript Library, Columbia University Libraries.

302 **"Pack your bags":** Kowalski to Terese Coe, Terese Coe Papers.

304 **"Tom was very paranoid":** Kowalski to Terese Coe, Terese Coe Papers.

306 **"He wanted to be their manager":** Holmstrom to Jon Savage, 1988 (courtesy of Jon Savage).

306 **"He was in the front":** Kowalski to Terese Coe, Terese Coe Papers.

307 **"He created an outlaw atmosphere":** Hilary White, "The Making of D.O.A." *Punk Special Edition: D.O.A.—the Official Filmbook*, April 1981.

308 **"The workers," he said:** Michael Chance, "Thomas King Forcade, Potfather," *Take Over*, November 9, 1979.

308 **"I can come around":** Joe Stevens to Jon Savage, 1988 (courtesy of Jon Savage).

309 **"the outcome of a manic-depressive":** Larry Flynt, with Kenneth Ross, *An Unseemly Man* (Dove Books, 1996).

309 **Flynt made moves:** Jim Stewart and Paul Lieberman, "Flynt's Staff Is Shrinking," *Atlanta Constitution*, March 27, 1978.

309 **Flynt's brother:** Paul Krassner, "The Pink Parables," *San Francisco Bay Guardian*, November 30, 1978.

309 **Soon he hit:** Stewart and Lieberman, "Flynt's Staff Is Shrinking."

309 **"They were plotting":** Thomas BeVier, "Born-Again Porn Tycoon Beset by Corporate Woes," *Detroit Free Press*, March 6, 1978.

310 **Flynt was the first:** Larry Kramer, "Flynt Gets into Magazine Distributing," *Washington Post*, November 17, 1977.

310 **Mark Lane, the lawyer:** Gene Miller, "Got a Conspiracy Theory? Get in Line," *Miami Herald*, March 12, 1978.

310 **"government agencies":** Cynthia Tucker and Tom Crawford, "Flynt Staff Investigates Shooting," *Atlanta Journal*, April 5, 1978.

310 **"I knew who did it":** "Gunning Down of Flynt Pal 3d Attack on Hustler Brass," New York *Daily News*, November 8, 1978.

310 **"desire not to be hassled":** Charles Powers, "Magazine of 'High Society' Hits Rich Vein," *Los Angeles Times*, July 7, 1978.

310 **"I feel like, in the end":** Transcript of Tom Forcade phone call with Albert Goldman, March 1978, Terese Coe Papers.

310 **Smuggler Tommy Sullivan:** Albert Goldman, *Grass Roots* (Harper & Row, 1979). See also Victor Bockris, "Tom Sullivan," *Interview*, October 1979; Margaret Trudeau, *Consequences* (Bantam, 1982); Anthony Haden-Guest, *The Last Party* (William Morrow & Co., 1997).

311   **"laying plans":** Albert Goldman, "Thomas King Forcade: Living and Dying the Great Adventure," *Conjunctions*, Fall 1991.

312   **stand of pine trees:** Ron Baygents, "Mystery Plane Crash Linked to Marijuana," *Ocala (FL) Star-Banner*, May 5, 1978; Jack Edger, "Georgian Identified as Pot Plane Victim," *Ocala (FL) Star-Banner*, May 23, 1978.

313   **"Though there was no hope":** Goldman, "Thomas King Forcade: Living and Dying."

314   **"If someone told me":** Tom Forcade to Albert Goldman, 1978, Box 61, Tape 2, Albert Goldman Papers, 1953–1994.

314   **"paraquat contamination may":** Associated Press, "Mexican Pot Lung Threat, HEW Warns," *Atlanta Constitution*, March 12, 1978.

315   **"If the risk exists":** "Poisoned Marijuana," *New Republic*, March 18, 1978.

315   **"You crazy fucker!":** Patrick Anderson, *High in America* (Viking, 1981), 251.

315   **"promoting paranoia":** Robert Levering, "The Story Behind the Paraquat Scare," *Straight Creek Journal*, May 4, 1978.

315   **"Since it's going to be such":** Michael Chance, "NORML & High Times Take the Bait: Paraquat Hoax Exposed," *Yipster Times*, June 1978.

316   **"There hasn't been":** "What's the Truth About Paraquat?" *High Times*, September 1978.

317   **The White House received:** "What's the Truth About Paraquat?" *High Times*, September 1978.

317   **"Are you sure this":** *Saturday Night Live*, May 13, 1978.

317   **"It may just be something":** Harry Wasserman and Carol Ryder, "Laraine Newman," *High Times*, July 1978.

317   **The paraphernalia industry:** Powers, "Magazine of 'High Society' Hits Rich Vein."

317   **Four states:** "Five Year Update," *New Times*, October 16, 1978.

317   **Peter Bourne set:** Richard D. Lyons, "Eye Study on Marijuana Sought," *New York Times*, November 30, 1978.

317   **"Paradoxically":** "Lines: Paraquat, Paranoia and Paramilitary Pot," *High Times*, September 1978.

318   **Then he resigned:** Jack Anderson, "Washington Merry-Go-Round: Changes Mind in Sugar Ads Fight," Washington Merry-Go-Round, July 14, 1978.

318   **"I get a very sick feeling":** Peggy Mann, "The Case Against Marijuana," *Washington Post*, July 30, 1978.

318   **anti-paraphernalia bills:** Michael Antonoff, "A Smoldering Battle over Rolling Paper Technology," *New York Times*, December 17, 1978.

318   **"what they are going to attempt":** "Lines: Paraquat, Paranoia and Paramilitary Pot," *High Times*, September 1978.

318   **"drug-related literature":** Mark Thellman, "Carter's Home State Outlaws Dope Press," *High Times*, August 1978.

318   **On July 19, 1978:** Lawrence Meyer and Alfred E. Lewis, "Carter Aide Signed Fake Quaalude Prescription," *Washington Post*, July 19, 1978.

318   **"high incidence":** James Wooten, "Carter's Top Drug Adviser Resigns in Conflict over False Prescription," *New York Times*, July 21, 1978.

318   **"Peter Bourne," said Keith Stroup:** "Bourne vs. Stroup Part II: One's KO'd, the Other's Reeling," *New Times*, August 21, 1978.

319   **"He lied through his teeth":** Craig Copetas to John Holmstrom (undated audiocassette), Box 117, Item 39002137167947, John Holmstrom Papers and Punk Magazine Records, General Collection, Beinecke Rare Book and Manuscript Library, Yale University.

319   **"My preference":** "Transcript of President's News Conference on Foreign and Domestic Matters," *New York Times*, July 21, 1978.

319   **"about the closest friend":** Kai Bird, *The Outlier: The Unfinished Presidency of Jimmy Carter* (Crown, 2021), 461.

319   **falsely claimed that marijuana:** Ronald J. Ostrow, "Drug Fighter Urges Congress to Triple Top Sentence for Marijuana Smugglers," *Los Angeles Times*, October 11, 1978. After the American Cancer Society insisted that marijuana was "far less carcinogenic than cigarettes," Bensinger said it was an "honest misunderstanding" (Jack Anderson, "Washington Merry-Go-Round," December 15, 1978).

319   **Dogoloff also solicited:** Dan Baum, *Smoke and Mirrors* (Back Bay Books, 1996), 120.

319   **There would be no more:** Baum, *Smoke and Mirrors*, 127.

320   **Jimmy Buffett skipped:** Anderson, *High in America*, 291.

320   **Chicago in the 1920s:** Patrick Riordan, "Smugglers Courting Death in Drive for High-Risk Profits," *Miami Herald*, April 17, 1978.

320   **"Don't worry," Forcade assured:** Anderson, *High in America*.

320   **Twenty-seven winners:** "Did Abbie Hoffman Appear at His Benefit?" *Baltimore Sun*, August 24, 1978.

320   **"Let's get a nice group picture":** Robert Sanford, "Yippie! Again and Again and Again and Again…" *St. Louis Post-Dispatch*, September 3, 1978.

321   **"Why don't they just":** Anne Keegan, "Yippies' 60s-Style Rally a Bust in 70s-Style Mood," *Chicago Tribune*, August 28, 1978.

321   **"Get some photos":** Shelley Levitt to Terese Coe, Terese Coe Papers.

321   **"I don't know what to do":** Shelley Levitt to Terese Coe, Terese Coe Papers. Mick Rock told a variation of the story in 2009: "I had my camera in the other room. I said, 'Oh shit!' because the pie had come off, and Andy said, 'Don't worry'—and he actually put the pie back on his head. He didn't care if you made him look a little ridiculous" (Chris Simunek, "Rock in a High Place," *High Times*, November 2009).

322   **"These girls came over":** Victor Bockris to John Holmstrom (undated audiocassette), Box 117, Item 39002137167996, John Holmstrom Papers and Punk Magazine Records.

322   **"My wife is my best friend":** Victor Bockris, "The Last Photograph of Tom Forcade," *Punk Special Edition: D.O.A.—the Official Filmbook*, April 1981.

323   **white pajama bottoms:** Victor Bockris, "Vagabond: Hollywood," *High Times*, June 1979.

324   **"He wasn't there at all":** Bockris, "The Last Photograph of Tom Forcade."

324   **"I think when you die":** Bockris, "The Last Photograph of Tom Forcade."

324   **"I never met a drug":** Gabrielle Schang-Forcade, "May the Forcade Be with You," *Overthrow*, April 1979.

325   **stadiums being used:** Michael Segell, "Thomas K. Forcade, 1945–1978," *Rolling Stone*, December 28, 1978–January 11, 1979.

325   **"It was really hard":** Shelley Levitt to Terese Coe, Terese Coe Papers.

325   **"RIP America?":** The editorial was originally written for the *Yipster Times* and eventually published as "Tom's Last Testament" in *Overthrow*, April 1979.

325   **"He went upstairs":** Bob Lemmo to Terese Coe, Terese Coe Papers.

325   **"Hey, man, could you":** Bockris, "The Last Photograph of Tom Forcade."

326   **only wanted to buy coke:** Maureen McFadden to Albert Goldman, November 30, 1978, Box 61, Tape 5, Albert Goldman Papers.

326   **"Do whatever you have to":** Shelley Levitt to Terese Coe, Terese Coe Papers.

326   **secretly implemented parts:** Ronald J. Ostrow, "Nixon Approved Break-Ins, Ex-FBI Aide Tells Court," *Washington Post*, November 16, 1978, 1.

327 **"Wait twenty minutes"**: Gabrielle Schang to Albert Goldman, Box A26, Folder 8, Albert Goldman Papers.

329 **The respirator:** Jane Perlez, "Suicide of a 'Media' Genius," *SoHo Weekly News*, November 23, 1978.

329 **The next day a wake:** Perlez, "Suicide of a 'Media' Genius."

329 **"He looked so together":** Bockris, "The Last Photograph of Tom Forcade."

329 **At the Diplomat Hotel:** Perlez, "Suicide of a 'Media' Genius."

329 **"He was a guy":** *High Times* Press Conference/Memorial Transcript, pages 3–4 (courtesy of John Holmstrom).

330 **"When people went":** Michael Antonoff, "The Thomas King Forcade Story," *Tucson's Mountain Newsreal*, December 1978.

330 **the Peoples Temple had supported:** Art Goldberg, "Charles Garry Discusses the Guns, Drugs, and Sex Used to Control Peoples Temple," *San Francisco Bay Guardian*, November 30, 1978.

330 **donated funds:** Peter N. Carroll, *It Seemed Like Nothing Happened: America in the 1970s* (Rutgers University Press, 2000), 249.

330 **bill that decriminalized:** "Cal Pot Bill May Pass," *Berkeley Barb*, June 27, 1975.

331 **"atop the World Trade Center":** Alex Williams, "High Times Wants to Be the Playboy of Pot," *New York Times*, April 2, 2016. Keith Stroup earlier made the claim that Forcade's ashes were smoked, in his first-person account, "Here's to High Times," *High Times*, November 2009.

Epilogue

333 **"Tom was the kind":** "Letters," *Village Voice*, January 1, 1979.

333 **"When I went":** Martin Torgoff, *Can't Find My Way Home: America in the Great Stoned Age, 1945–2000* (Simon & Schuster, 2003).

333 **"Breaking into Forcade's loft:"** A. J. Weberman, "Tom Forcade: Death of a Radical Romantic," *Village Voice*, November 27, 1978.

333 **"mysterious black cars":** Bill Weinberg, "The Life & Strange Trips of *High Times* Founder Tom Forcade," *Cannabis Culture*, January–February 2007.

334 **"CIA's inquiry":** Senate Select Committee to Study Governmental Operations with Respect to Intelligence Activities, *Final Report: Book III: Supplementary Detailed Staff Reports on Intelligence Activities and the Rights of Americans*, S. Rep. 94-755 (1976), 691.

334 **"John Thomas Mason":** Don Wirtshafter, *Report to the NORML Board on the Trans-High Corporate Trust*, April 16, 2001, and copies of Trans-High documents viewed by the author.

335 **Jean-Michel Basquiat and Keith Haring:** Victor Bockris, "Visions of the Seventies," *Gadfly*, January–February 2001.

335 **"We didn't realize":** Marcus D. Niski, "Interview with Sylvère Lotringer on the Nova Convention," RealityStudio.org, September 14, 2012.

335 **"His associate/antagonist":** Abbie Hoffman, "Fugitive on the Town," *Village Voice*, December 18, 1978.

336 **"We want the right":** "Highwitness News: NORML Calls for Legal Pot," *High Times*, March 1979.

336 **plied with Dom Pérignon:** Patrick Anderson, *High in America* (Viking, 1981).

336 **"Watch the light":** "Letters," *High Times*, February 1979.

336 **Big Top:** "Frisco's Most Righteous Dealer Runs for Harvey Milk's Seat," *High Times*, October 1979.

336 **expressed shock:** Russ Cone, "Board: Halt Paraquat Spraying," *San Francisco Examiner*, July 18, 1978.

336 **agreed to coordinate:** Tom Fiedler, "White House Plans Crackdown on South Florida Drug Traffic," *Akron (OH) Beacon Journal*, July 6, 1978; Robert M. Press, "White House Maps Attack on Drug Smuggling," *Christian Science Monitor*, July 21, 1978.

336 **first big fish:** Al Messerschmidt and Joe Crankshaw, "Drug Ring Is Busted, Called Giant in Trade," *Miami Herald*, May 2, 1979.

336 **Trans-High Market Quotations:** Robert Platshorn, "My pot smuggling career began at…" Facebook post, May 30, 2017 (no longer available online).

337 **largest retail business:** Donald Neff, "The Colombian Connection," *Time*, January 29, 1979.

337 **CIA-trained Cuban exiles:** Hyde Post, "CIA-Trained Cubans Are New Breed of Drug Smugglers," *Atlanta Constitution*, August 16, 1979; Helga Silva, "Villaverde Drug Charges Shock Followers in Cuban Community," *Miami Herald*, August 6, 1981.

337 **drug-related homicides increased:** Bud Newman, "Pot Seizures Up Since Crackdown," *Palm Beach Post*, February 7, 1979.

337 **"As those who have gotten":** "Lines," *High Times*, November 1, 1976.

337 **Marijuana flourished:** Melinda Beck, "Homegrown Grass," *Newsweek*, October 30, 1978.

337 **a third of the grass:** John Hurst and Phil Garlington, "Pot: The Price and Potency Are Way Up," *Los Angeles Times*, November 25, 1979.

337 **Proposition 215:** Martin A. Lee, *Smoke Signals* (Scribner, 2012), 247.

337 **"Each dealer would have":** "Lines," *High Times*, August 1975.

338 **"When Forcade shot":** Daniel Machalaba, "The Pot Trade: High Times Magazine, Hated by Drug Foes, Suffers Hard Times," *Wall Street Journal*, July 29, 1980.

338 **The next few years:** UPI, "Power Struggle Rocks Drug Culture Bible," *Macon News*, August 19, 1979.

338 **"pot of gold":** Tim Weiner, "Bad Trip at *High Times*," *Soho Weekly News*, August 16, 1979.

338 **In July:** Weiner, "Bad Trip at *High Times*."

338 **drug bazaars:** Machalaba, "The Pot Trade."

338 **"fairly impressive display":** UPI, "Power Struggle Rocks Drug Culture Bible."

338 **"I think it was hard":** Katy Butler, "She's High on Her 'High Times,'" *San Francisco Chronicle*, October 29, 1979.

339 **Bricks crashed:** Robert Sam Anson, "Mixed Media," *Soho Weekly News*, undated clipping, 1980 (in author's possession).

339 **planned articles:** N. R. Kleinfield, "Advertising: High Times Seeks New Readers," *New York Times*, August 22, 1979.

339 **more than 90 percent:** Machalaba, "The Pot Trade."

339 **the DEA was targeting:** Michael Isikoff, "Justice Dept. Targets High Times: Ad for Marijuana Seed Catalogue Leads to Grand Jury Probe," *Washington Post*, July 16, 1990; Dexter Filkins, "Garden Suppliers Caught in Middle of War on Pot," *Miami Herald*, October 21, 1991.

339 **internal lawsuits:** "First Amendment to Merger Agreement" between Origo Acquisition, High Times Holding Corp., et al., September 27, 2017.

339 **Models posed:** "The Reincarnation of High Style," HighTimes.com, October 11, 2016. See also the photo spread at "Defying Gravity & the Trump Administration," HighTimes.com, March 14, 2017.

339 **branded furniture and casinos:** Alex Williams, "High Times Wants to Be the Playboy of Pot," *New York Times*, April 2, 2016.

340 **Its CEO donated:** Kali Hays, "Memo Pad: Inside Out," *Women's Wear Daily*, October 18, 2018.

340 **"platform for cannabis entrepreneurs":** Aaron Smith, "The New CEO of High Times Most Definitely Inhales," CNN.com, June 6, 2017.

340 **resignations and layoffs:** Ben Schreckinger, "The Long Fall of High Times," *Politico*, September 4, 2020.

340 **"The same people that own":** Tom Forcade to Albert Goldman, Spring 1978, transcribed by Terese Coe in 1980.

INDEX